STORY AND ART BY

Nene Yukimori

4

Kubo Won't Let Me Be Invisible

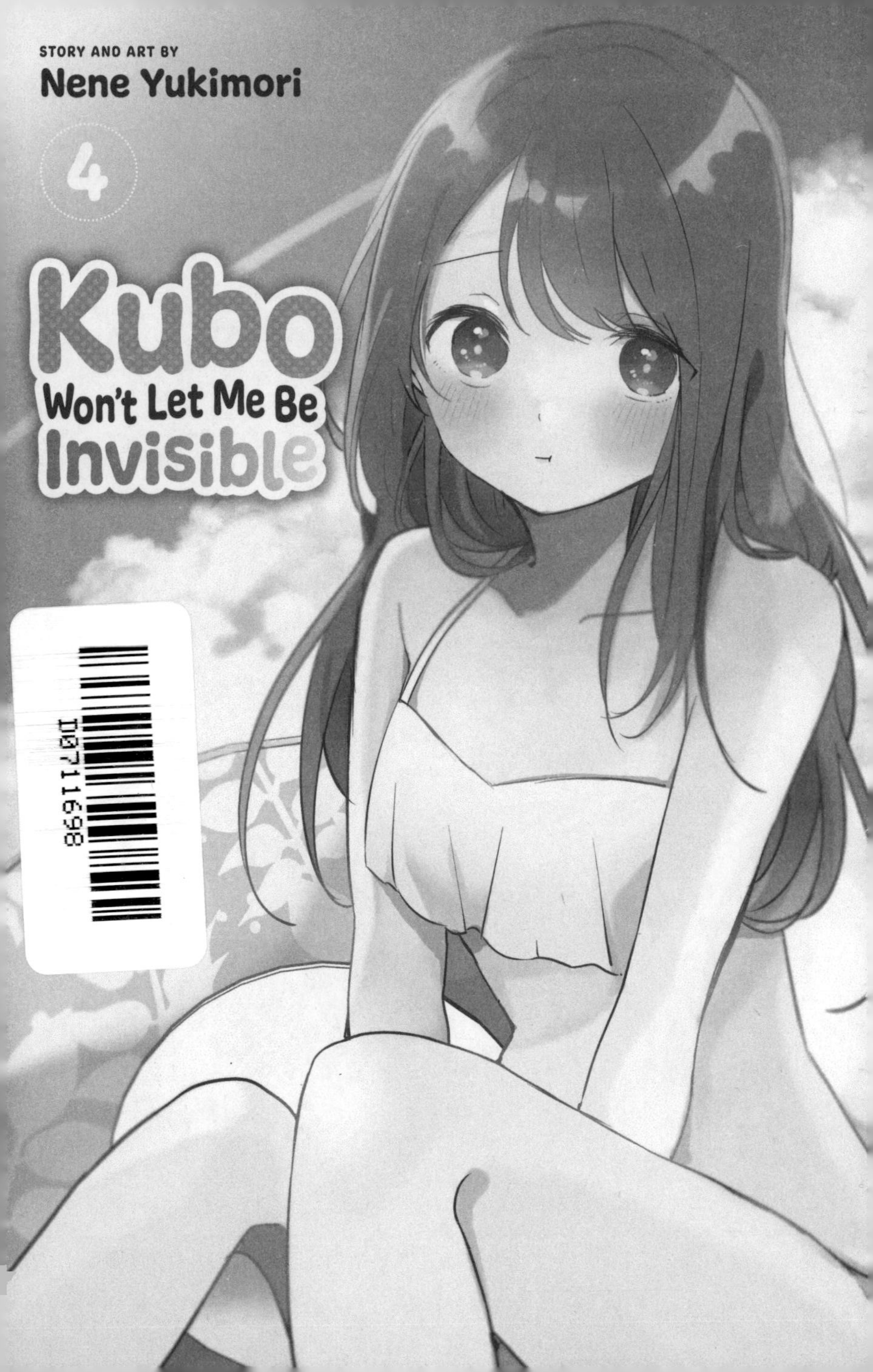

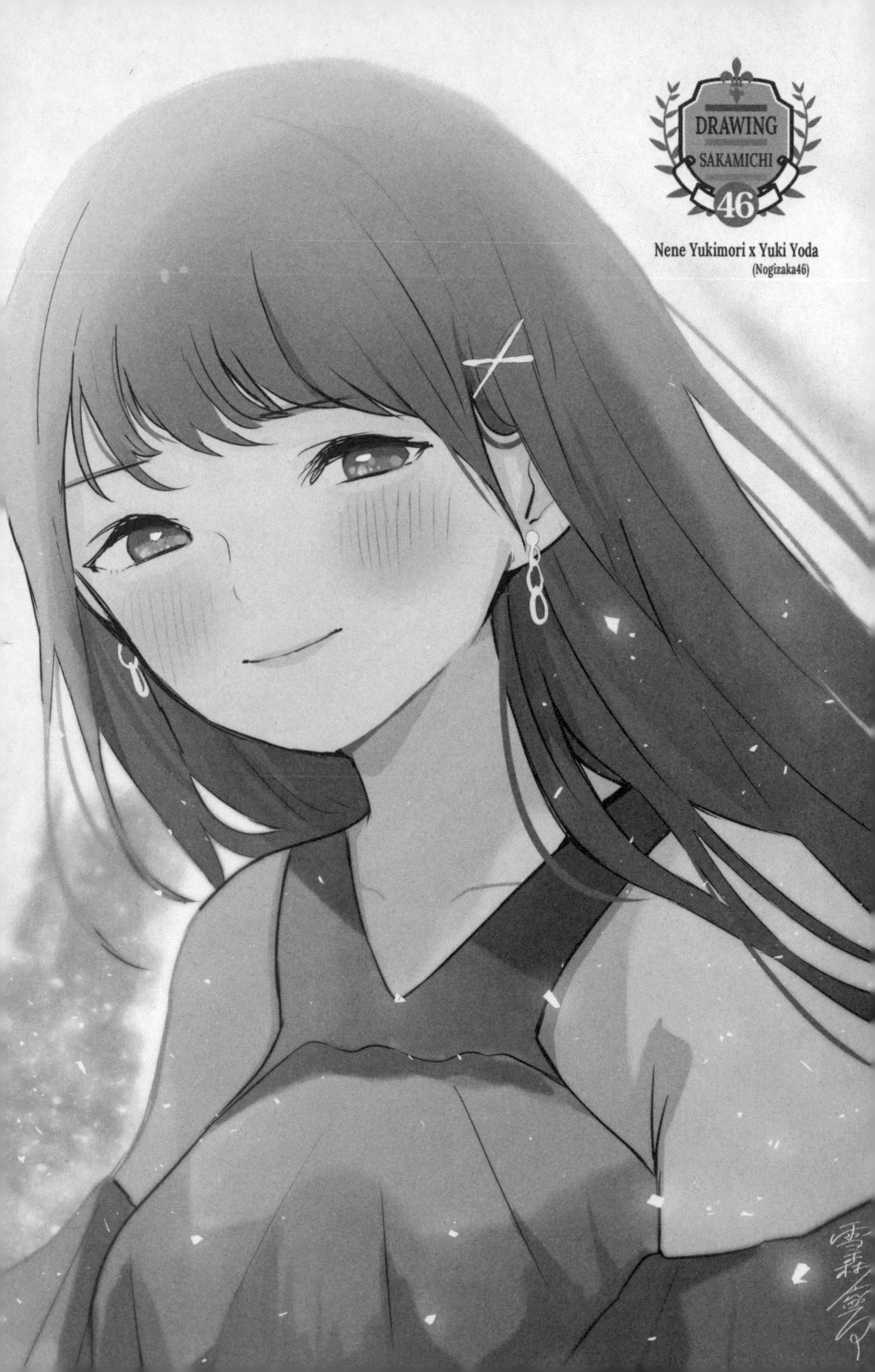
DRAWING
SAKAMICHI
46
Nene Yukimori x Yuki Yoda
(Nogizaka46)

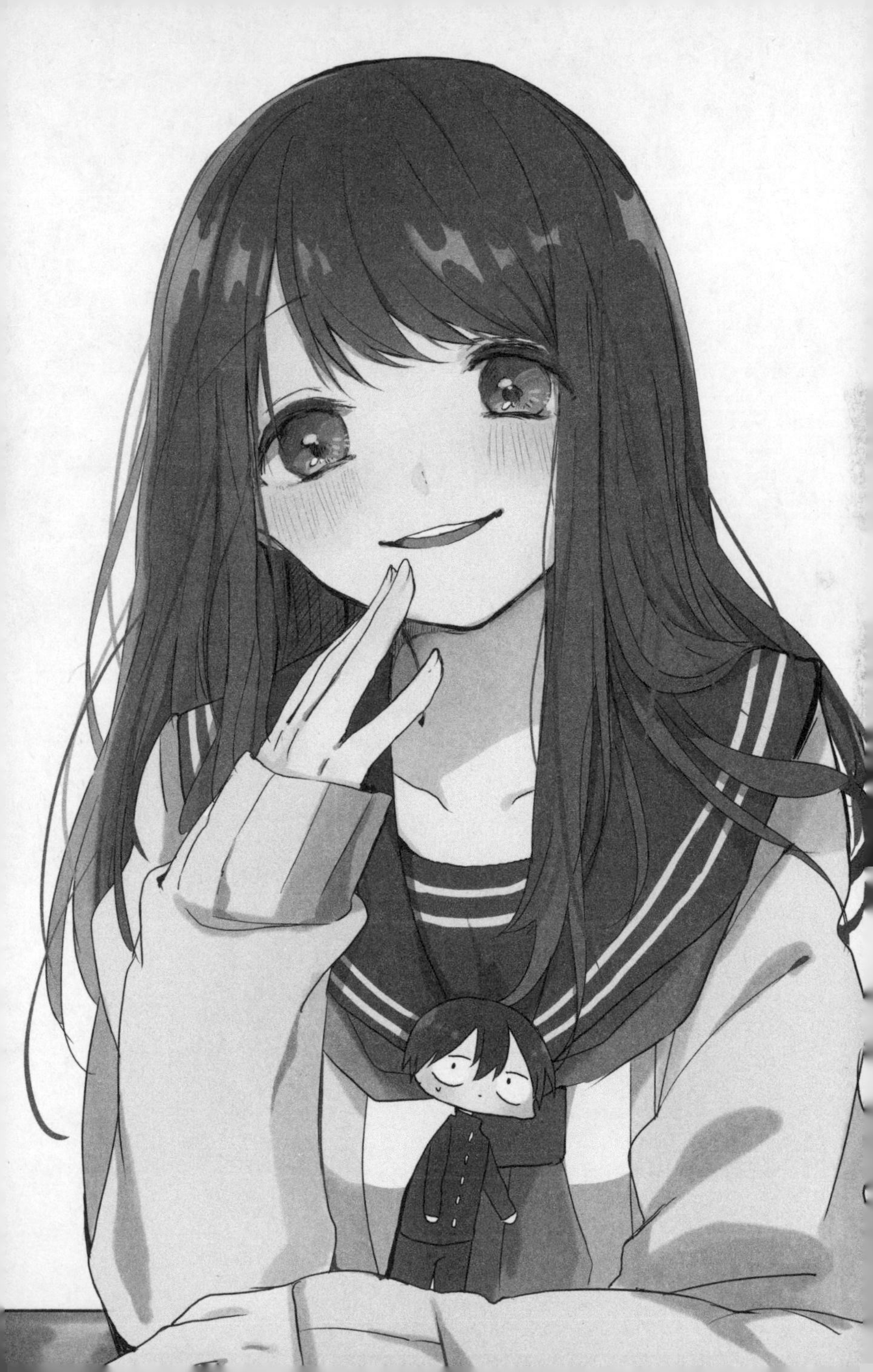

CONTENTS

episode 033

COMMITTEE AND FLOWER BEDS

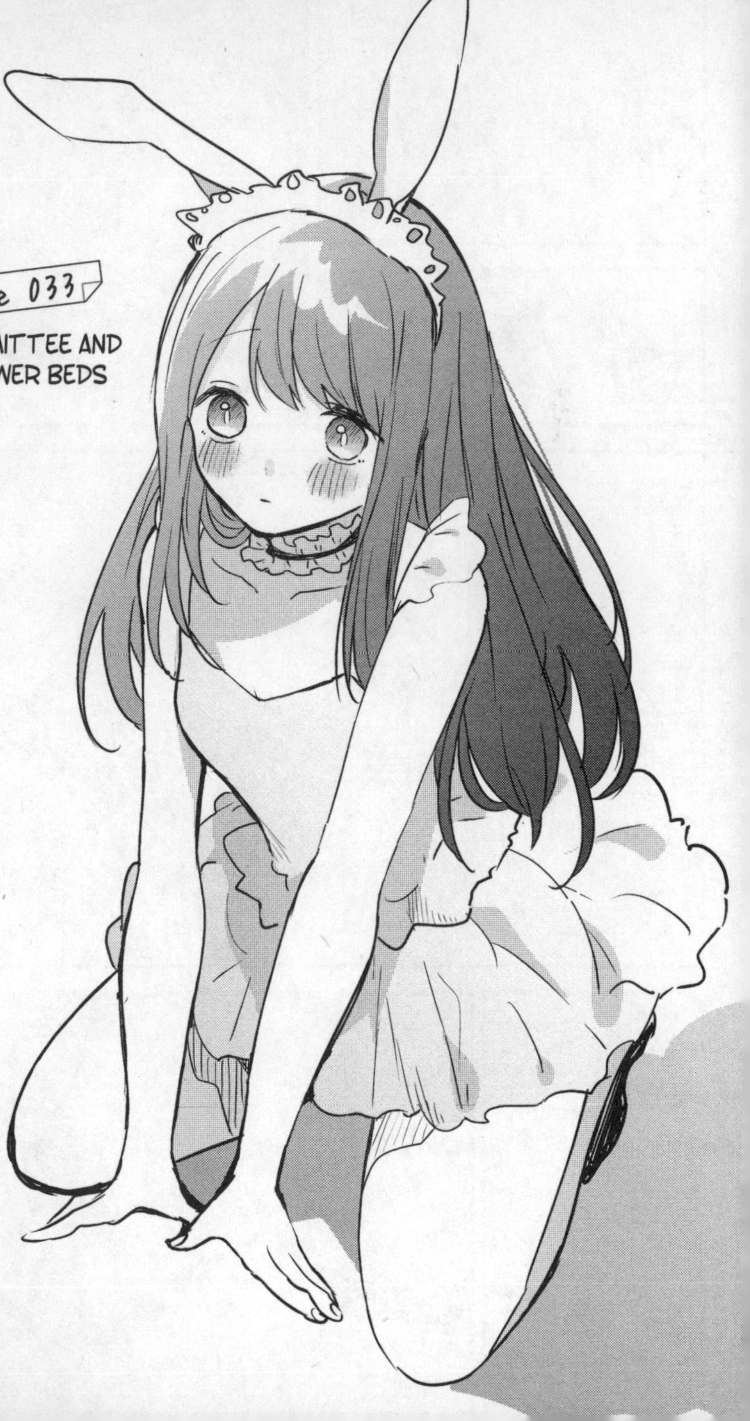

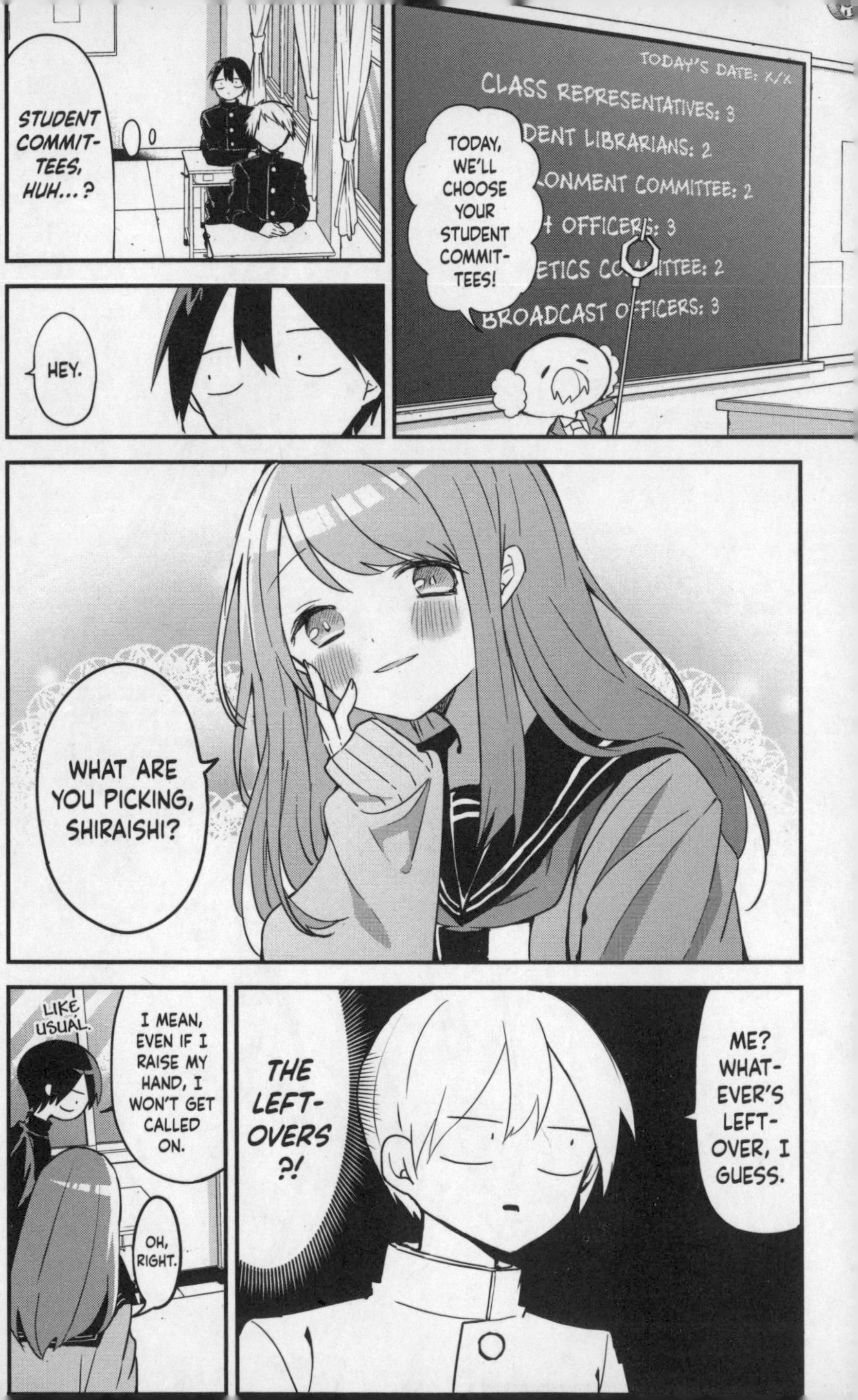
TODAY'S DATE: X/X
CLASS REPRESENTATIVES: 3
DENT LIBRARIANS: 2
ONMENT COMMITTEE: 2
OFFICERS: 3
ETICS COMMITTEE: 2
BROADCAST OFFICERS: 3
TODAY, WE'LL CHOOSE YOUR STUDENT COMMITTEES!
STUDENT COMMITTEES, HUH...?
HEY.
WHAT ARE YOU PICKING, SHIRAISHI?
ME? WHATEVER'S LEFTOVER, I GUESS.
THE LEFTOVERS?!
I MEAN, EVEN IF I RAISE MY HAND, I WON'T GET CALLED ON.
LIKE USUAL.
OH, RIGHT.

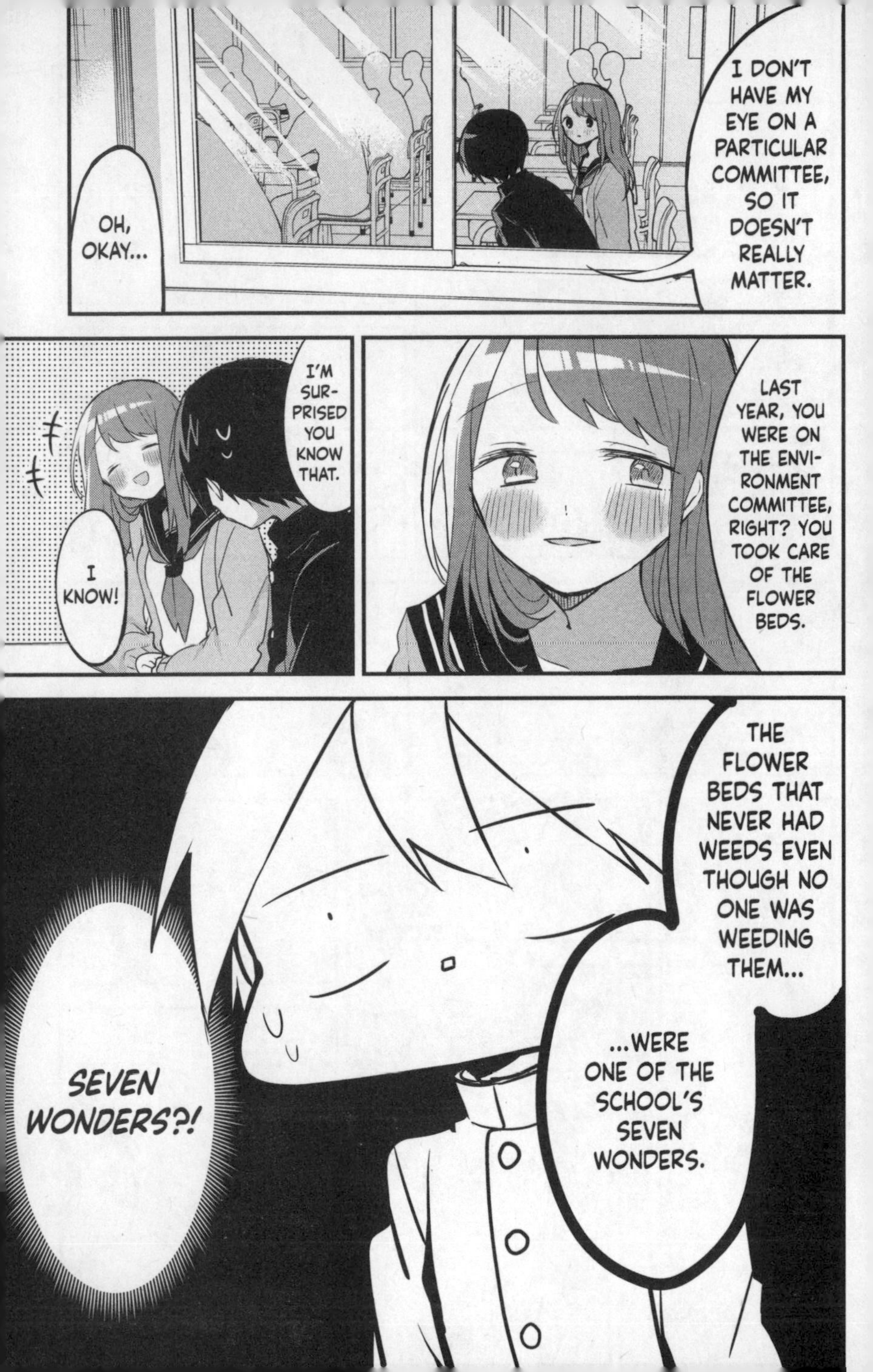
I DON'T HAVE MY EYE ON A PARTICULAR COMMITTEE, SO IT DOESN'T REALLY MATTER.
OH, OKAY...
LAST YEAR, YOU WERE ON THE ENVIRONMENT COMMITTEE, RIGHT? YOU TOOK CARE OF THE FLOWER BEDS.
I'M SURPRISED YOU KNOW THAT.
I KNOW!
THE FLOWER BEDS THAT NEVER HAD WEEDS EVEN THOUGH NO ONE WAS WEEDING THEM...
...WERE ONE OF THE SCHOOL'S SEVEN WONDERS.
SEVEN WONDERS?!

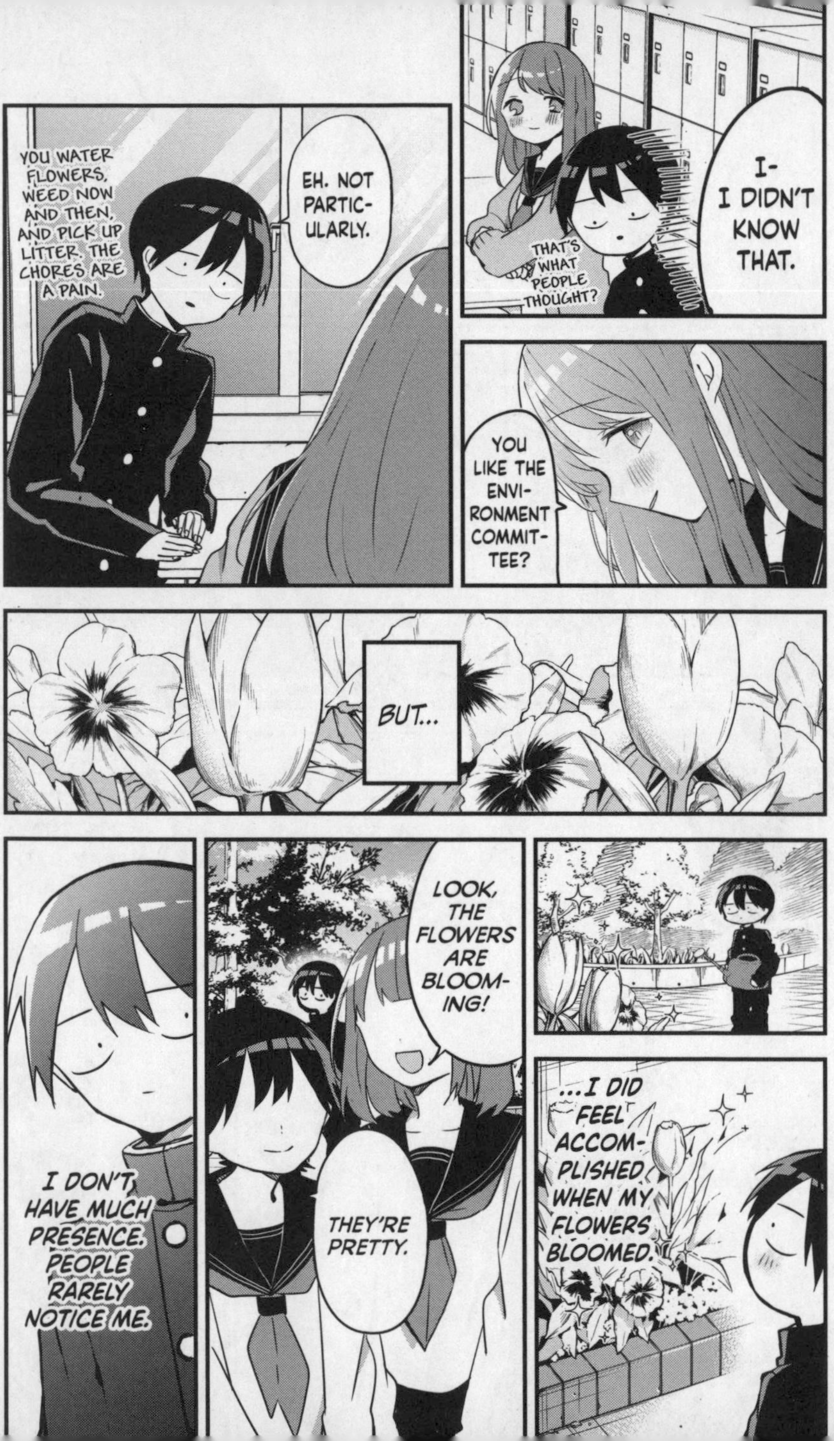
I- I DIDN'T KNOW THAT.
THAT'S WHAT PEOPLE THOUGHT?
YOU LIKE THE ENVIRONMENT COMMITTEE?
EH. NOT PARTICULARLY.
YOU WATER FLOWERS, WEED NOW AND THEN, AND PICK UP LITTER. THE CHORES ARE A PAIN.
BUT...
...I DID FEEL ACCOMPLISHED WHEN MY FLOWERS BLOOMED.
LOOK, THE FLOWERS ARE BLOOMING!
THEY'RE PRETTY.
I DON'T HAVE MUCH PRESENCE. PEOPLE RARELY NOTICE ME.

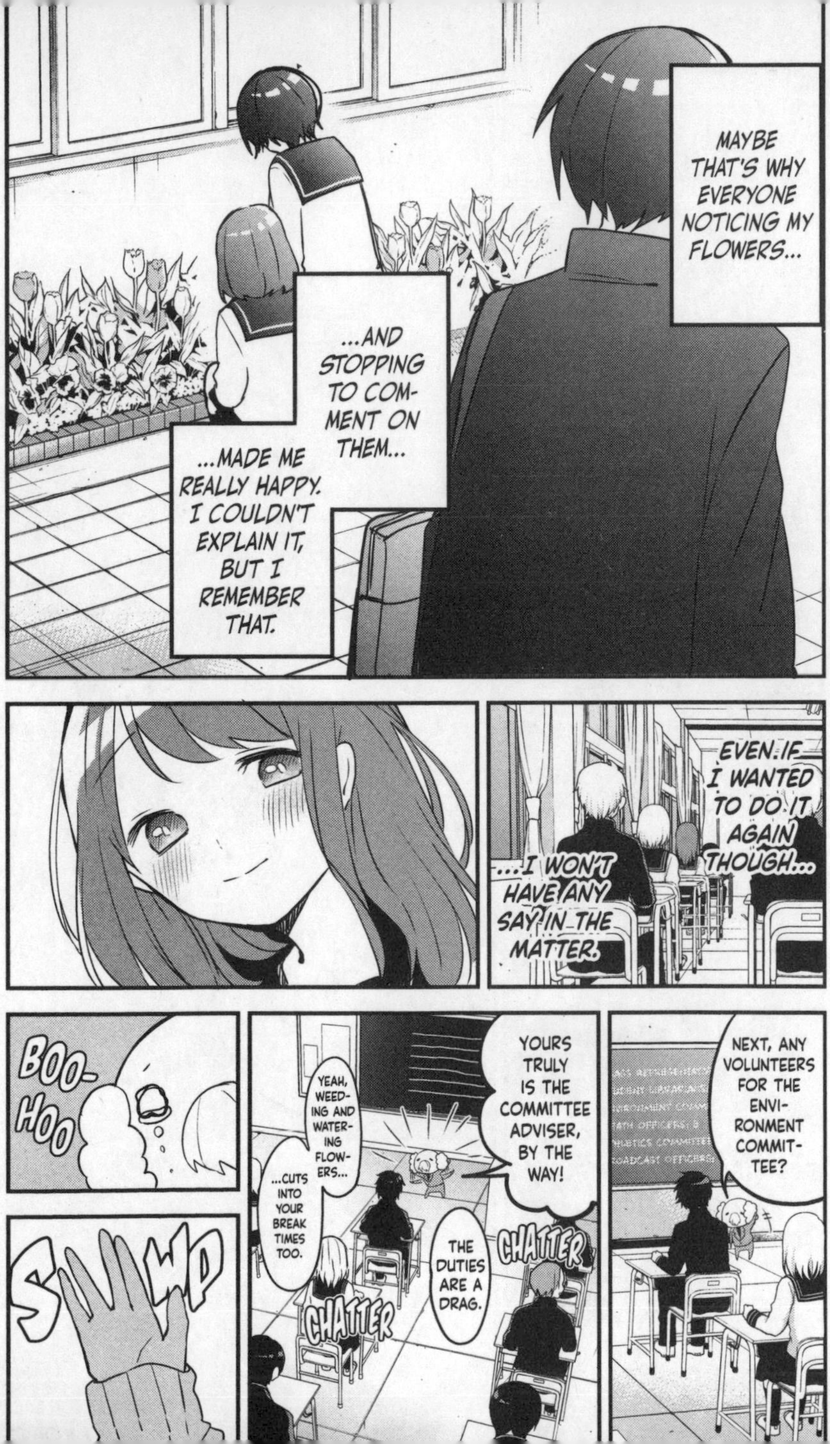
MAYBE THAT'S WHY EVERYONE NOTICING MY FLOWERS...
...AND STOPPING TO COMMENT ON THEM...
...MADE ME REALLY HAPPY. I COULDN'T EXPLAIN IT, BUT I REMEMBER THAT.
EVEN IF I WANTED TO DO IT AGAIN THOUGH...
...I WON'T HAVE ANY SAY IN THE MATTER.
NEXT, ANY VOLUNTEERS FOR THE ENVIRONMENT COMMITTEE?
YOURS TRULY IS THE COMMITTEE ADVISER, BY THE WAY!
CHATTER
THE DUTIES ARE A DRAG.
YEAH, WEEDING AND WATERING FLOWERS...
...CUTS INTO YOUR BREAK TIMES TOO.
CHATTER
BOO-HOO

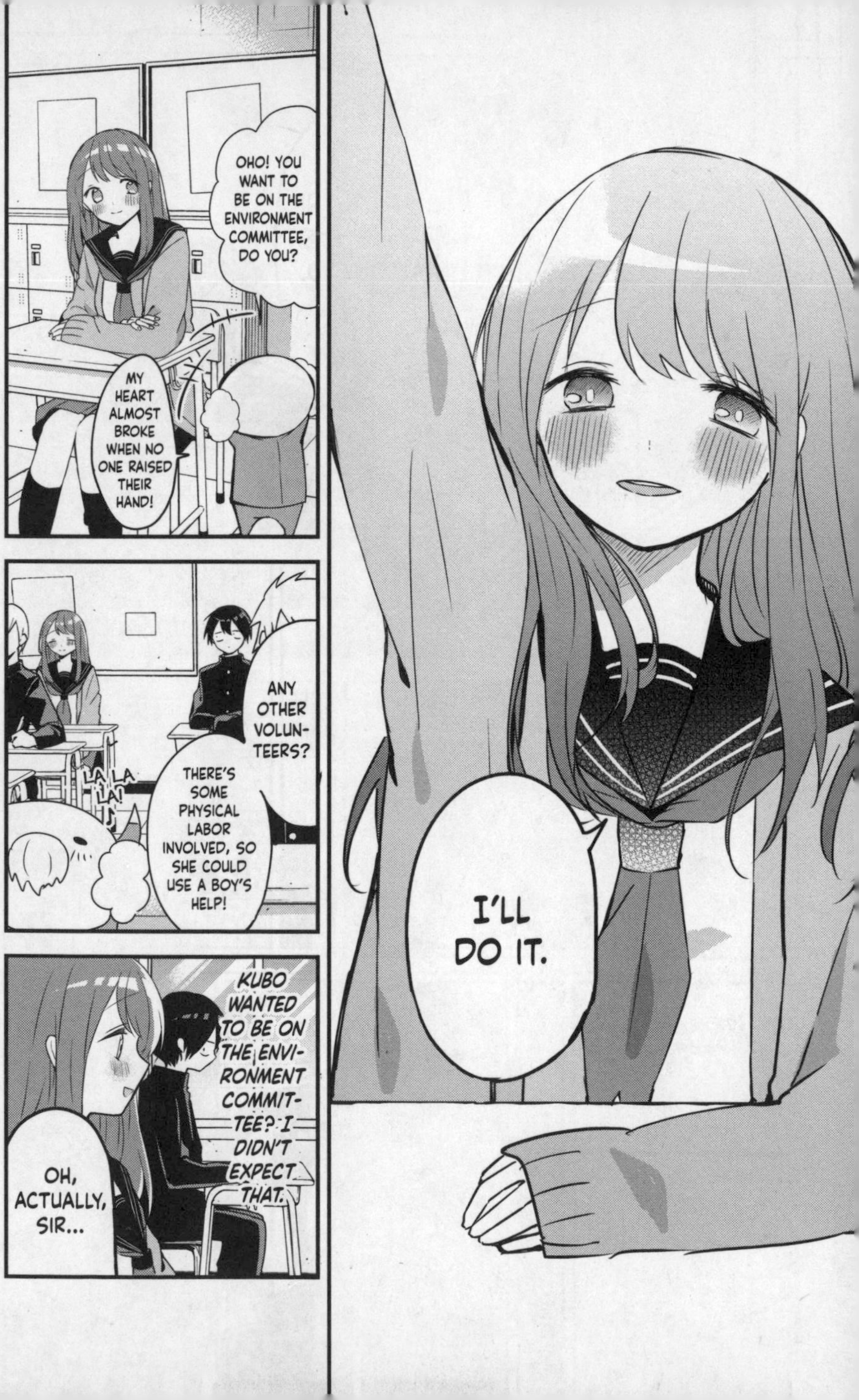
OHO! YOU WANT TO BE ON THE ENVIRONMENT COMMITTEE, DO YOU?
MY HEART ALMOST BROKE WHEN NO ONE RAISED THEIR HAND!
ANY OTHER VOLUNTEERS?
THERE'S SOME PHYSICAL LABOR INVOLVED, SO SHE COULD USE A BOY'S HELP!
LA LA LA! ♪
KUBO WANTED TO BE ON THE ENVIRONMENT COMMITTEE? I DIDN'T EXPECT THAT.
OH, ACTUALLY, SIR...
I'LL DO IT.

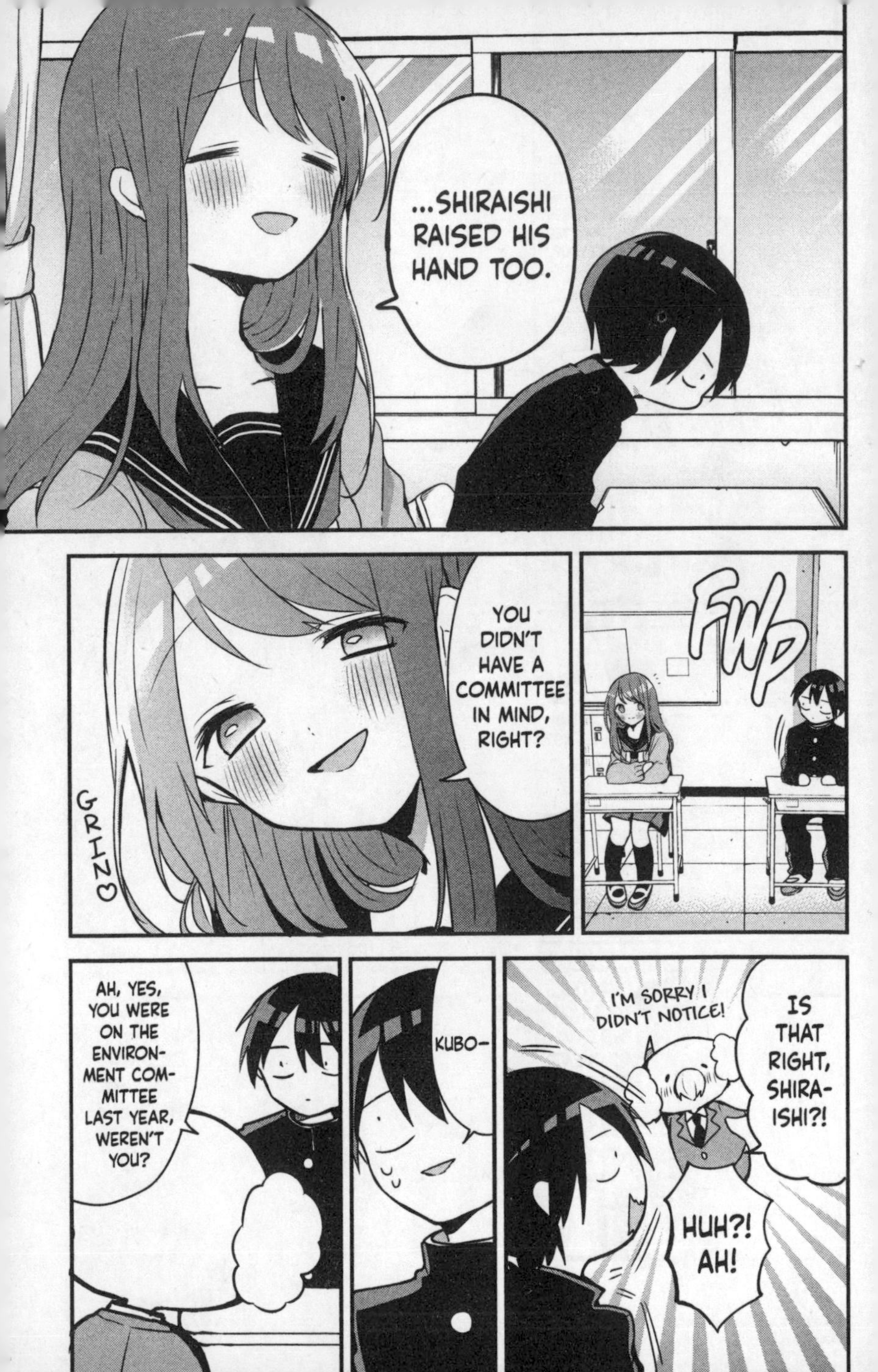
...SHIRAISHI RAISED HIS HAND TOO.
FWP
YOU DIDN'T HAVE A COMMITTEE IN MIND, RIGHT?
GRIN♡
IS THAT RIGHT, SHIRA-ISHI?!
I'M SORRY I DIDN'T NOTICE!
HUH?! AH!
KUBO-
AH, YES, YOU WERE ON THE ENVIRON-MENT COM-MITTEE LAST YEAR, WEREN'T YOU?

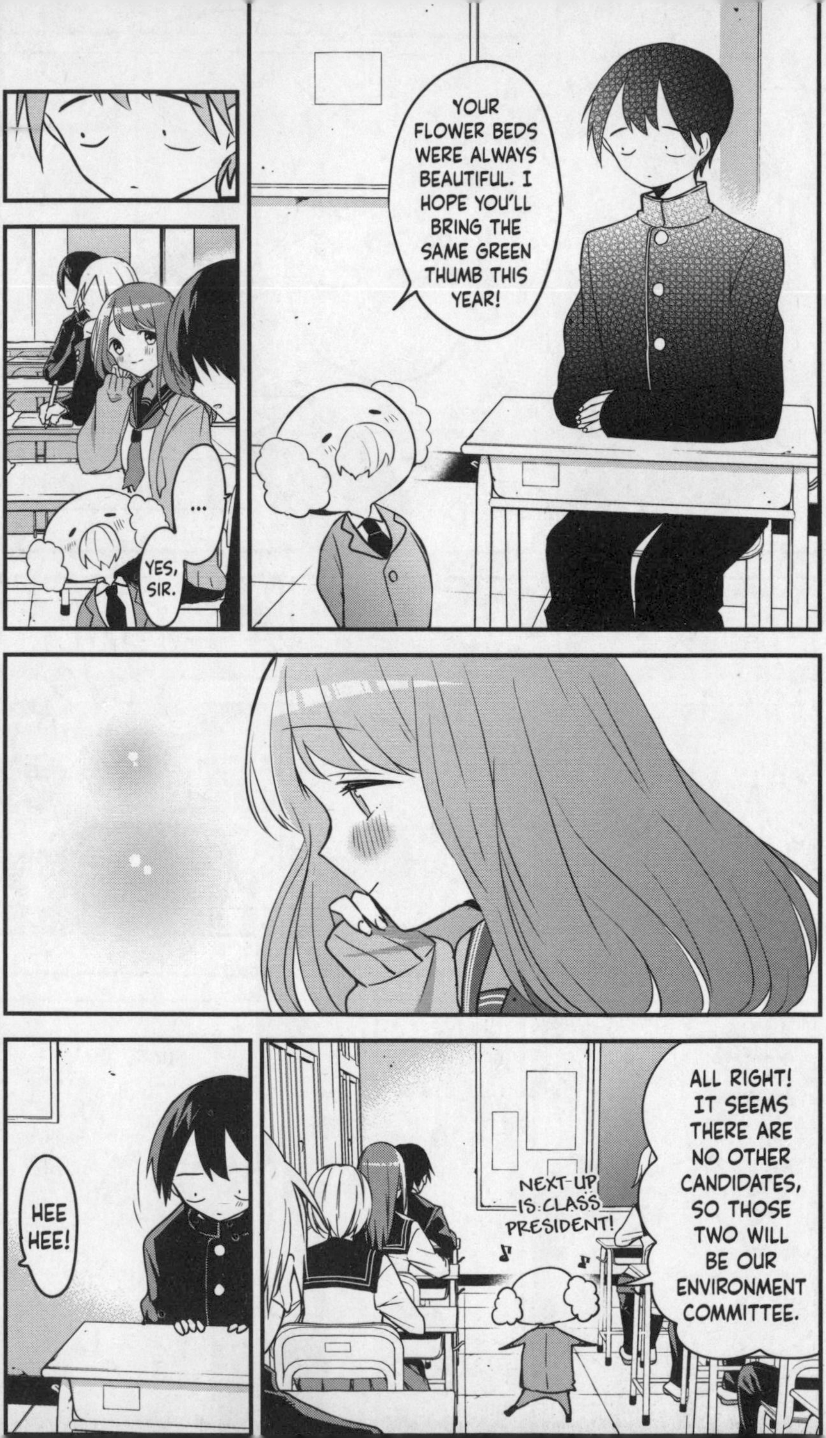
YOUR FLOWER BEDS WERE ALWAYS BEAUTIFUL. I HOPE YOU'LL BRING THE SAME GREEN THUMB THIS YEAR!
...
YES, SIR.
ALL RIGHT! IT SEEMS THERE ARE NO OTHER CANDIDATES, SO THOSE TWO WILL BE OUR ENVIRONMENT COMMITTEE.
NEXT-UP IS CLASS PRESIDENT!
HEE HEE!

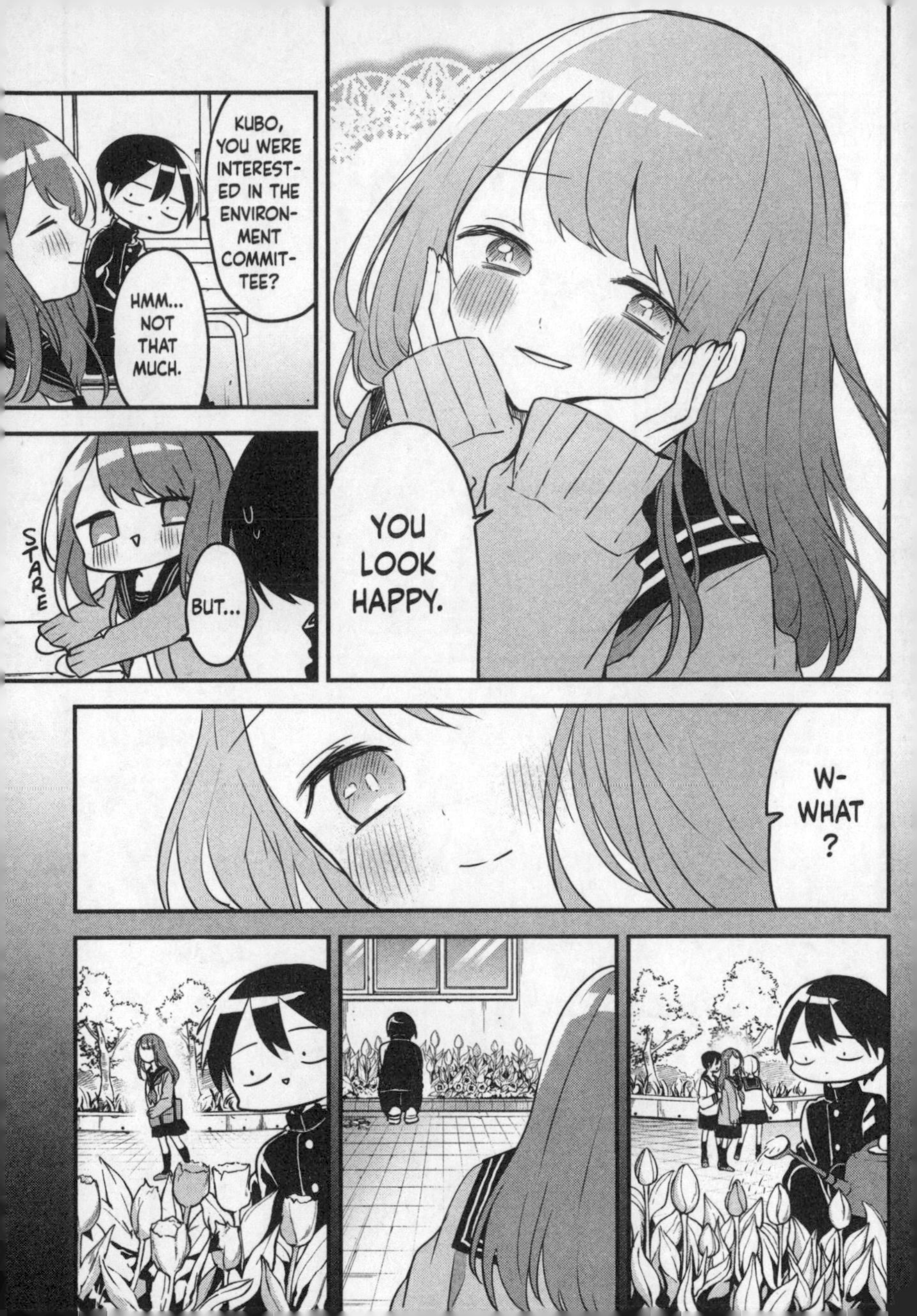
YOU LOOK HAPPY.
KUBO, YOU WERE INTEREST-ED IN THE ENVIRON-MENT COMMIT-TEE?
HMM... NOT THAT MUCH.
BUT...
STARE
W-WHAT?

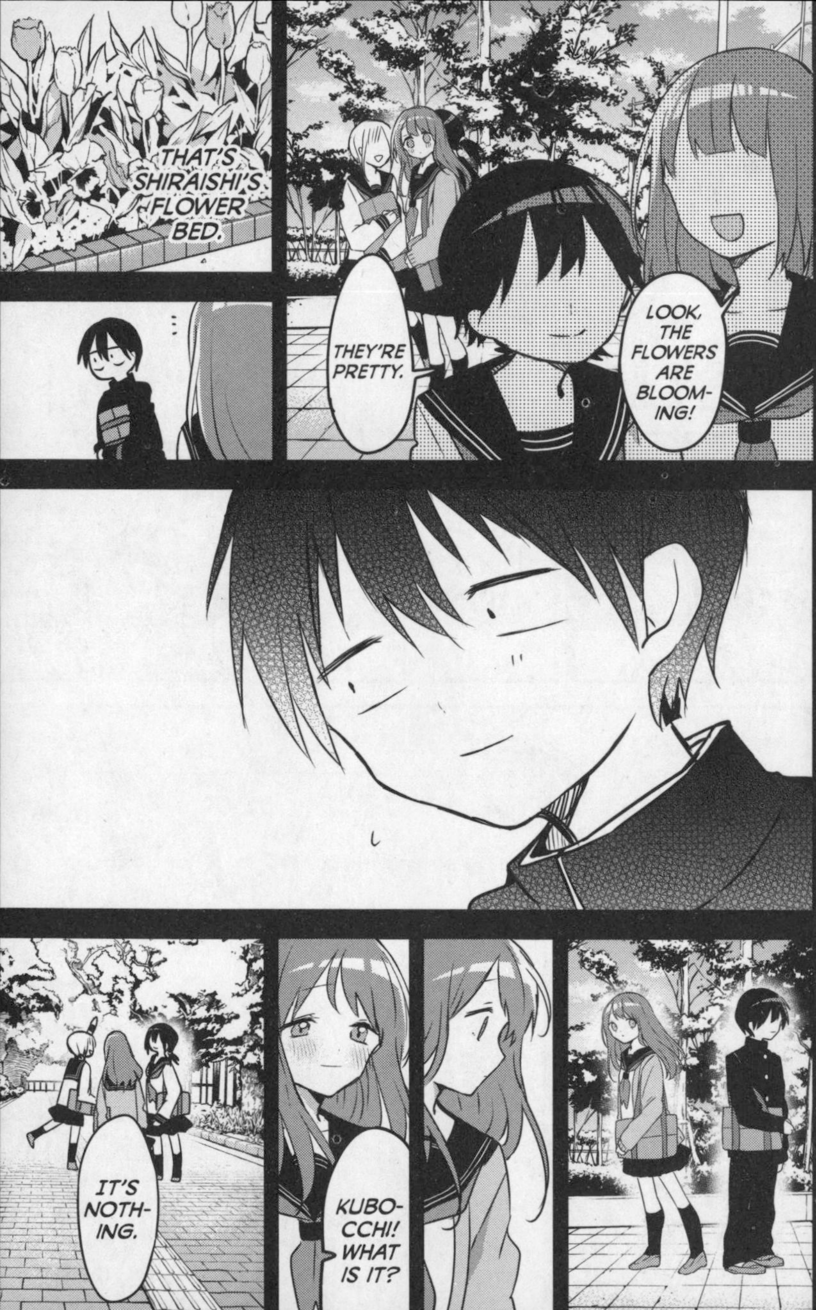
LOOK, THE FLOWERS ARE BLOOM-ING!
THEY'RE PRETTY.
THAT'S SHIRAISHI'S FLOWER BED.
...
KUBO-CCHI! WHAT IS IT?
IT'S NOTH-ING.

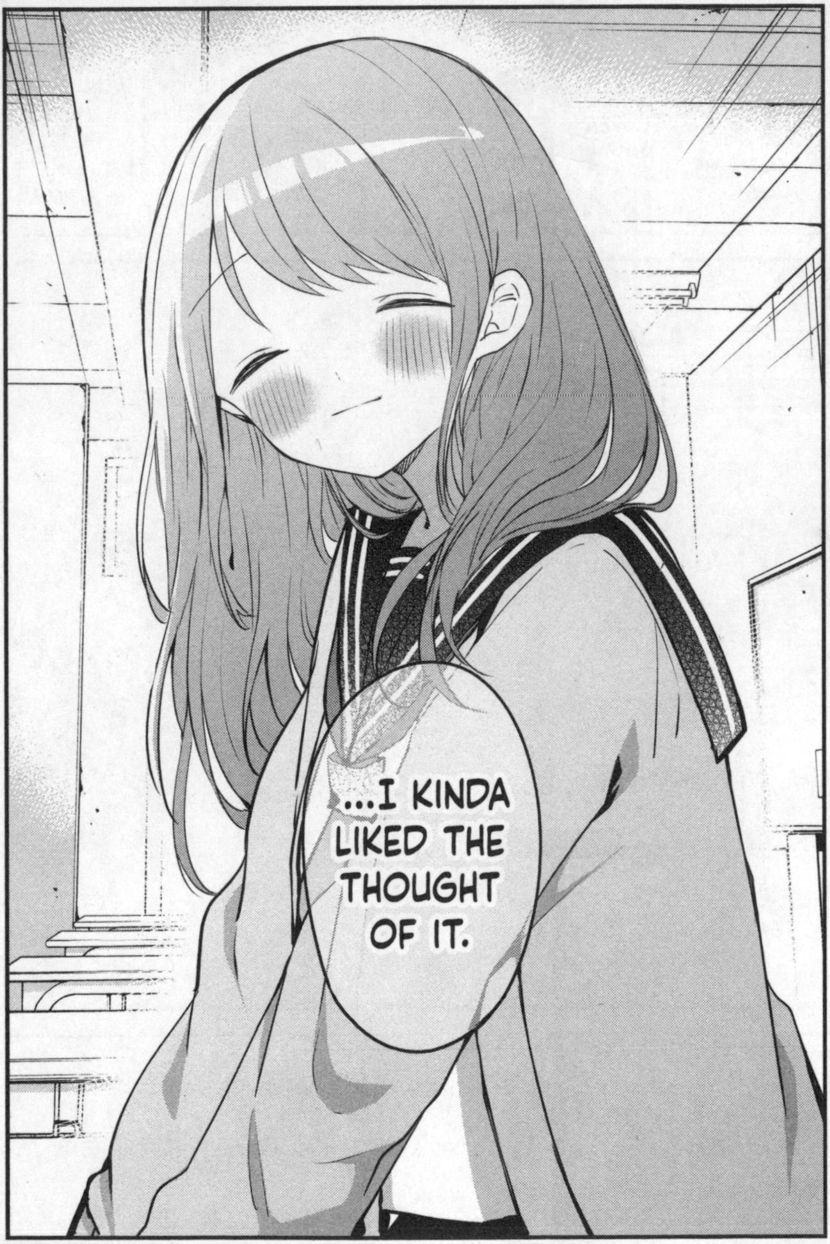
...I KINDA LIKED THE THOUGHT OF IT.

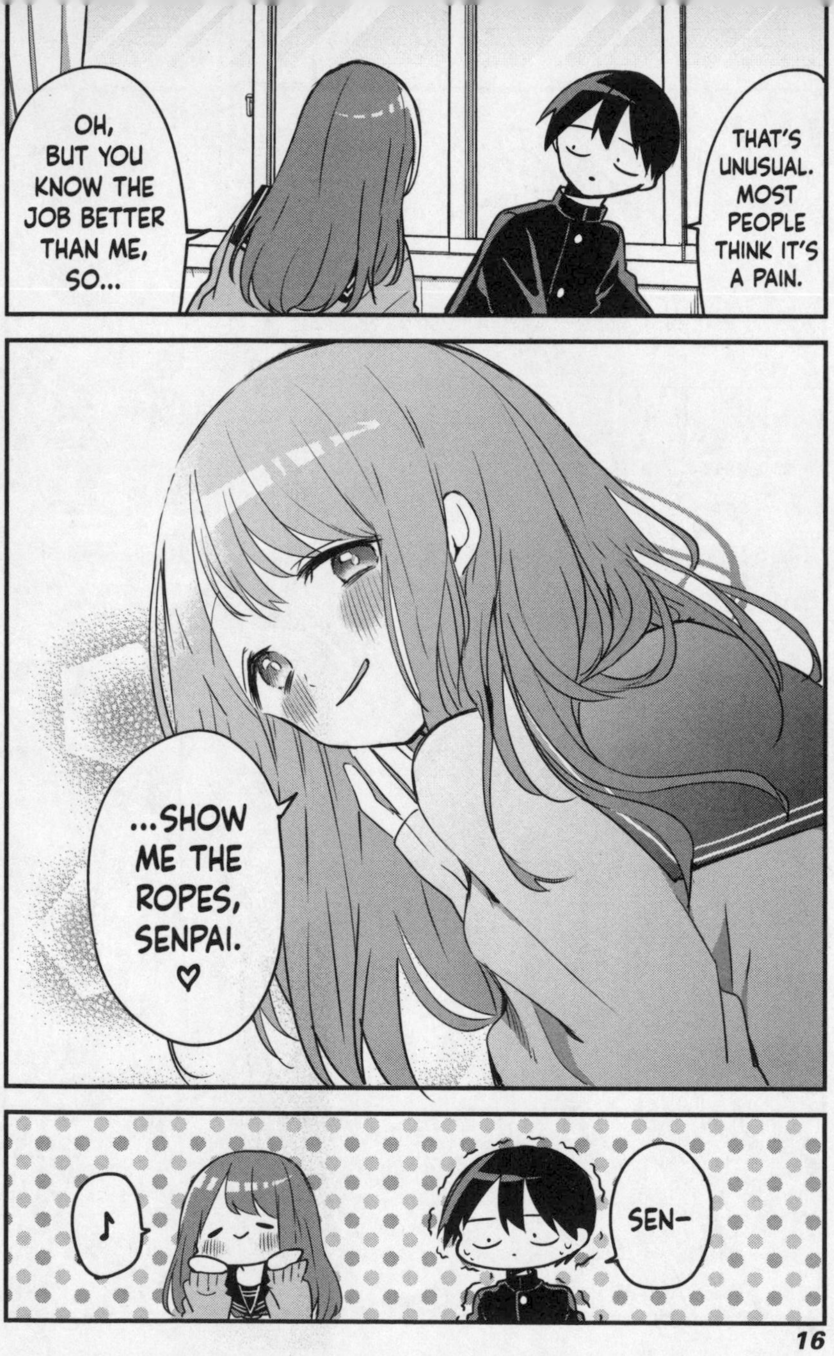
THAT'S UNUSUAL. MOST PEOPLE THINK IT'S A PAIN.
OH, BUT YOU KNOW THE JOB BETTER THAN ME, SO...
...SHOW ME THE ROPES, SENPAI. ♡
SEN-
♪

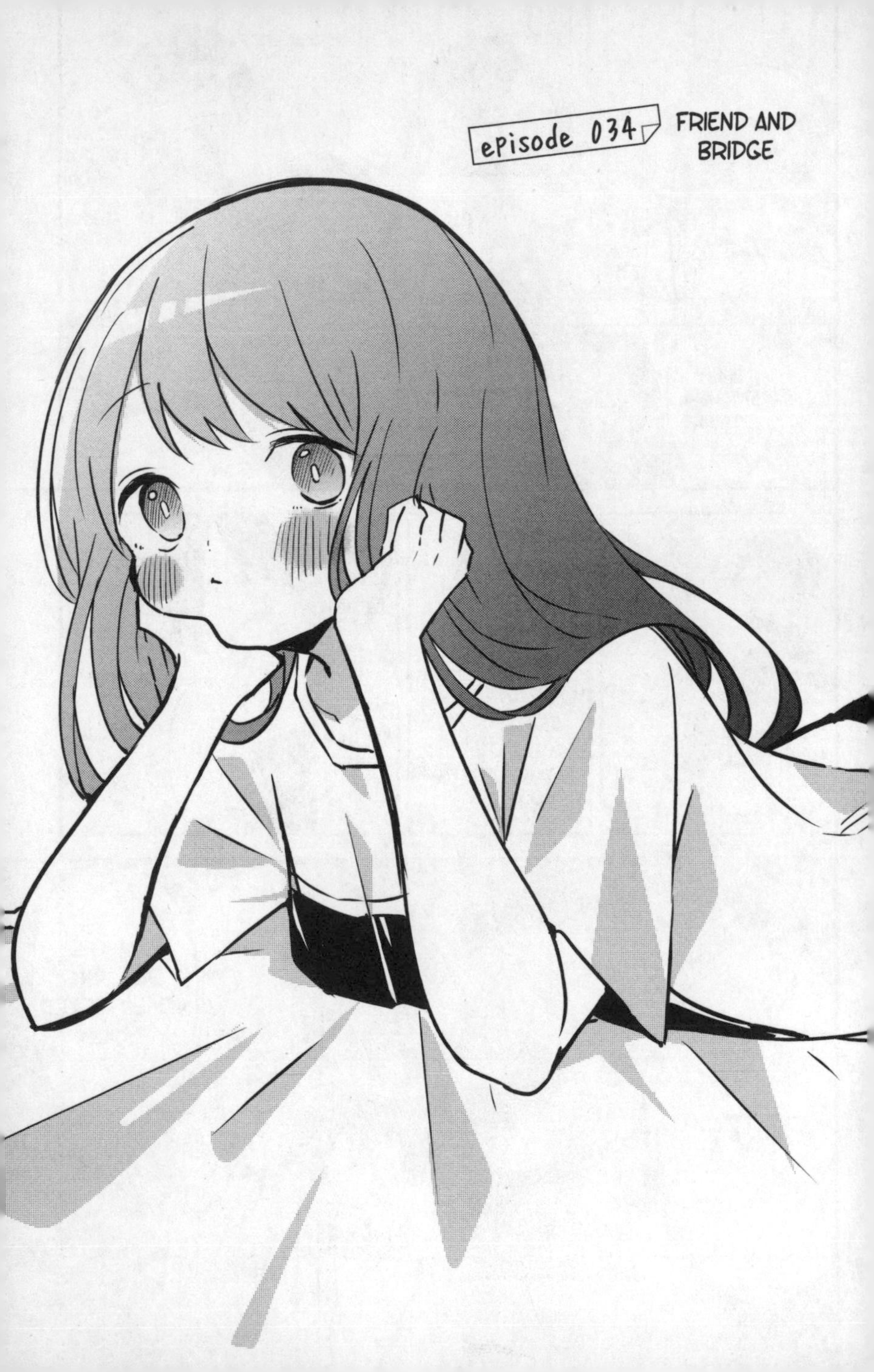
episode 034
FRIEND AND BRIDGE

YEAH. TAKING CARE OF FLOWERS— THAT SUITS HER.

WHO WAS THE OTHER PERSON AGAIN?

UHHH, SHIRAISHI, I THINK?

SPEAKING OF, WHICH COMMITTEE WAS KUBO ON? THE ENVIRONMENT COMMITTEE?

YOU GET TO DO COMMITTEE DUTIES WITH A GIRL? LUCKY!

THE ATHLETICS COMMITTEE IS ALL DUDES.

SORRY...

KUBO...

I CAN'T BLAME THEM FOR THINKING THAT.

I CAN SEE HIM DOING THAT.

YEAH.

OHH, SHIRAISHI. HE PROBABLY VOLUNTEERED FOR IT CUZ KUBO DID.

FACTS.

I'M THE ONE WHO VOLUNTEERED YOU.

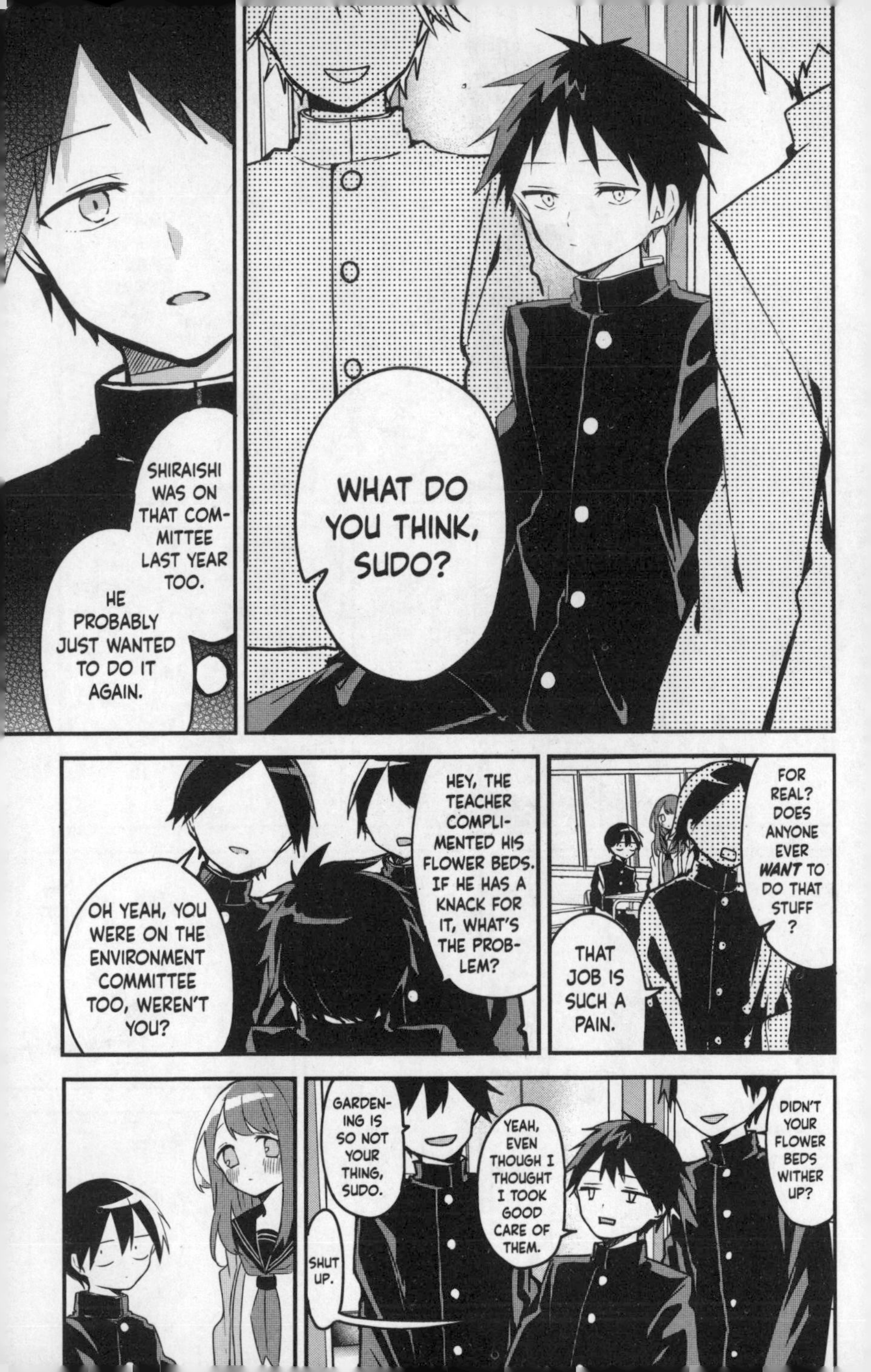
WHAT DO YOU THINK, SUDO?
SHIRAISHI WAS ON THAT COMMITTEE LAST YEAR TOO.
HE PROBABLY JUST WANTED TO DO IT AGAIN.
FOR REAL? DOES ANYONE EVER *WANT* TO DO THAT STUFF?
THAT JOB IS SUCH A PAIN.
HEY, THE TEACHER COMPLIMENTED HIS FLOWER BEDS. IF HE HAS A KNACK FOR IT, WHAT'S THE PROBLEM?
OH YEAH, YOU WERE ON THE ENVIRONMENT COMMITTEE TOO, WEREN'T YOU?
DIDN'T YOUR FLOWER BEDS WITHER UP?
YEAH, EVEN THOUGH I THOUGHT I TOOK GOOD CARE OF THEM.
GARDENING IS SO NOT YOUR THING, SUDO.
SHUT UP.

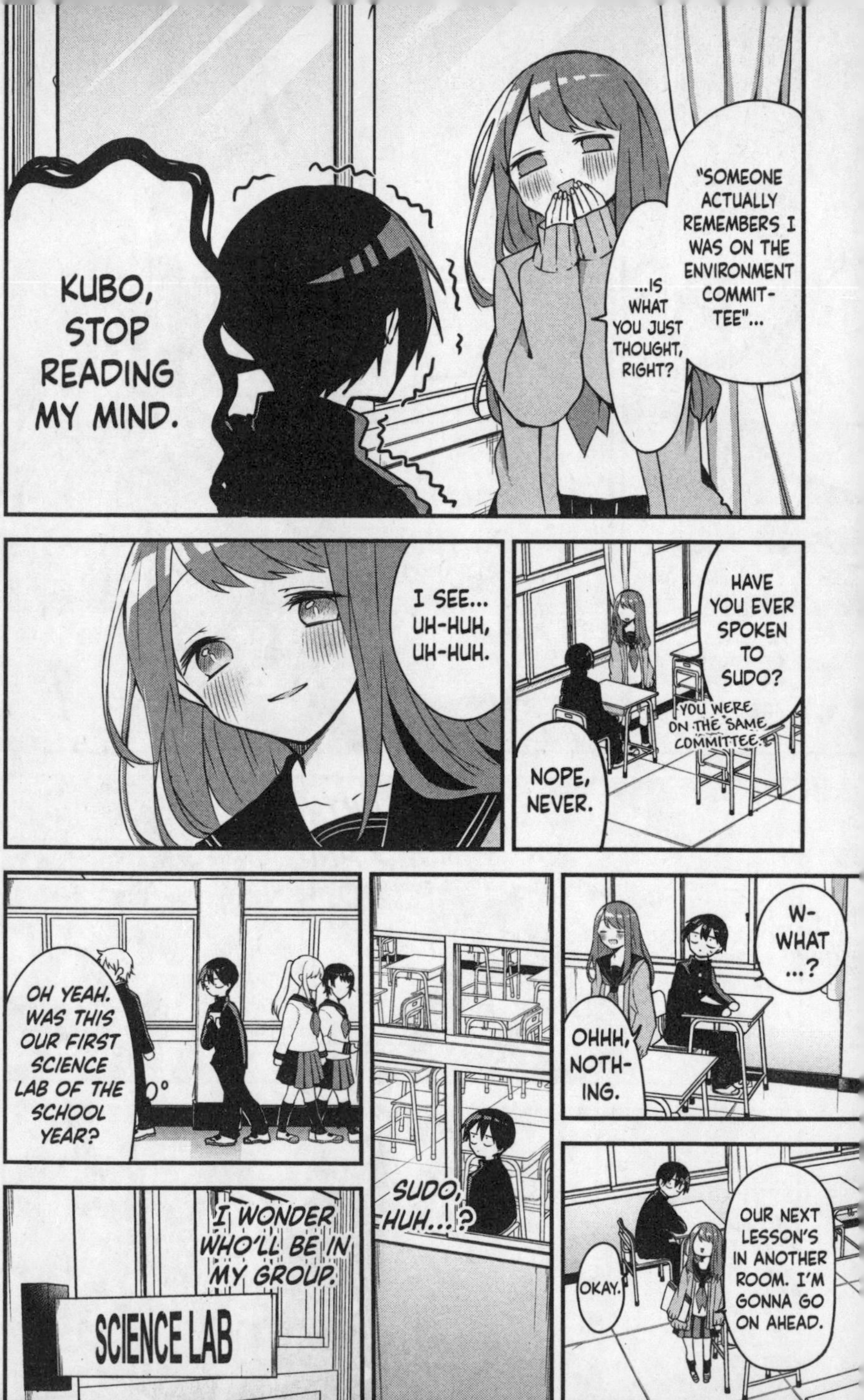
"SOMEONE ACTUALLY REMEMBERS I WAS ON THE ENVIRONMENT COMMIT-TEE"...
...IS WHAT YOU JUST THOUGHT, RIGHT?
KUBO, STOP READING MY MIND.
HAVE YOU EVER SPOKEN TO SUDO?
YOU WERE ON THE SAME COMMITTEE.
NOPE, NEVER.
I SEE... UH-HUH, UH-HUH.
W-WHAT ...?
OHHH, NOTH-ING.
OUR NEXT LESSON'S IN ANOTHER ROOM. I'M GONNA GO ON AHEAD.
OKAY.
SUDO, HUH...!?
OH YEAH. WAS THIS OUR FIRST SCIENCE LAB OF THE SCHOOL YEAR?
I WONDER WHO'LL BE IN MY GROUP.
SCIENCE LAB

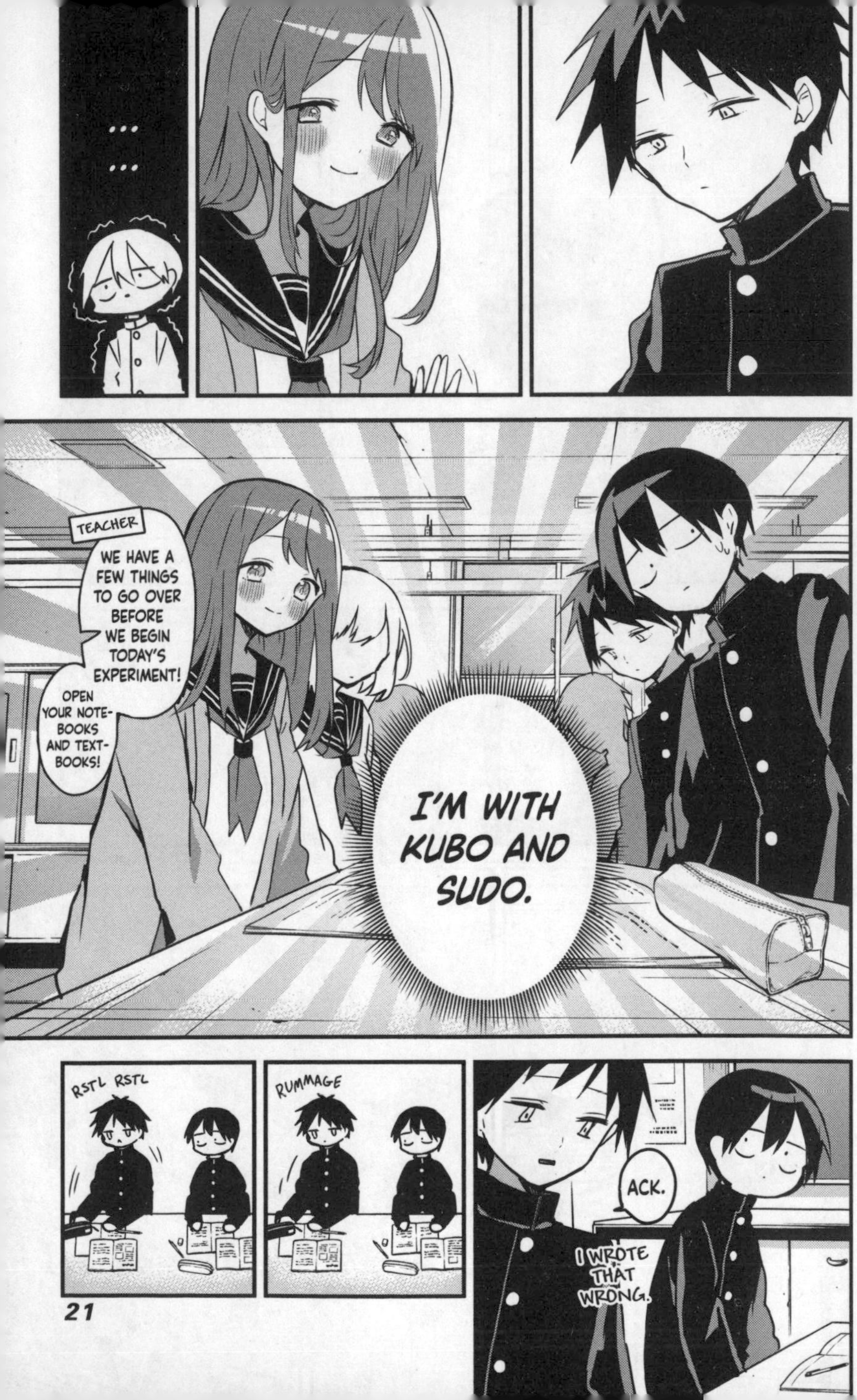
......
TEACHER
WE HAVE A FEW THINGS TO GO OVER BEFORE WE BEGIN TODAY'S EXPERIMENT!
OPEN YOUR NOTE-BOOKS AND TEXT-BOOKS!
I'M WITH KUBO AND SUDO.
ACK.
I WROTE THAT WRONG.
RUMMAGE
RSTL RSTL

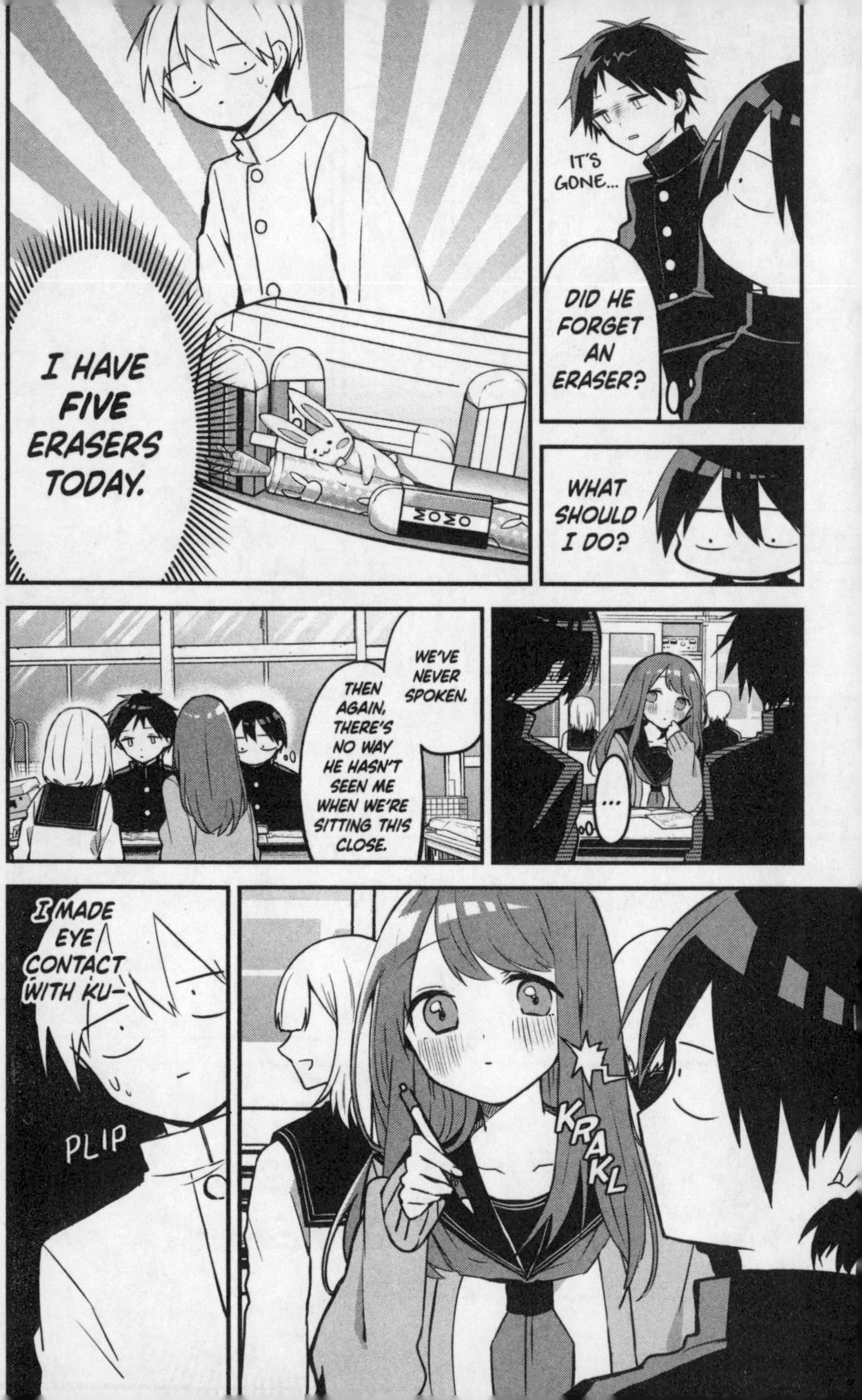
IT'S GONE...
DID HE FORGET AN ERASER?
WHAT SHOULD I DO?
I HAVE FIVE ERASERS TODAY.
...
WE'VE NEVER SPOKEN.
THEN AGAIN, THERE'S NO WAY HE HASN'T SEEN ME WHEN WE'RE SITTING THIS CLOSE.
KRAKL
I MADE EYE CONTACT WITH KU–
PLIP

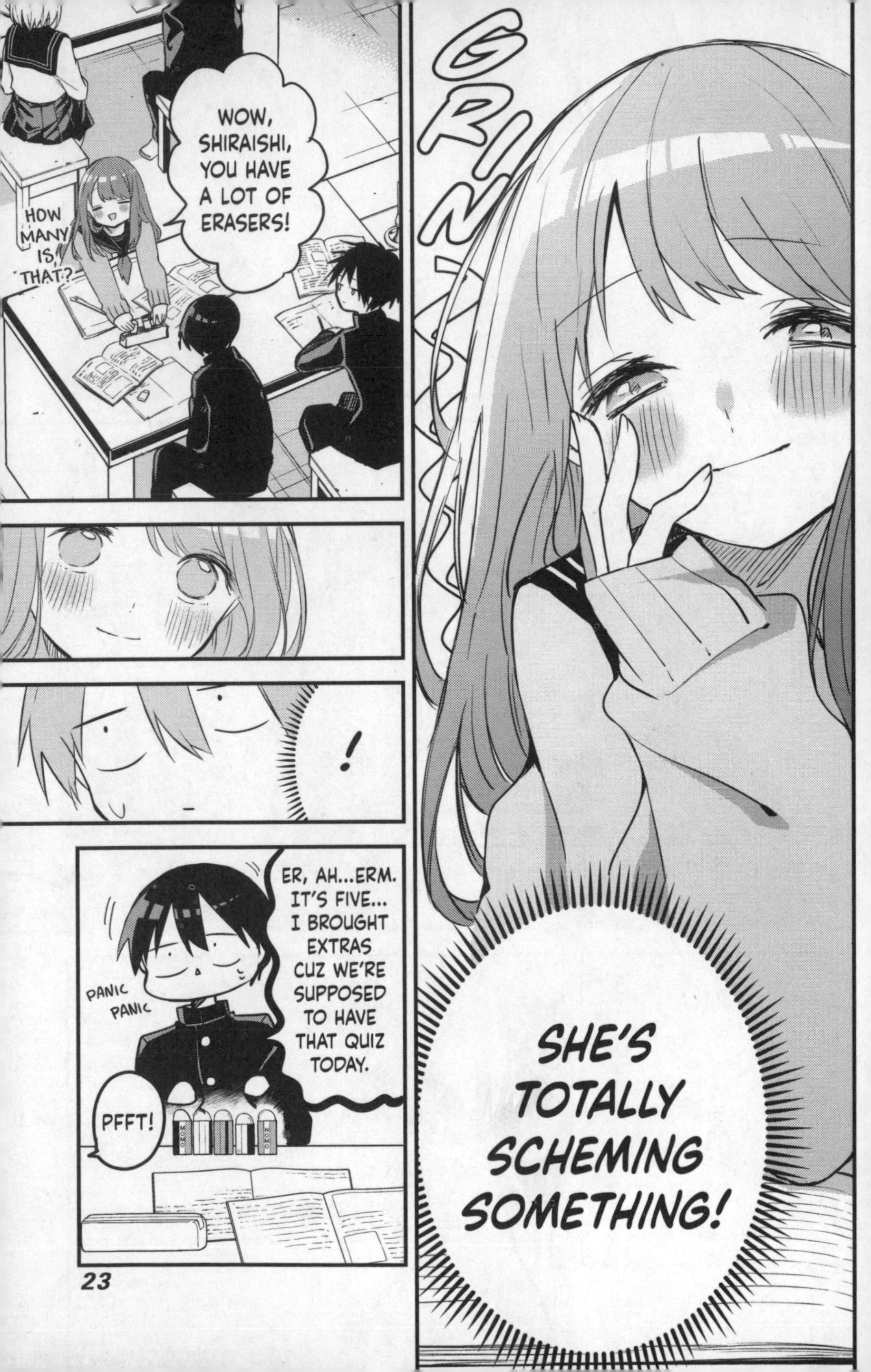
GRIN
SHE'S TOTALLY SCHEMING SOMETHING!
WOW, SHIRAISHI, YOU HAVE A LOT OF ERASERS!
HOW MANY IS THAT?
!
ER, AH...ERM. IT'S FIVE... I BROUGHT EXTRAS CUZ WE'RE SUPPOSED TO HAVE THAT QUIZ TODAY.
PANIC PANIC
PFFT!
MOMO
MOMO

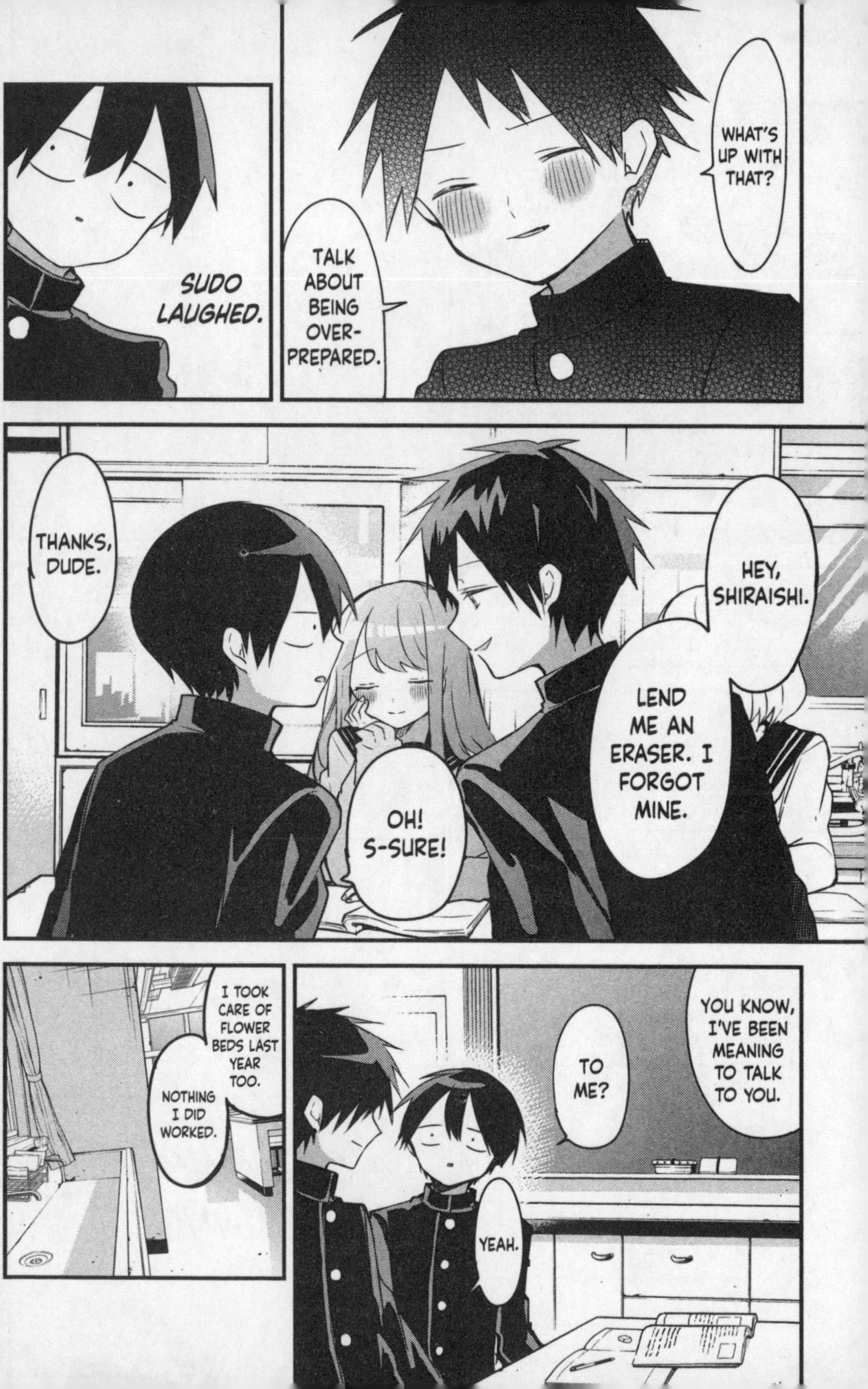
WHAT'S UP WITH THAT?
TALK ABOUT BEING OVER-PREPARED.
SUDO LAUGHED.
HEY, SHIRAISHI.
LEND ME AN ERASER. I FORGOT MINE.
OH! S-SURE!
THANKS, DUDE.
YOU KNOW, I'VE BEEN MEANING TO TALK TO YOU.
TO ME?
YEAH.
I TOOK CARE OF FLOWER BEDS LAST YEAR TOO.
NOTHING I DID WORKED.

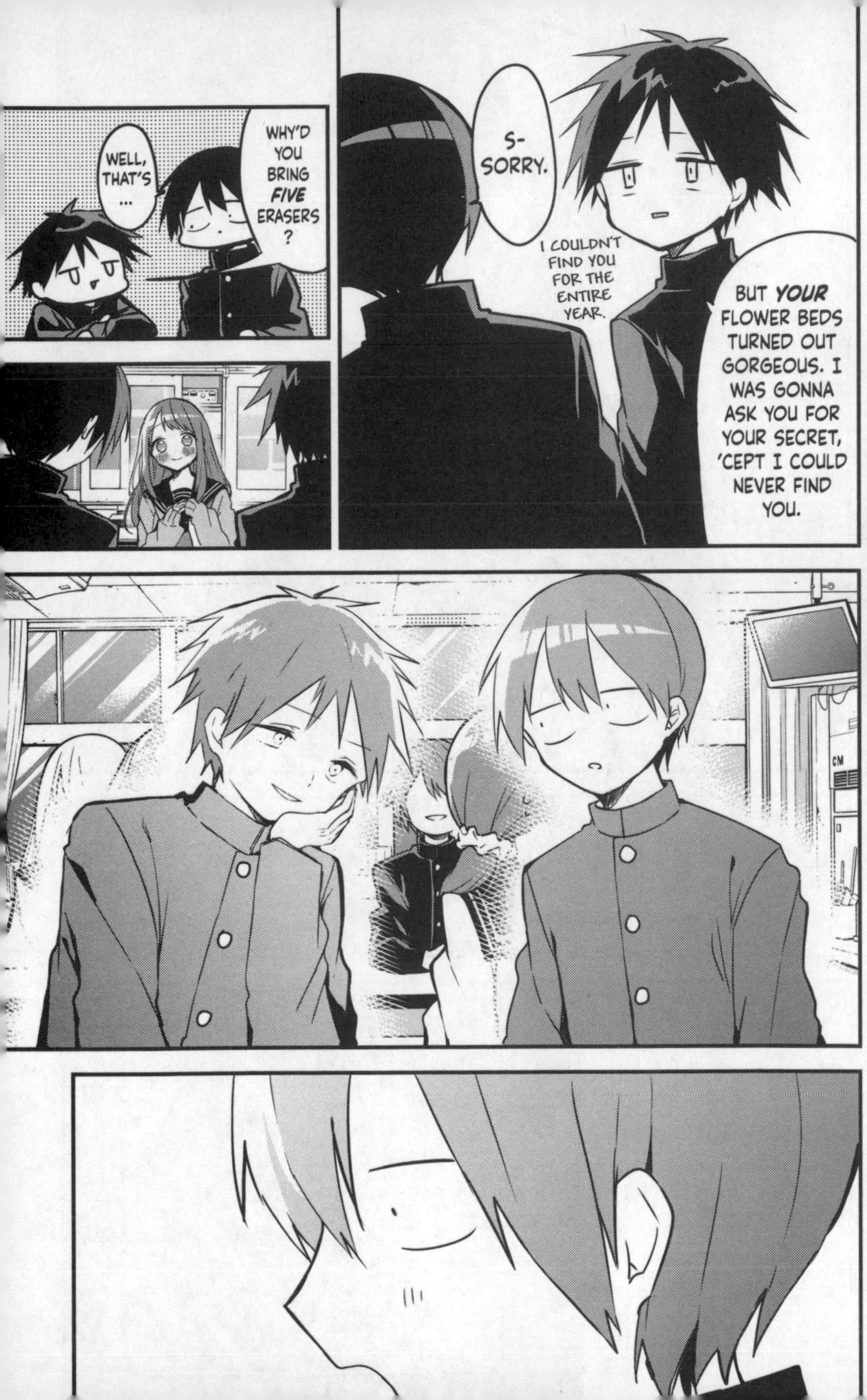
S-SORRY.
I COULDN'T FIND YOU FOR THE ENTIRE YEAR.
BUT YOUR FLOWER BEDS TURNED OUT GORGEOUS. I WAS GONNA ASK YOU FOR YOUR SECRET, 'CEPT I COULD NEVER FIND YOU.
WHY'D YOU BRING FIVE ERASERS?
WELL, THAT'S ...

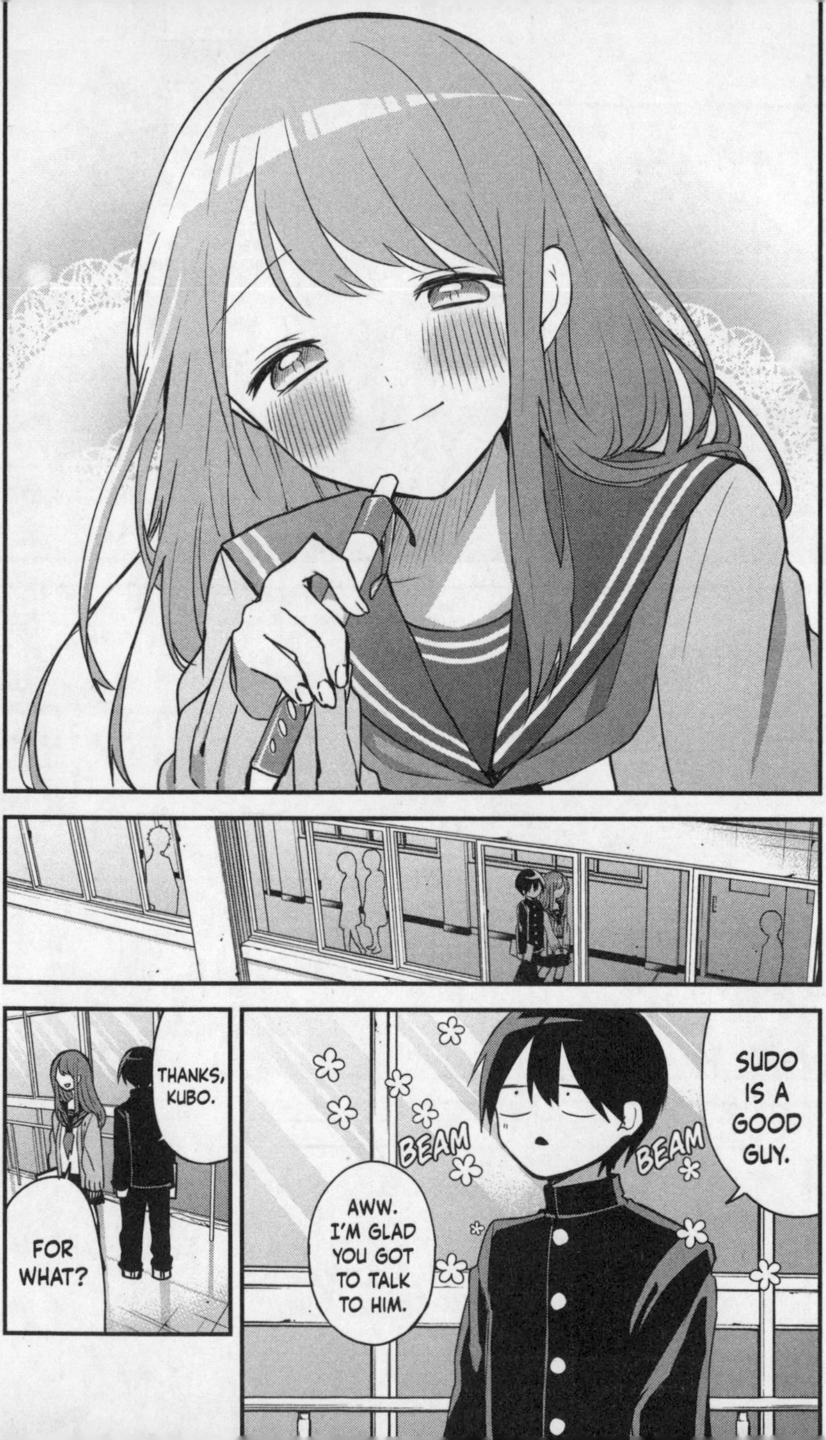
SUDO IS A GOOD GUY.
BEAM
BEAM
AWW. I'M GLAD YOU GOT TO TALK TO HIM.
THANKS, KUBO.
FOR WHAT?

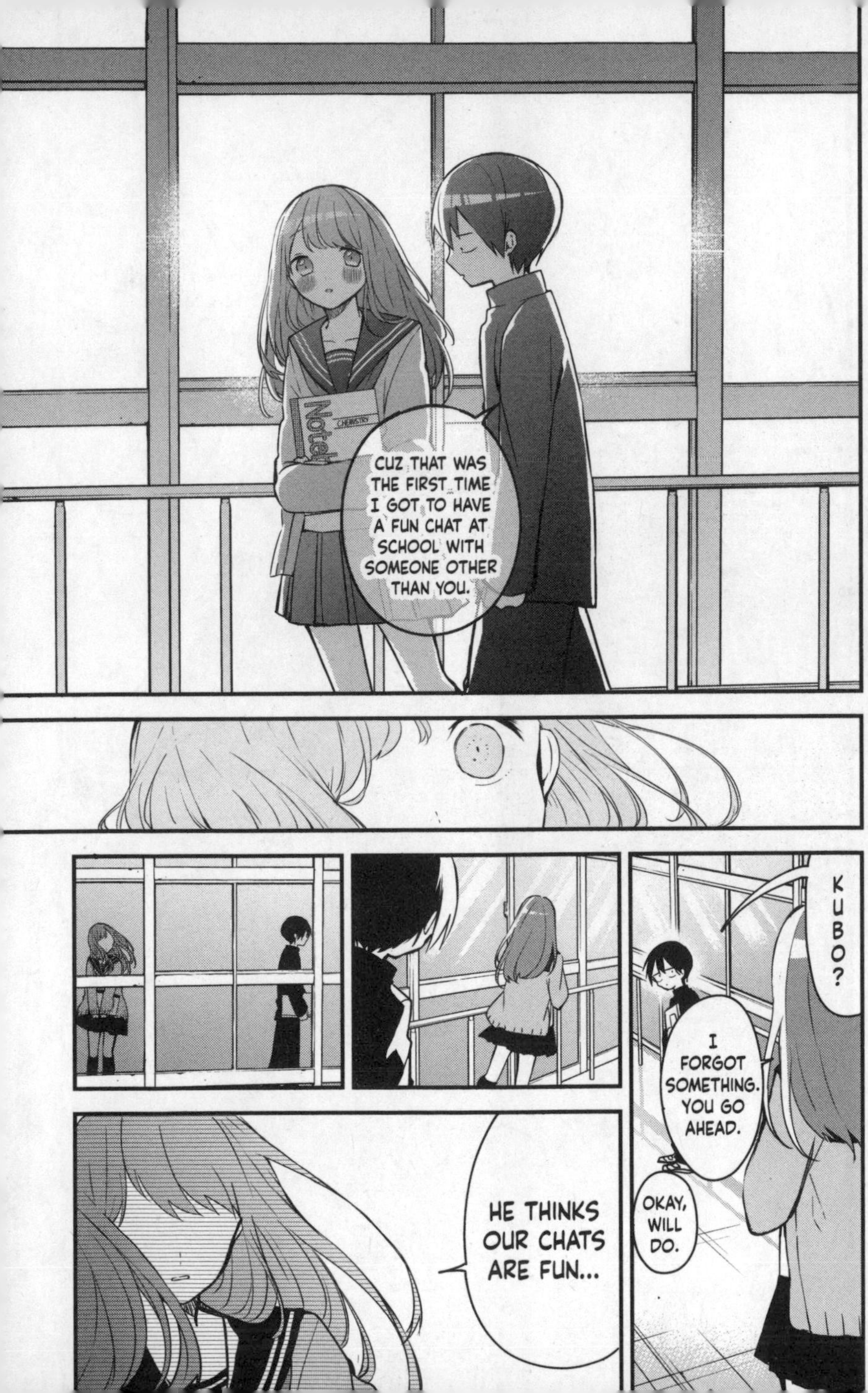
CUZ THAT WAS THE FIRST TIME I GOT TO HAVE A FUN CHAT AT SCHOOL WITH SOMEONE OTHER THAN YOU.
KUBO?
I FORGOT SOMETHING. YOU GO AHEAD.
OKAY, WILL DO.
HE THINKS OUR CHATS ARE FUN...

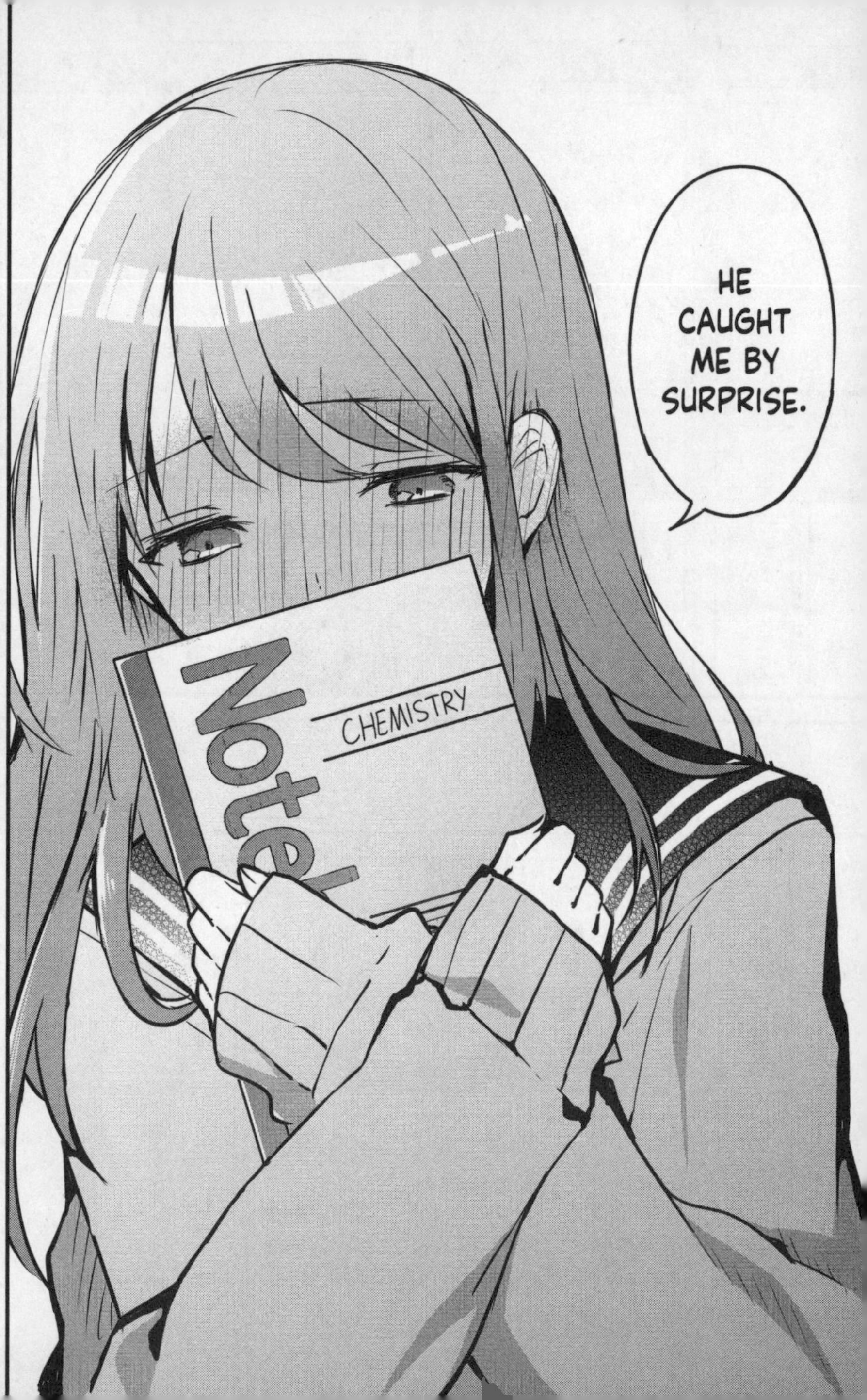
HE CAUGHT ME BY SURPRISE.
Note
CHEMISTRY

IS JUNTA SHIRAISHI HERE?
NOPE, I HAVEN'T SEEN HIM TODAY.
IS SHIRAISHI HERE TODAY?
I HAVEN'T SEEN HIM.
AH! HEY, SUDO. I SPOTTED SHIRAISHI YESTERDAY.
WHAT ABOUT TODAY?
HAVEN'T SEEN HIM.
IN THE END, I DIDN'T GET TO SEE HIM FOR THAT ENTIRE YEAR.

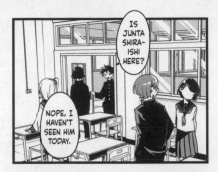

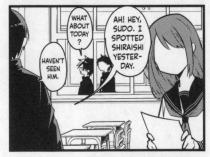

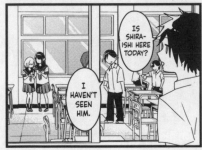

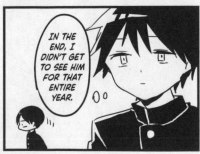

THEY
BLOOMED.

episode 035

LEMON AND YOUTH

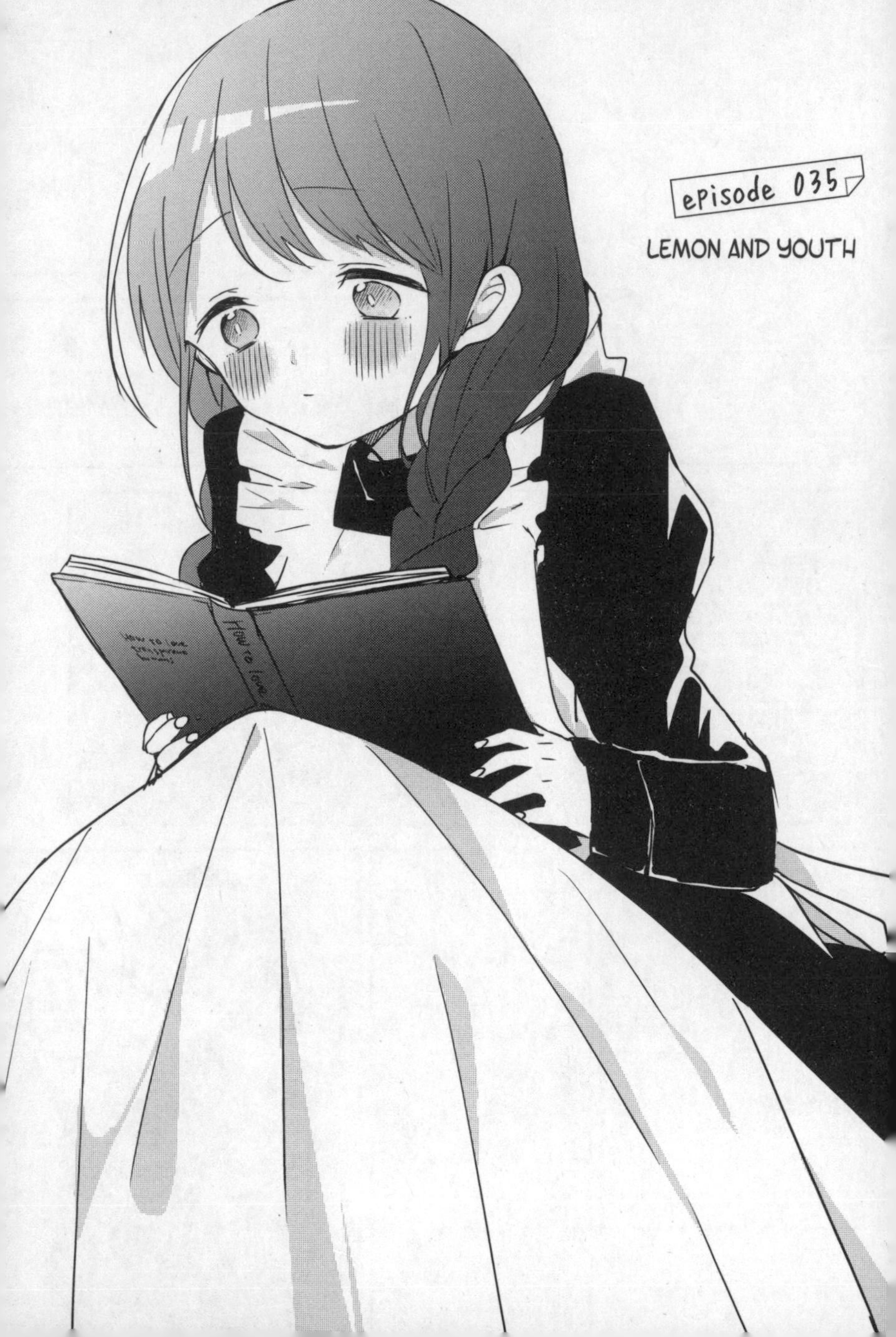
How to love

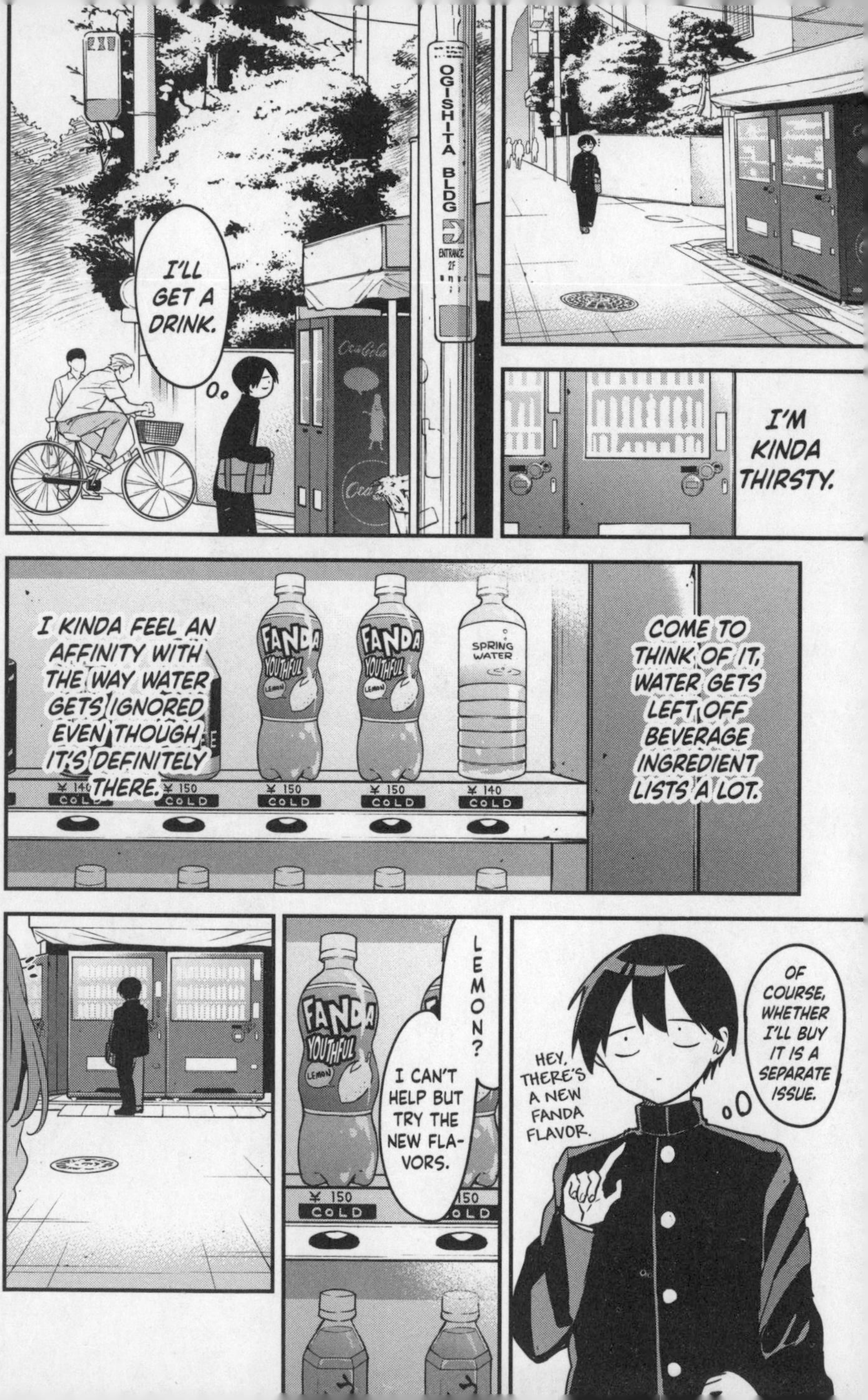
I'M KINDA THIRSTY.
OGISHITA BLDG
ENTRANCE 2F
I'LL GET A DRINK.
COME TO THINK OF IT, WATER GETS LEFT OFF BEVERAGE INGREDIENT LISTS A LOT.
SPRING WATER
¥ 140 COLD
FANDA YOUTHFUL LEMON
¥ 150 COLD
FANDA YOUTHFUL LEMON
¥ 150 COLD
¥ 150 COLD
¥ 140 COLD
I KINDA FEEL AN AFFINITY WITH THE WAY WATER GETS IGNORED EVEN THOUGH IT'S DEFINITELY THERE.
OF COURSE, WHETHER I'LL BUY IT IS A SEPARATE ISSUE.
HEY, THERE'S A NEW FANDA FLAVOR.
LEMON?
I CAN'T HELP BUT TRY THE NEW FLA-VORS.
FANDA YOUTHFUL LEMON
¥ 150 COLD

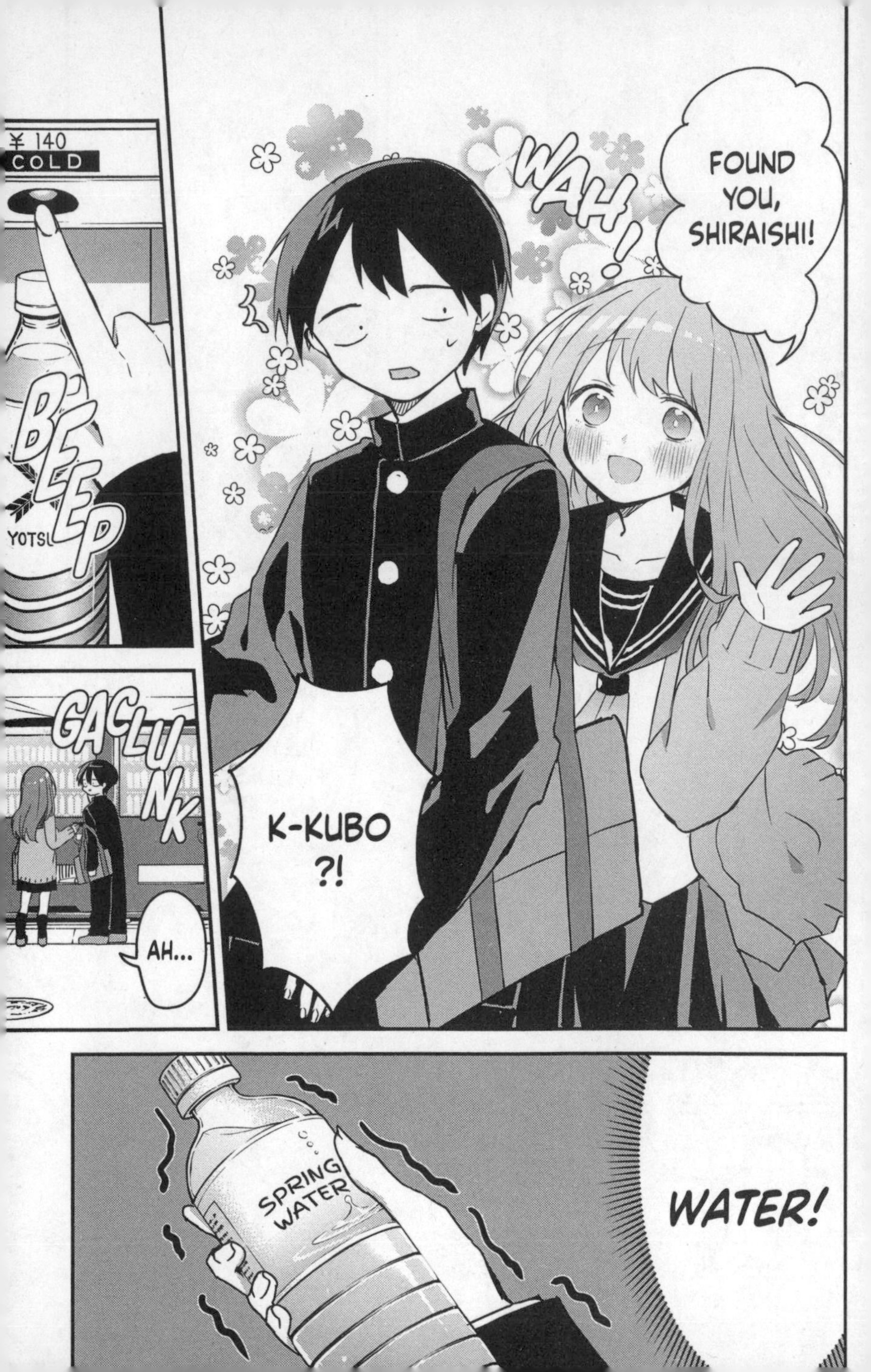
FOUND YOU, SHIRAISHI!
WAH!
K-KUBO ?!
¥ 140
COLD
BEEP
GACLUNK
AH...
SPRING WATER
WATER!

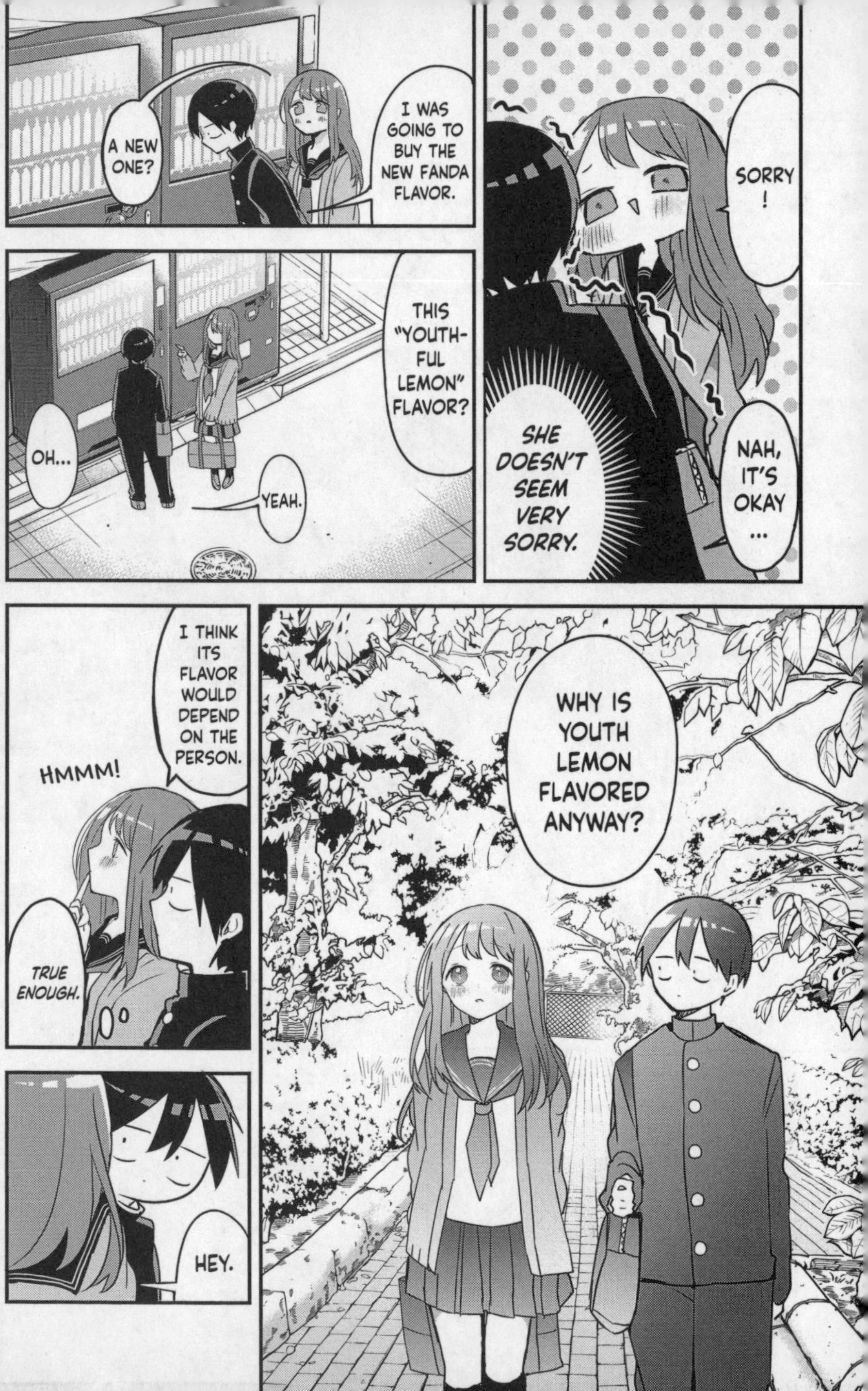
SORRY!
NAH, IT'S OKAY...
SHE DOESN'T SEEM VERY SORRY.
I WAS GOING TO BUY THE NEW FANDA FLAVOR.
A NEW ONE?
THIS "YOUTH-FUL LEMON" FLAVOR?
OH...
YEAH.
WHY IS YOUTH LEMON FLAVORED ANYWAY?
I THINK ITS FLAVOR WOULD DEPEND ON THE PERSON.
HMMM!
TRUE ENOUGH.
HEY.

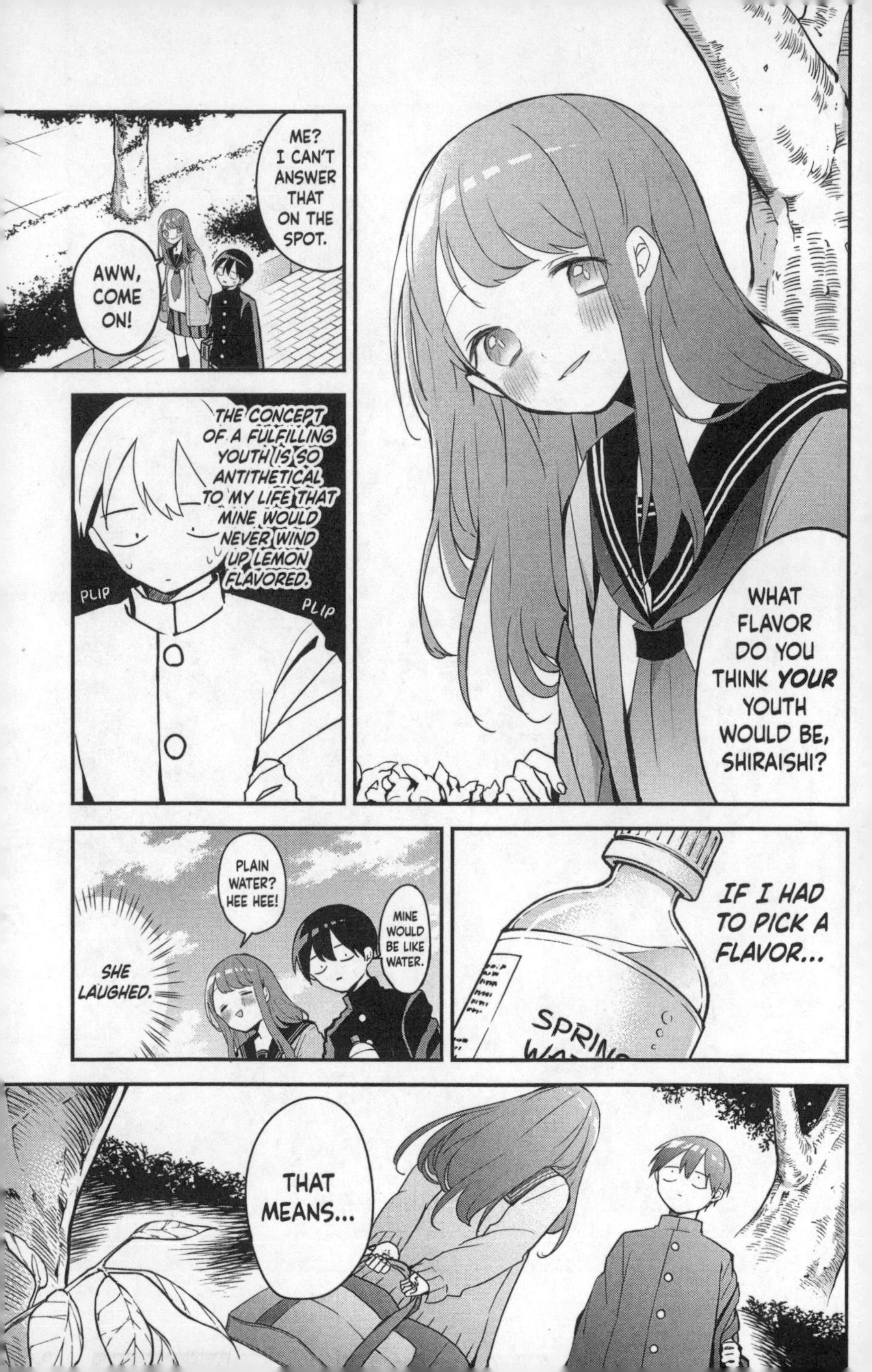
WHAT FLAVOR DO YOU THINK *YOUR* YOUTH WOULD BE, SHIRAISHI?
ME? I CAN'T ANSWER THAT ON THE SPOT.
AWW, COME ON!
THE CONCEPT OF A FULFILLING YOUTH IS SO ANTITHETICAL TO MY LIFE THAT MINE WOULD NEVER WIND UP LEMON FLAVORED.
PLIP
PLIP
IF I HAD TO PICK A FLAVOR...
MINE WOULD BE LIKE WATER.
PLAIN WATER? HEE HEE!
SHE LAUGHED.
THAT MEANS...

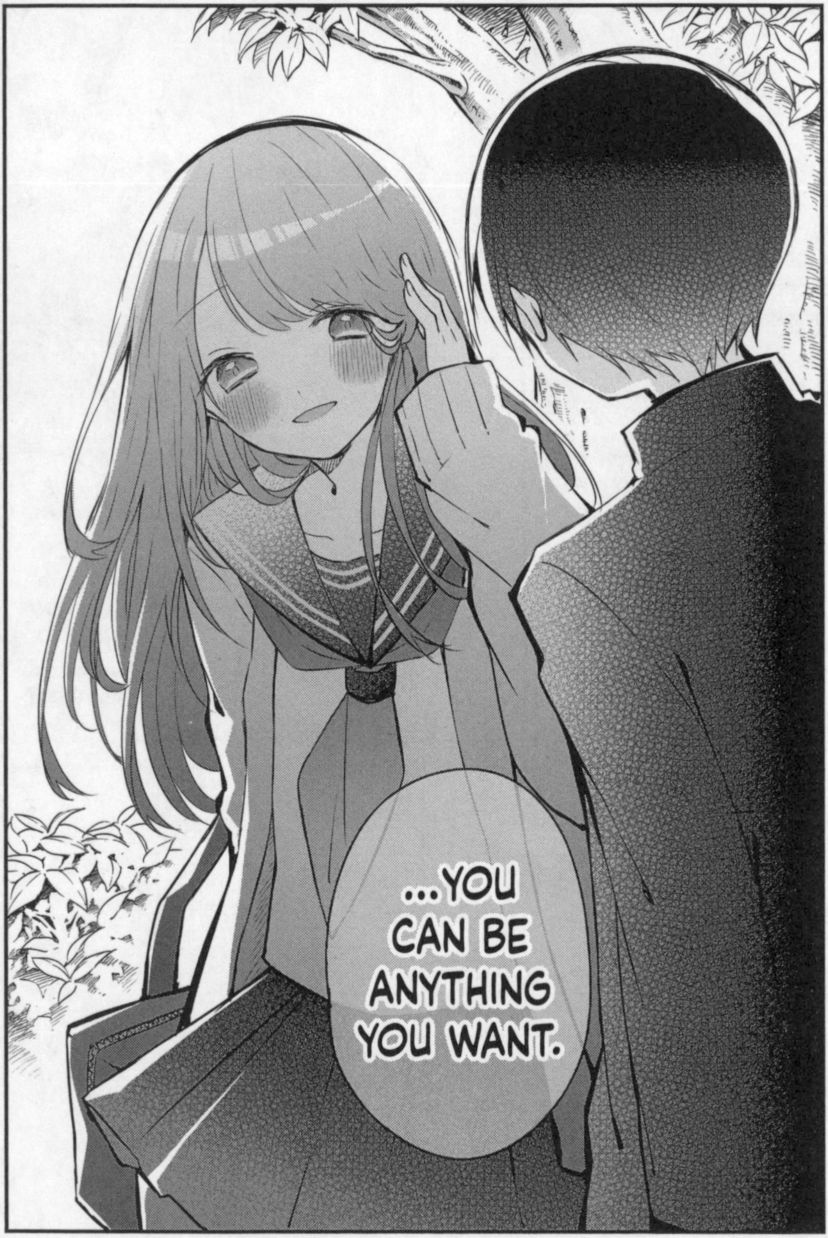
...YOU CAN BE ANYTHING YOU WANT.

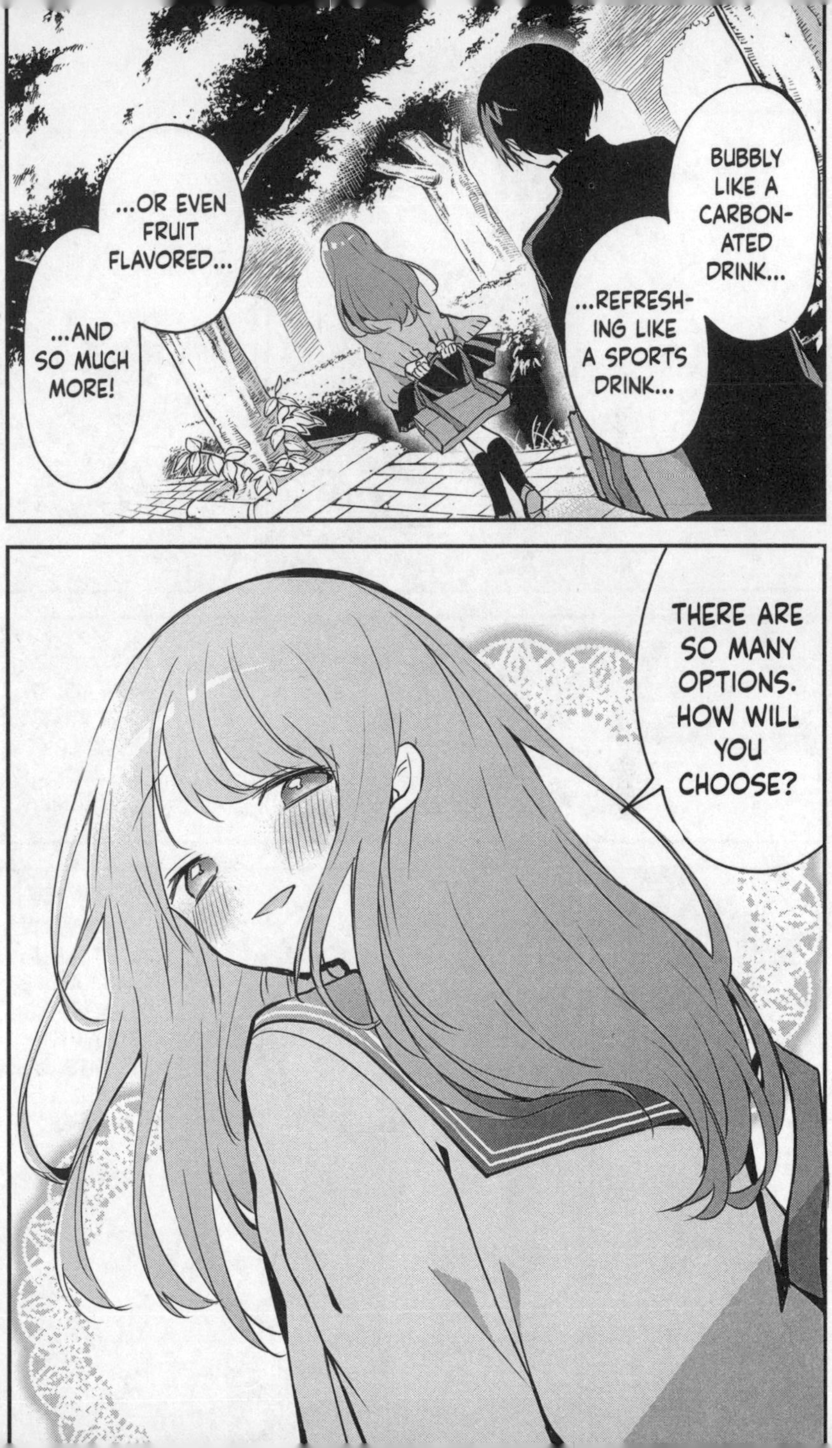
BUBBLY LIKE A CARBON-ATED DRINK...
...REFRESH-ING LIKE A SPORTS DRINK...
...OR EVEN FRUIT FLAVORED...
...AND SO MUCH MORE!
THERE ARE SO MANY OPTIONS. HOW WILL YOU CHOOSE?

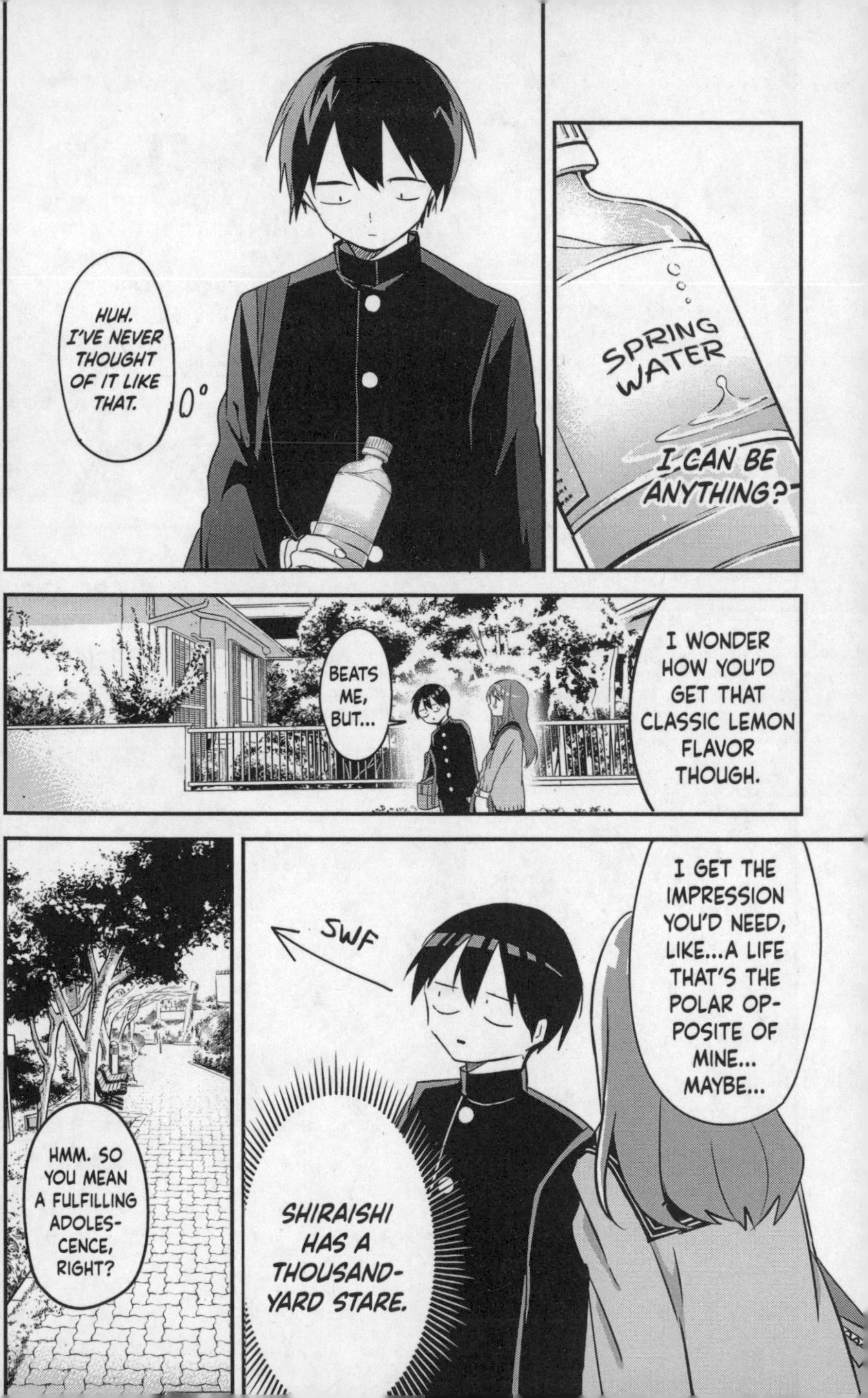
SPRING WATER
I CAN BE ANYTHING?
HUH. I'VE NEVER THOUGHT OF IT LIKE THAT.
I WONDER HOW YOU'D GET THAT CLASSIC LEMON FLAVOR THOUGH.
BEATS ME, BUT...
I GET THE IMPRESSION YOU'D NEED, LIKE...A LIFE THAT'S THE POLAR OP-POSITE OF MINE... MAYBE...
SWF
SHIRAISHI HAS A THOUSAND-YARD STARE.
HMM. SO YOU MEAN A FULFILLING ADOLES-CENCE, RIGHT?

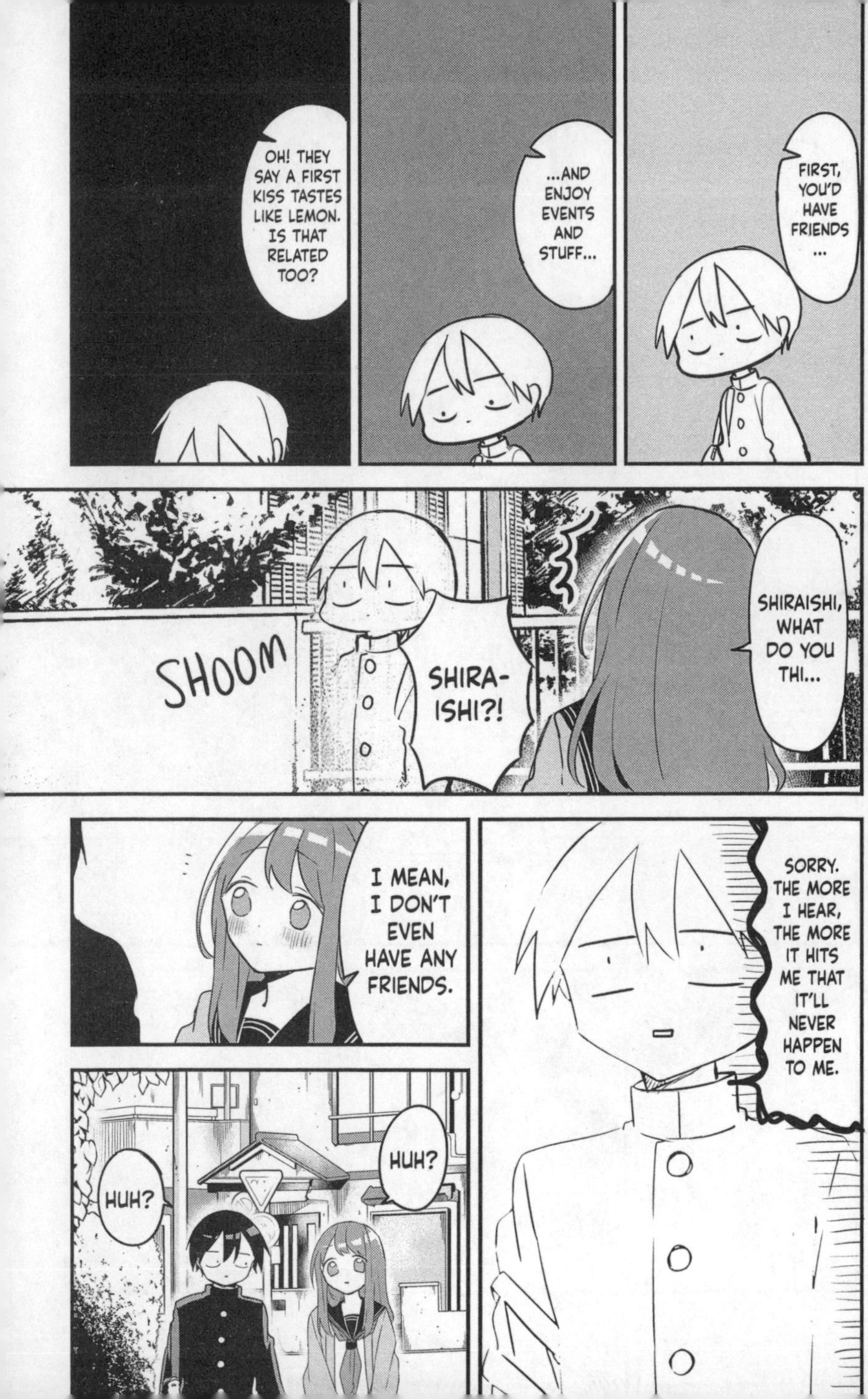
FIRST, YOU'D HAVE FRIENDS ...
...AND ENJOY EVENTS AND STUFF...
OH! THEY SAY A FIRST KISS TASTES LIKE LEMON. IS THAT RELATED TOO?
SHIRAISHI, WHAT DO YOU THI...
SHIRA-ISHI?!
SHOOM
SORRY. THE MORE I HEAR, THE MORE IT HITS ME THAT IT'LL NEVER HAPPEN TO ME.
I MEAN, I DON'T EVEN HAVE ANY FRIENDS.
HUH?
HUH?

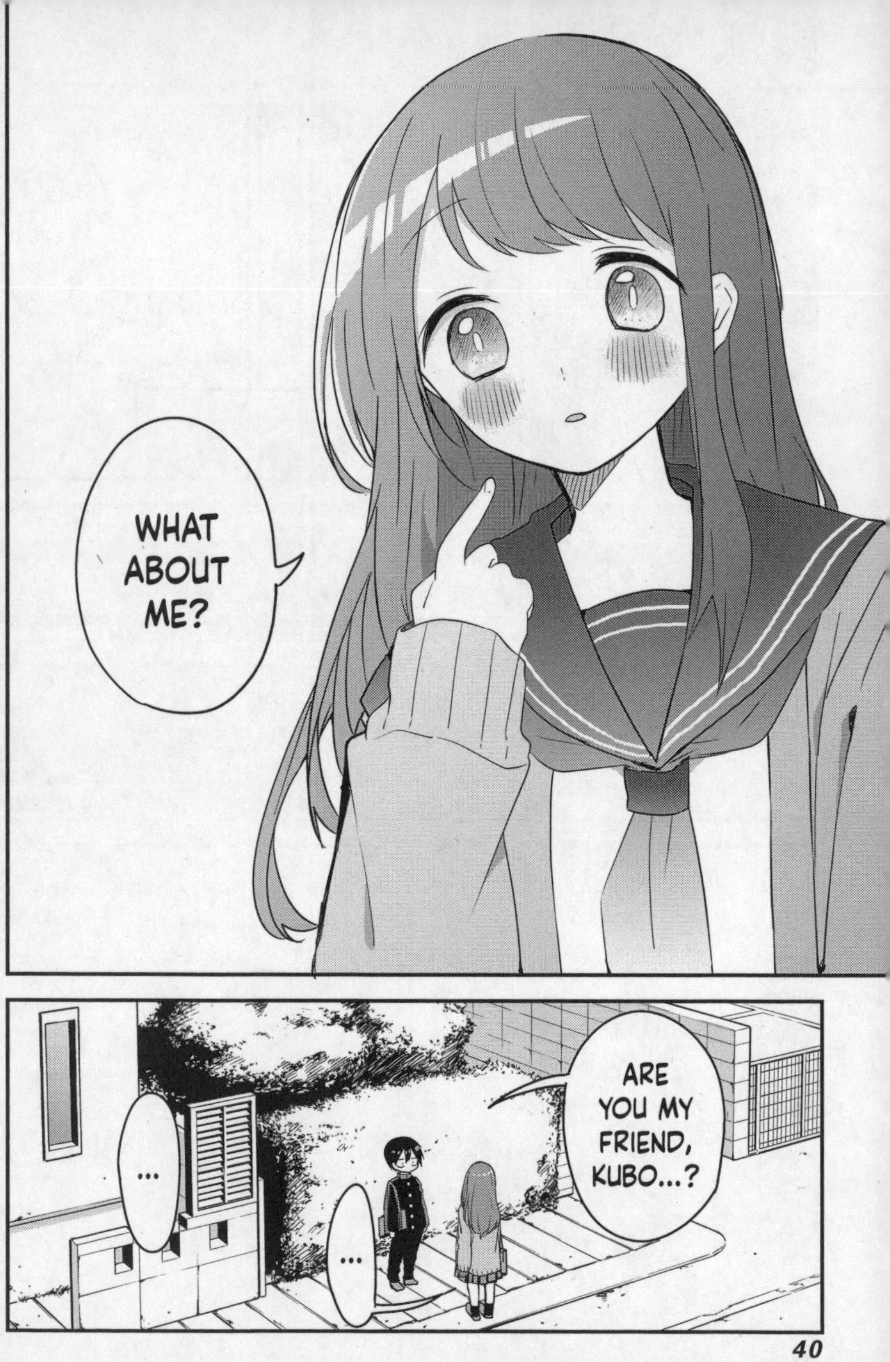
WHAT ABOUT ME?
ARE YOU MY FRIEND, KUBO...?
...
...

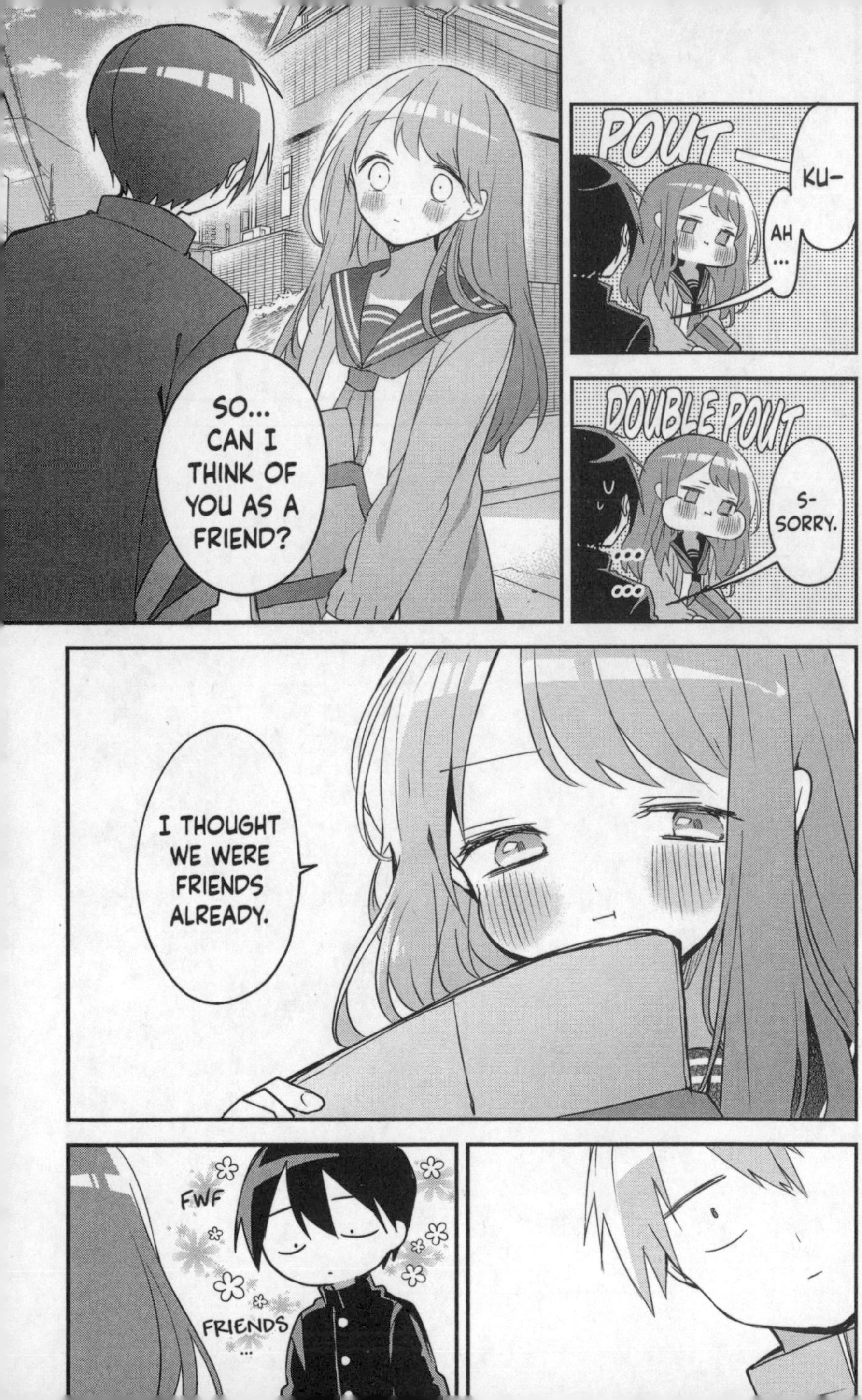
POUT
KU-
AH ...
DOUBLE POUT
S-SORRY.
SO... CAN I THINK OF YOU AS A FRIEND?
I THOUGHT WE WERE FRIENDS ALREADY.
FWF
FRIENDS ...

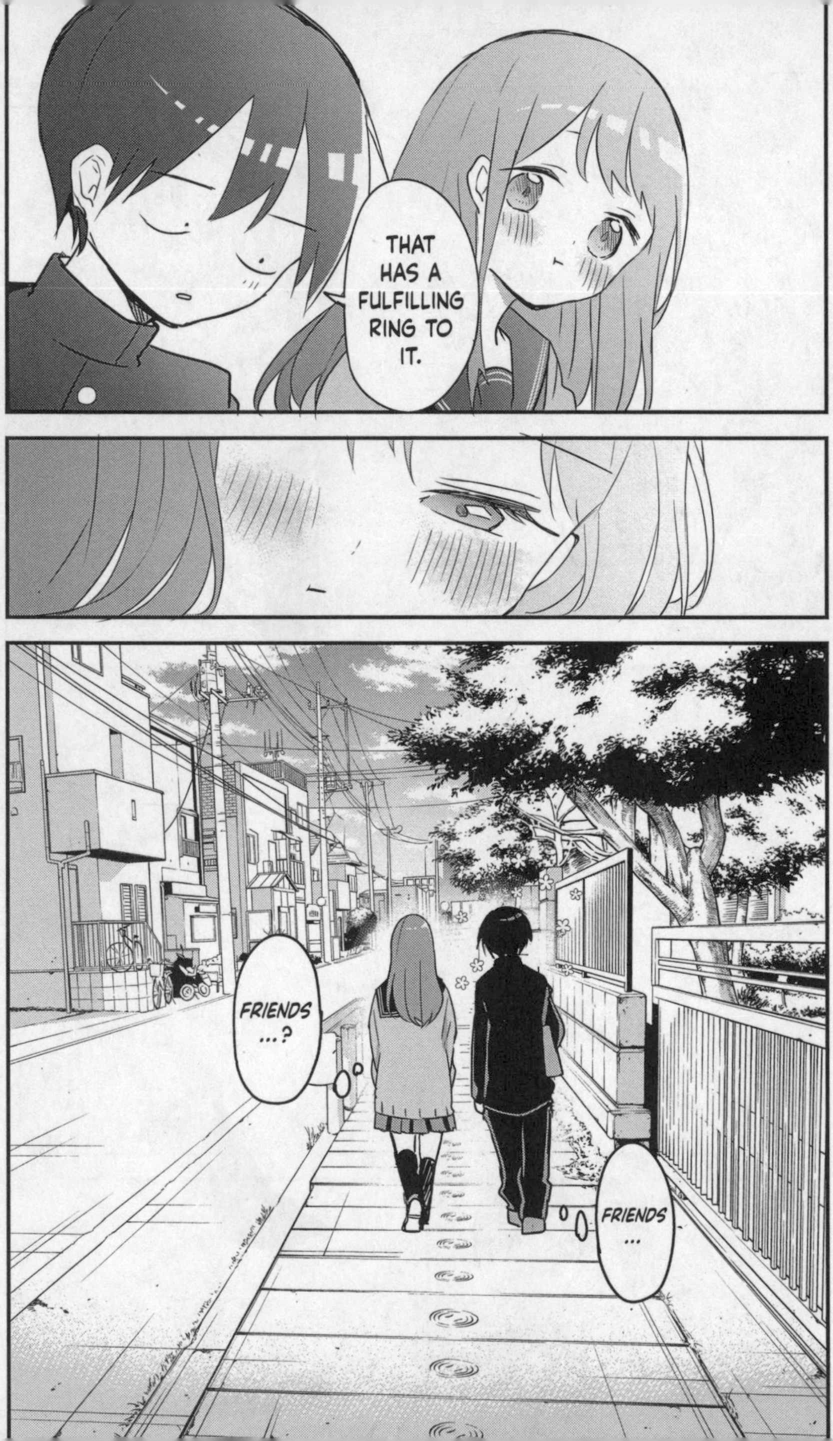
THAT HAS A FULFILLING RING TO IT.
FRIENDS ...?
FRIENDS ...

episode 036

CHALKBOARD ERASERS AND FAVORITE HAIRSTYLE

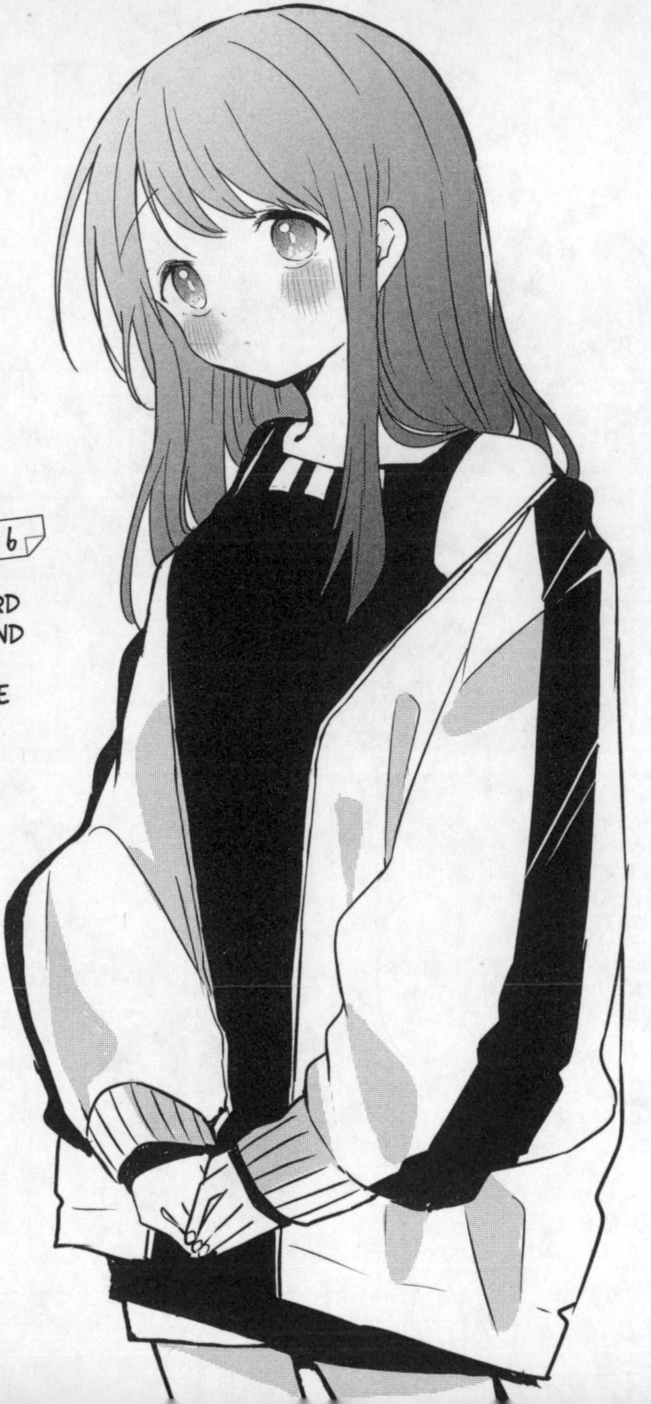

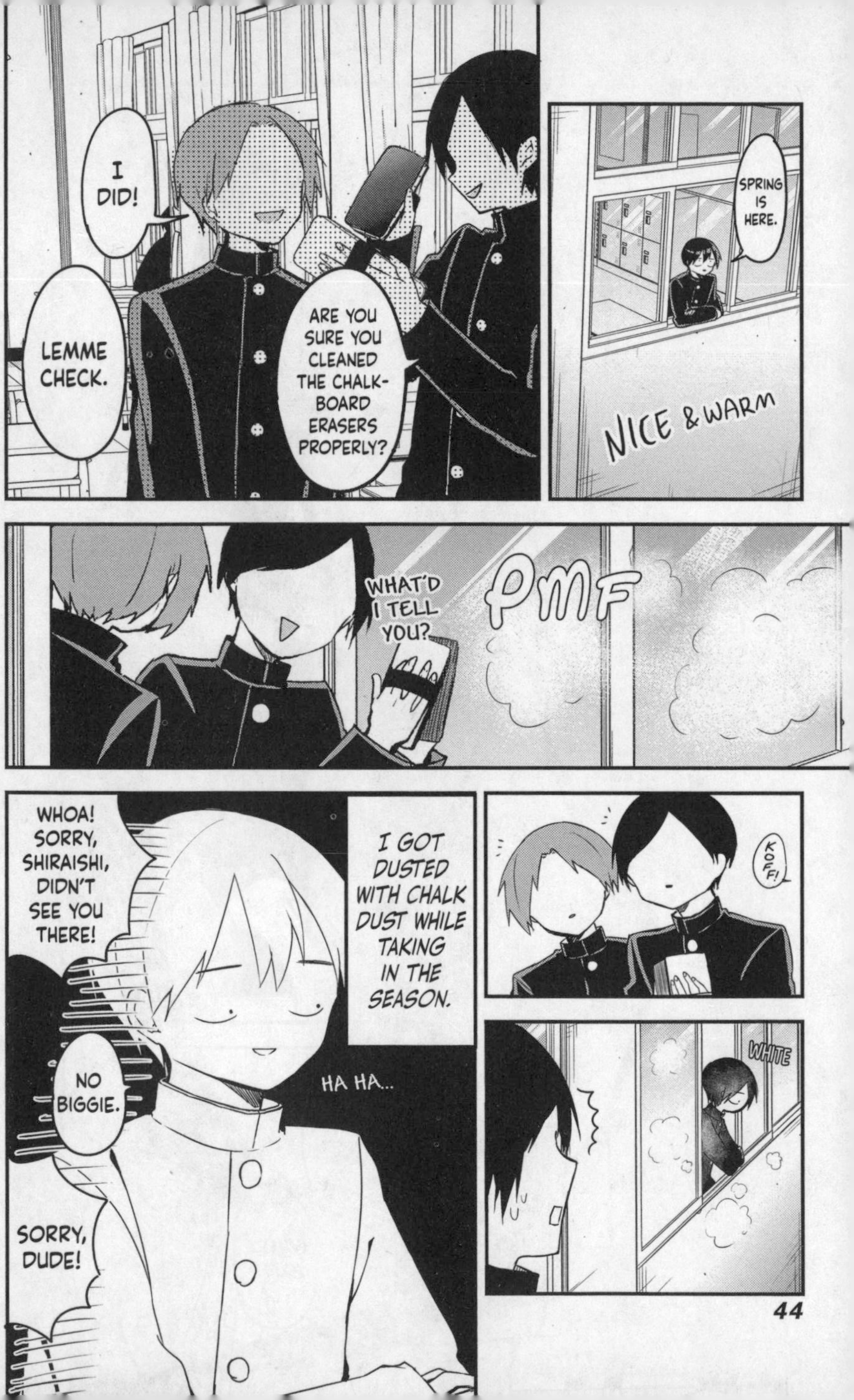
SPRING IS HERE.
NICE & WARM
ARE YOU SURE YOU CLEANED THE CHALK-BOARD ERASERS PROPERLY?
I DID!
LEMME CHECK.
PMF
WHAT'D I TELL YOU?
KOFF!
WHITE
I GOT DUSTED WITH CHALK DUST WHILE TAKING IN THE SEASON.
WHOA! SORRY, SHIRAISHI, DIDN'T SEE YOU THERE!
HA HA...
NO BIGGIE.
SORRY, DUDE!

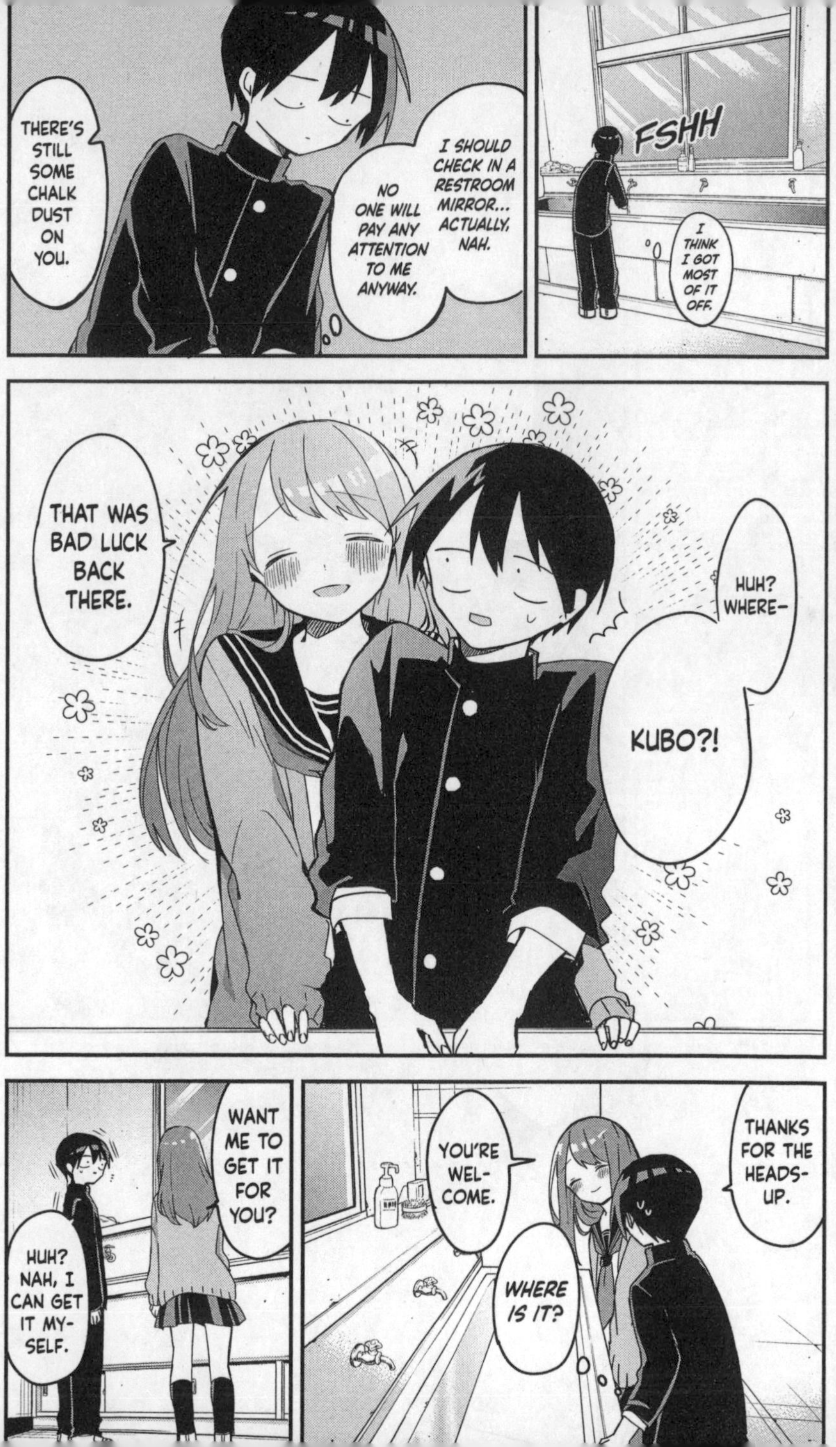
FSHH
I THINK I GOT MOST OF IT OFF.
I SHOULD CHECK IN A RESTROOM MIRROR... ACTUALLY, NAH.
NO ONE WILL PAY ANY ATTENTION TO ME ANYWAY.
THERE'S STILL SOME CHALK DUST ON YOU.
HUH? WHERE-
KUBO?!
THAT WAS BAD LUCK BACK THERE.
THANKS FOR THE HEADS-UP.
YOU'RE WEL-COME.
WHERE IS IT?
WANT ME TO GET IT FOR YOU?
HUH? NAH, I CAN GET IT MY-SELF.

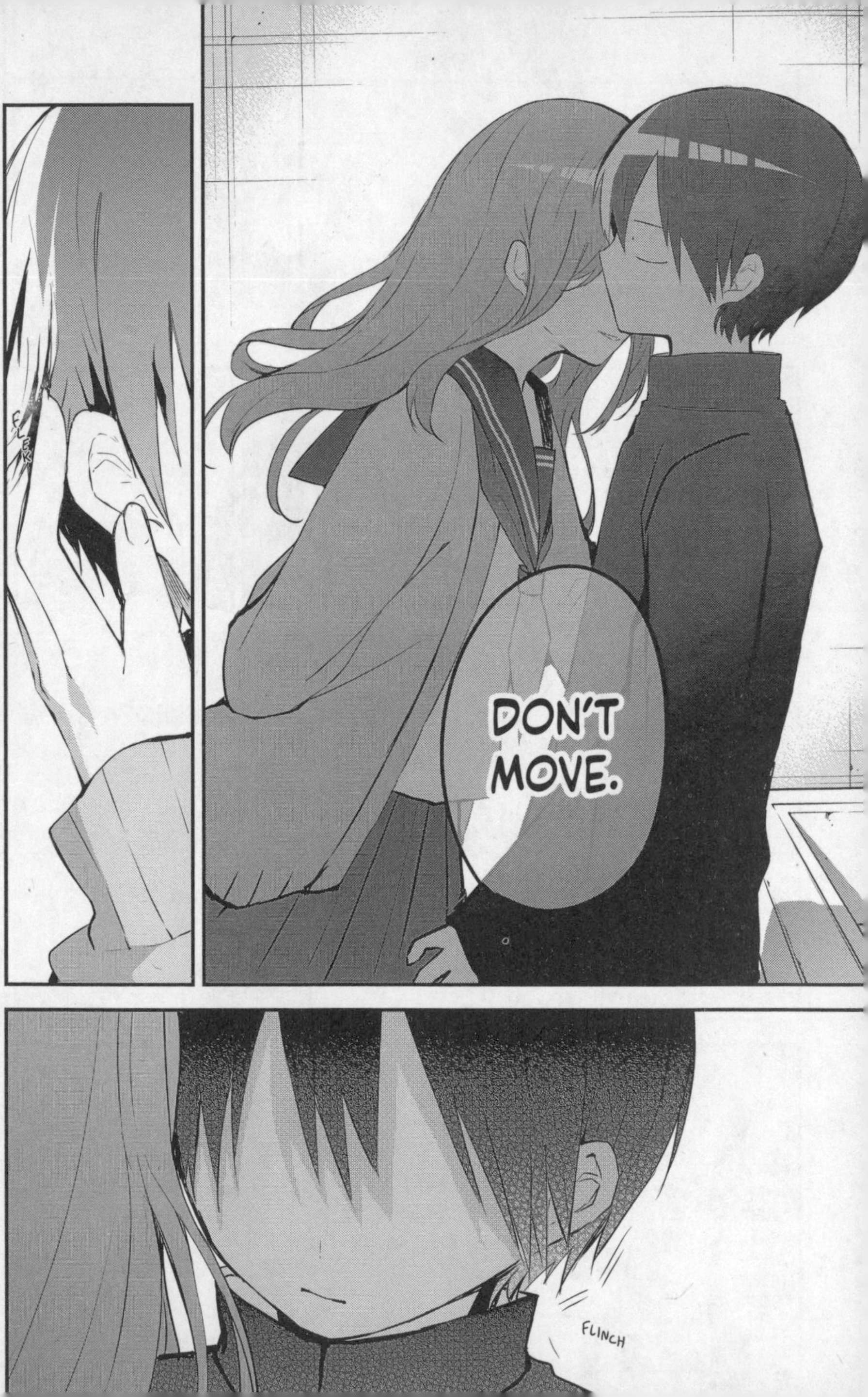
DON'T MOVE.
FLEK
FLINCH

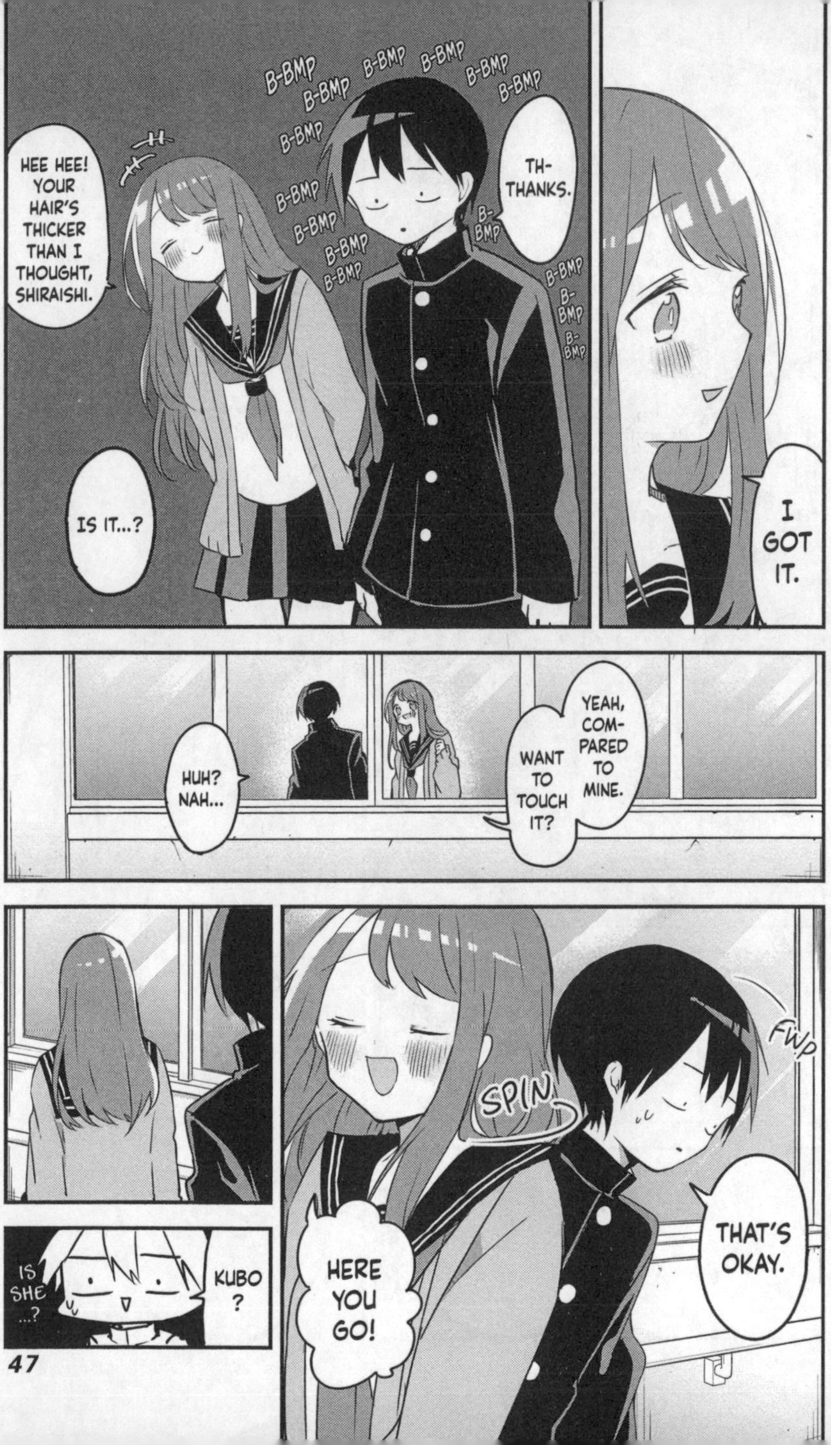
I GOT IT.
B-BMP B-BMP B-BMP B-BMP B-BMP B-BMP B-BMP B-BMP B-BMP B-BMP B-BMP B-BMP
TH-THANKS.
B-BMP B-BMP B-BMP B-BMP
HEE HEE! YOUR HAIR'S THICKER THAN I THOUGHT, SHIRAISHI.
IS IT...?
YEAH, COMPARED TO MINE.
WANT TO TOUCH IT?
HUH? NAH...
FWP
SPIN
THAT'S OKAY.
HERE YOU GO!
KUBO ?
IS SHE ...?

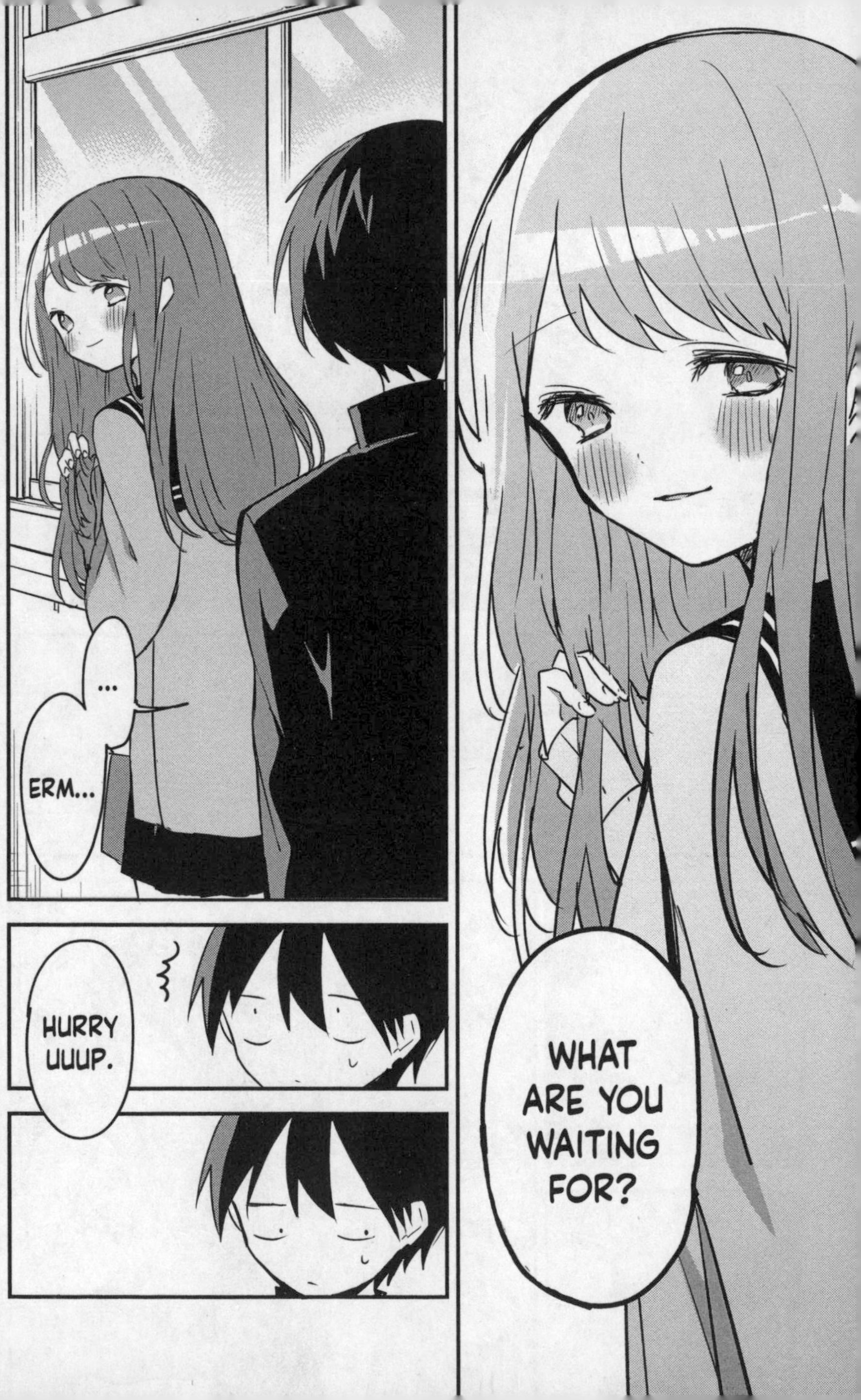
WHAT ARE YOU WAITING FOR?
...
ERM...
HURRY UUUP.

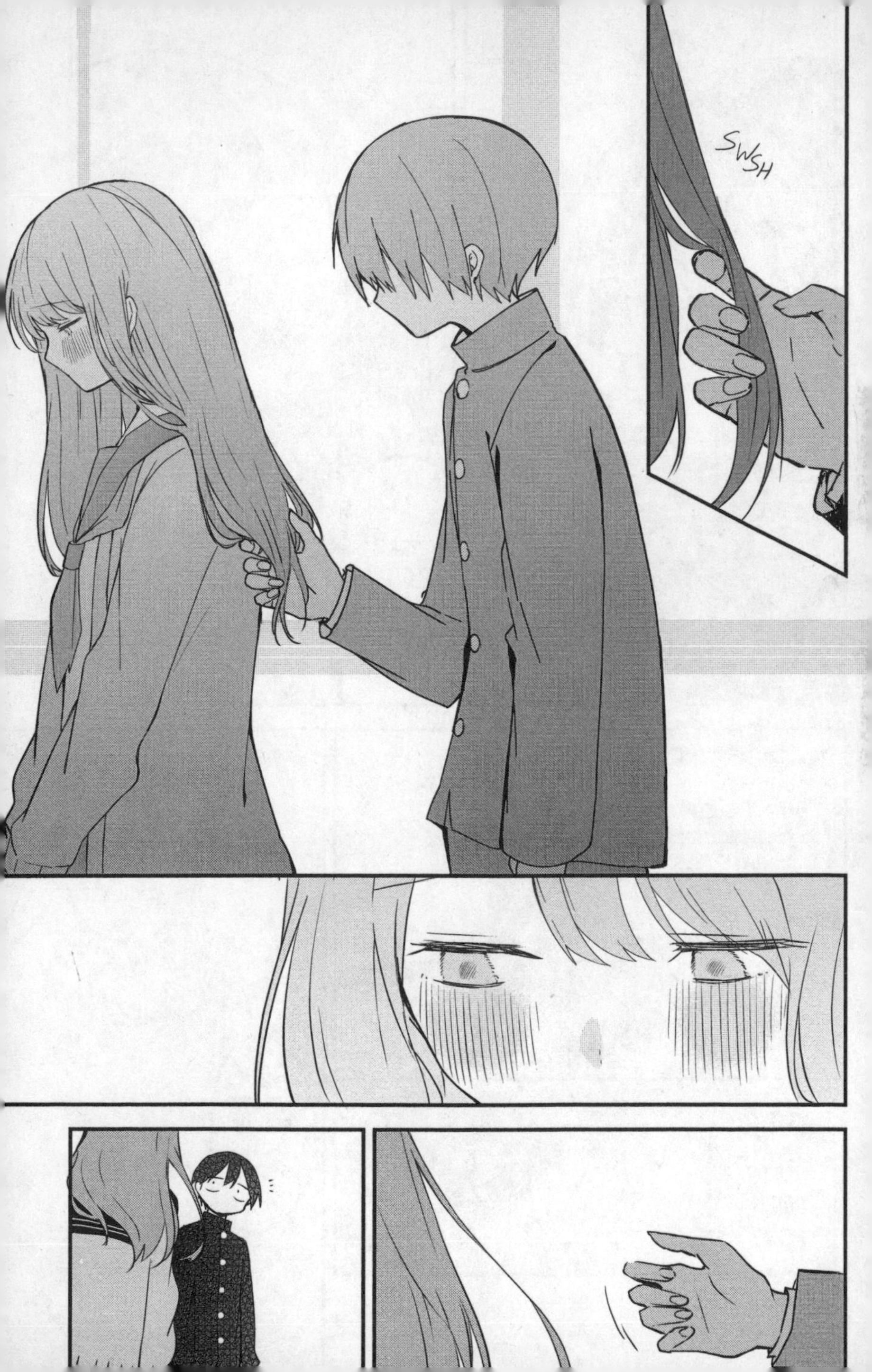
SWSH

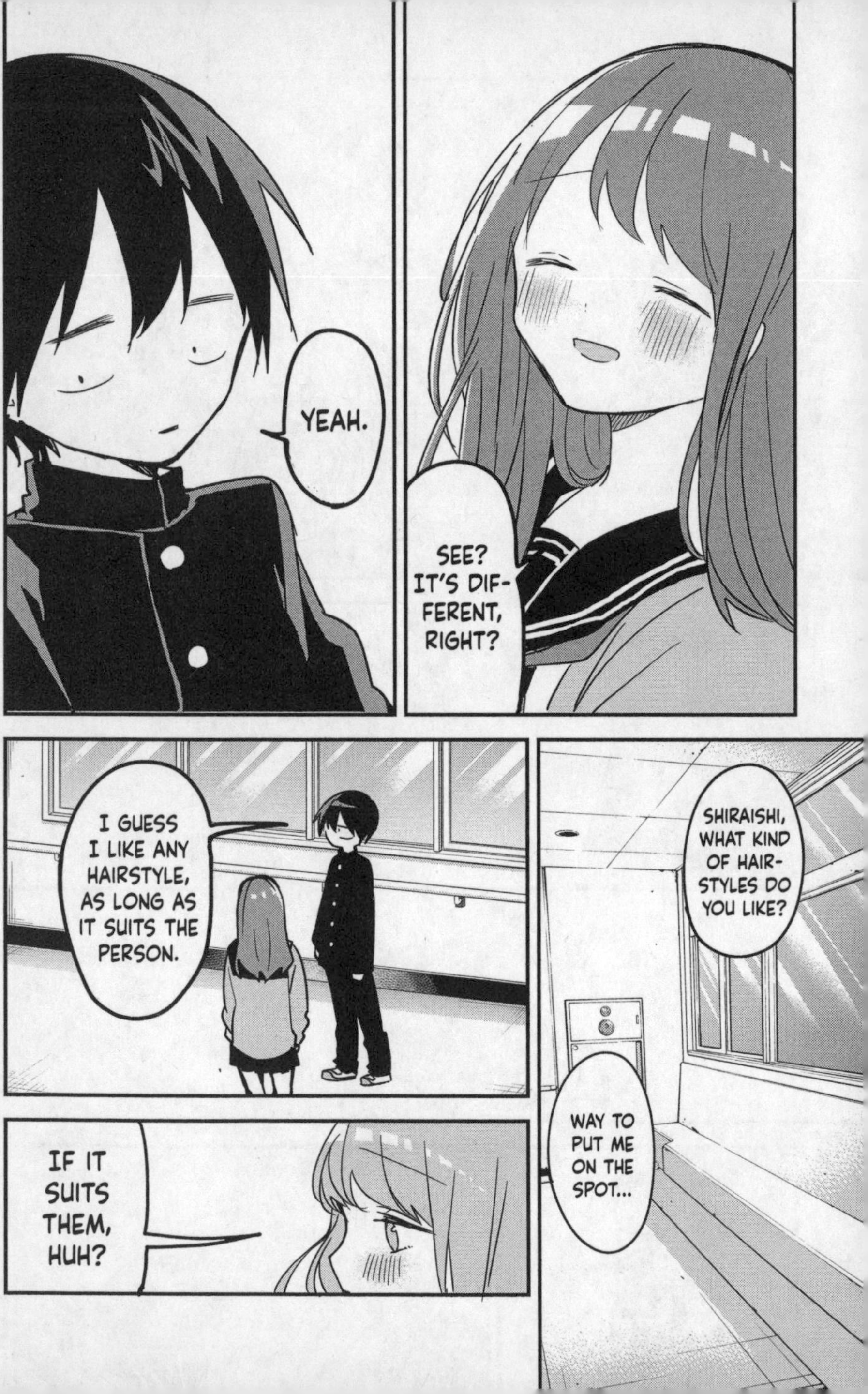
SEE? IT'S DIF-FERENT, RIGHT?
YEAH.
SHIRAISHI, WHAT KIND OF HAIR-STYLES DO YOU LIKE?
WAY TO PUT ME ON THE SPOT...
I GUESS I LIKE ANY HAIRSTYLE, AS LONG AS IT SUITS THE PERSON.
IF IT SUITS THEM, HUH?

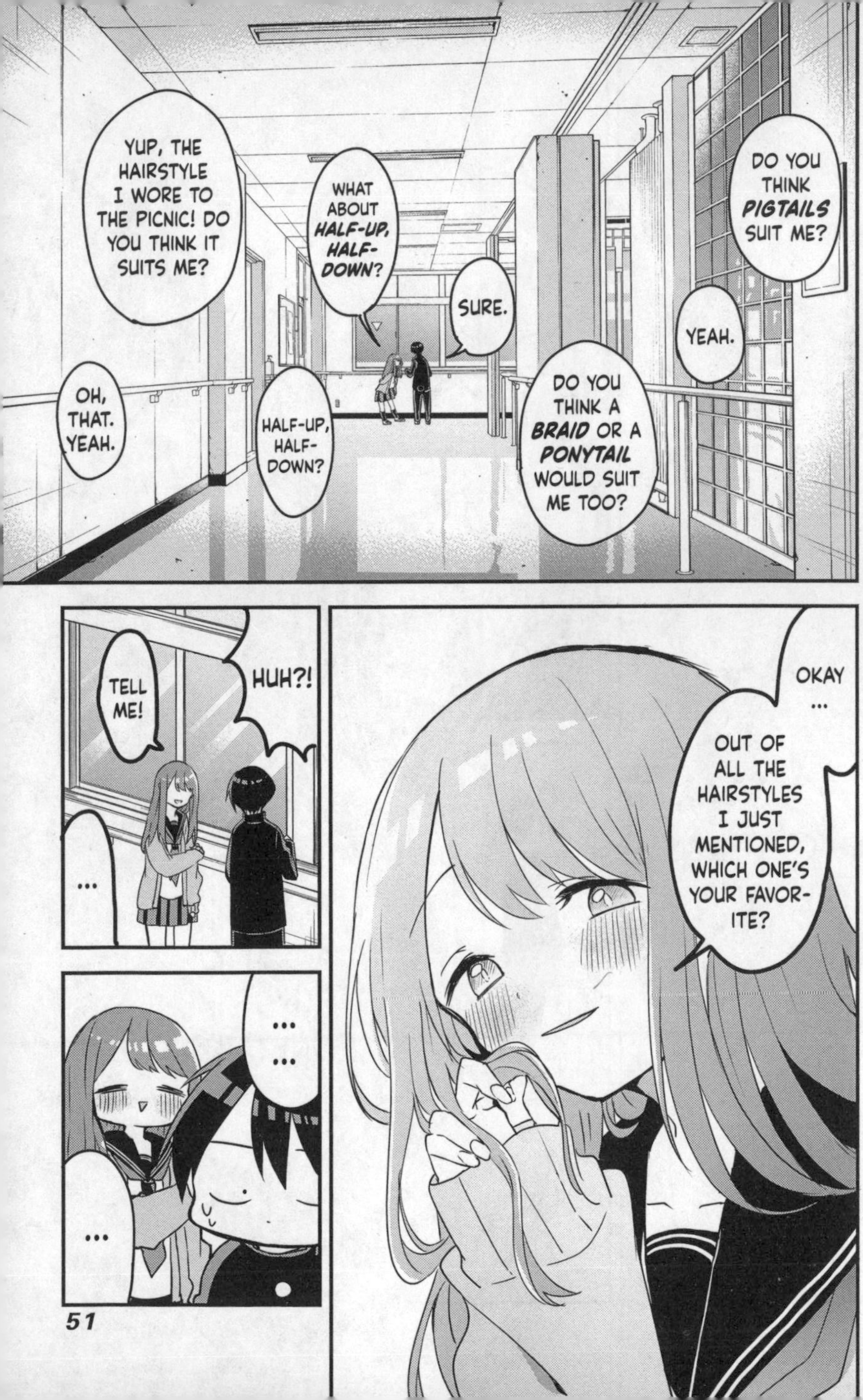
DO YOU THINK PIGTAILS SUIT ME?
YEAH.
DO YOU THINK A BRAID OR A PONYTAIL WOULD SUIT ME TOO?
SURE.
WHAT ABOUT HALF-UP, HALF-DOWN?
HALF-UP, HALF-DOWN?
YUP, THE HAIRSTYLE I WORE TO THE PICNIC! DO YOU THINK IT SUITS ME?
OH, THAT. YEAH.
OKAY ...
OUT OF ALL THE HAIRSTYLES I JUST MENTIONED, WHICH ONE'S YOUR FAVORITE?
HUH?!
TELL ME!
...
... ...
...

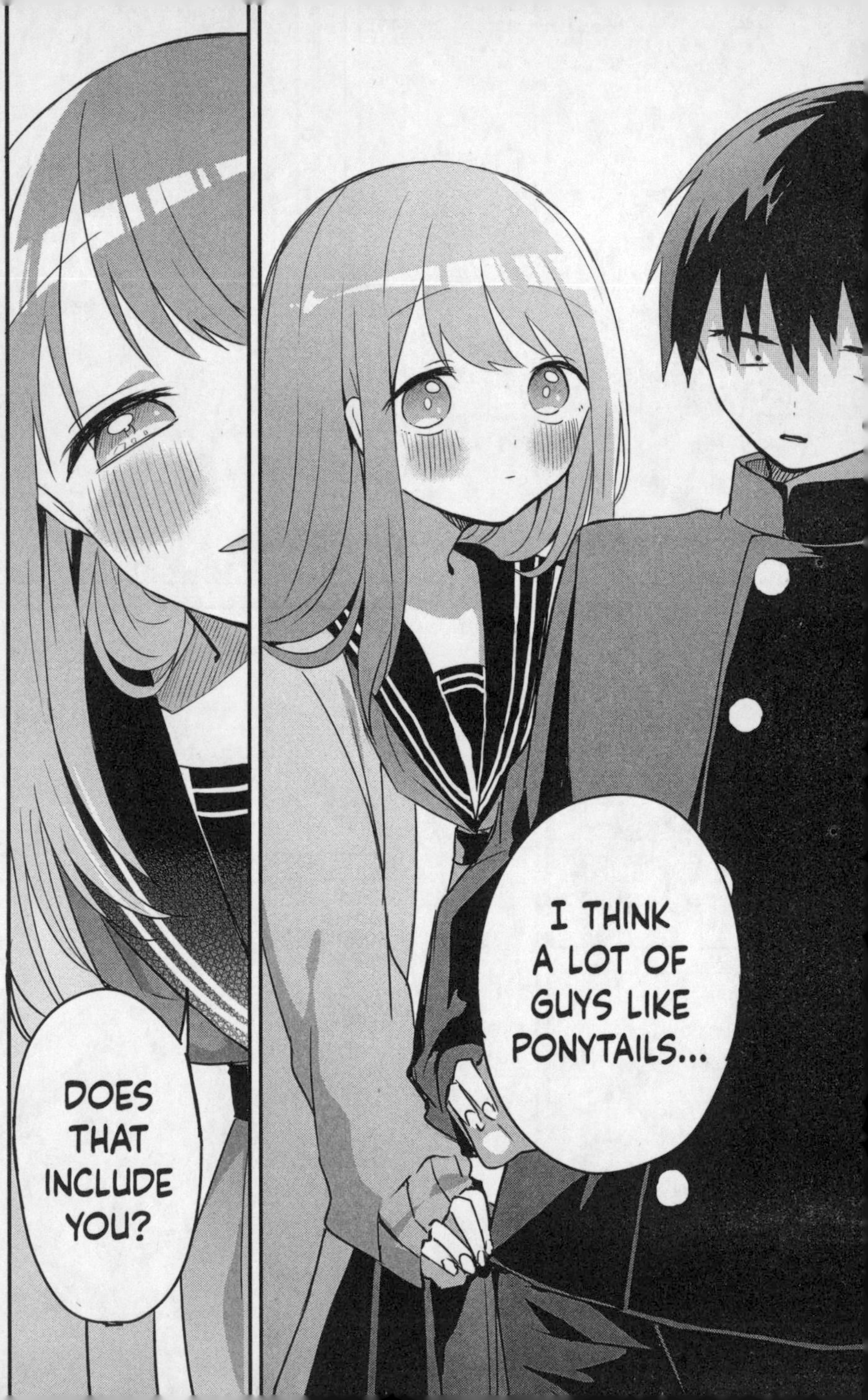
I THINK A LOT OF GUYS LIKE PONYTAILS...
DOES THAT INCLUDE YOU?

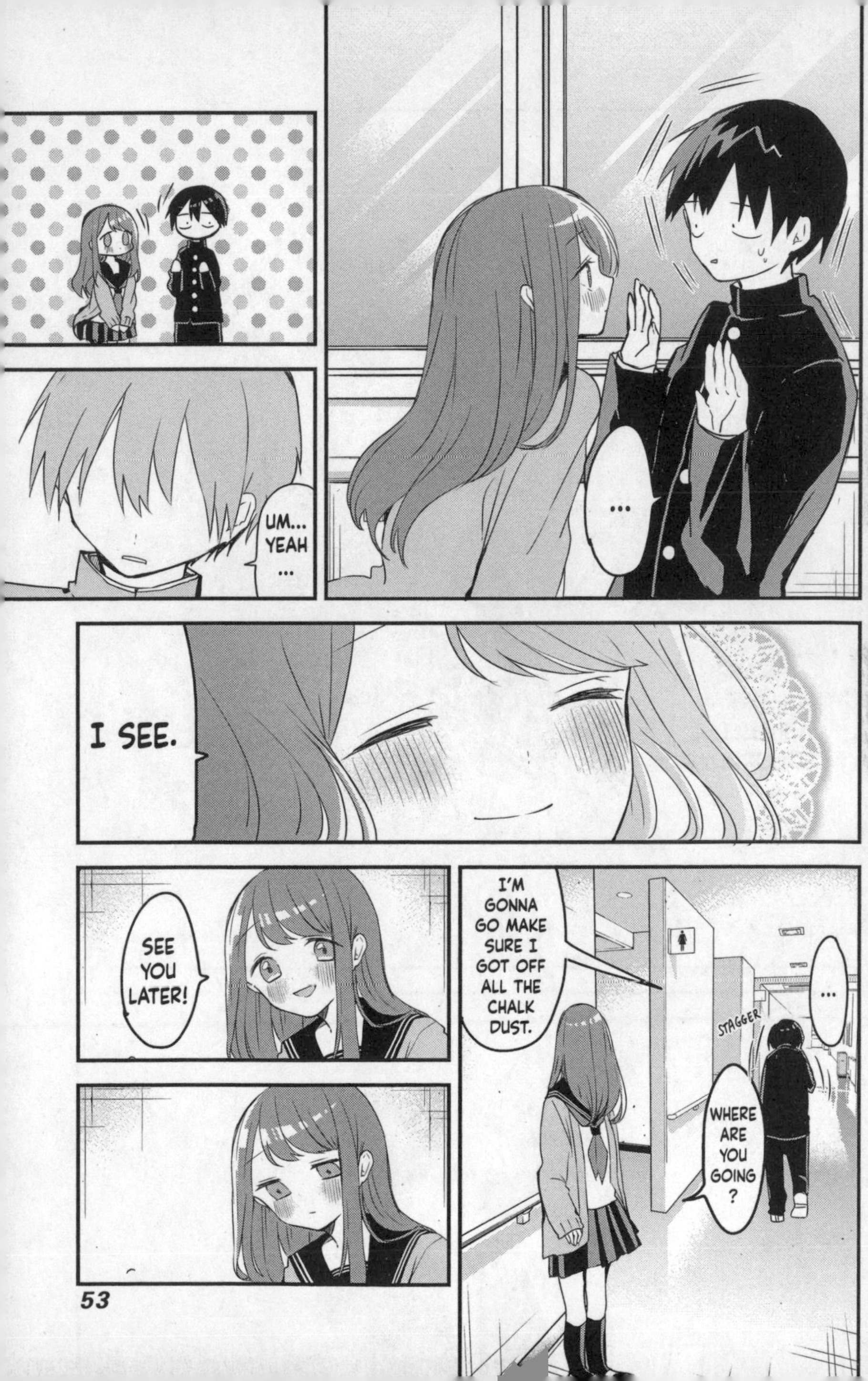
...
UM... YEAH ...
I SEE.
I'M GONNA GO MAKE SURE I GOT OFF ALL THE CHALK DUST.
...
STAGGER
WHERE ARE YOU GOING?
SEE YOU LATER!

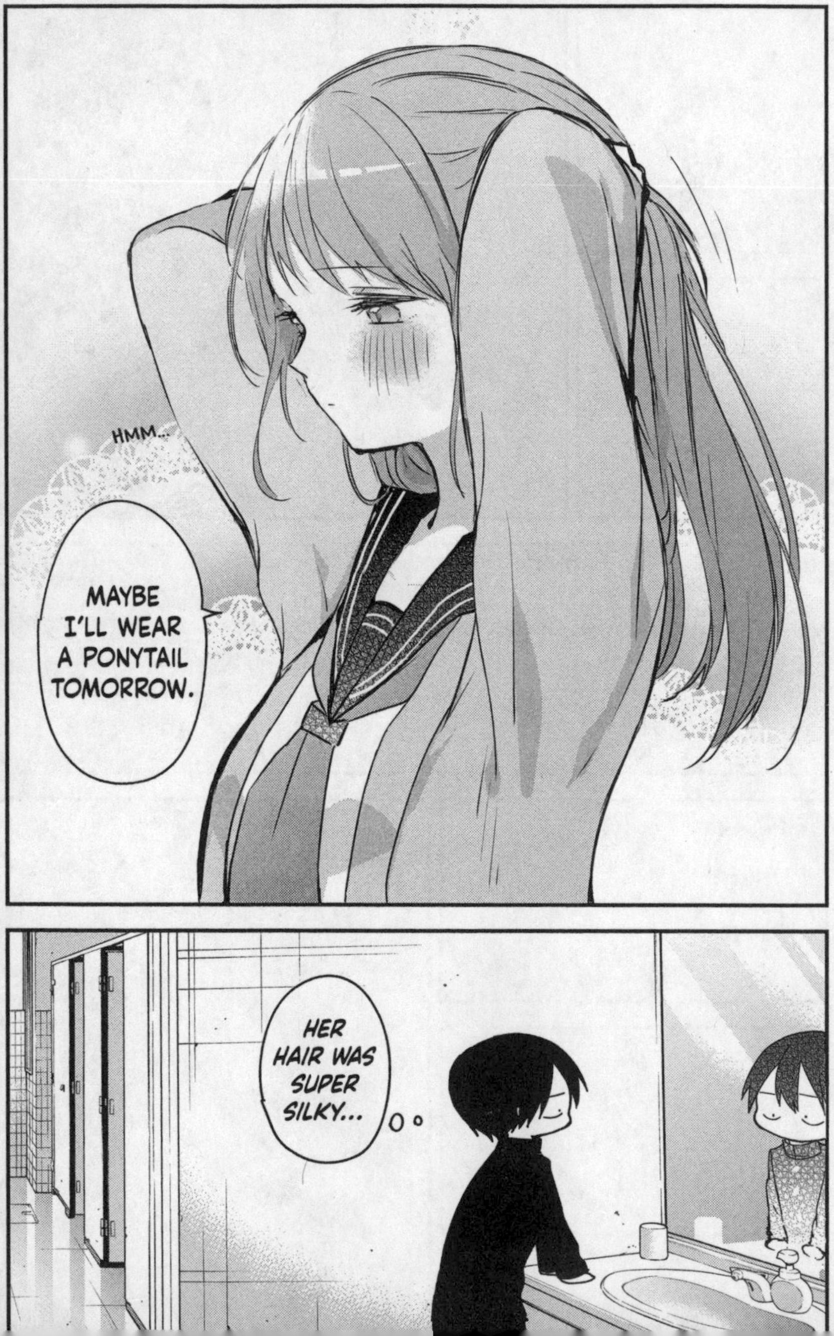
HMM...
MAYBE I'LL WEAR A PONYTAIL TOMORROW.
HER HAIR WAS SUPER SILKY...

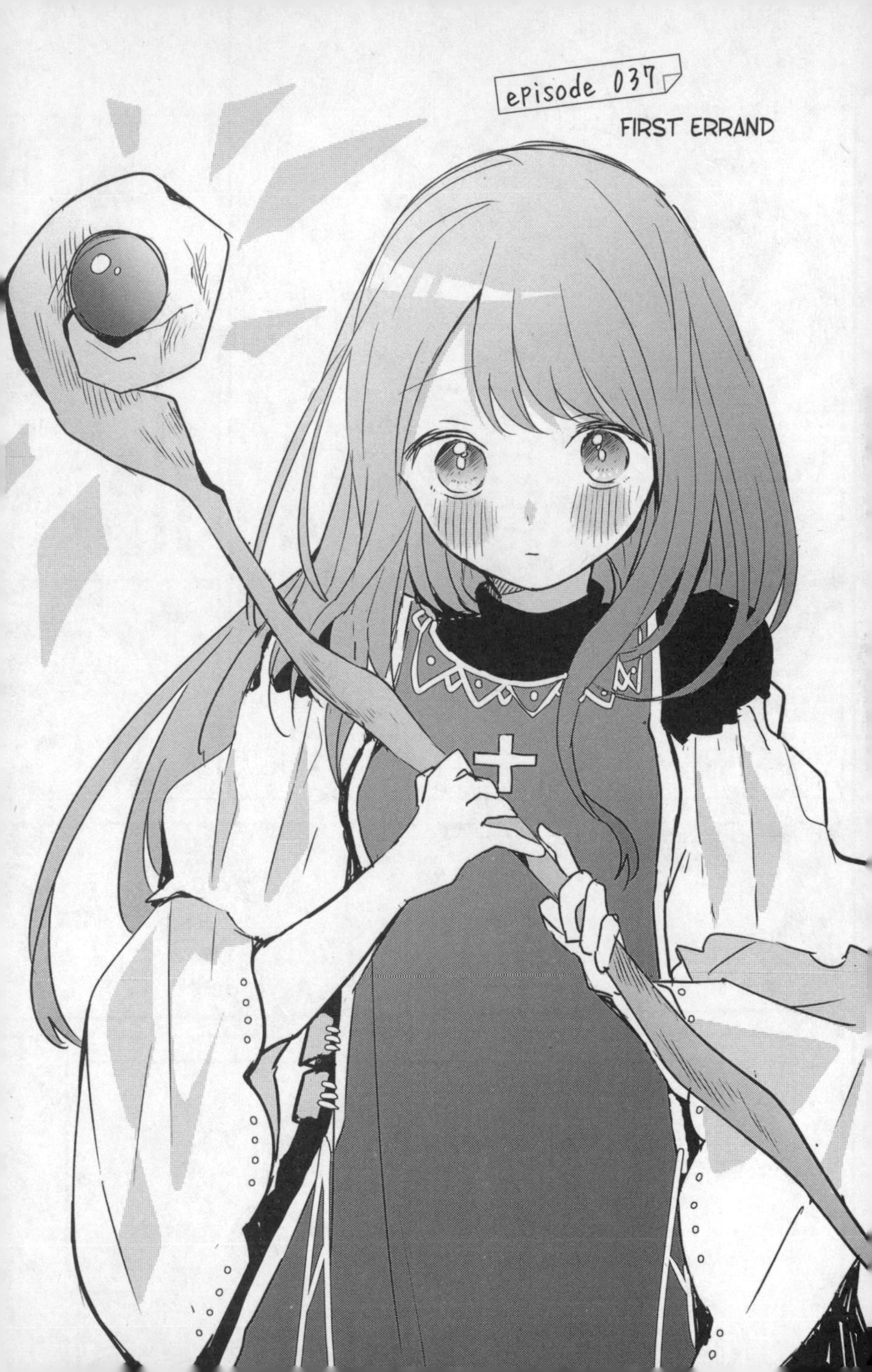
episode 037
FIRST ERRAND

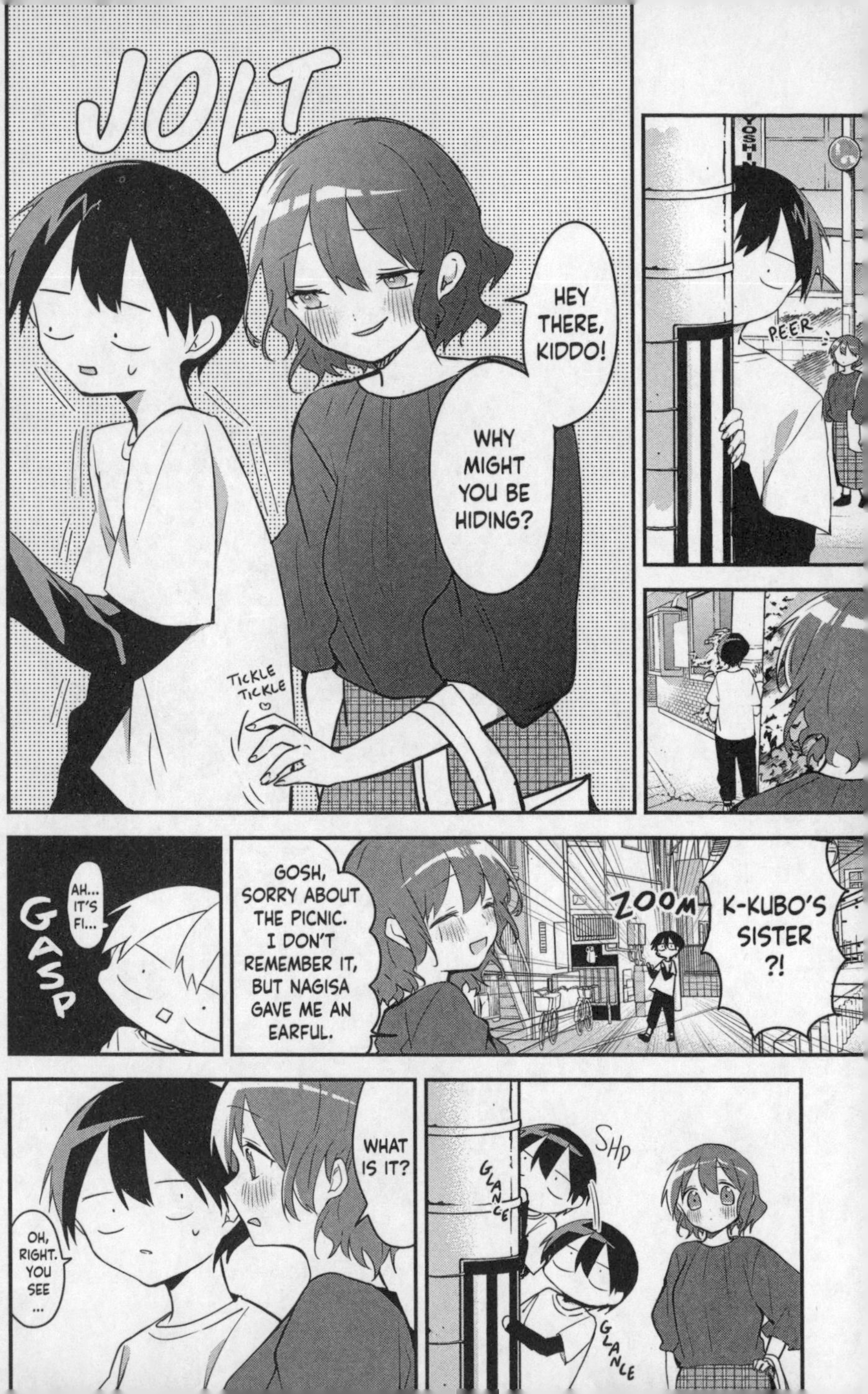
PEER
JOLT
HEY THERE, KIDDO!
WHY MIGHT YOU BE HIDING?
TICKLE TICKLE
ZOOM
K-KUBO'S SISTER ?!
GOSH, SORRY ABOUT THE PICNIC. I DON'T REMEMBER IT, BUT NAGISA GAVE ME AN EARFUL.
AH... IT'S FI...
GASP
SHP
GLANCE
GLANCE
WHAT IS IT?
OH, RIGHT. YOU SEE ...

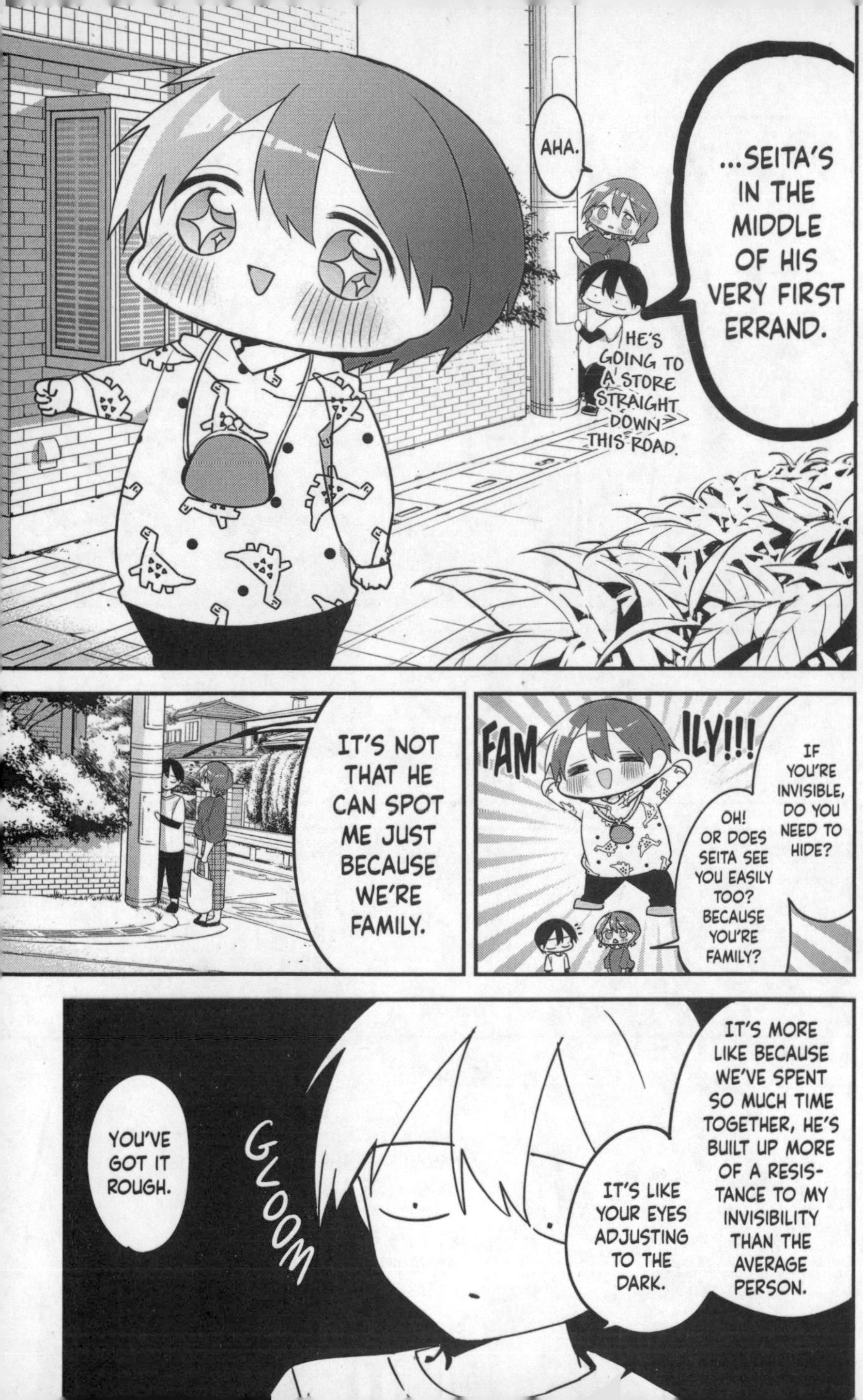
...SEITA'S IN THE MIDDLE OF HIS VERY FIRST ERRAND.
AHA.
HE'S GOING TO A STORE STRAIGHT DOWN THIS ROAD.
IF YOU'RE INVISIBLE, DO YOU NEED TO HIDE?
OH! OR DOES SEITA SEE YOU EASILY TOO? BECAUSE YOU'RE FAMILY?
FAMILY!!!
IT'S NOT THAT HE CAN SPOT ME JUST BECAUSE WE'RE FAMILY.
IT'S MORE LIKE BECAUSE WE'VE SPENT SO MUCH TIME TOGETHER, HE'S BUILT UP MORE OF A RESIS-TANCE TO MY INVISIBILITY THAN THE AVERAGE PERSON.
IT'S LIKE YOUR EYES ADJUSTING TO THE DARK.
GLOOM
YOU'VE GOT IT ROUGH.

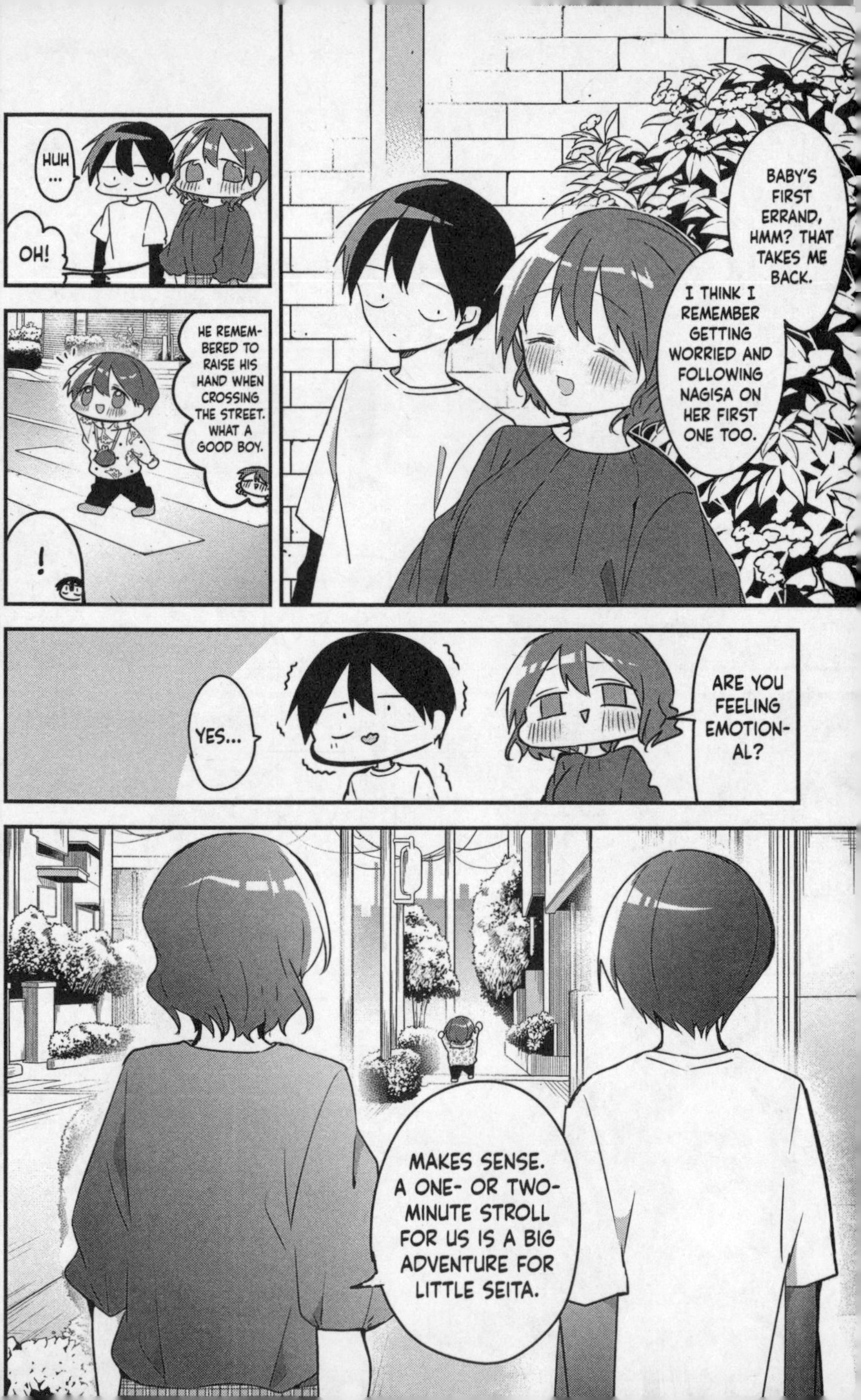
BABY'S FIRST ERRAND, HMM? THAT TAKES ME BACK.
I THINK I REMEMBER GETTING WORRIED AND FOLLOWING NAGISA ON HER FIRST ONE TOO.
HUH ...
OH!
HE REMEMBERED TO RAISE HIS HAND WHEN CROSSING THE STREET. WHAT A GOOD BOY.
!
ARE YOU FEELING EMOTIONAL?
YES...
MAKES SENSE. A ONE- OR TWO-MINUTE STROLL FOR US IS A BIG ADVENTURE FOR LITTLE SEITA.

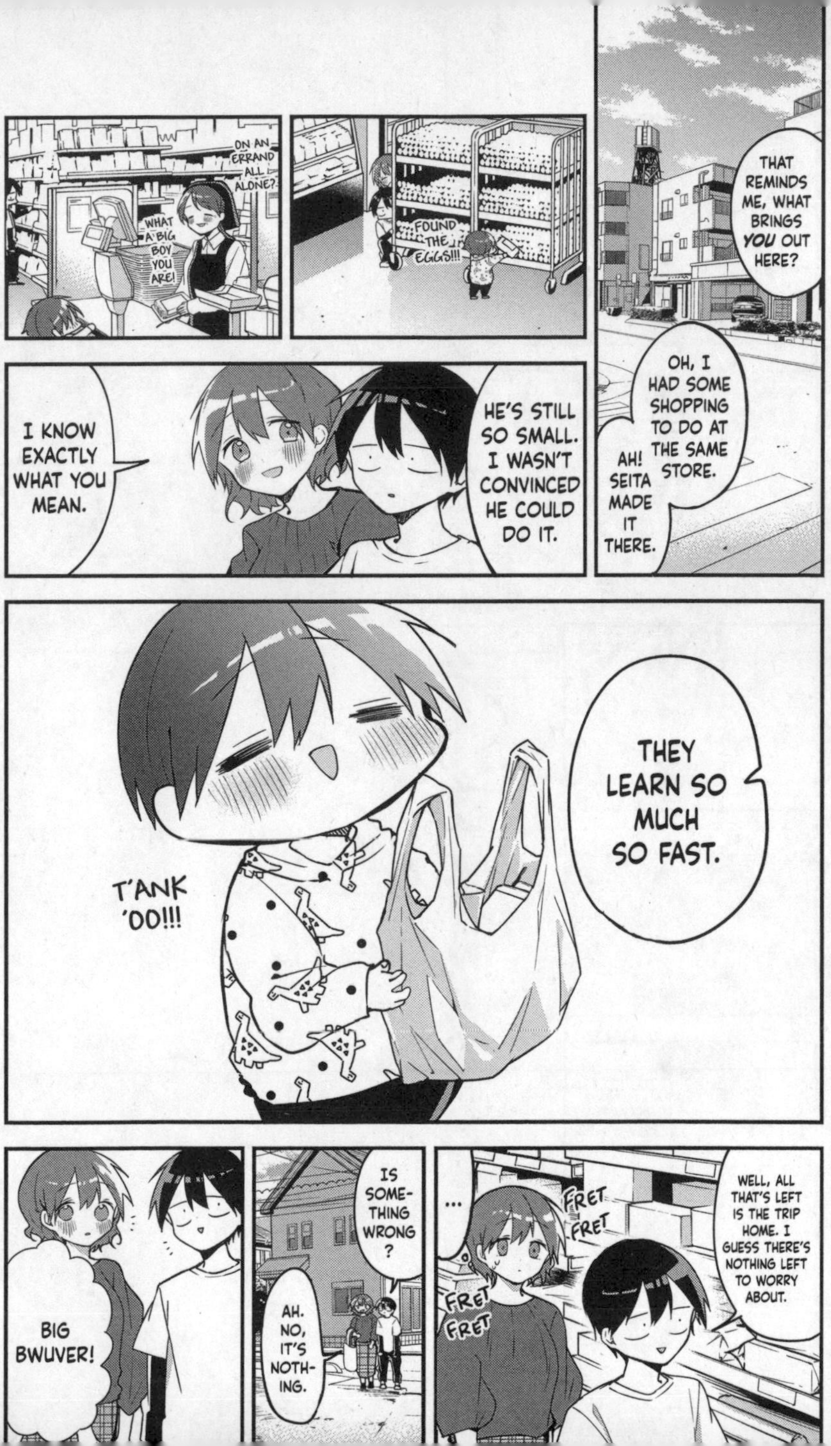
THAT REMINDS ME, WHAT BRINGS YOU OUT HERE?
OH, I HAD SOME SHOPPING TO DO AT THE SAME STORE.
AH! SEITA MADE IT THERE.
FOUND THE EGGS!!!
ON AN ERRAND ALL ALONE?
WHAT A BIG BOY YOU ARE!
HE'S STILL SO SMALL. I WASN'T CONVINCED HE COULD DO IT.
I KNOW EXACTLY WHAT YOU MEAN.
THEY LEARN SO MUCH SO FAST.
T'ANK 'OO!!!
WELL, ALL THAT'S LEFT IS THE TRIP HOME. I GUESS THERE'S NOTHING LEFT TO WORRY ABOUT.
FRET FRET
FRET FRET
...
IS SOMETHING WRONG?
AH. NO, IT'S NOTHING.
BIG BWUVER!

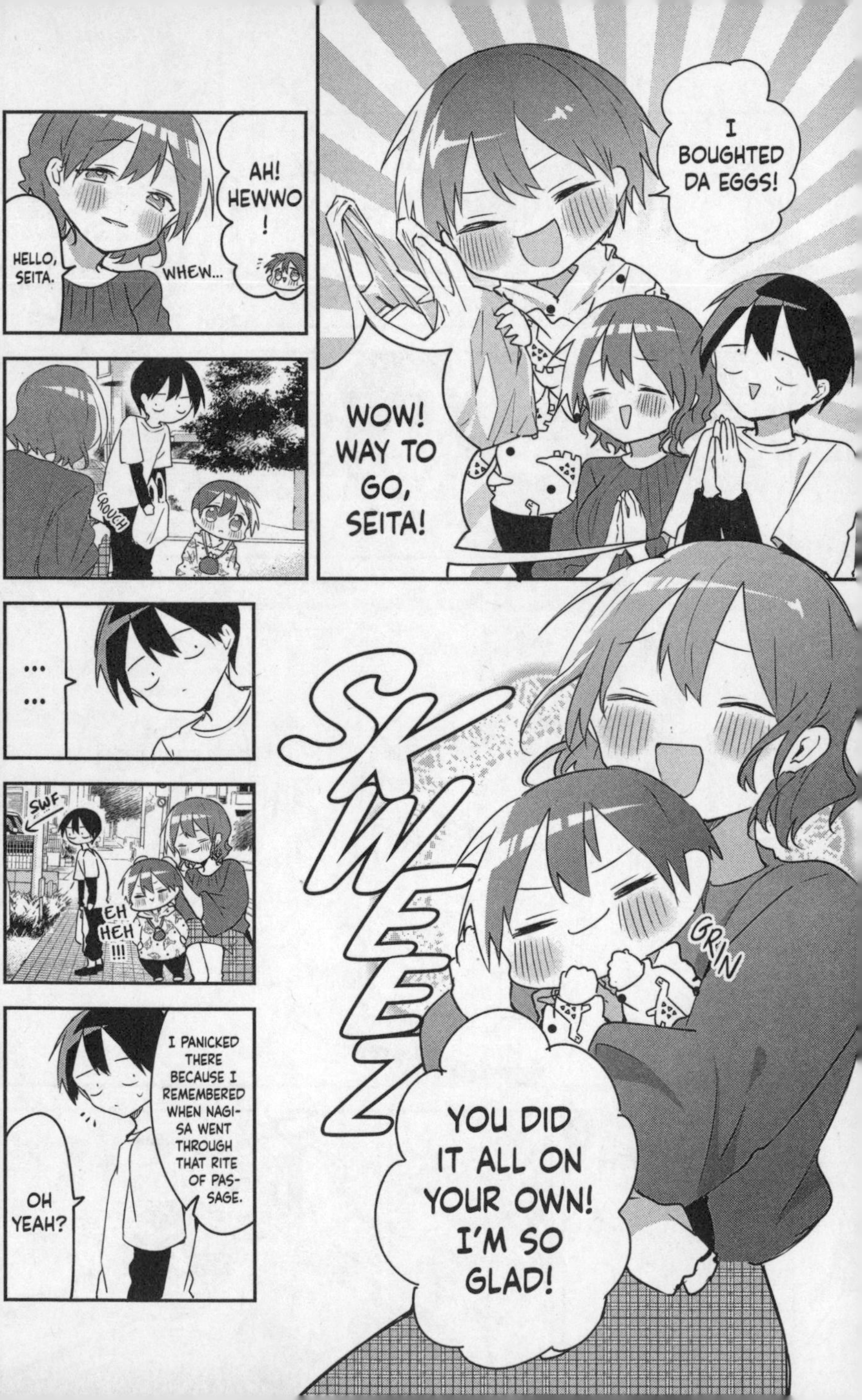
I BOUGHTED DA EGGS!
WOW! WAY TO GO, SEITA!
AH! HEWWO !
WHEW...
HELLO, SEITA.
CROUCH
GRIN
SKWEEZ
YOU DID IT ALL ON YOUR OWN! I'M SO GLAD!
... ...
SWF
EH HEH !!!
I PANICKED THERE BECAUSE I REMEMBERED WHEN NAGI-SA WENT THROUGH THAT RITE OF PAS-SAGE.
OH YEAH?

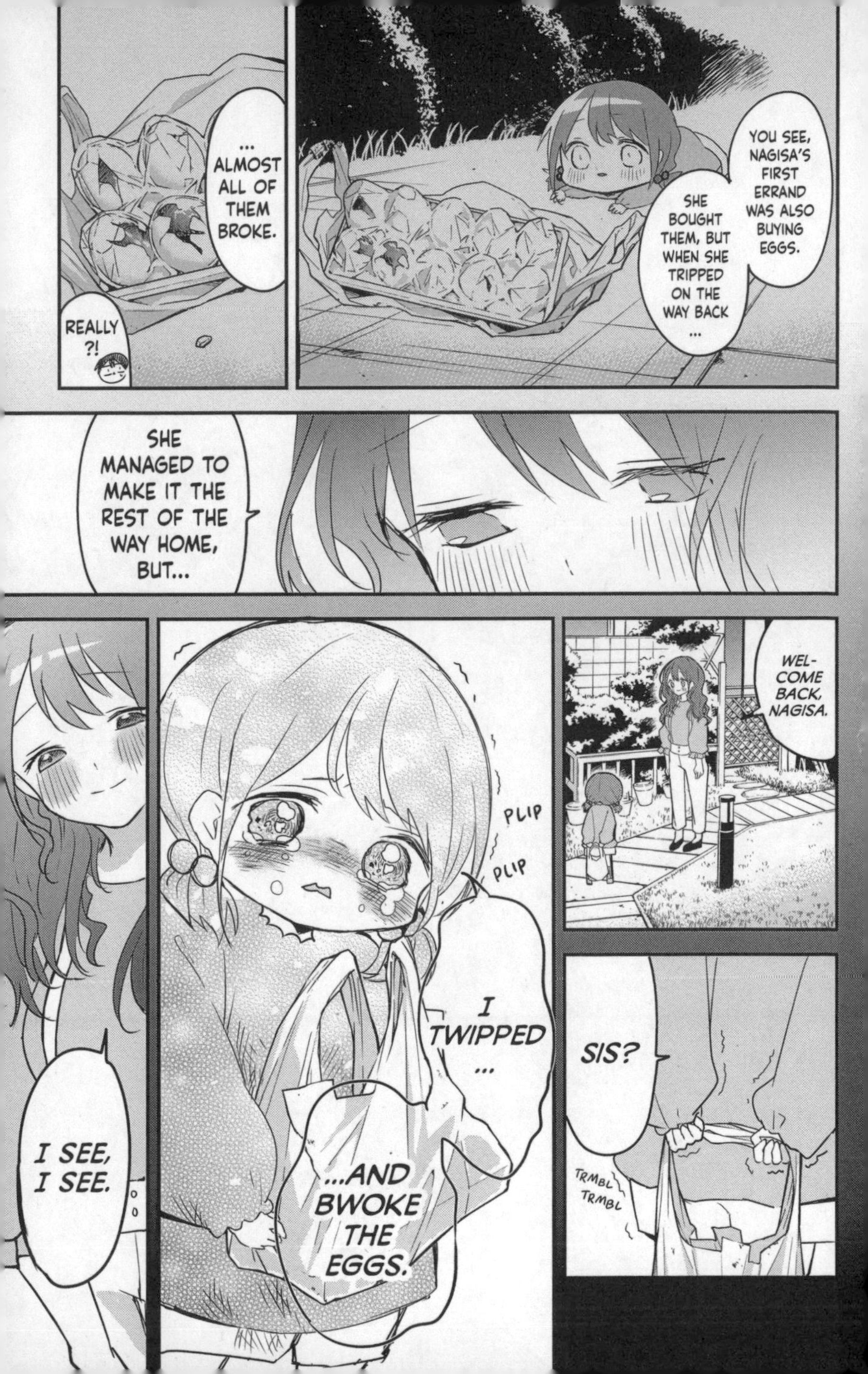
YOU SEE, NAGISA'S FIRST ERRAND WAS ALSO BUYING EGGS.
SHE BOUGHT THEM, BUT WHEN SHE TRIPPED ON THE WAY BACK ...
... ALMOST ALL OF THEM BROKE.
REALLY ?!
SHE MANAGED TO MAKE IT THE REST OF THE WAY HOME, BUT...
WEL-COME BACK, NAGISA.
SIS?
TRMBL TRMBL
PLIP
PLIP
I TWIPPED ...
...AND BWOKE THE EGGS.
I SEE, I SEE.

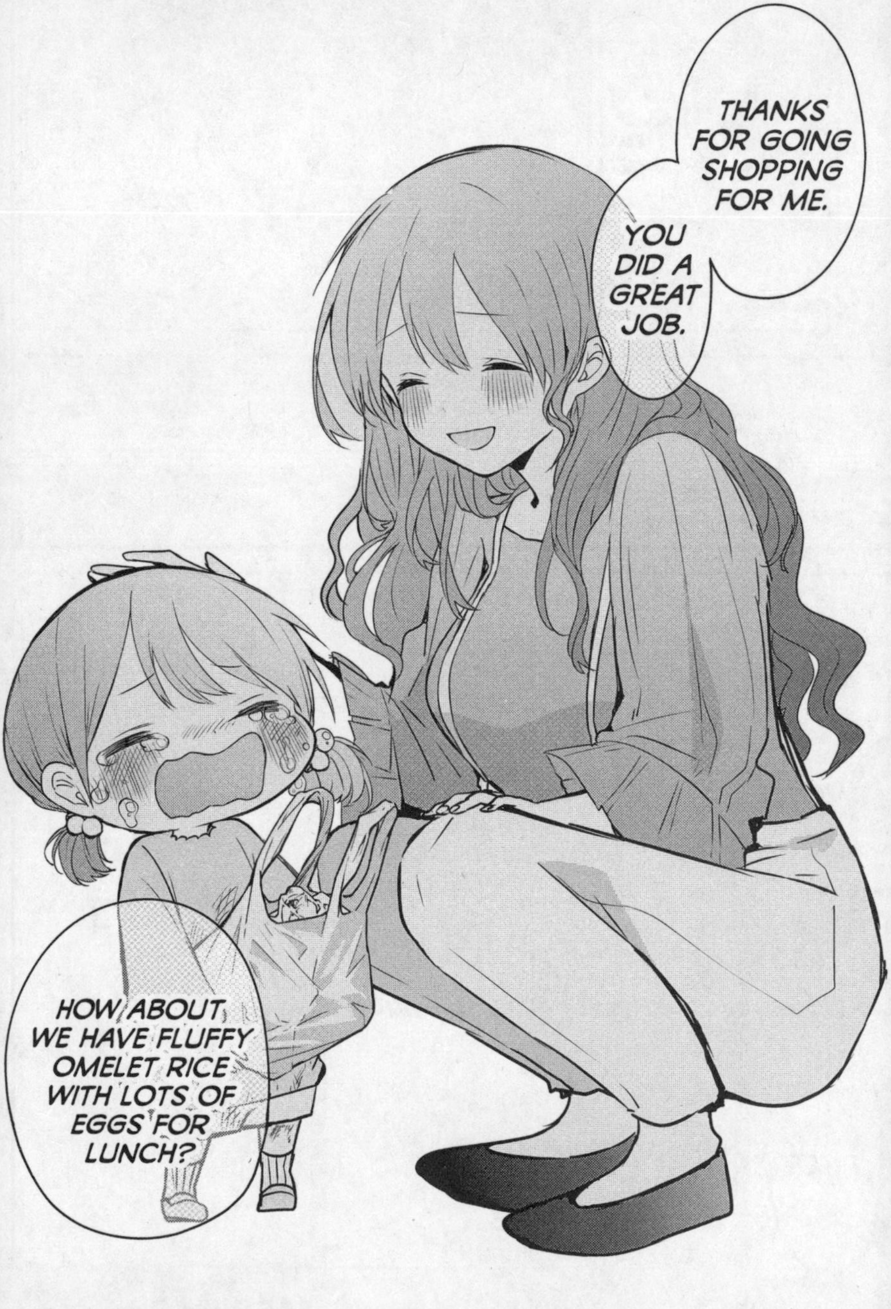
THANKS FOR GOING SHOPPING FOR ME.
YOU DID A GREAT JOB.
HOW ABOUT WE HAVE FLUFFY OMELET RICE WITH LOTS OF EGGS FOR LUNCH?

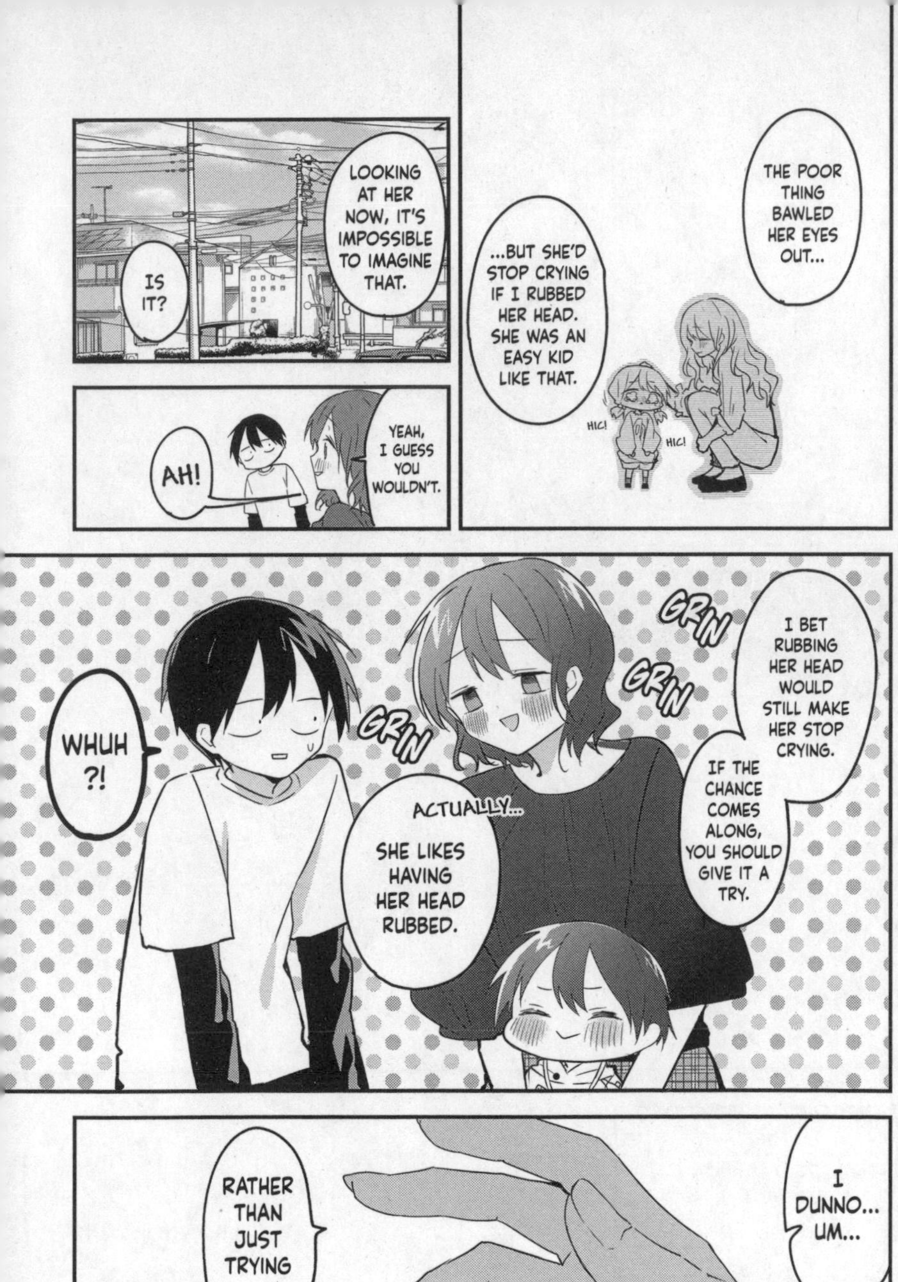
THE POOR THING BAWLED HER EYES OUT...
...BUT SHE'D STOP CRYING IF I RUBBED HER HEAD. SHE WAS AN EASY KID LIKE THAT.
HIC!
HIC!
LOOKING AT HER NOW, IT'S IMPOSSIBLE TO IMAGINE THAT.
IS IT?
YEAH, I GUESS YOU WOULDN'T.
AH!
I BET RUBBING HER HEAD WOULD STILL MAKE HER STOP CRYING.
GRIN
GRIN
IF THE CHANCE COMES ALONG, YOU SHOULD GIVE IT A TRY.
GRIN
ACTUALLY...
SHE LIKES HAVING HER HEAD RUBBED.
WHUH ?!
I DUNNO... UM...
RATHER THAN JUST TRYING ...

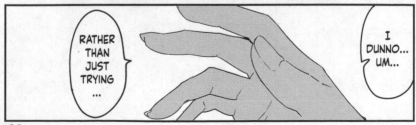

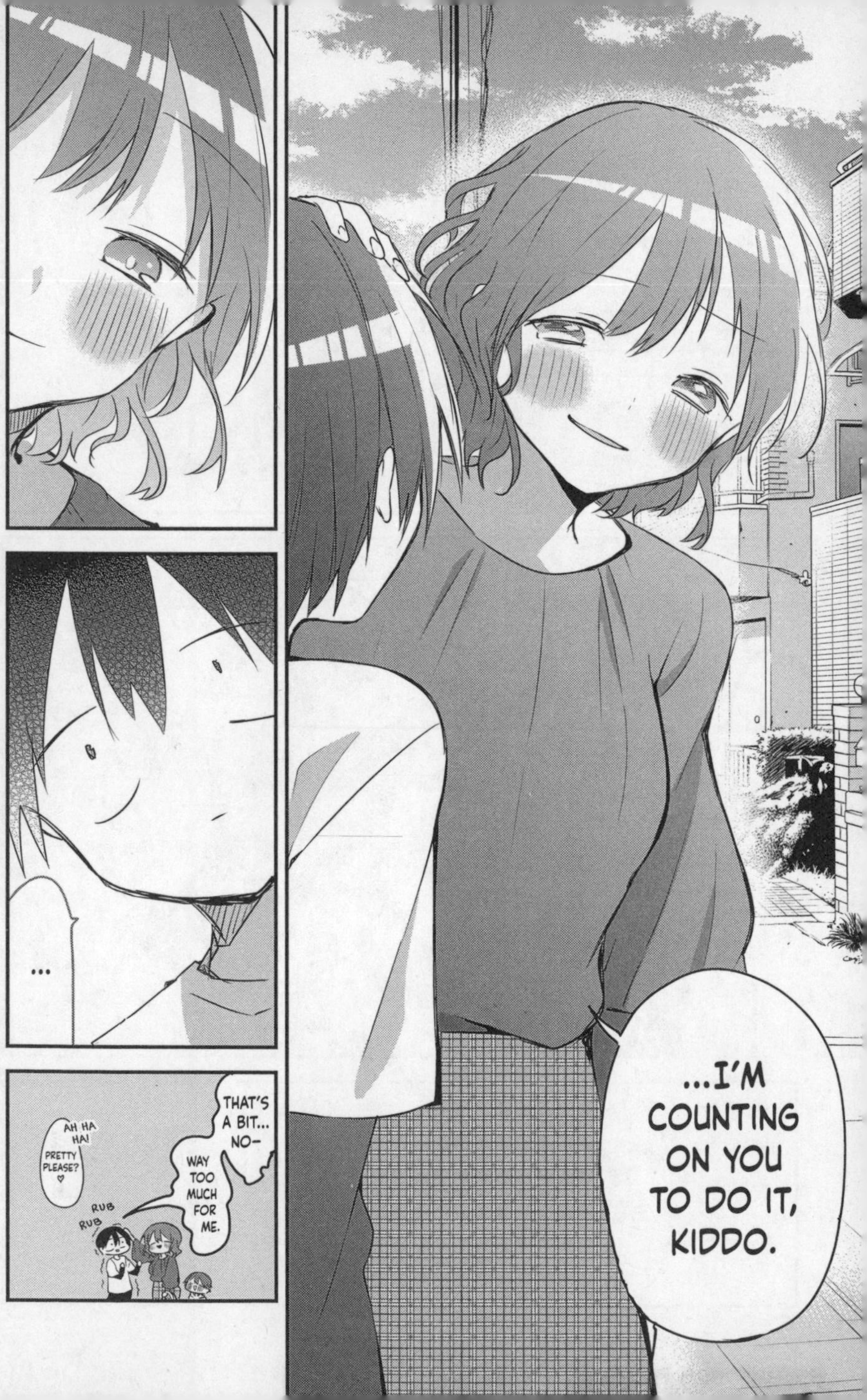
...I'M COUNTING ON YOU TO DO IT, KIDDO.
...
THAT'S A BIT... NO–
WAY TOO MUCH FOR ME.
RUB RUB
AH HA HA! PRETTY PLEASE? ♡

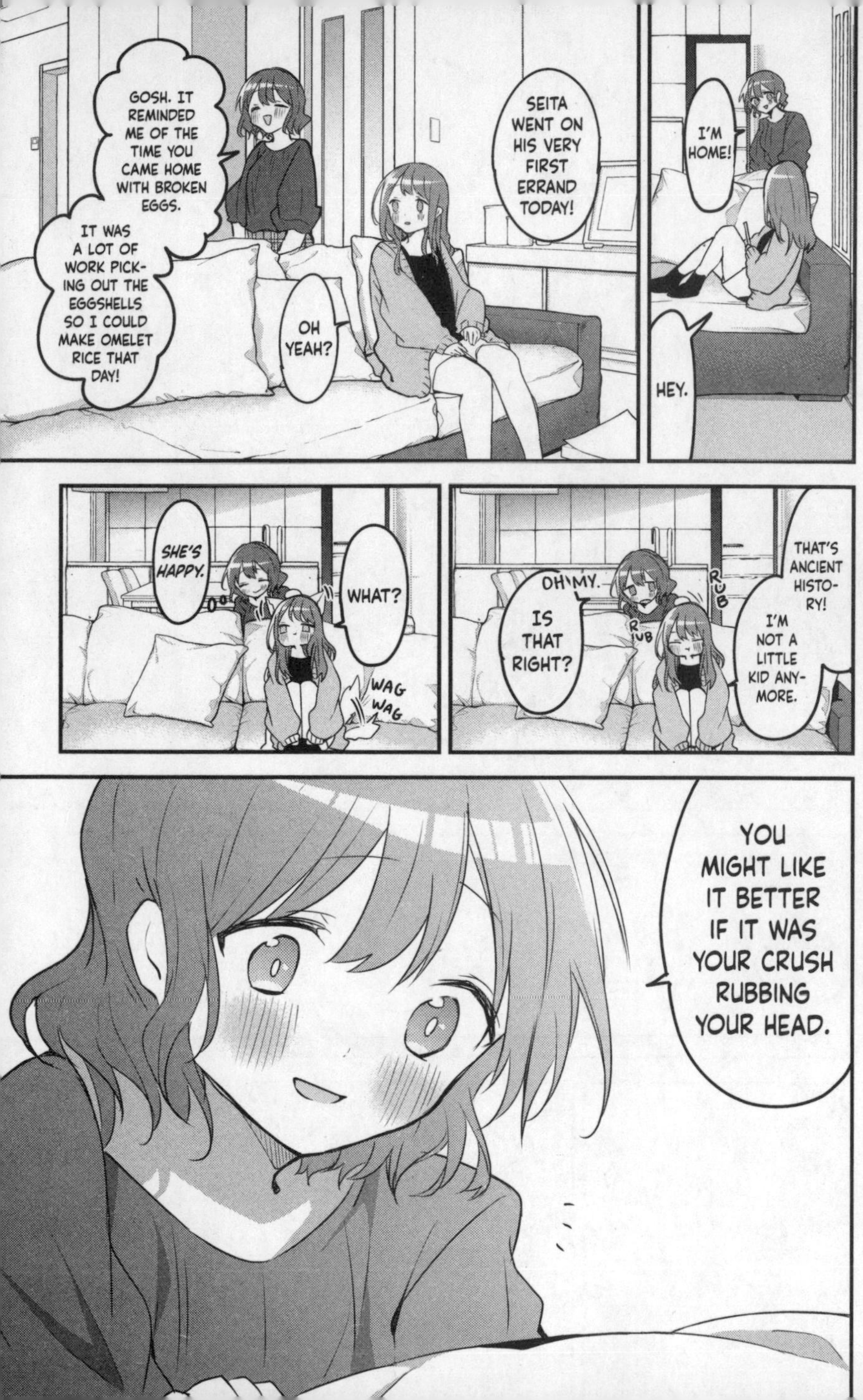
I'M HOME!
HEY.
SEITA WENT ON HIS VERY FIRST ERRAND TODAY!
OH YEAH?
GOSH. IT REMINDED ME OF THE TIME YOU CAME HOME WITH BROKEN EGGS.
IT WAS A LOT OF WORK PICK-ING OUT THE EGGSHELLS SO I COULD MAKE OMELET RICE THAT DAY!
THAT'S ANCIENT HISTORY!
I'M NOT A LITTLE KID ANY-MORE.
RUB
RUB
OH MY.
IS THAT RIGHT?
WHAT?
WAG WAG
SHE'S HAPPY.
YOU MIGHT LIKE IT BETTER IF IT WAS YOUR CRUSH RUBBING YOUR HEAD.

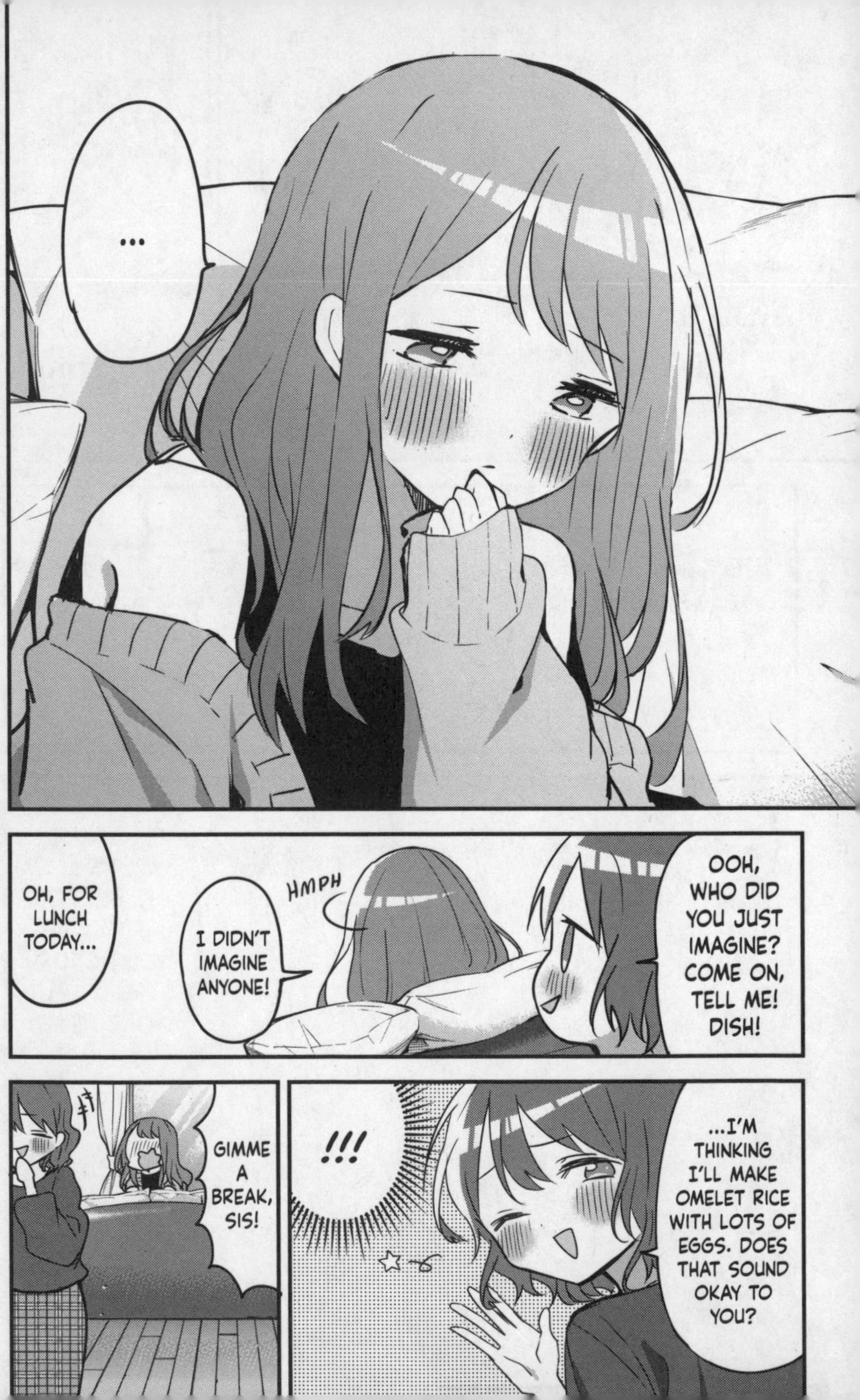
...
OOH, WHO DID YOU JUST IMAGINE? COME ON, TELL ME! DISH!
HMPH
I DIDN'T IMAGINE ANYONE!
OH, FOR LUNCH TODAY...
...I'M THINKING I'LL MAKE OMELET RICE WITH LOTS OF EGGS. DOES THAT SOUND OKAY TO YOU?
!!!
GIMME A BREAK, SIS!

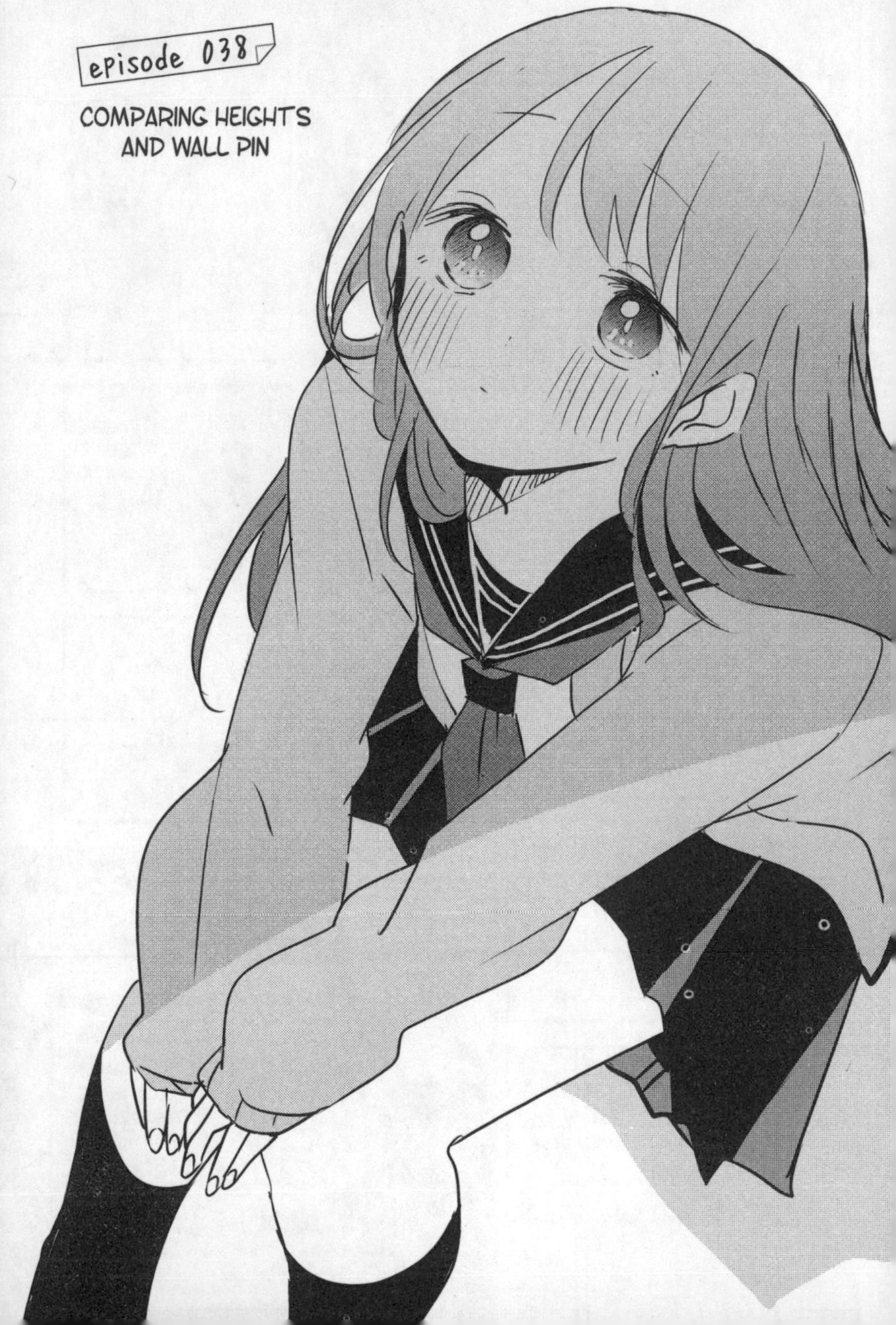
episode 038
COMPARING HEIGHTS
AND WALL PIN

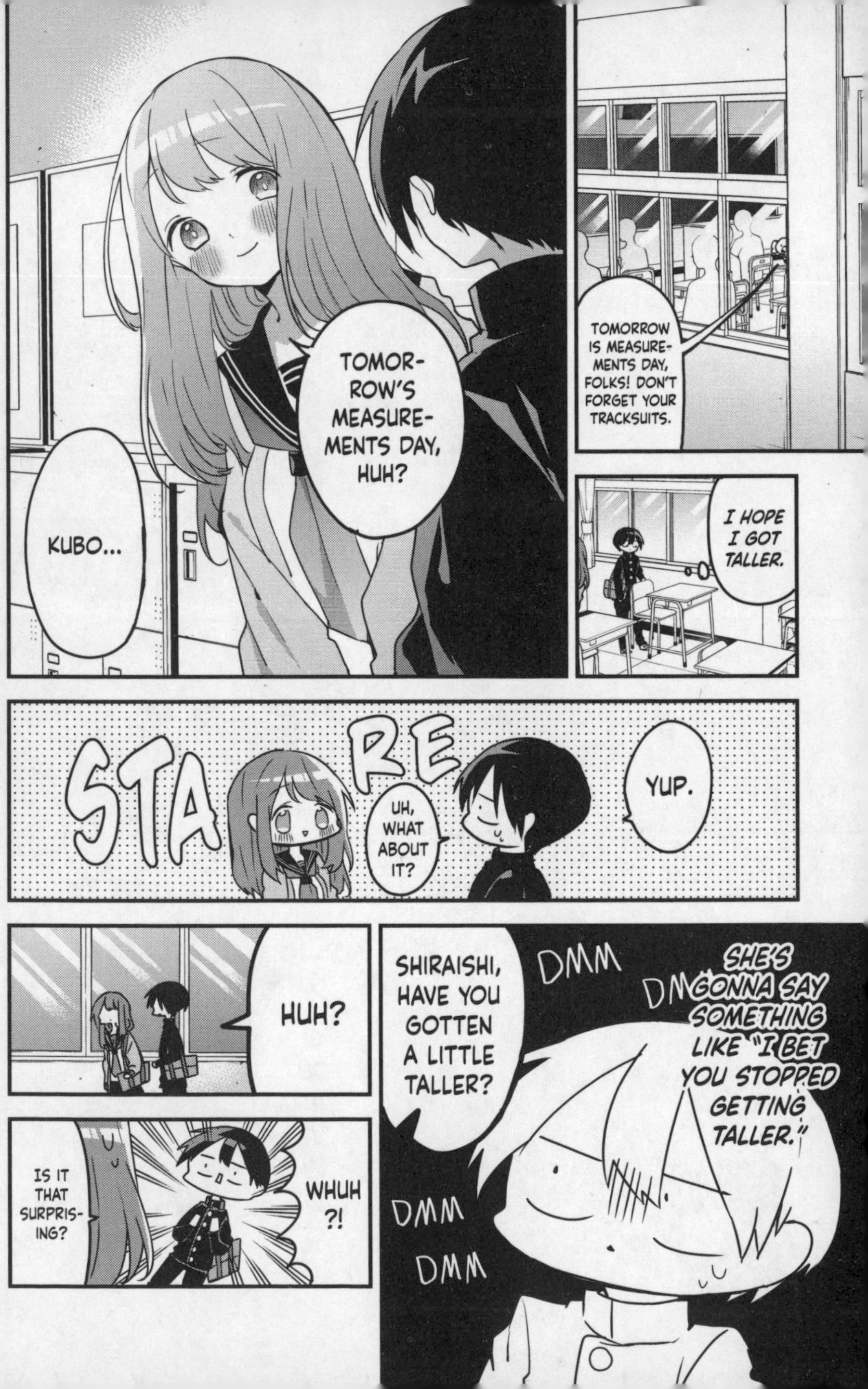

TOMORROW IS MEASUREMENTS DAY, FOLKS! DON'T FORGET YOUR TRACKSUITS.
I HOPE I GOT TALLER.
TOMORROW'S MEASUREMENTS DAY, HUH?
KUBO...
YUP.
STARE
UH, WHAT ABOUT IT?
SHE'S GONNA SAY SOMETHING LIKE "I BET YOU STOPPED GETTING TALLER."
DMM
DM
SHIRAISHI, HAVE YOU GOTTEN A LITTLE TALLER?
DMM
DMM
HUH?
WHUH ?!
IS IT THAT SURPRISING?

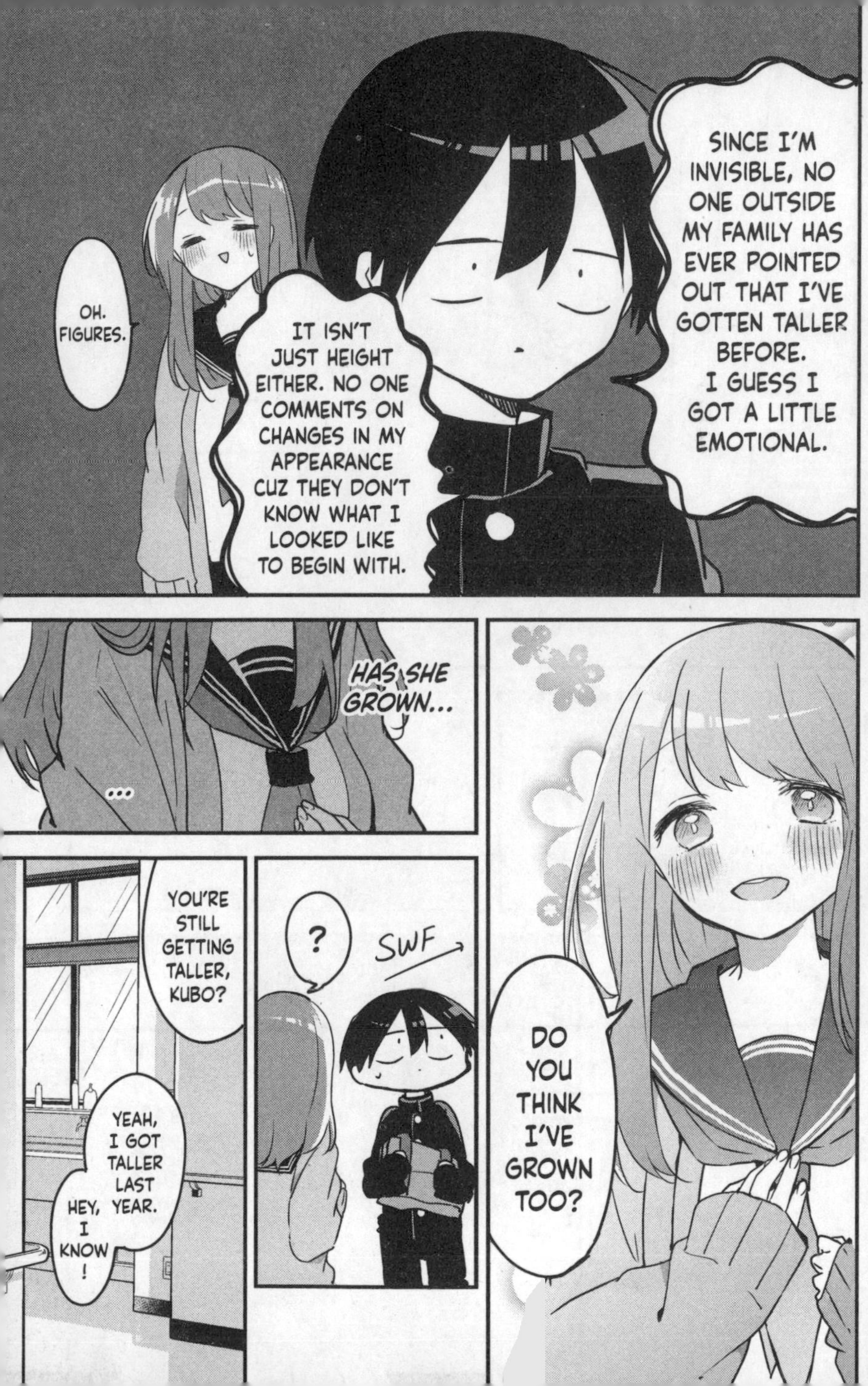
SINCE I'M INVISIBLE, NO ONE OUTSIDE MY FAMILY HAS EVER POINTED OUT THAT I'VE GOTTEN TALLER BEFORE. I GUESS I GOT A LITTLE EMOTIONAL.
IT ISN'T JUST HEIGHT EITHER. NO ONE COMMENTS ON CHANGES IN MY APPEARANCE CUZ THEY DON'T KNOW WHAT I LOOKED LIKE TO BEGIN WITH.
OH. FIGURES.
DO YOU THINK I'VE GROWN TOO?
HAS SHE GROWN...
...
?
SWF
YOU'RE STILL GETTING TALLER, KUBO?
YEAH, I GOT TALLER LAST YEAR.
HEY, I KNOW!

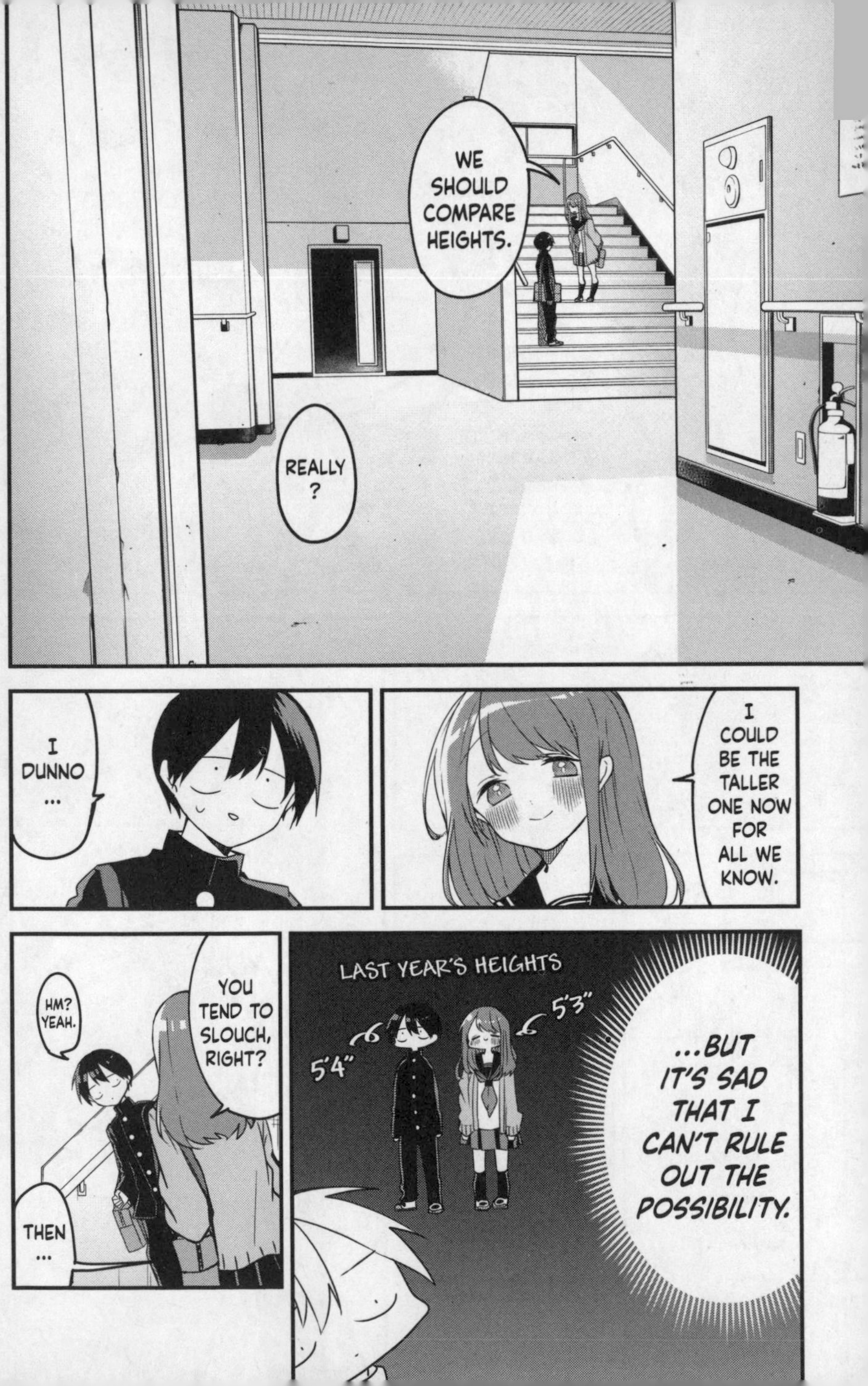
WE SHOULD COMPARE HEIGHTS.
REALLY?
I COULD BE THE TALLER ONE NOW FOR ALL WE KNOW.
I DUNNO...
LAST YEAR'S HEIGHTS
5'3"
5'4"
...BUT IT'S SAD THAT I CAN'T RULE OUT THE POSSIBILITY.
YOU TEND TO SLOUCH, RIGHT?
HM? YEAH.
THEN...

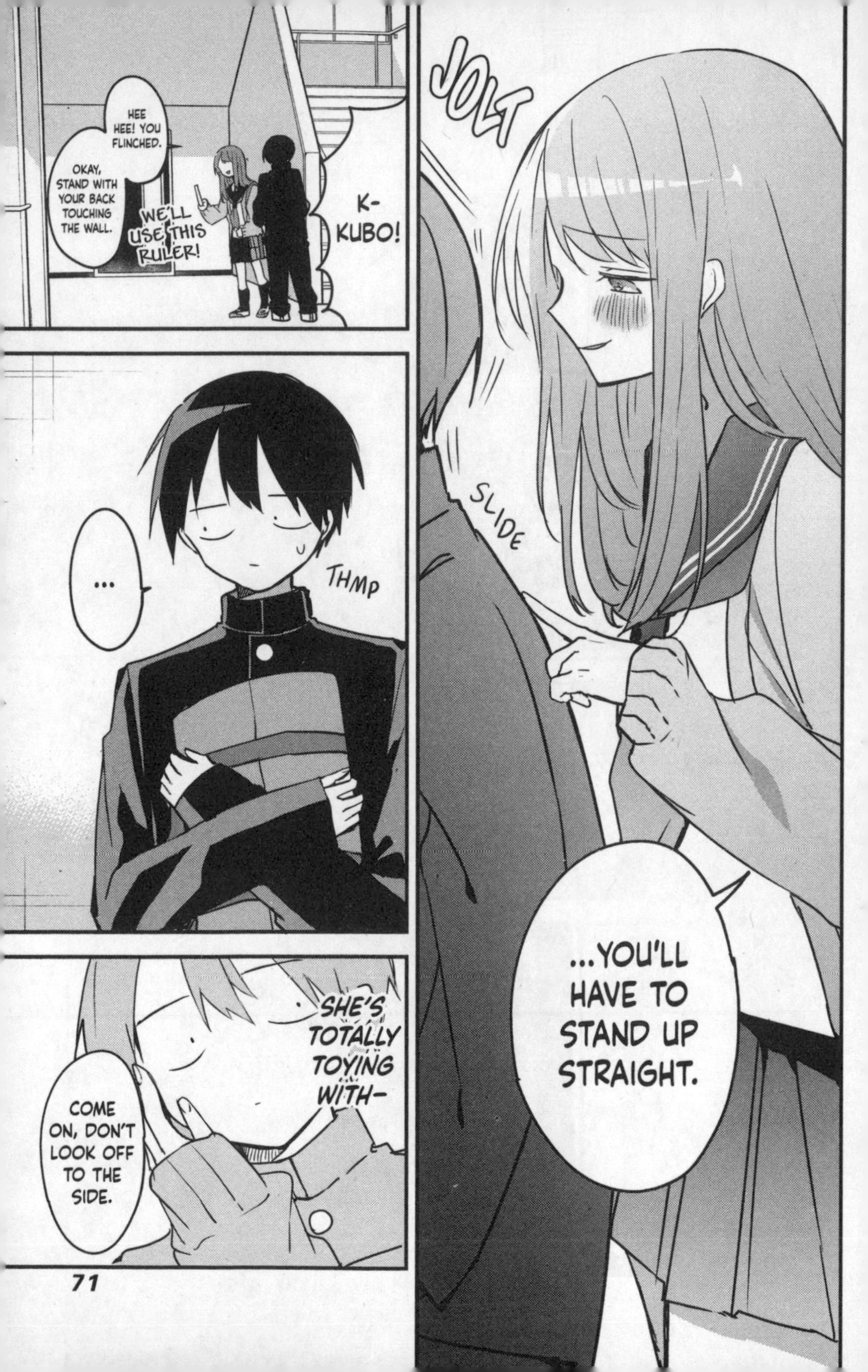
JOLT
SLIDE
...YOU'LL HAVE TO STAND UP STRAIGHT.
K-KUBO!
HEE HEE! YOU FLINCHED.
OKAY, STAND WITH YOUR BACK TOUCHING THE WALL.
WE'LL USE THIS RULER!
THMP
...
SHE'S TOTALLY TOYING WITH-
COME ON, DON'T LOOK OFF TO THE SIDE.

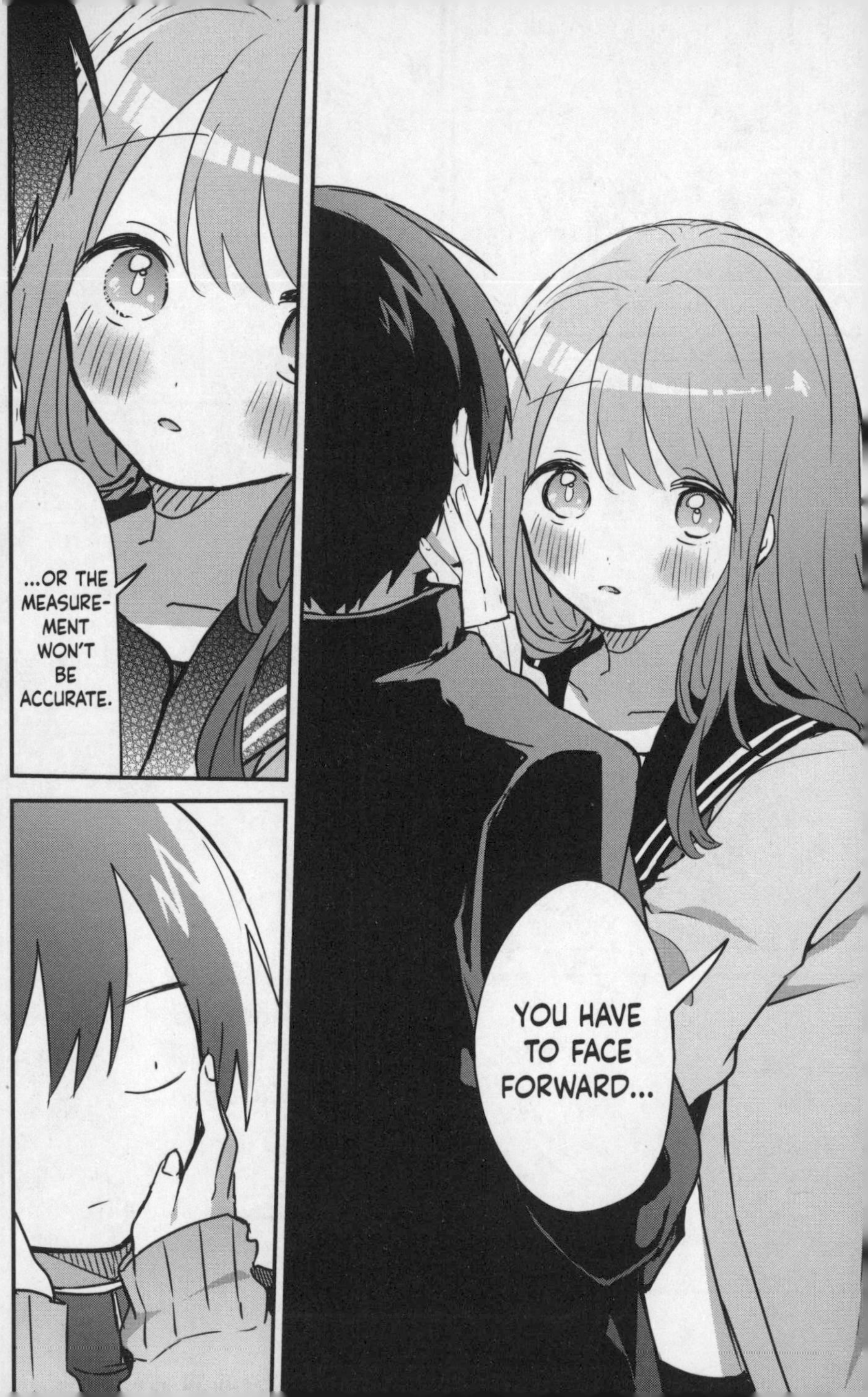
YOU HAVE TO FACE FORWARD...
...OR THE MEASUREMENT WON'T BE ACCURATE.

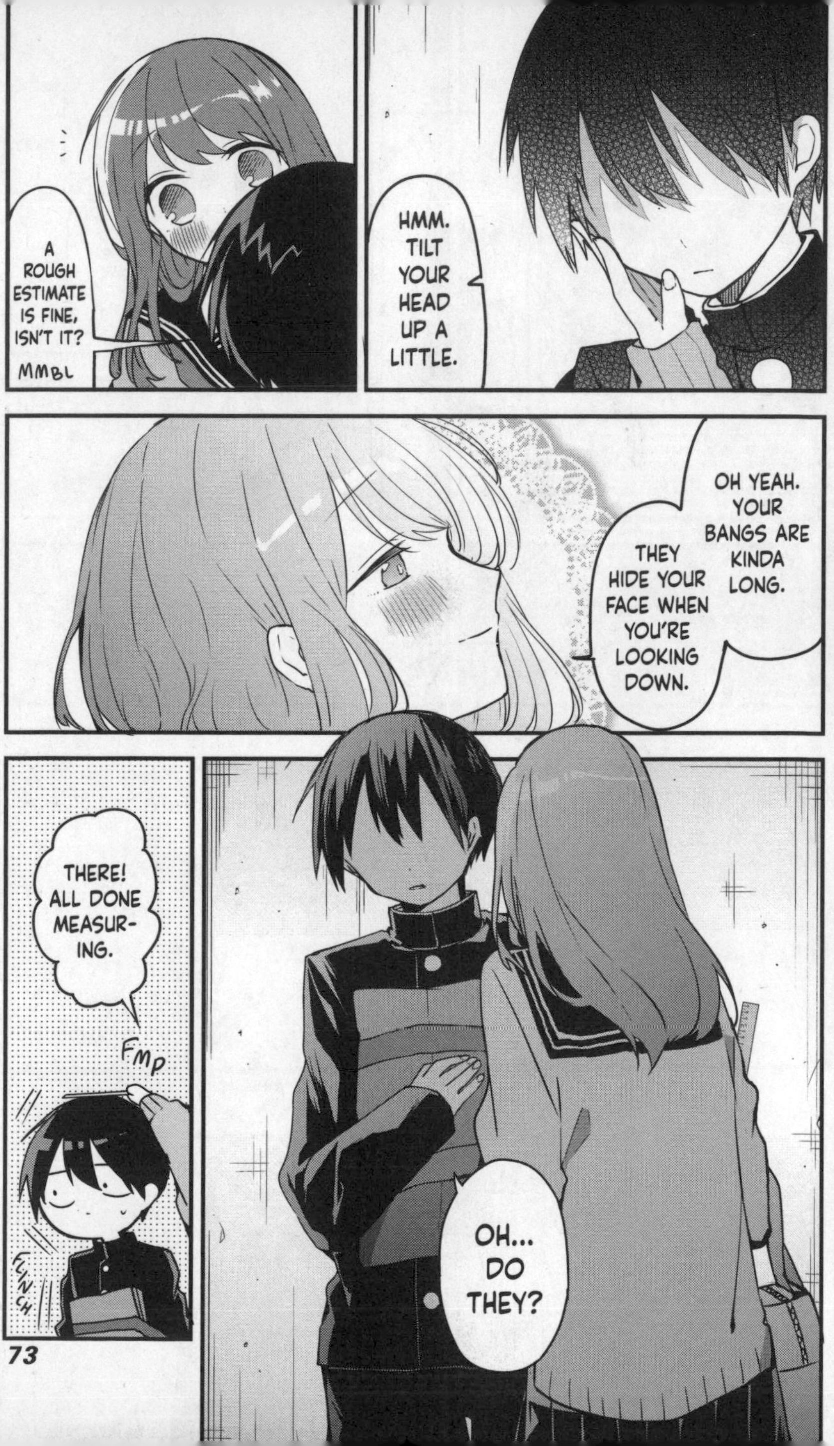
HMM. TILT YOUR HEAD UP A LITTLE.
A ROUGH ESTIMATE IS FINE, ISN'T IT?
MMBL
OH YEAH. YOUR BANGS ARE KINDA LONG.
THEY HIDE YOUR FACE WHEN YOU'RE LOOKING DOWN.
OH... DO THEY?
THERE! ALL DONE MEASUR-ING.
FMP
FLINCH

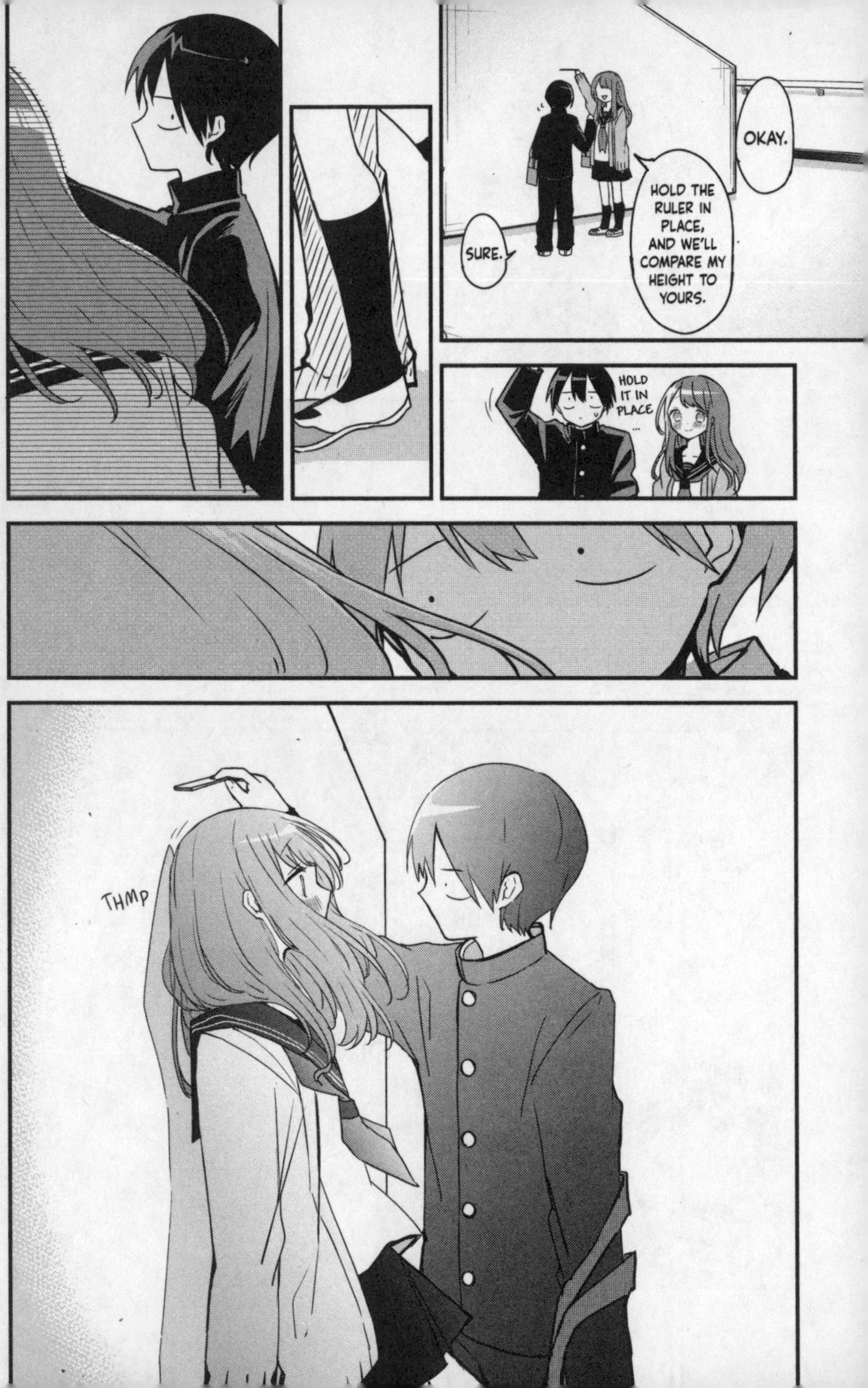
OKAY.
HOLD THE RULER IN PLACE, AND WE'LL COMPARE MY HEIGHT TO YOURS.
SURE.
HOLD IT IN PLACE ...
THMP

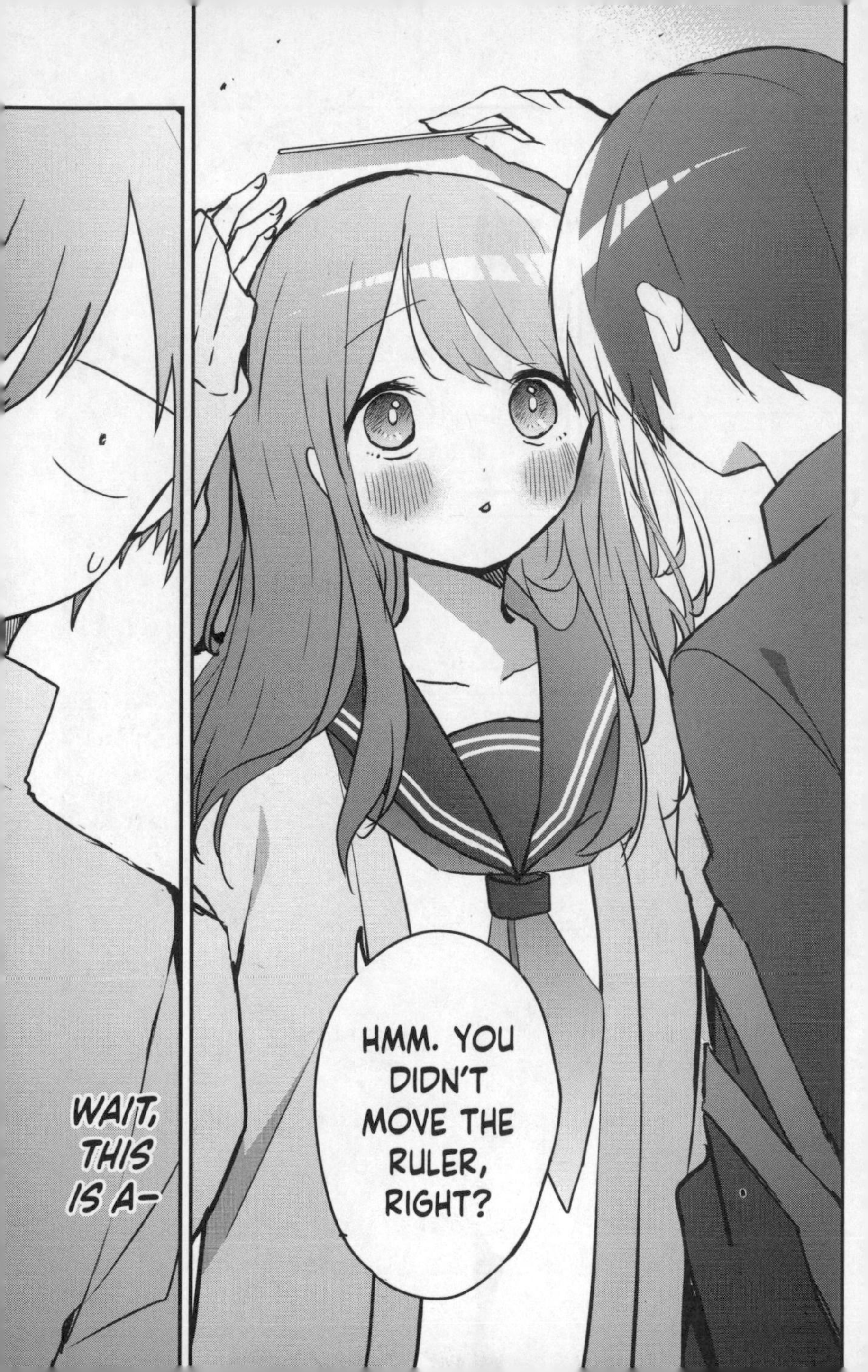
HMM. YOU DIDN'T MOVE THE RULER, RIGHT?
WAIT, THIS IS A-

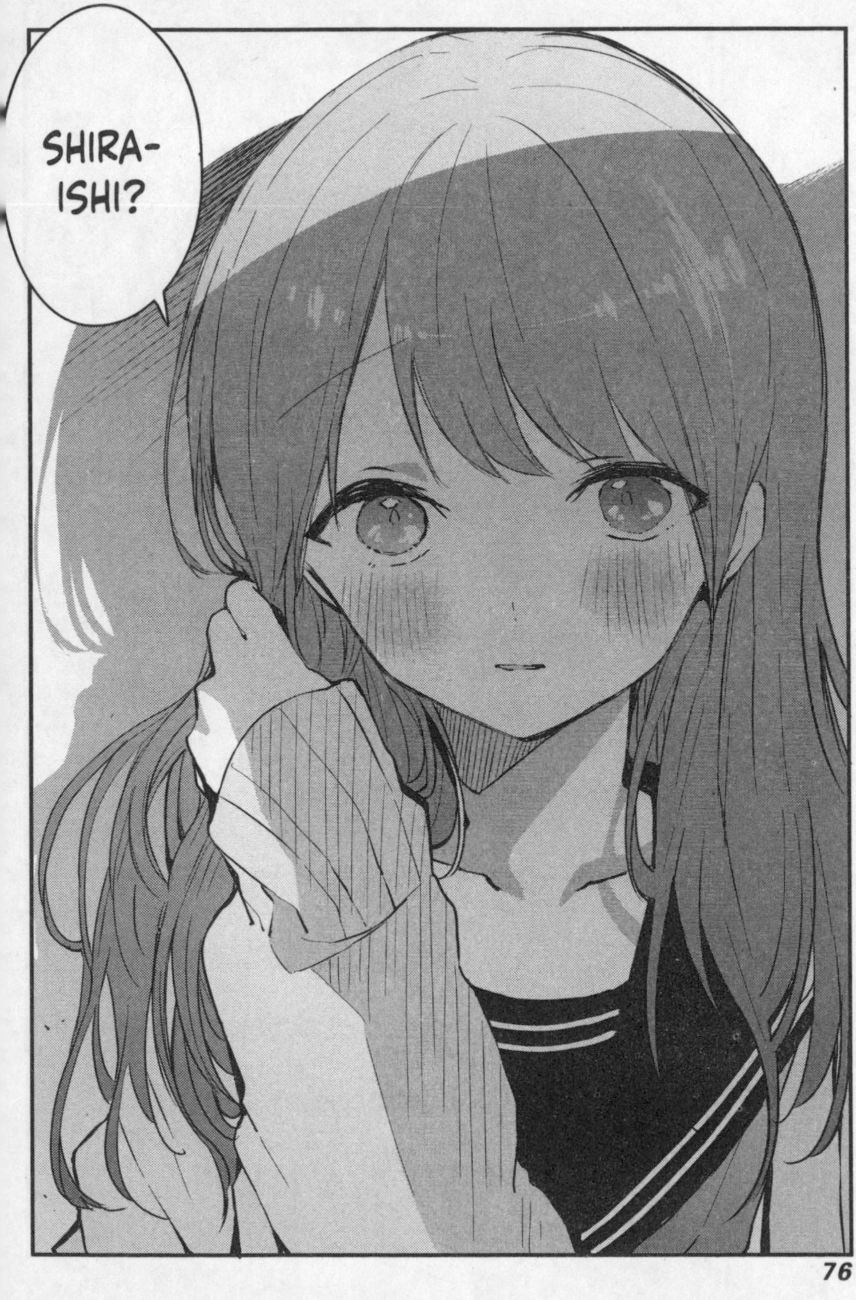
SHIRA-ISHI?

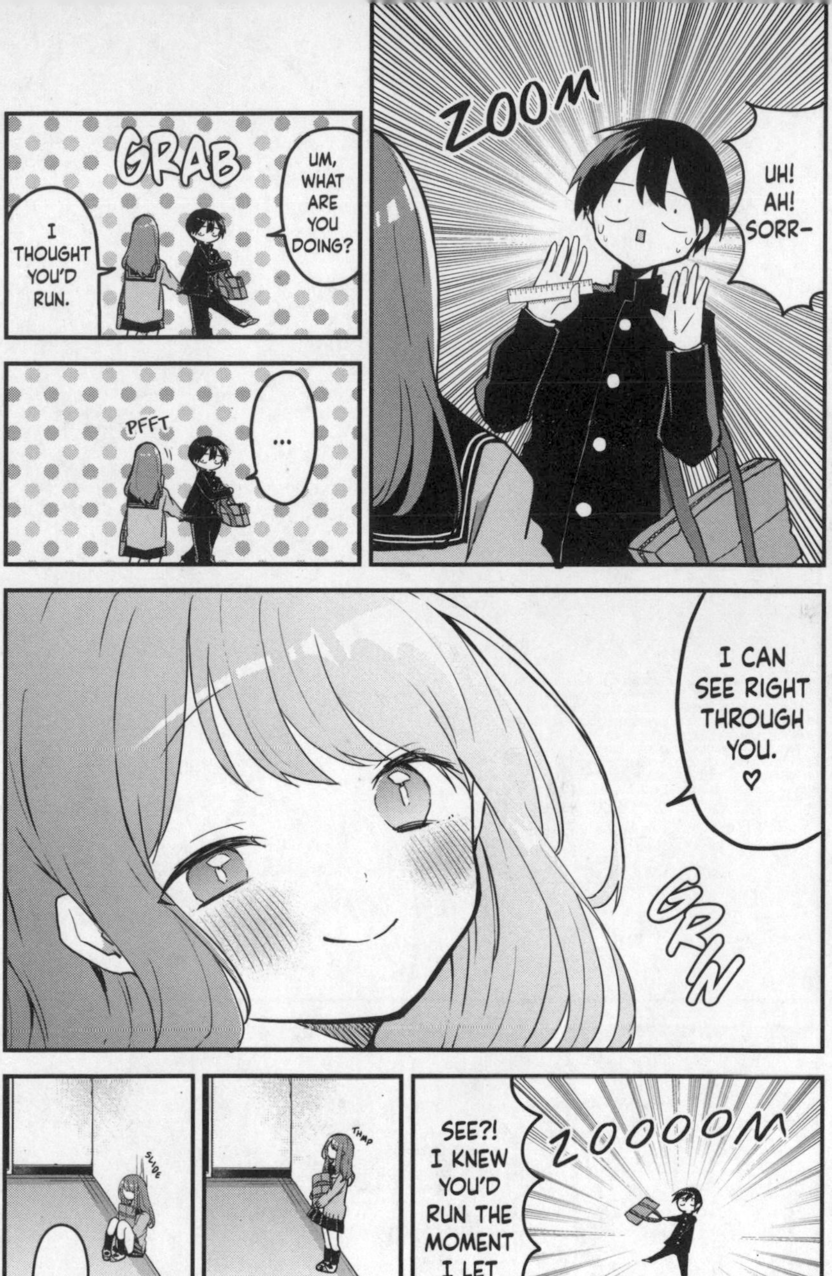
ZOOM
UH! AH! SORR-
GRAB
UM, WHAT ARE YOU DOING?
I THOUGHT YOU'D RUN.
PFFT
...
I CAN SEE RIGHT THROUGH YOU. ♡
GRIN
ZOOOOOM
SEE?! I KNEW YOU'D RUN THE MOMENT I LET GO!
THMP
SLIDE
...

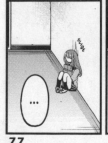

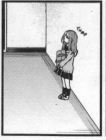

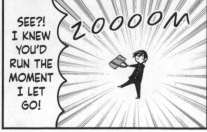

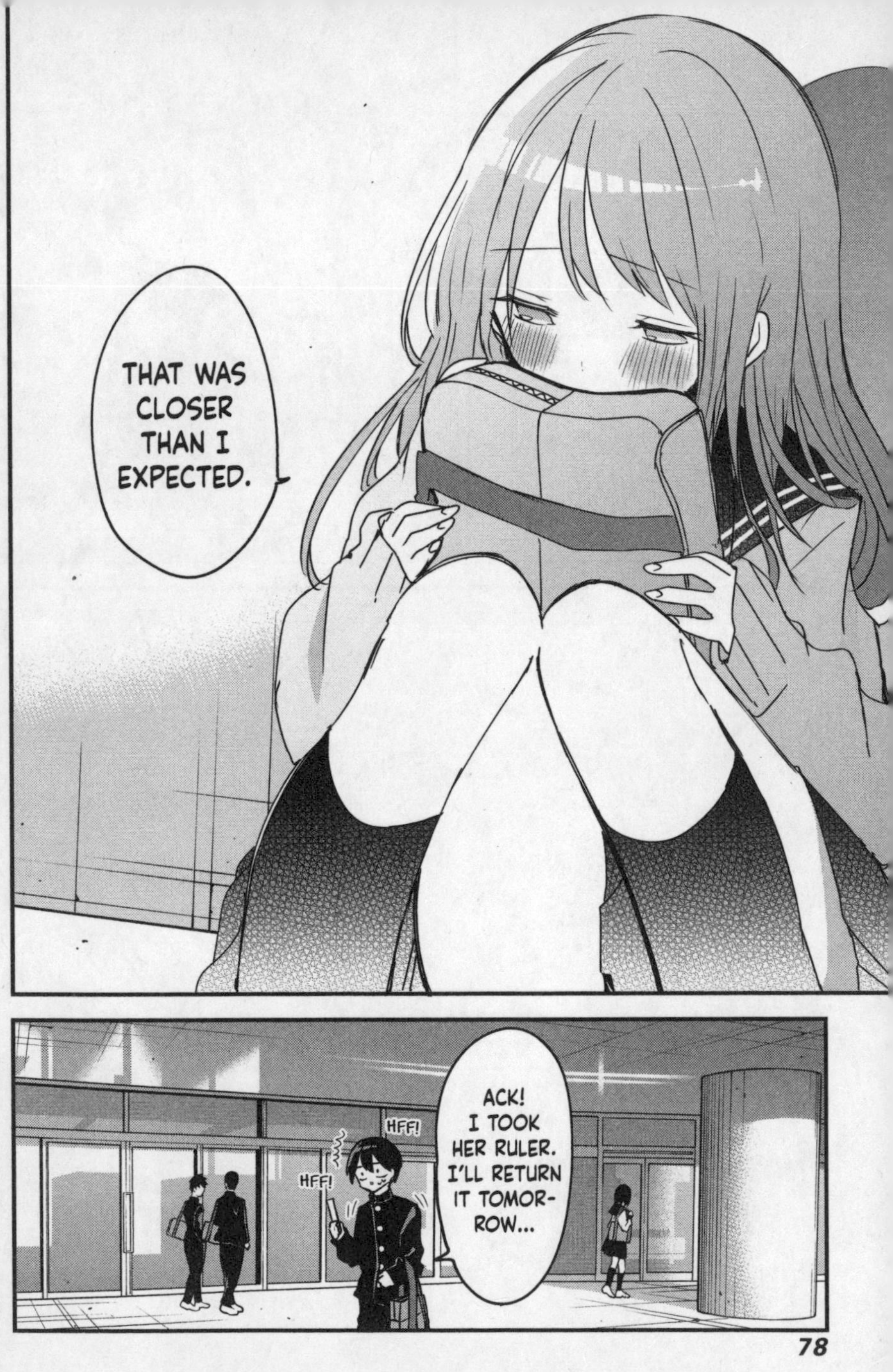
THAT WAS CLOSER THAN I EXPECTED.
ACK! I TOOK HER RULER. I'LL RETURN IT TOMORROW...
HFF!
HFF!

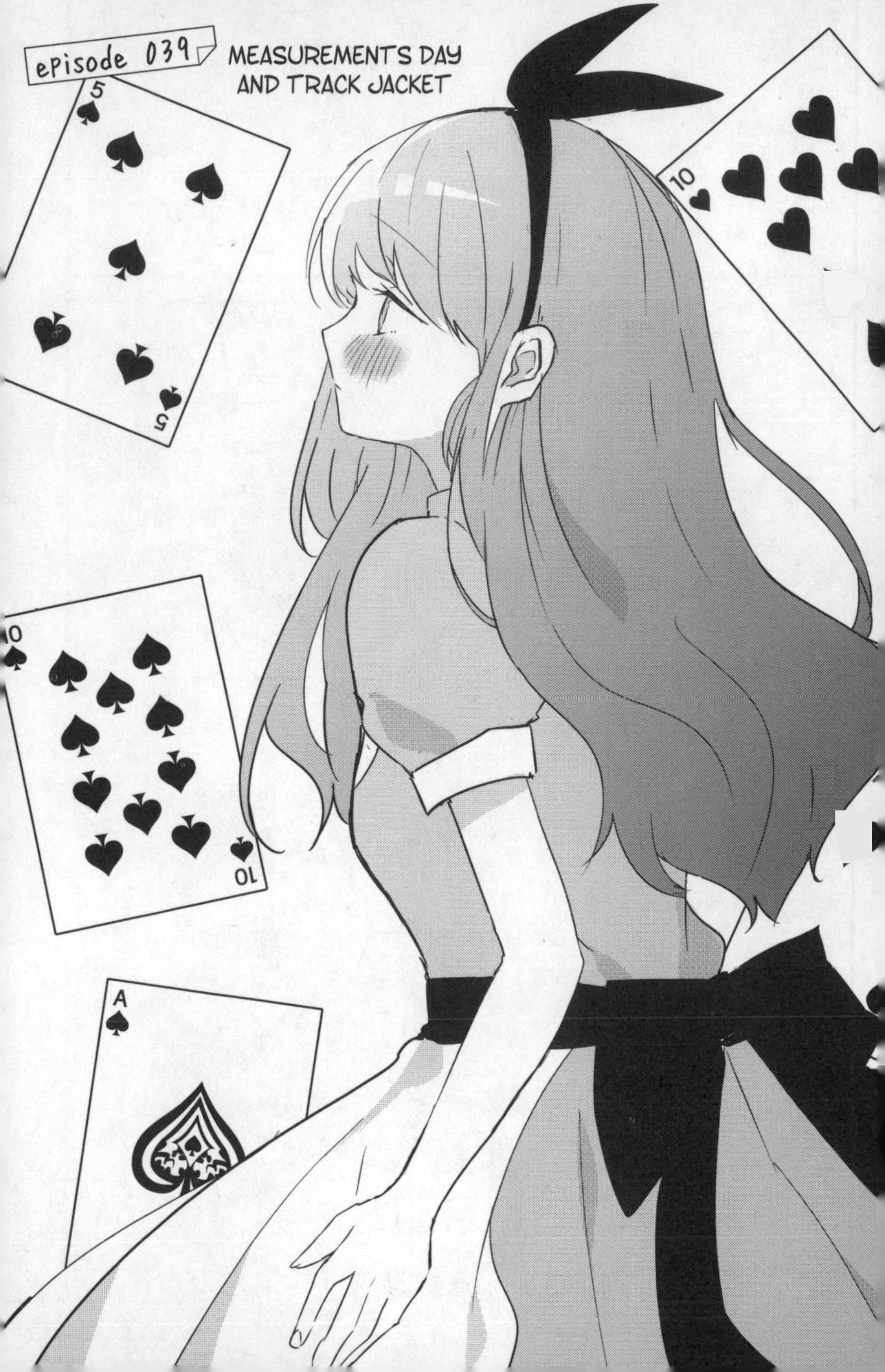
episode 039
MEASUREMENTS DAY AND TRACK JACKET

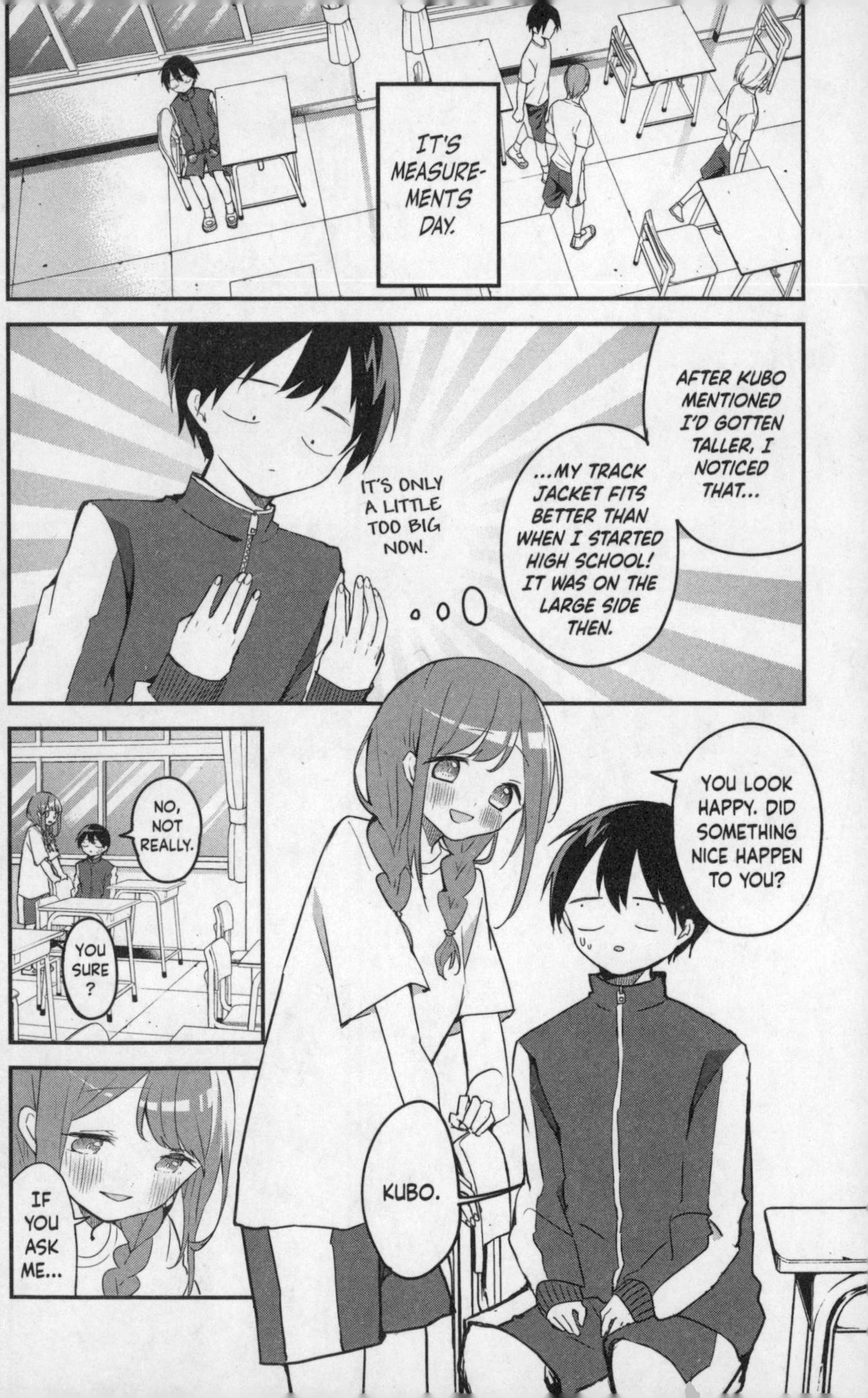
IT'S MEASURE-MENTS DAY.
AFTER KUBO MENTIONED I'D GOTTEN TALLER, I NOTICED THAT...
...MY TRACK JACKET FITS BETTER THAN WHEN I STARTED HIGH SCHOOL! IT WAS ON THE LARGE SIDE THEN.
IT'S ONLY A LITTLE TOO BIG NOW.
YOU LOOK HAPPY. DID SOMETHING NICE HAPPEN TO YOU?
KUBO.
NO, NOT REALLY.
YOU SURE?
IF YOU ASK ME...

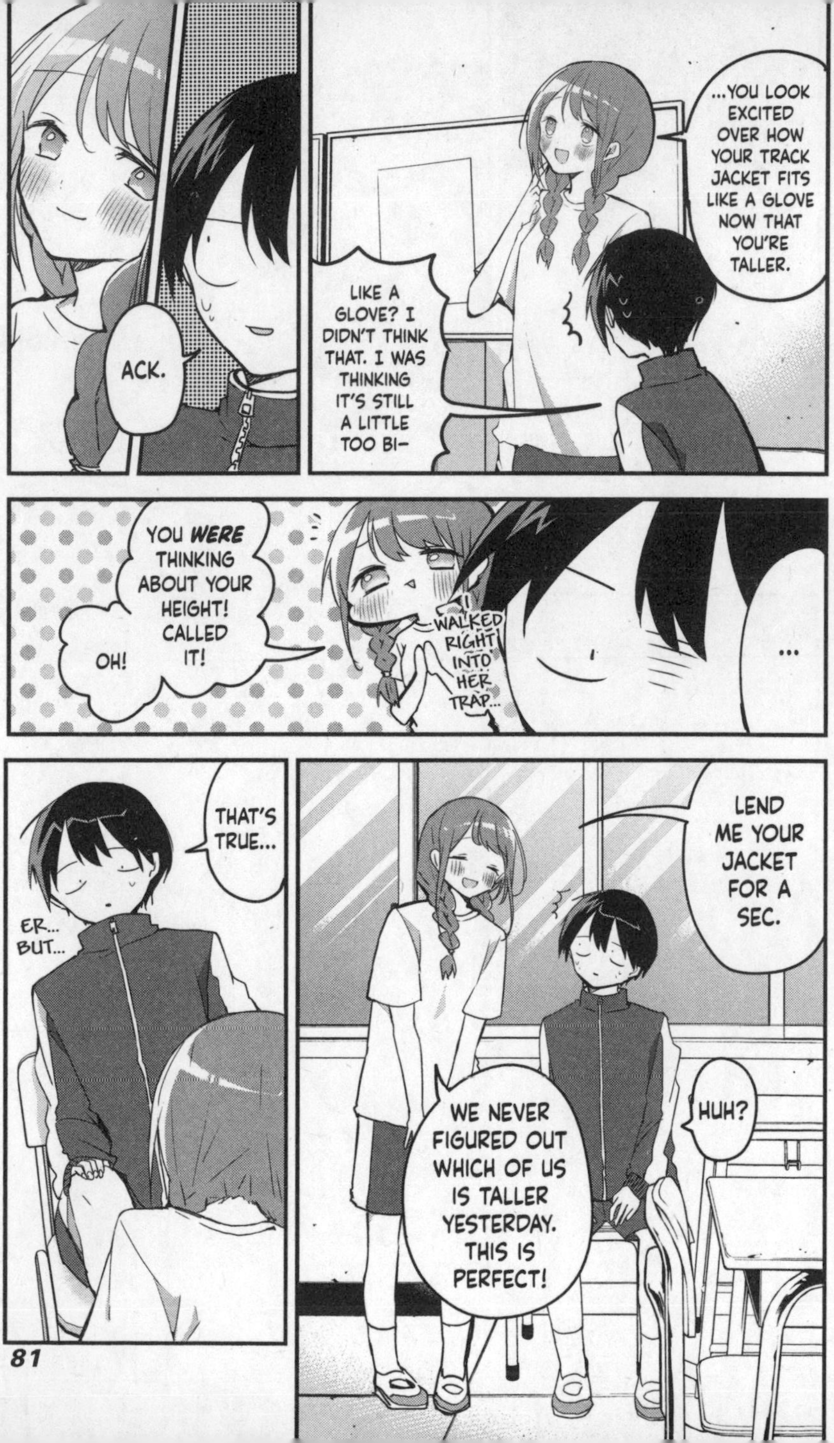
...YOU LOOK EXCITED OVER HOW YOUR TRACK JACKET FITS LIKE A GLOVE NOW THAT YOU'RE TALLER.
LIKE A GLOVE? I DIDN'T THINK THAT. I WAS THINKING IT'S STILL A LITTLE TOO BI–
ACK.
...
I WALKED RIGHT INTO HER TRAP...
YOU *WERE* THINKING ABOUT YOUR HEIGHT! CALLED IT!
OH!
LEND ME YOUR JACKET FOR A SEC.
HUH?
WE NEVER FIGURED OUT WHICH OF US IS TALLER YESTERDAY. THIS IS PERFECT!
THAT'S TRUE...
ER... BUT...

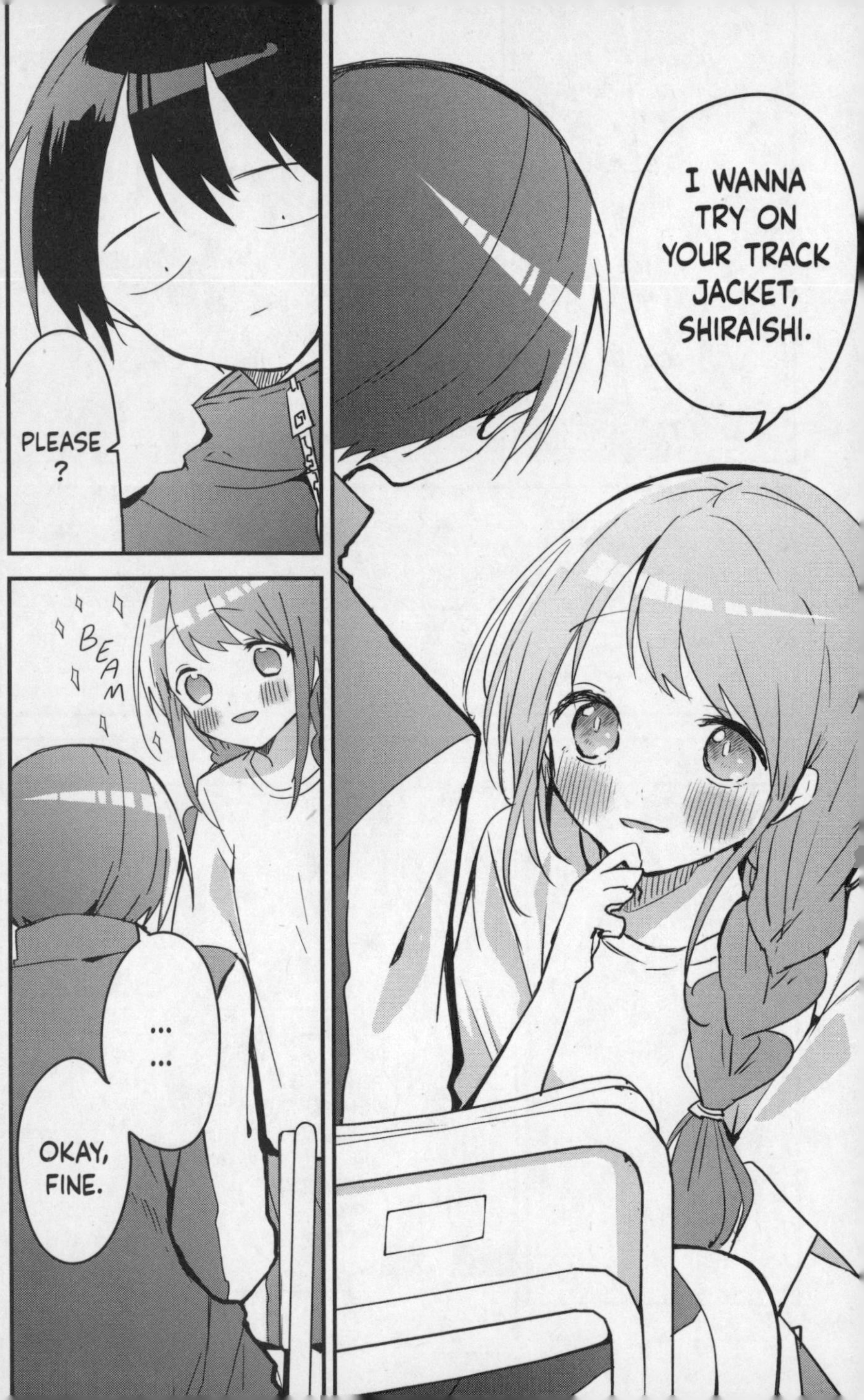
I WANNA TRY ON YOUR TRACK JACKET, SHIRAISHI.
PLEASE?
BEAM
... ... OKAY, FINE.

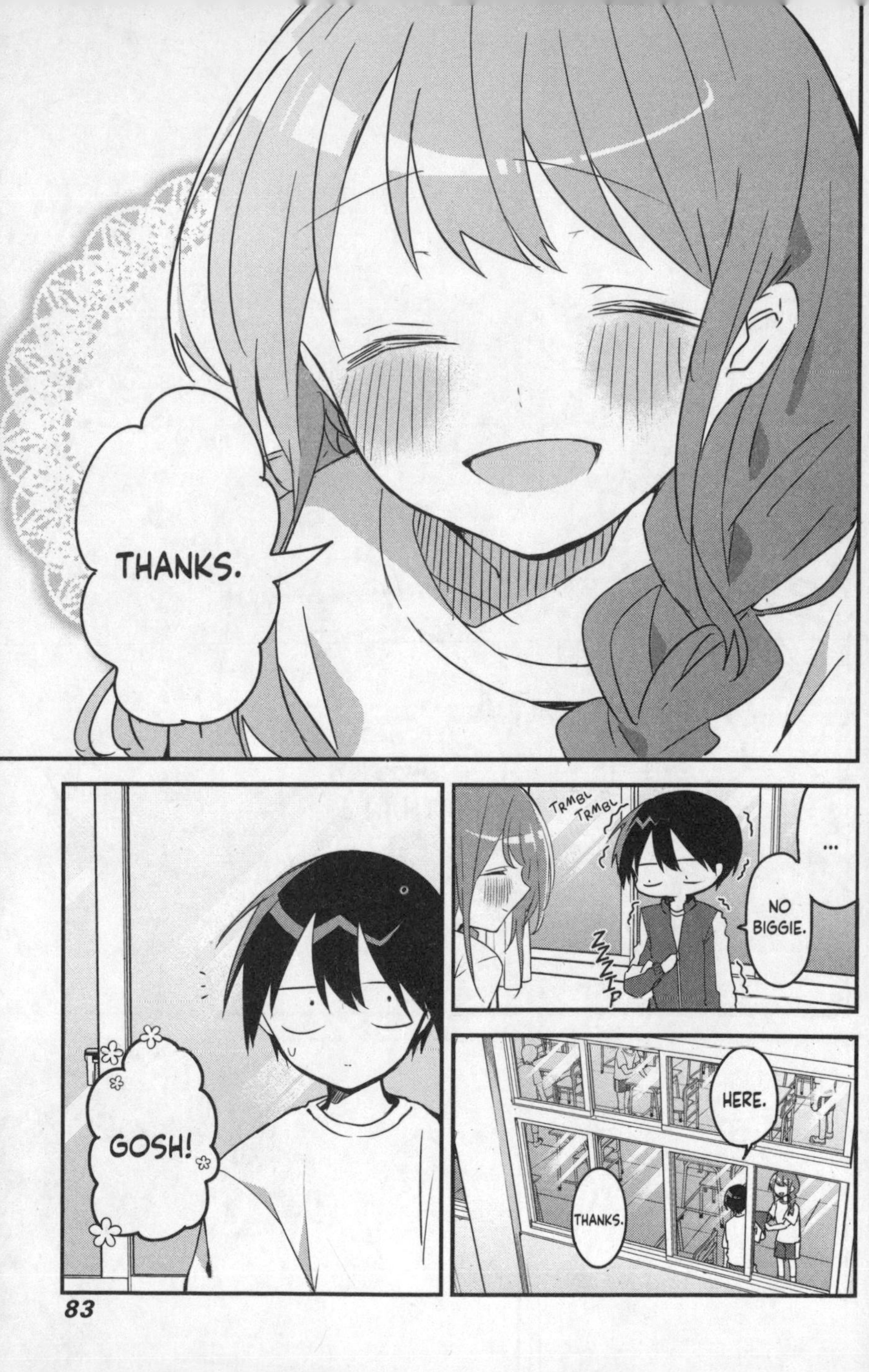
THANKS.
...
NO BIGGIE.
TRMBL TRMBL
ZZZZIP
HERE.
THANKS.
GOSH!

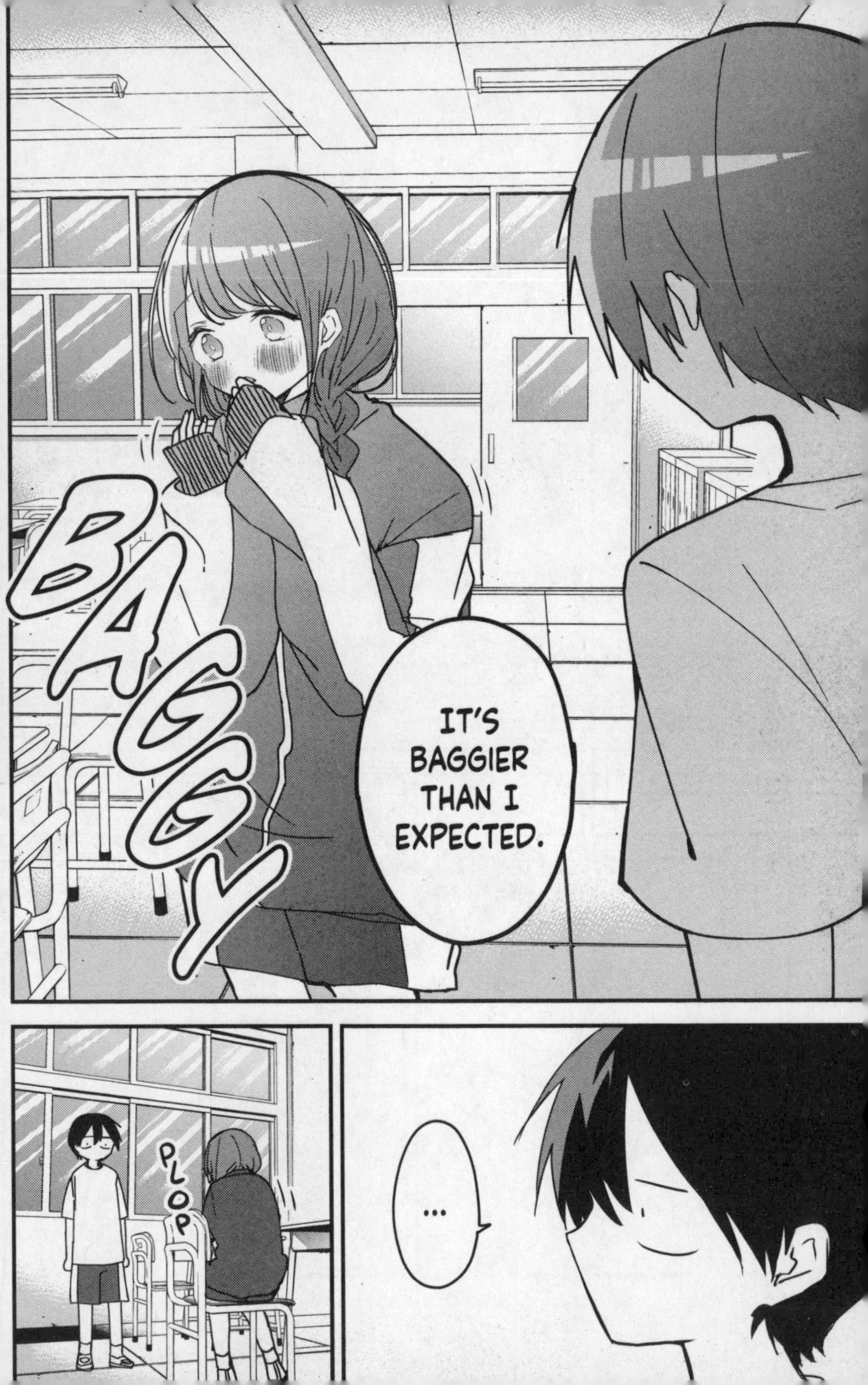
BAGGY
IT'S BAGGIER THAN I EXPECTED.
...
PLOP

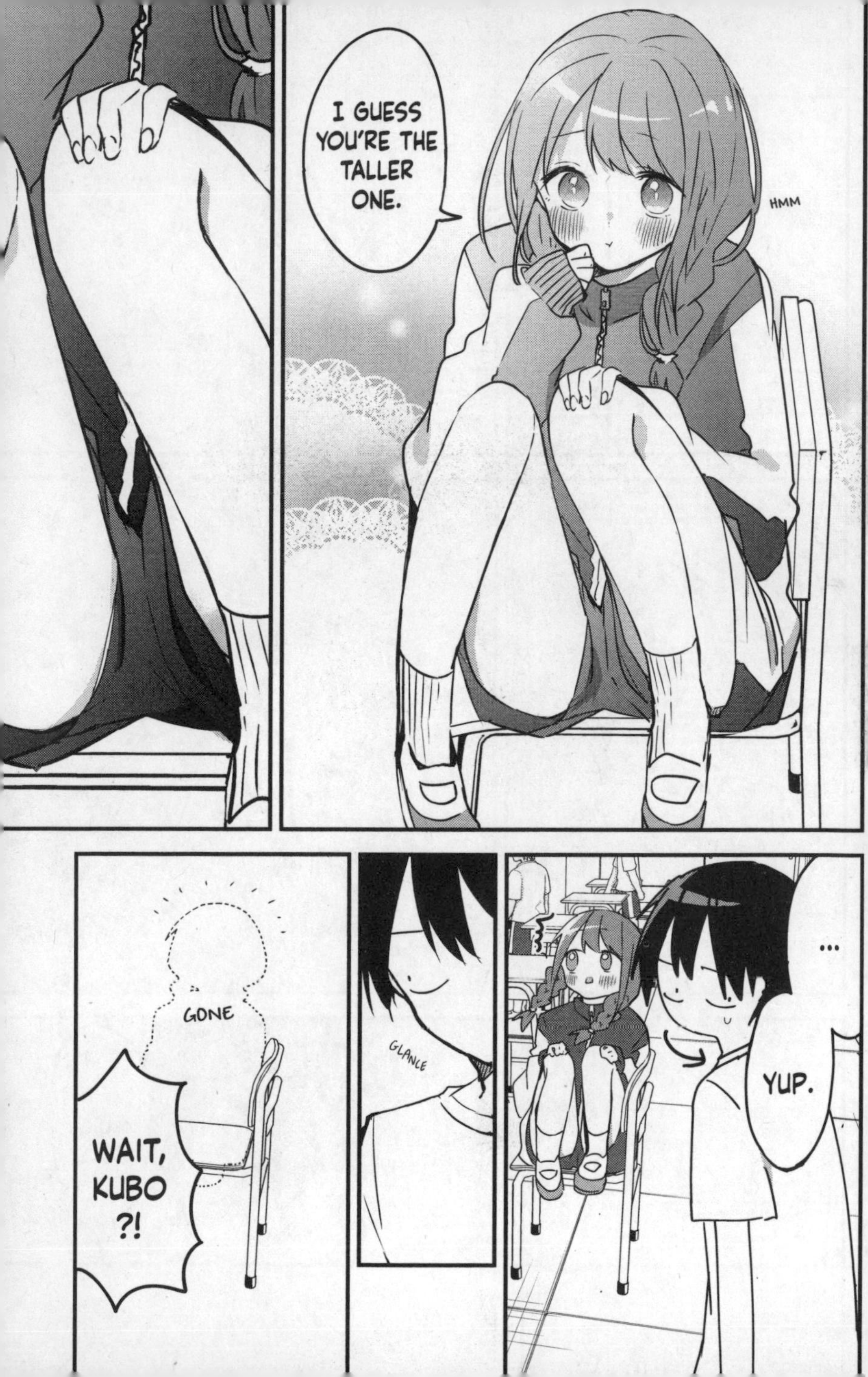
I GUESS YOU'RE THE TALLER ONE.
HMM
...
YUP.
GLANCE
GONE
WAIT, KUBO?!

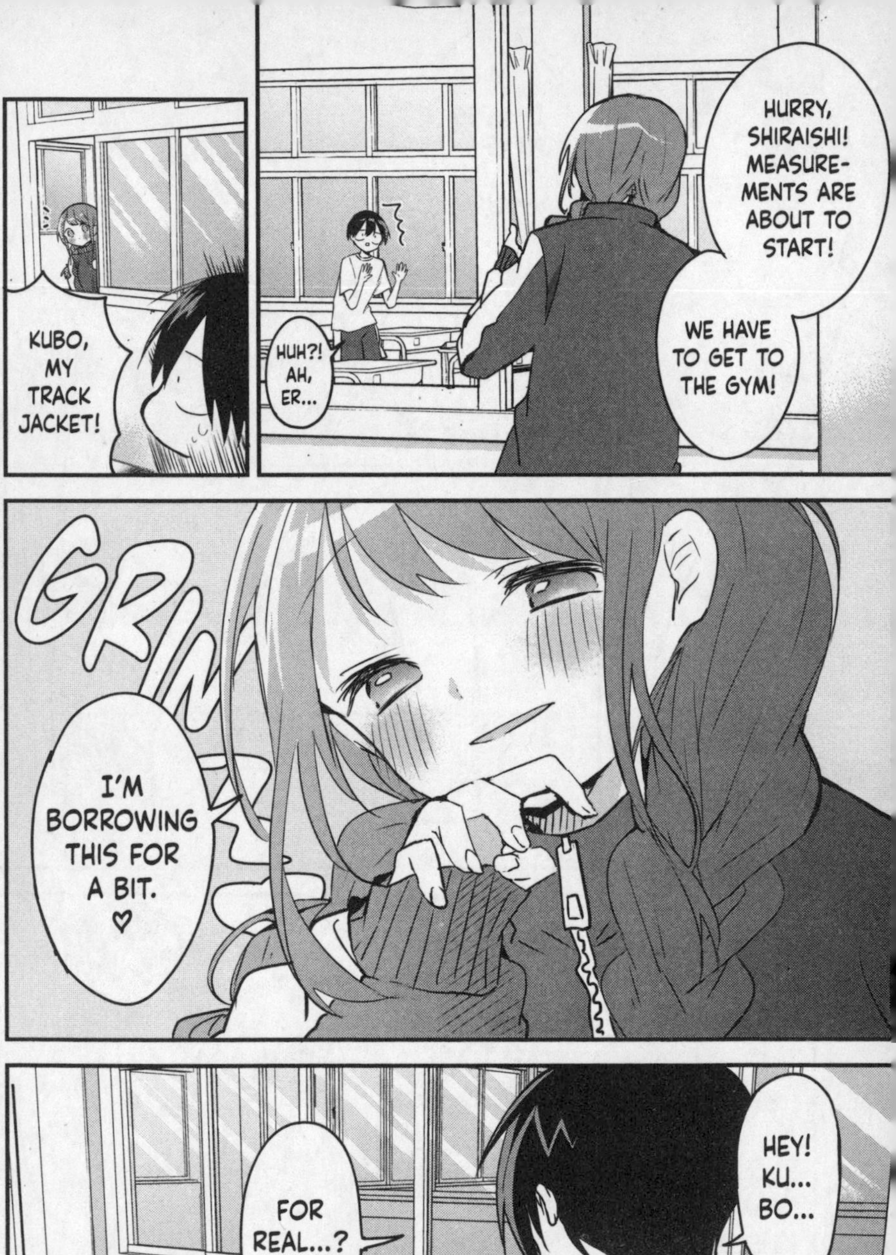
HURRY, SHIRAISHI! MEASUREMENTS ARE ABOUT TO START!
WE HAVE TO GET TO THE GYM!
HUH?! AH, ER...
KUBO, MY TRACK JACKET!
GRIN
I'M BORROWING THIS FOR A BIT. ♡
HEY! KU... BO...
FOR REAL...?

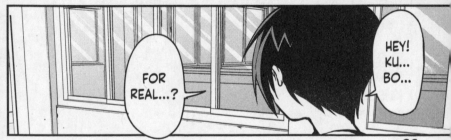

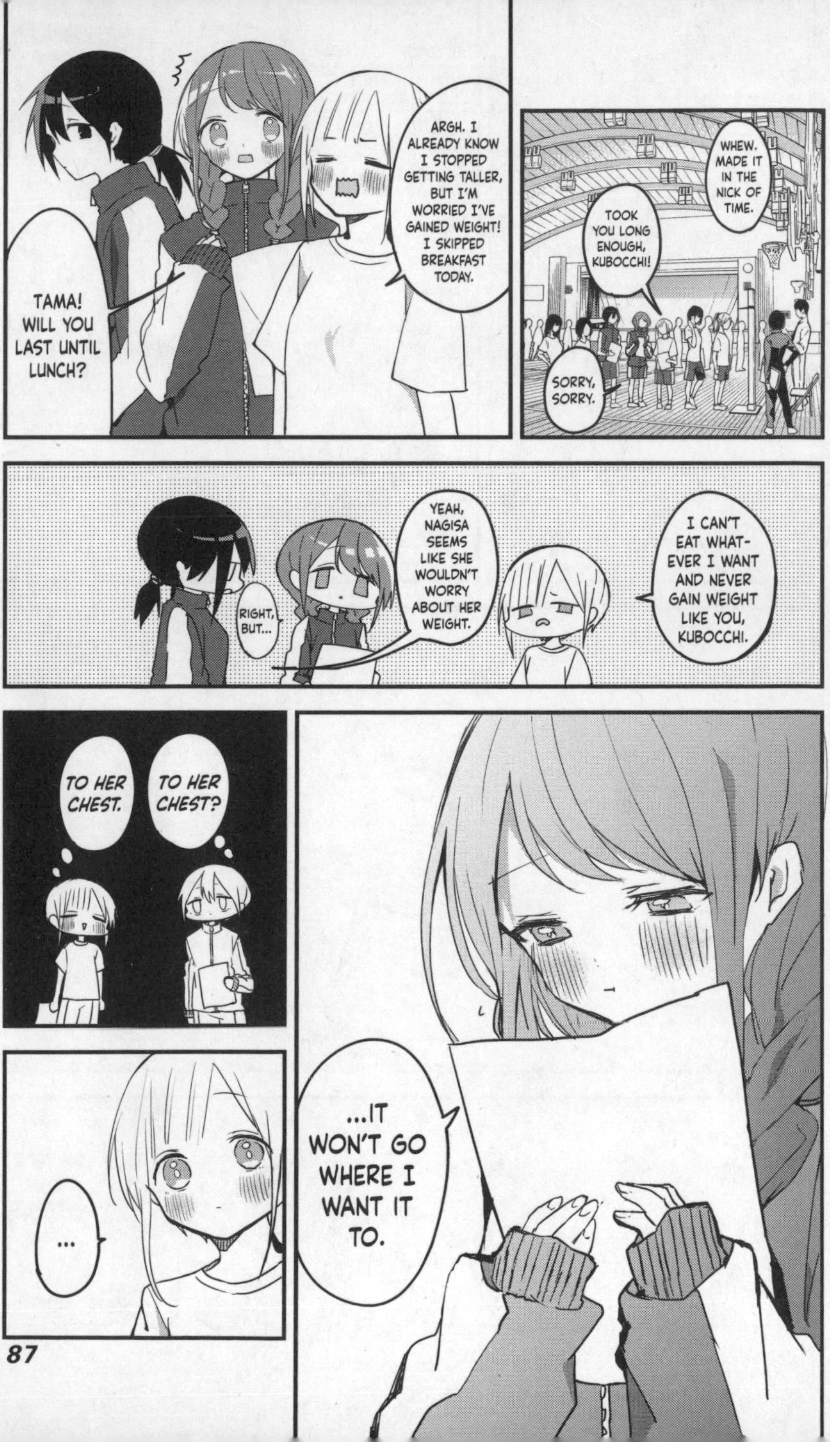
WHEW. MADE IT IN THE NICK OF TIME.
TOOK YOU LONG ENOUGH, KUBOCCHI!
SORRY, SORRY.
ARGH. I ALREADY KNOW I STOPPED GETTING TALLER, BUT I'M WORRIED I'VE GAINED WEIGHT! I SKIPPED BREAKFAST TODAY.
TAMA! WILL YOU LAST UNTIL LUNCH?
I CAN'T EAT WHAT-EVER I WANT AND NEVER GAIN WEIGHT LIKE YOU, KUBOCCHI.
YEAH, NAGISA SEEMS LIKE SHE WOULDN'T WORRY ABOUT HER WEIGHT.
RIGHT, BUT...
...IT WON'T GO WHERE I WANT IT TO.
TO HER CHEST?
TO HER CHEST.
...

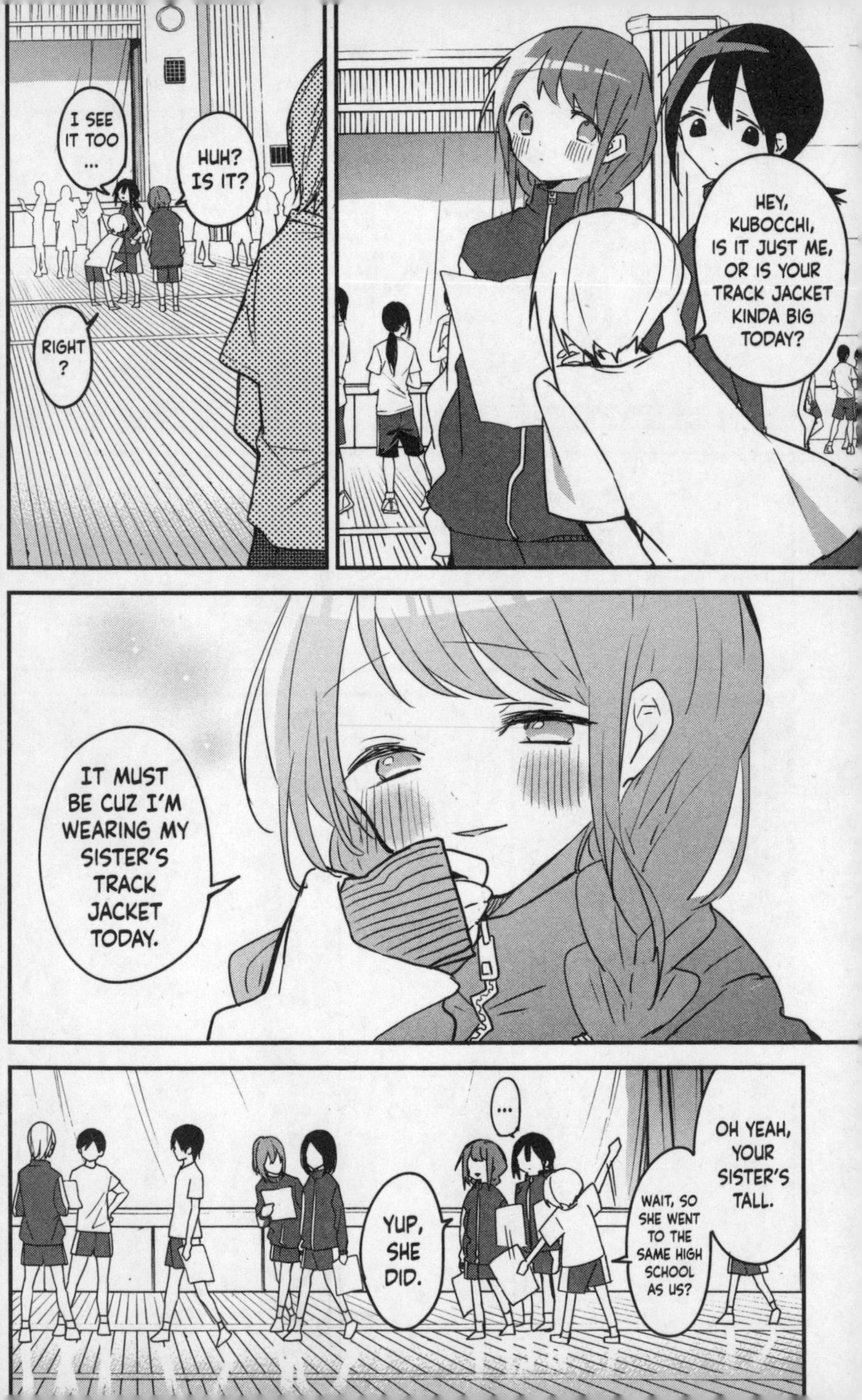
HEY, KUBOCCHI, IS IT JUST ME, OR IS YOUR TRACK JACKET KINDA BIG TODAY?
I SEE IT TOO ...
HUH? IS IT?
RIGHT ?
IT MUST BE CUZ I'M WEARING MY SISTER'S TRACK JACKET TODAY.
OH YEAH, YOUR SISTER'S TALL.
...
WAIT, SO SHE WENT TO THE SAME HIGH SCHOOL AS US?
YUP, SHE DID.

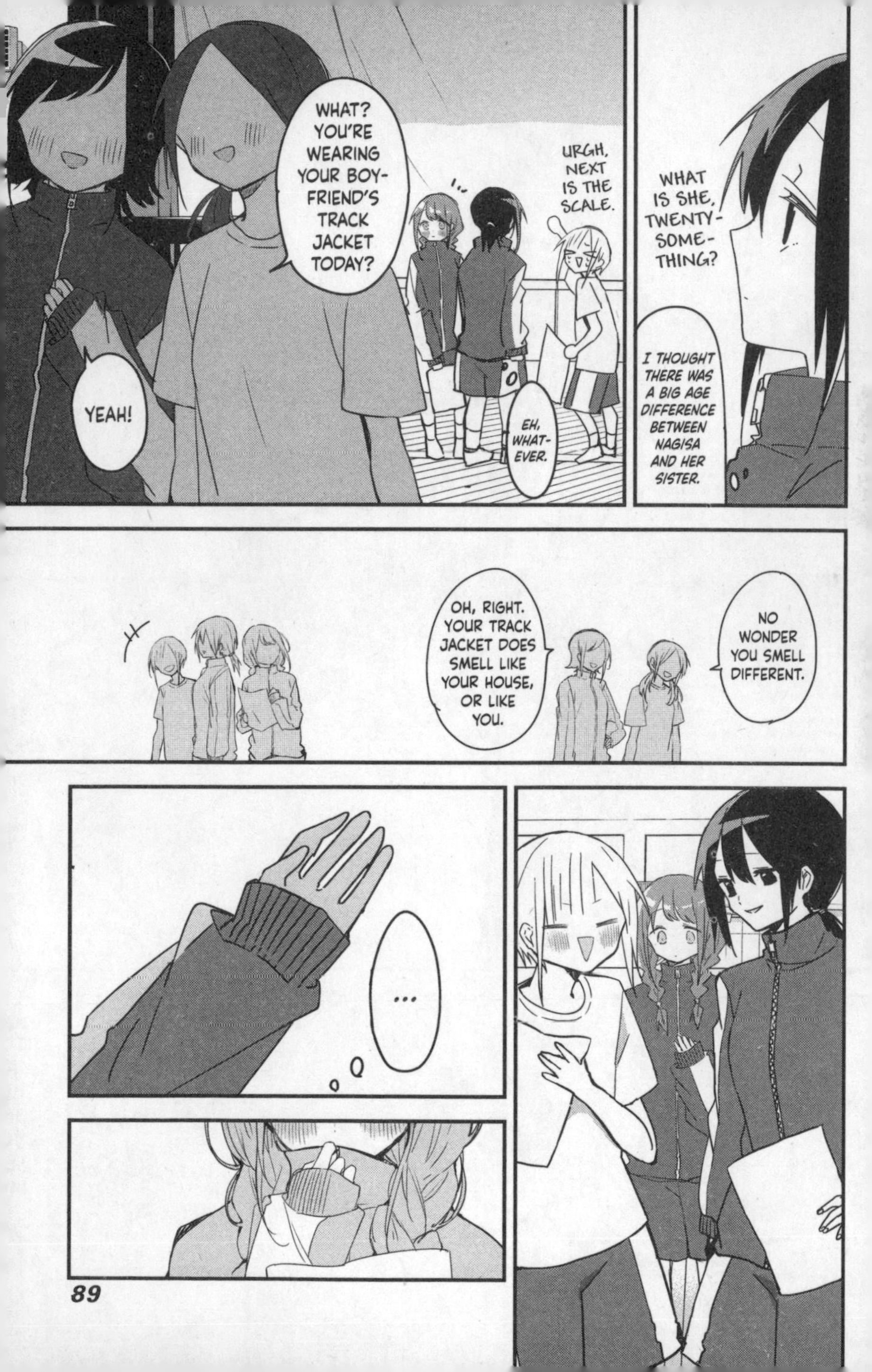
WHAT IS SHE, TWENTY-SOMETHING?
I THOUGHT THERE WAS A BIG AGE DIFFERENCE BETWEEN NAGISA AND HER SISTER.
URGH, NEXT IS THE SCALE.
WHAT? YOU'RE WEARING YOUR BOY-FRIEND'S TRACK JACKET TODAY?
EH, WHATEVER.
YEAH!
NO WONDER YOU SMELL DIFFERENT.
OH, RIGHT. YOUR TRACK JACKET DOES SMELL LIKE YOUR HOUSE, OR LIKE YOU.
...

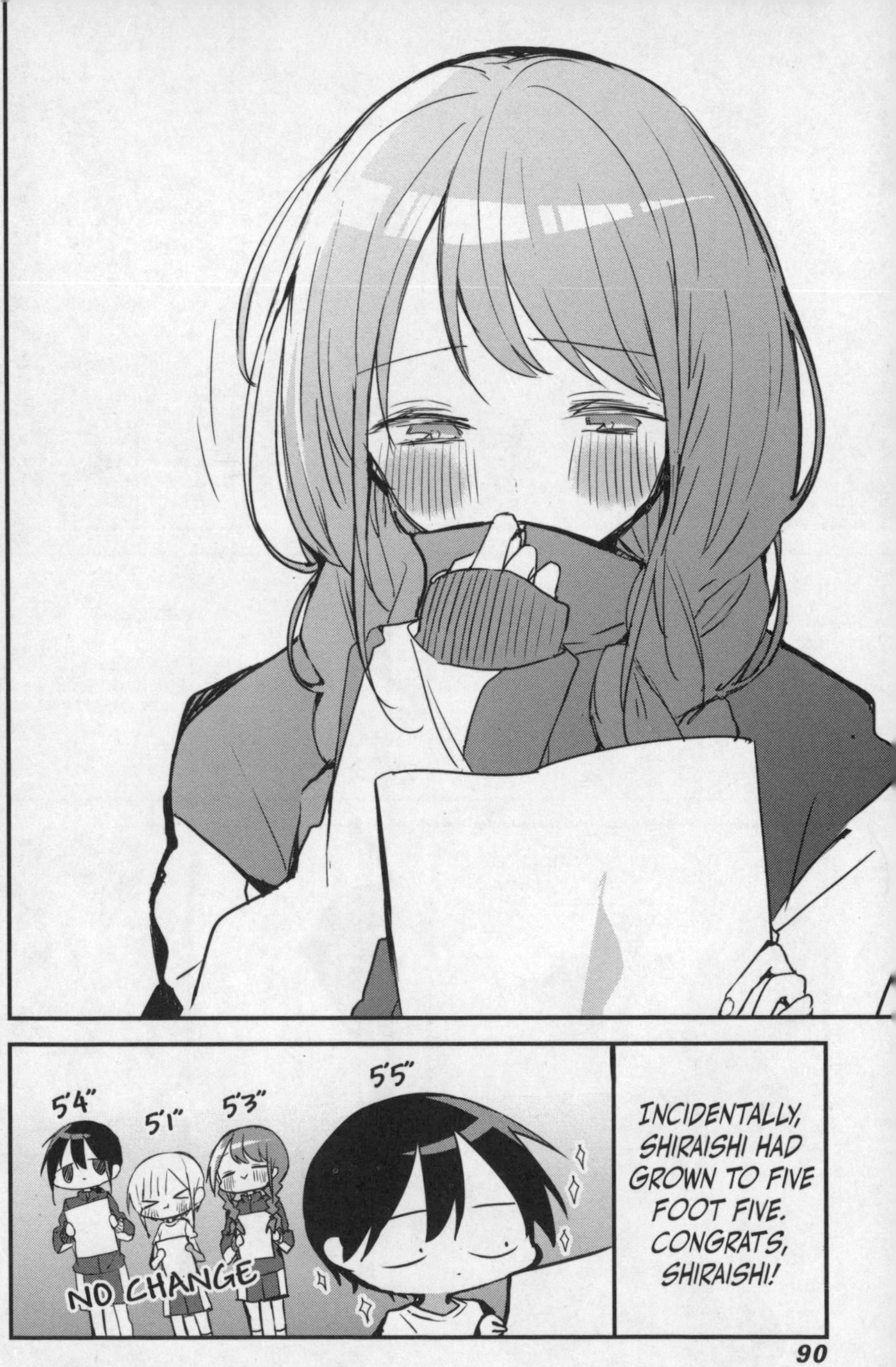
INCIDENTALLY, SHIRAISHI HAD GROWN TO FIVE FOOT FIVE. CONGRATS, SHIRAISHI!
5'5"
5'3"
5'1"
5'4"
NO CHANGE

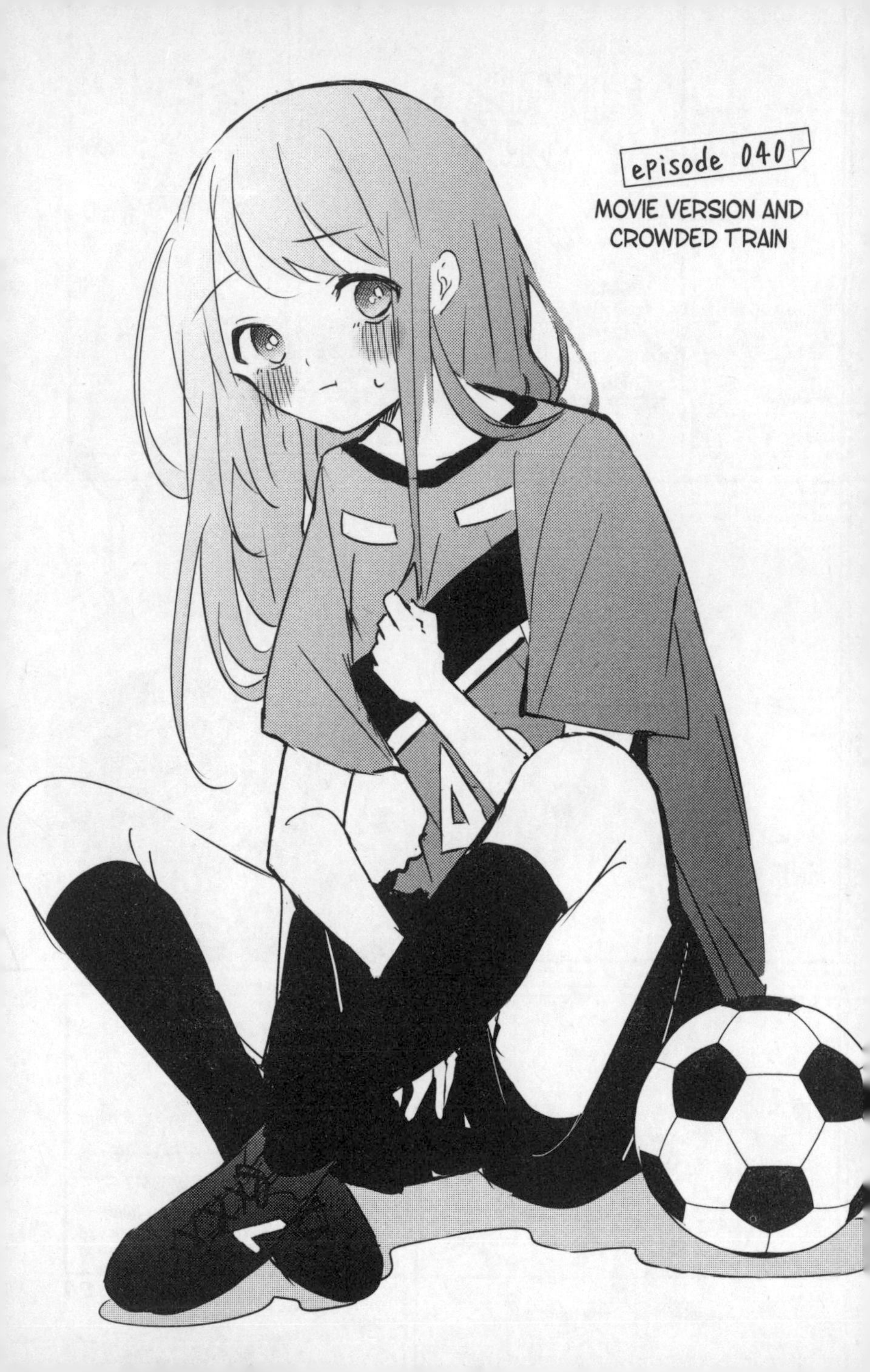
episode 040
MOVIE VERSION AND
CROWDED TRAIN

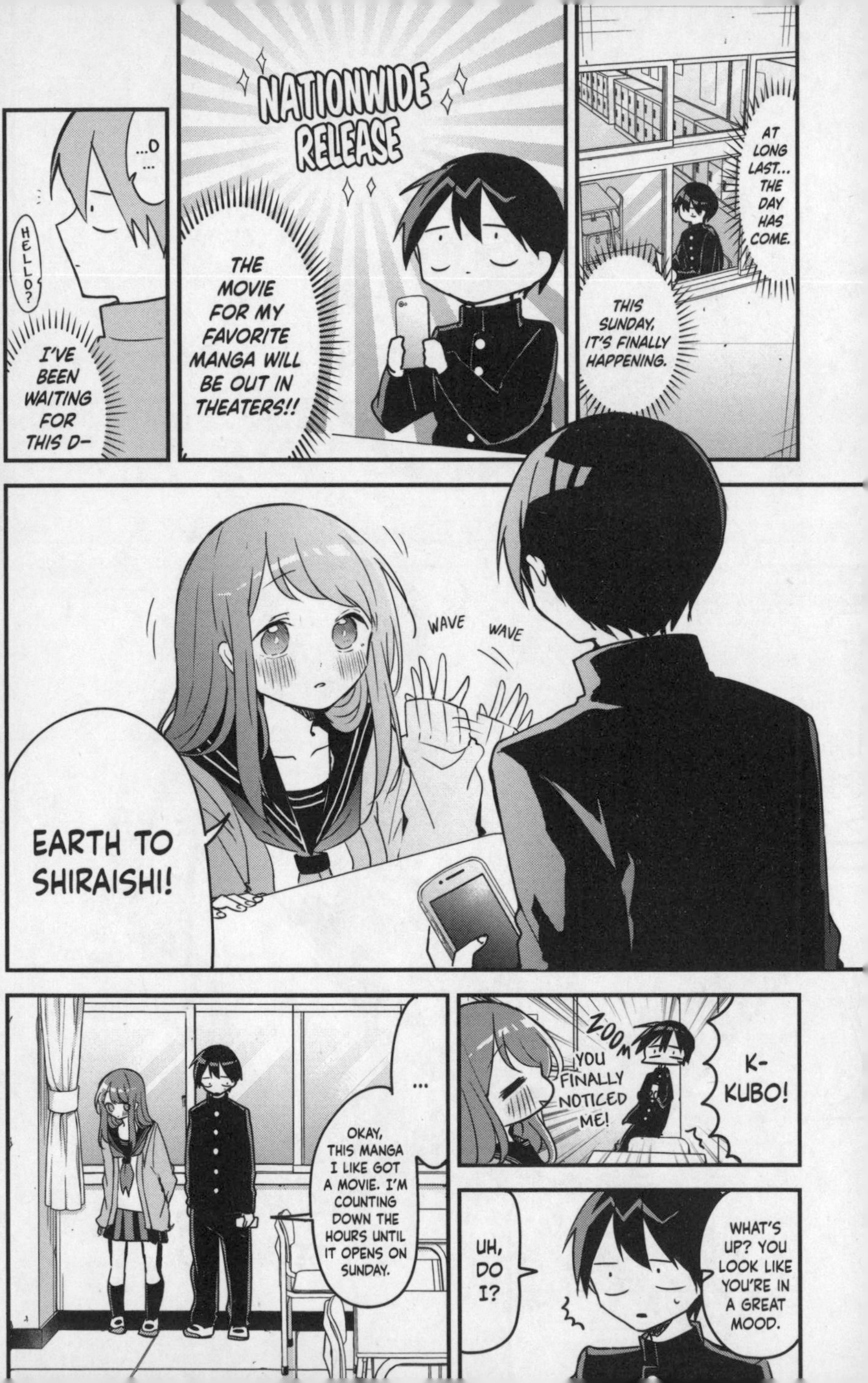
AT LONG LAST... THE DAY HAS COME.
THIS SUNDAY, IT'S FINALLY HAPPENING.
NATIONWIDE RELEASE
THE MOVIE FOR MY FAVORITE MANGA WILL BE OUT IN THEATERS!!
...D ...
HELLO?
I'VE BEEN WAITING FOR THIS D-
WAVE
WAVE
EARTH TO SHIRAISHI!
K-KUBO!
ZOOM
YOU FINALLY NOTICED ME!
WHAT'S UP? YOU LOOK LIKE YOU'RE IN A GREAT MOOD.
UH, DO I?
...
OKAY, THIS MANGA I LIKE GOT A MOVIE. I'M COUNTING DOWN THE HOURS UNTIL IT OPENS ON SUNDAY.

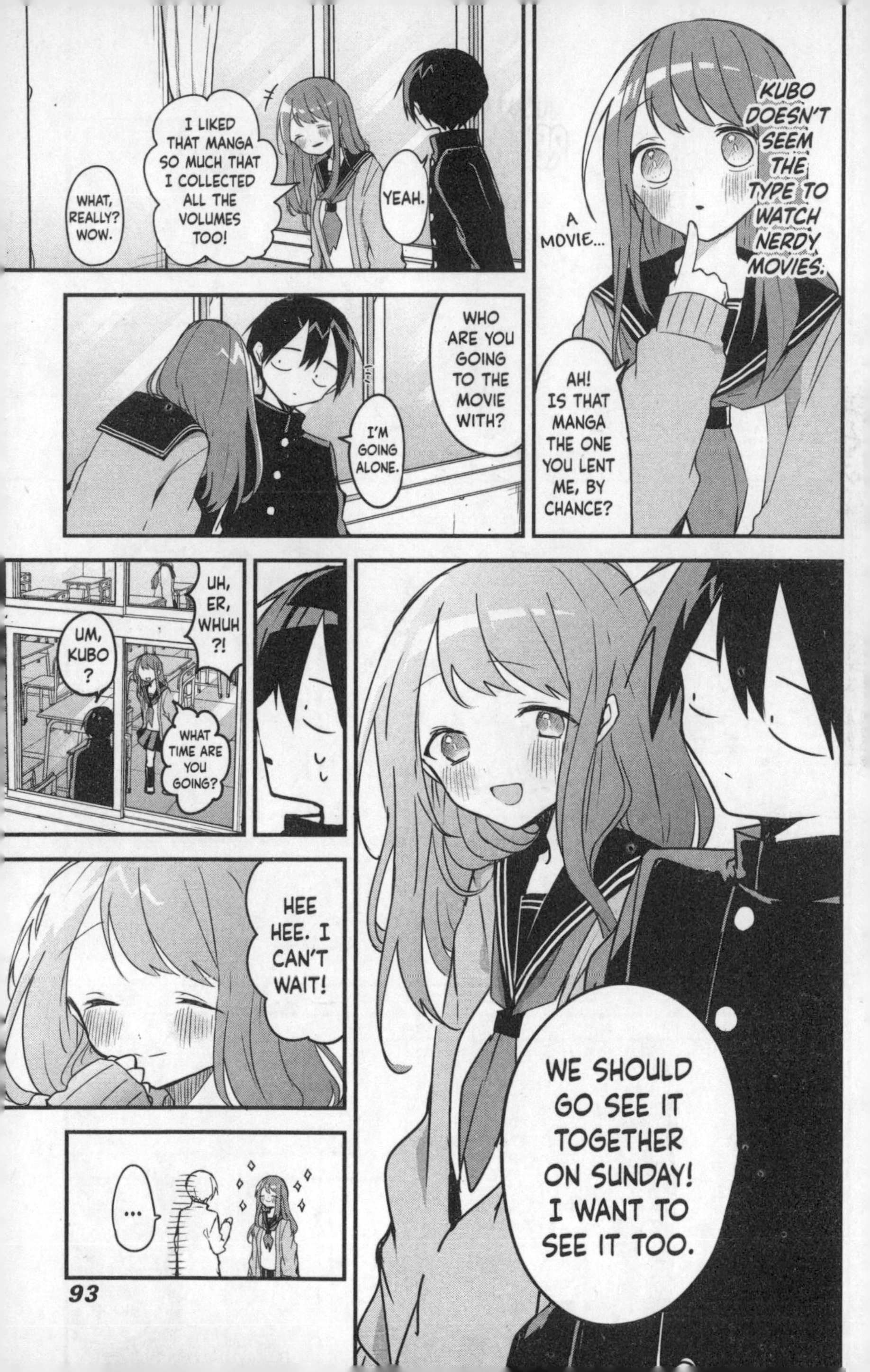
A MOVIE...
KUBO DOESN'T SEEM THE TYPE TO WATCH NERDY MOVIES.
AH! IS THAT MANGA THE ONE YOU LENT ME, BY CHANCE?
YEAH.
I LIKED THAT MANGA SO MUCH THAT I COLLECTED ALL THE VOLUMES TOO!
WHAT, REALLY? WOW.
WHO ARE YOU GOING TO THE MOVIE WITH?
I'M GOING ALONE.
WE SHOULD GO SEE IT TOGETHER ON SUNDAY! I WANT TO SEE IT TOO.
UH, ER, WHUH ?!
UM, KUBO ?
WHAT TIME ARE YOU GOING?
HEE HEE. I CAN'T WAIT!
...

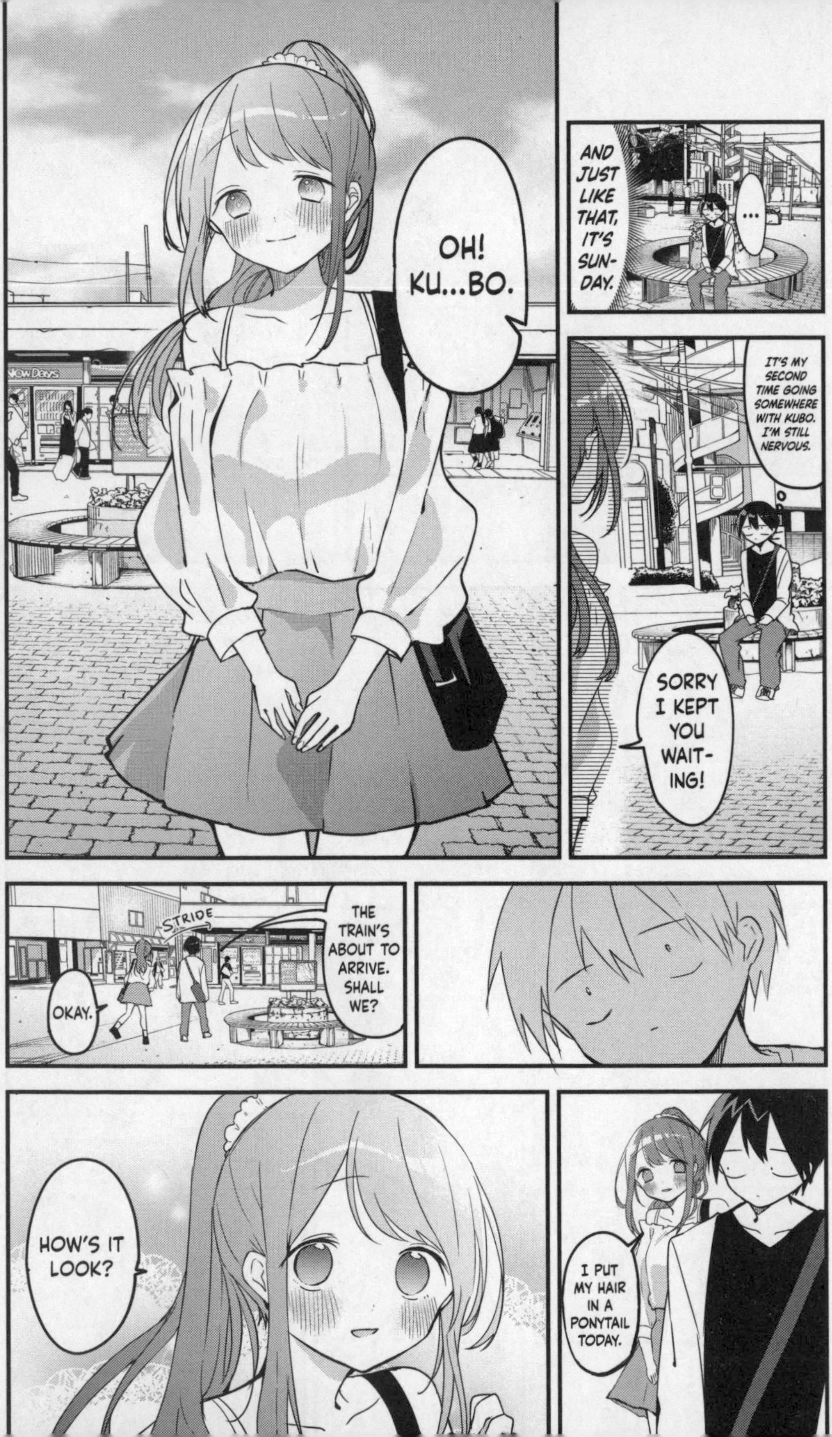
AND JUST LIKE THAT, IT'S SUNDAY.
...
IT'S MY SECOND TIME GOING SOMEWHERE WITH KUBO. I'M STILL NERVOUS.
SORRY I KEPT YOU WAITING!
OH! KU...BO.
THE TRAIN'S ABOUT TO ARRIVE. SHALL WE?
STRIDE
OKAY.
I PUT MY HAIR IN A PONYTAIL TODAY.
HOW'S IT LOOK?

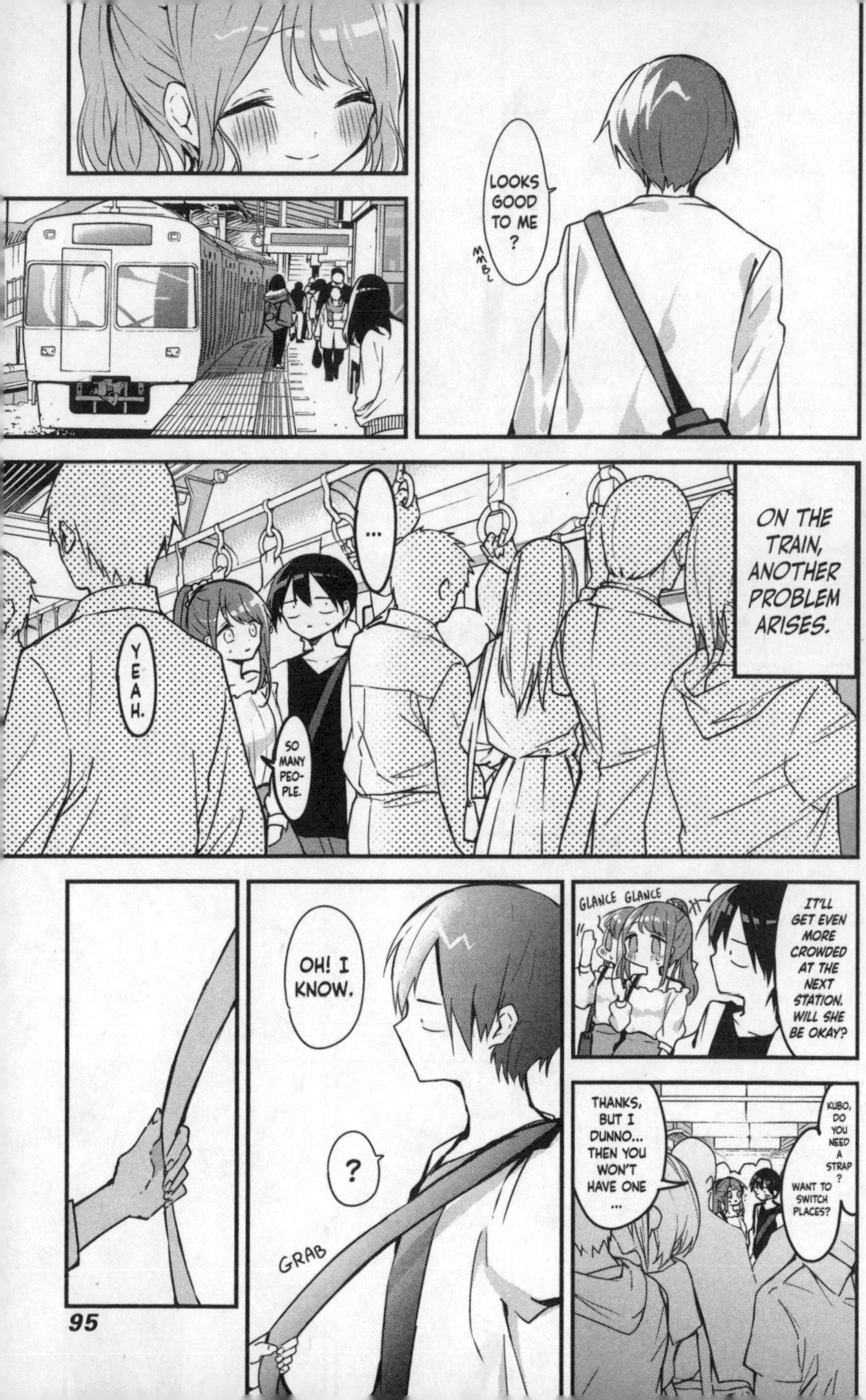
LOOKS GOOD TO ME?
MMBL
ON THE TRAIN, ANOTHER PROBLEM ARISES.
...
YEAH.
SO MANY PEO-PLE.
IT'LL GET EVEN MORE CROWDED AT THE NEXT STATION. WILL SHE BE OKAY?
GLANCE GLANCE
KUBO, DO YOU NEED A STRAP?
WANT TO SWITCH PLACES?
THANKS, BUT I DUNNO... THEN YOU WON'T HAVE ONE...
OH! I KNOW.
?
GRAB

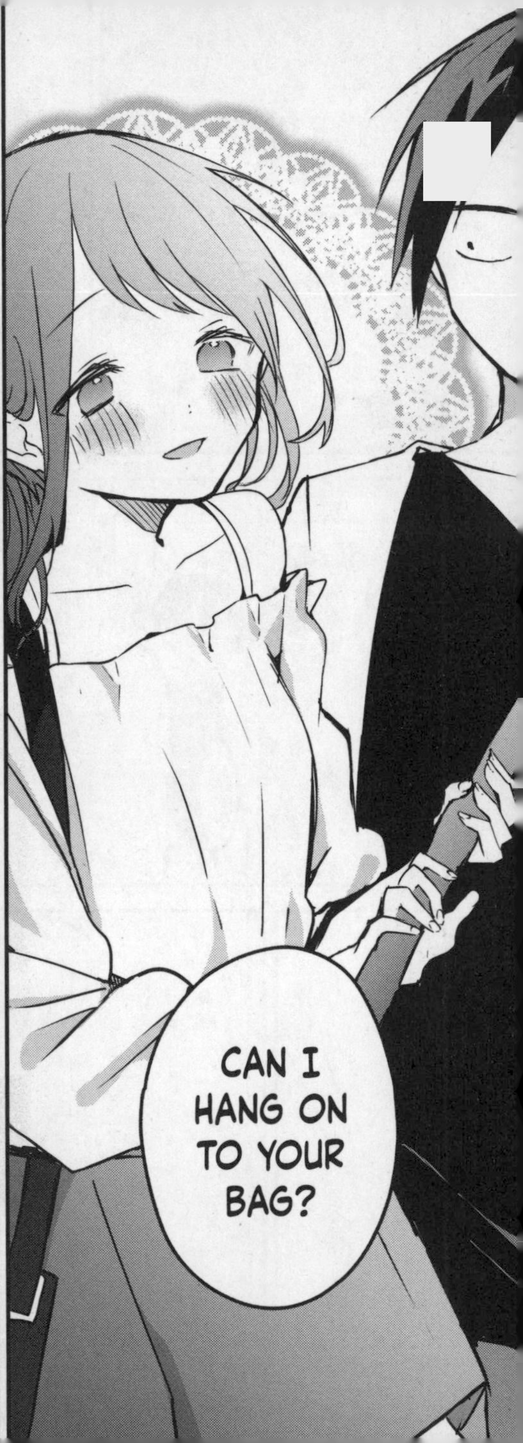
CAN I HANG ON TO YOUR BAG?

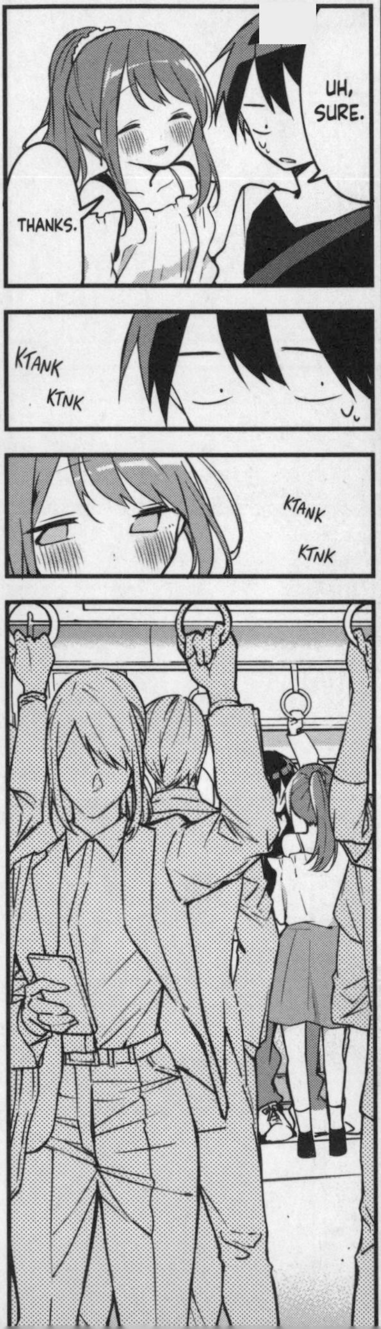
UH, SURE.
THANKS.
KTANK
KTNK
KTANK
KTNK

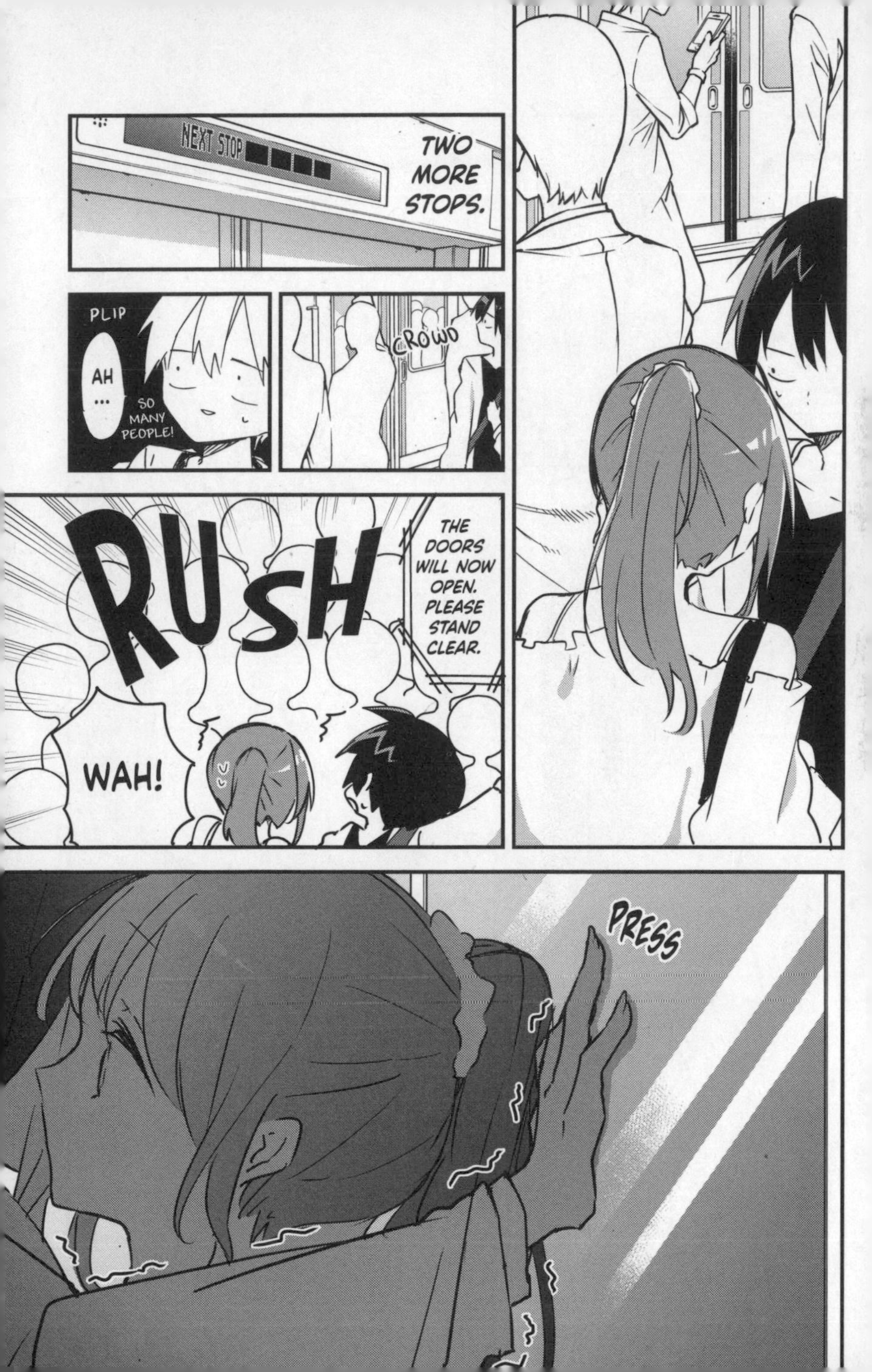
NEXT STOP [redacted]
TWO MORE STOPS.
CROWD
PLIP
AH...
SO MANY PEOPLE!
THE DOORS WILL NOW OPEN. PLEASE STAND CLEAR.
RUSH
WAH!
PRESS

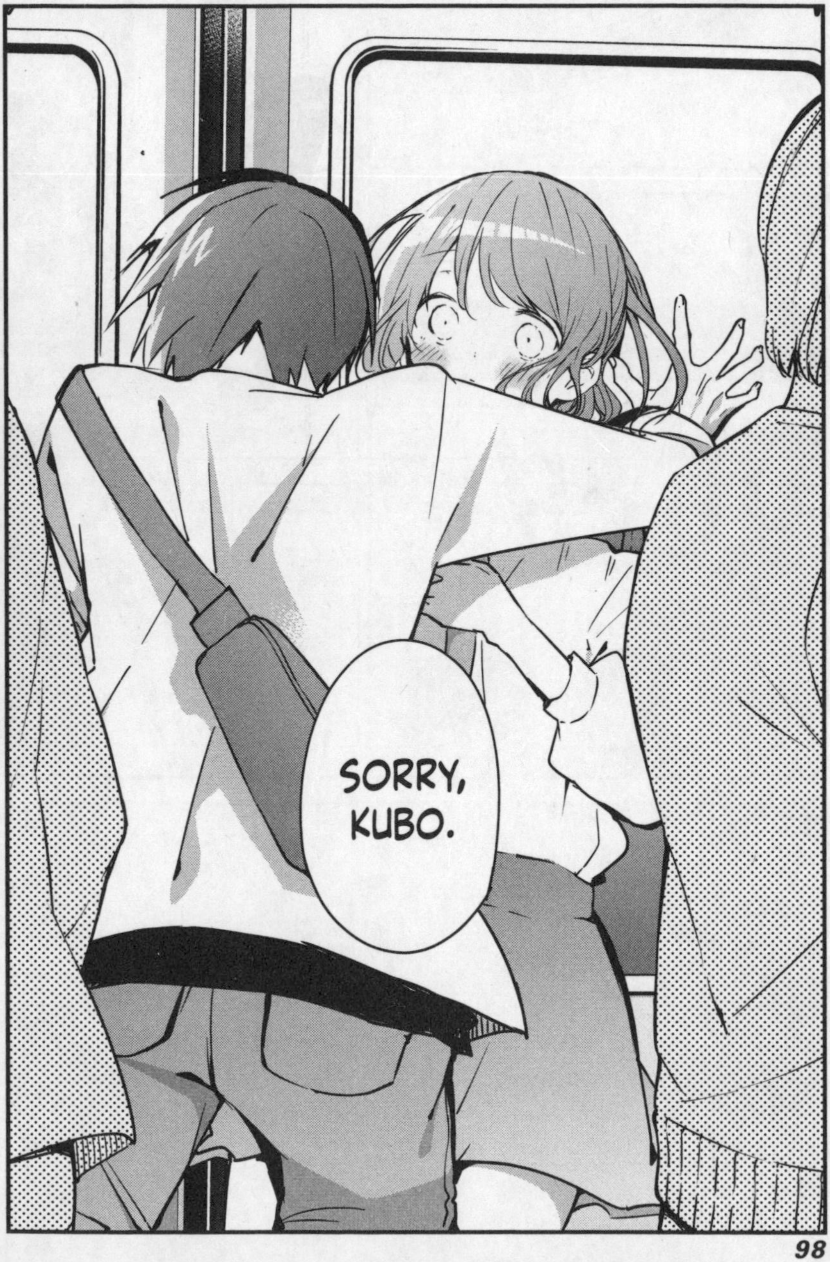
SORRY, KUBO.

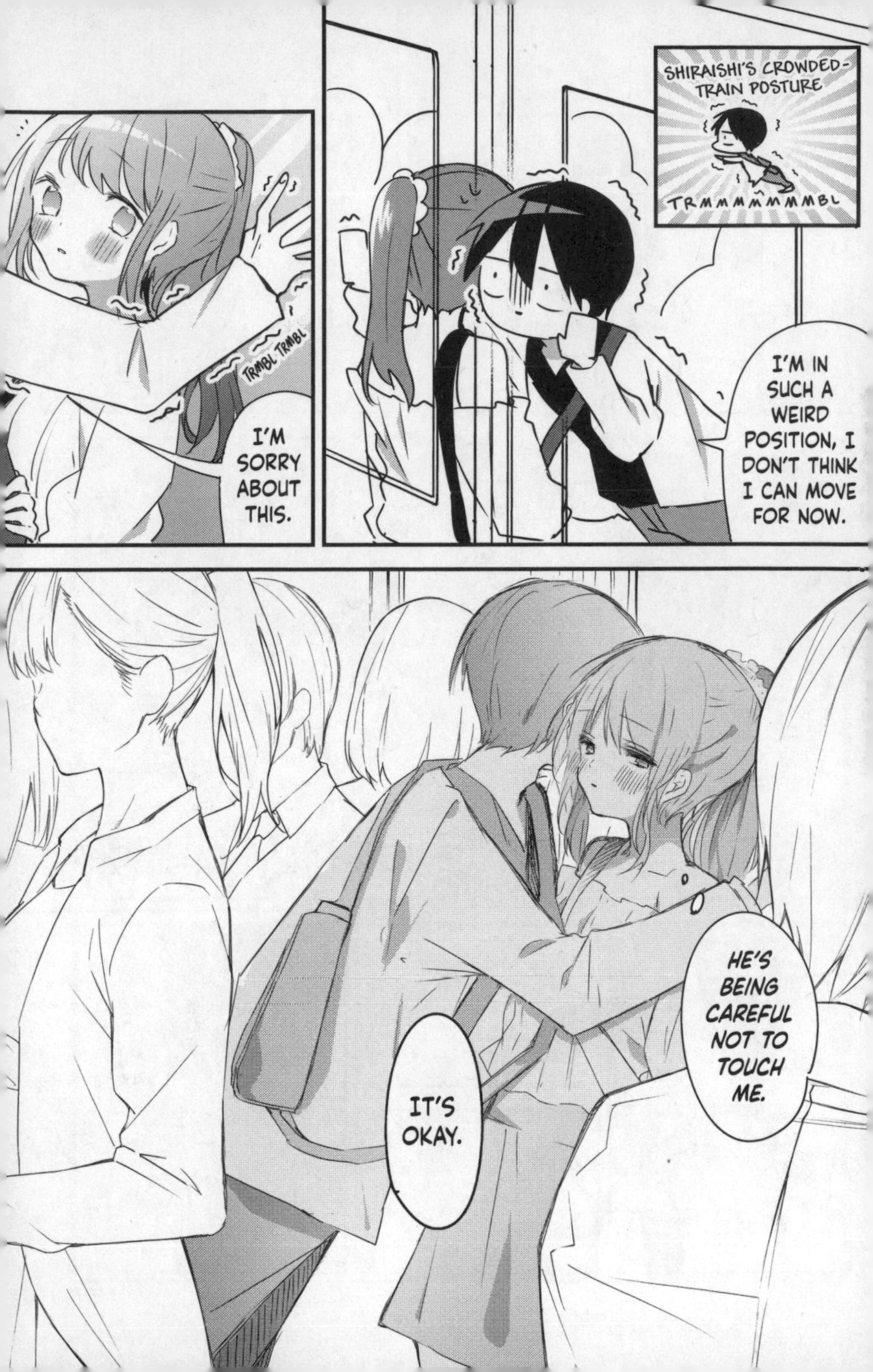
SHIRAISHI'S CROWDED-TRAIN POSTURE
TRMMMMMMMBL
I'M IN SUCH A WEIRD POSITION, I DON'T THINK I CAN MOVE FOR NOW.
TRMBL TRMBL
I'M SORRY ABOUT THIS.
HE'S BEING CAREFUL NOT TO TOUCH ME.
IT'S OKAY.

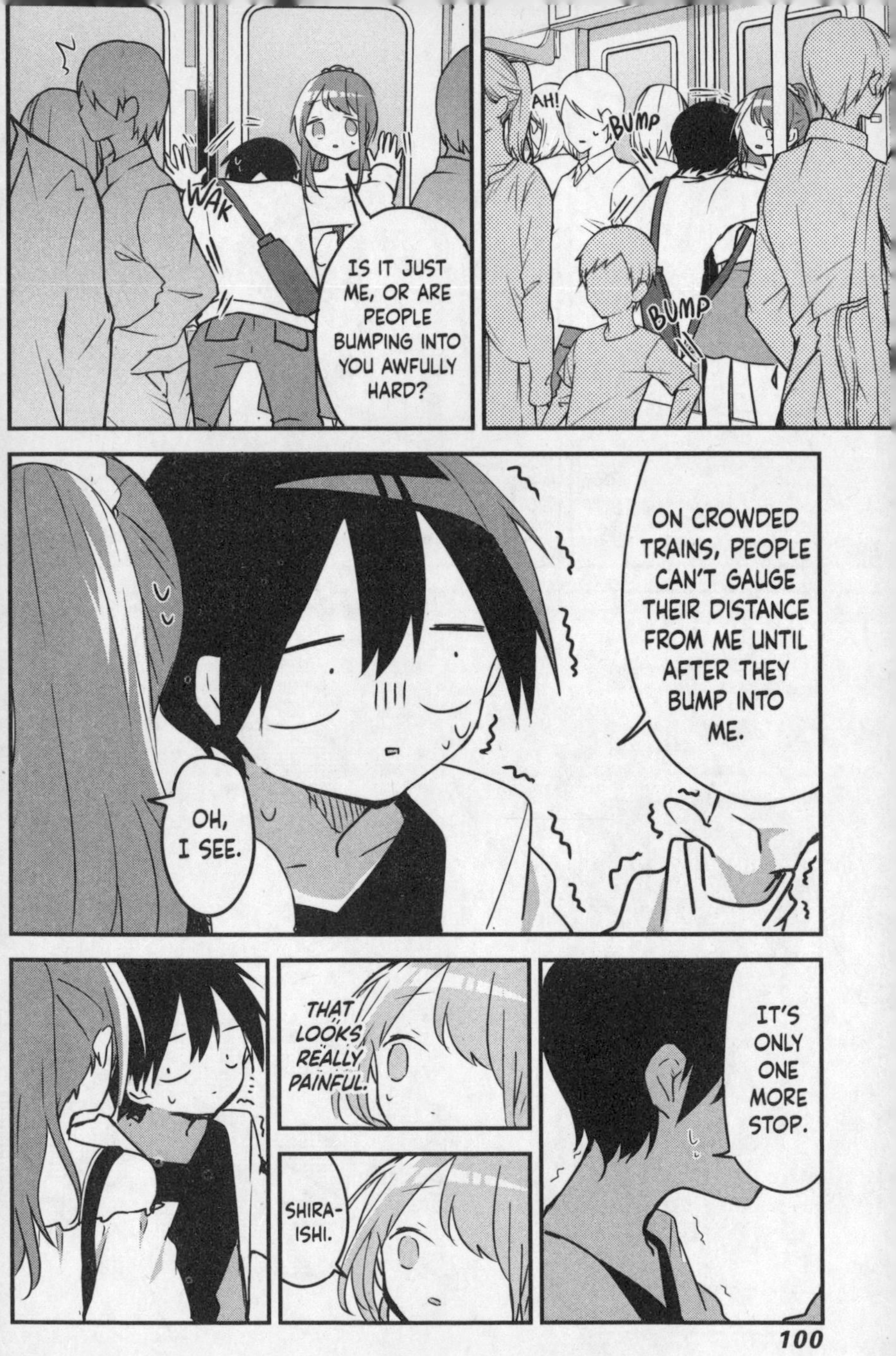
AH!
BUMP
BUMP
WAK
IS IT JUST ME, OR ARE PEOPLE BUMPING INTO YOU AWFULLY HARD?
ON CROWDED TRAINS, PEOPLE CAN'T GAUGE THEIR DISTANCE FROM ME UNTIL AFTER THEY BUMP INTO ME.
OH, I SEE.
IT'S ONLY ONE MORE STOP.
THAT LOOKS REALLY PAINFUL.
SHIRA-ISHI.

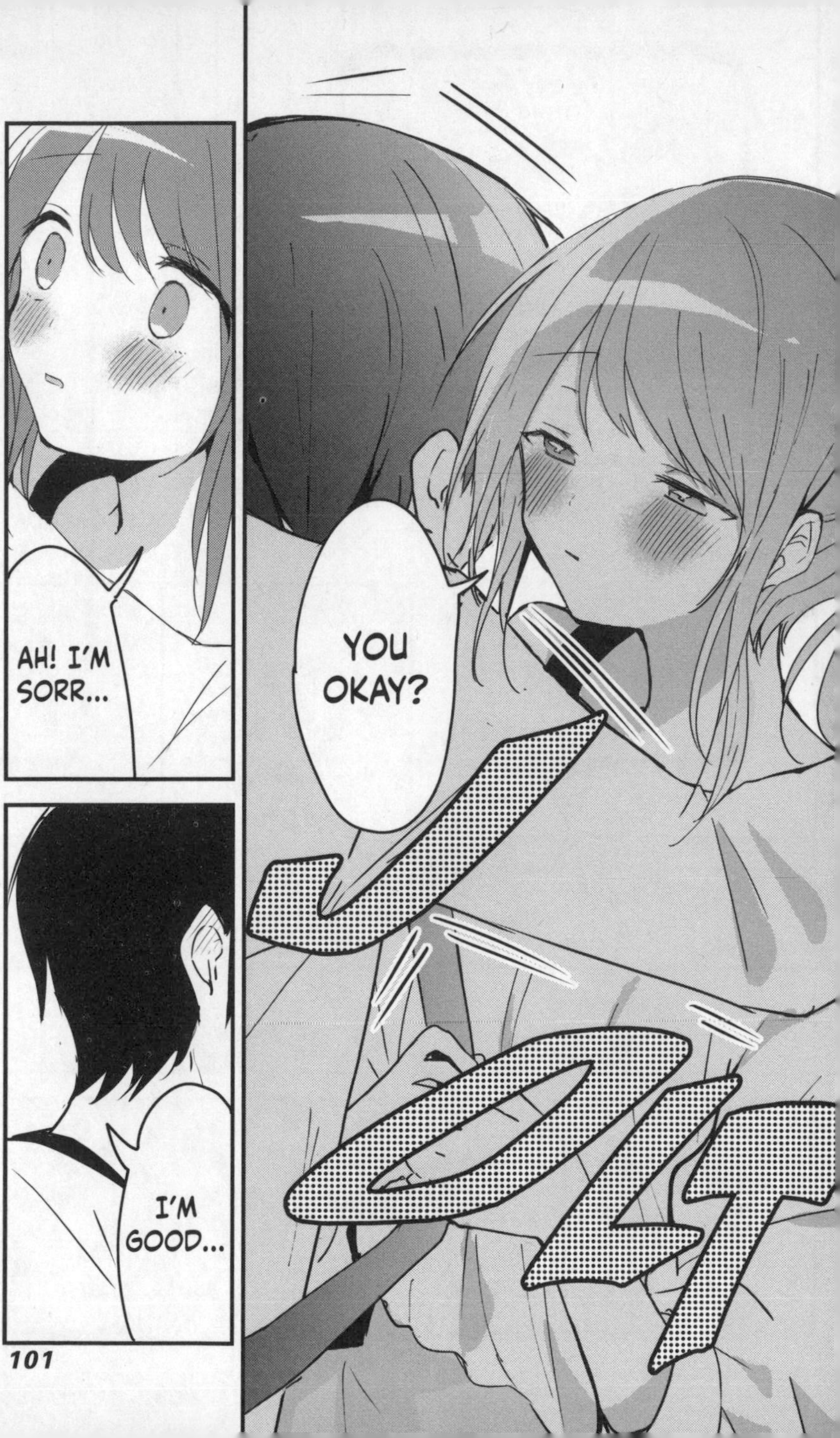
YOU OKAY?
AH! I'M SORR...
I'M GOOD...

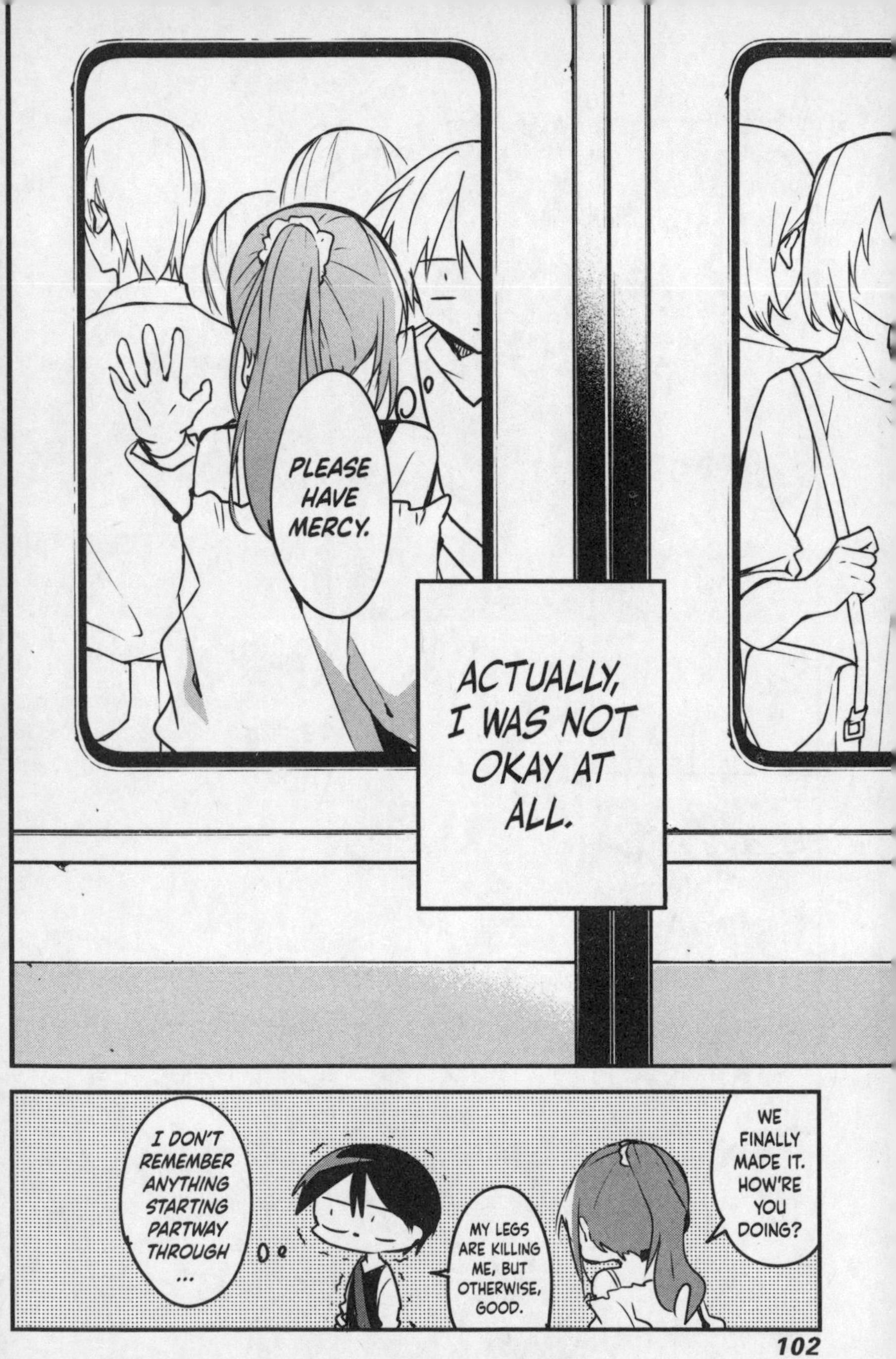
PLEASE HAVE MERCY.
ACTUALLY, I WAS NOT OKAY AT ALL.
WE FINALLY MADE IT. HOW'RE YOU DOING?
MY LEGS ARE KILLING ME, BUT OTHERWISE, GOOD.
I DON'T REMEMBER ANYTHING STARTING PARTWAY THROUGH ...

episode 041

CHATTED UP AND MOVIE LENGTH

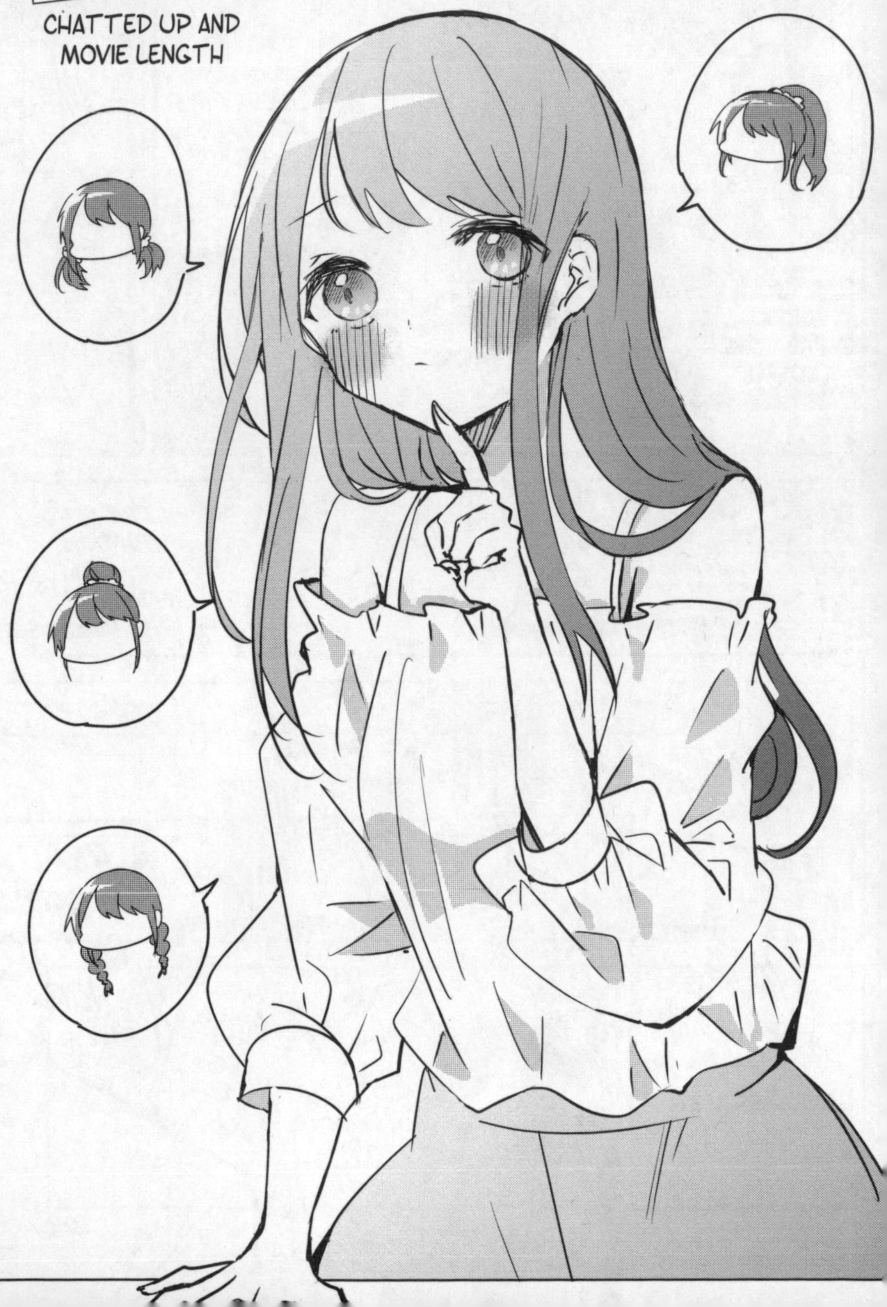

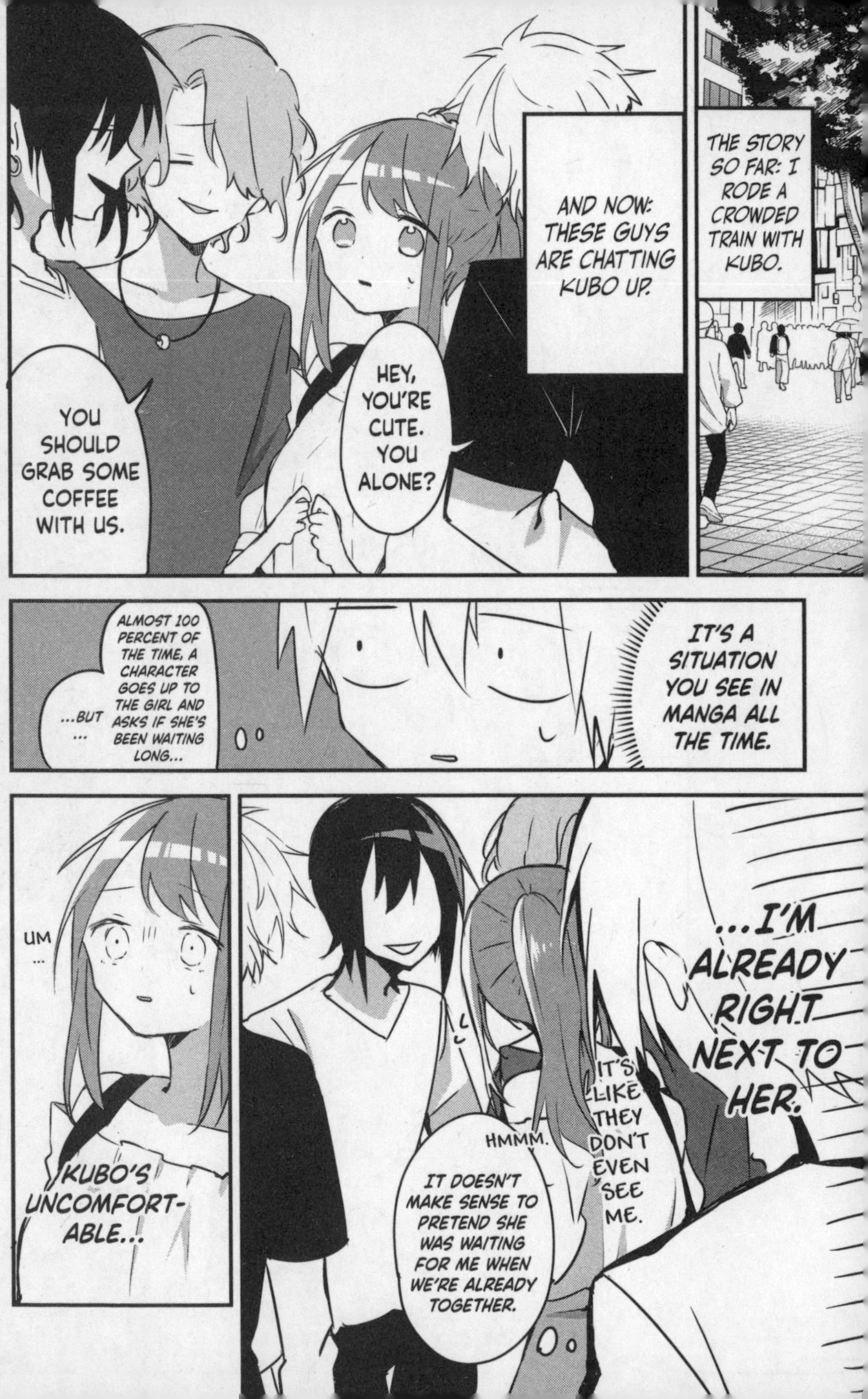
THE STORY SO FAR: I RODE A CROWDED TRAIN WITH KUBO.
AND NOW: THESE GUYS ARE CHATTING KUBO UP.
HEY, YOU'RE CUTE. YOU ALONE?
YOU SHOULD GRAB SOME COFFEE WITH US.
IT'S A SITUATION YOU SEE IN MANGA ALL THE TIME.
ALMOST 100 PERCENT OF THE TIME, A CHARACTER GOES UP TO THE GIRL AND ASKS IF SHE'S BEEN WAITING LONG...
...BUT ...
...I'M ALREADY RIGHT NEXT TO HER.
IT'S LIKE THEY DON'T EVEN SEE ME.
HMMM.
IT DOESN'T MAKE SENSE TO PRETEND SHE WAS WAITING FOR ME WHEN WE'RE ALREADY TOGETHER.
UM ...
KUBO'S UNCOMFORT-ABLE...

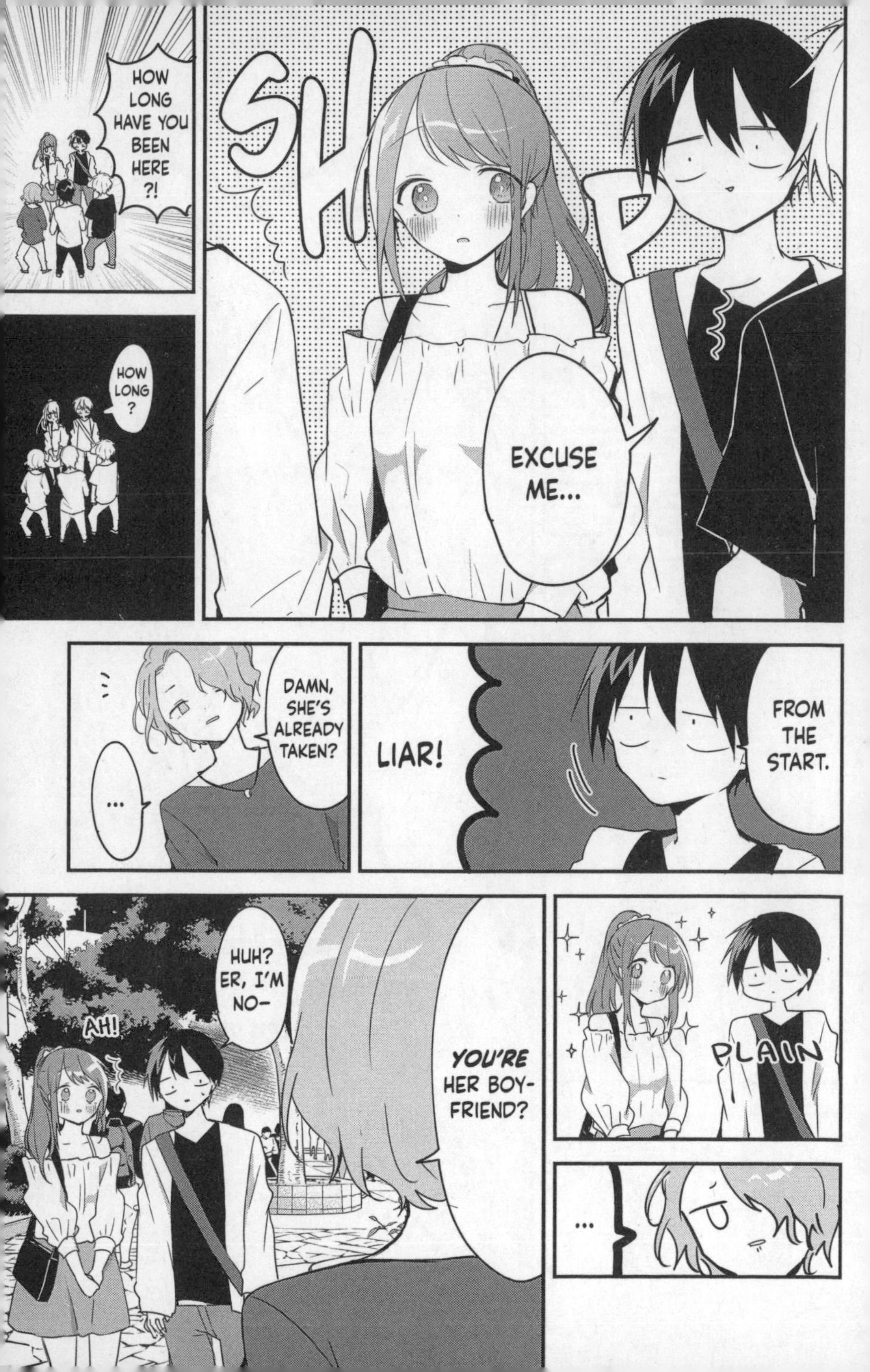
SHP
EXCUSE ME...
HOW LONG HAVE YOU BEEN HERE ?!
HOW LONG ?
FROM THE START.
LIAR!
DAMN, SHE'S ALREADY TAKEN?
...
PLAIN
...
YOU'RE HER BOY-FRIEND?
HUH? ER, I'M NO—
AH!

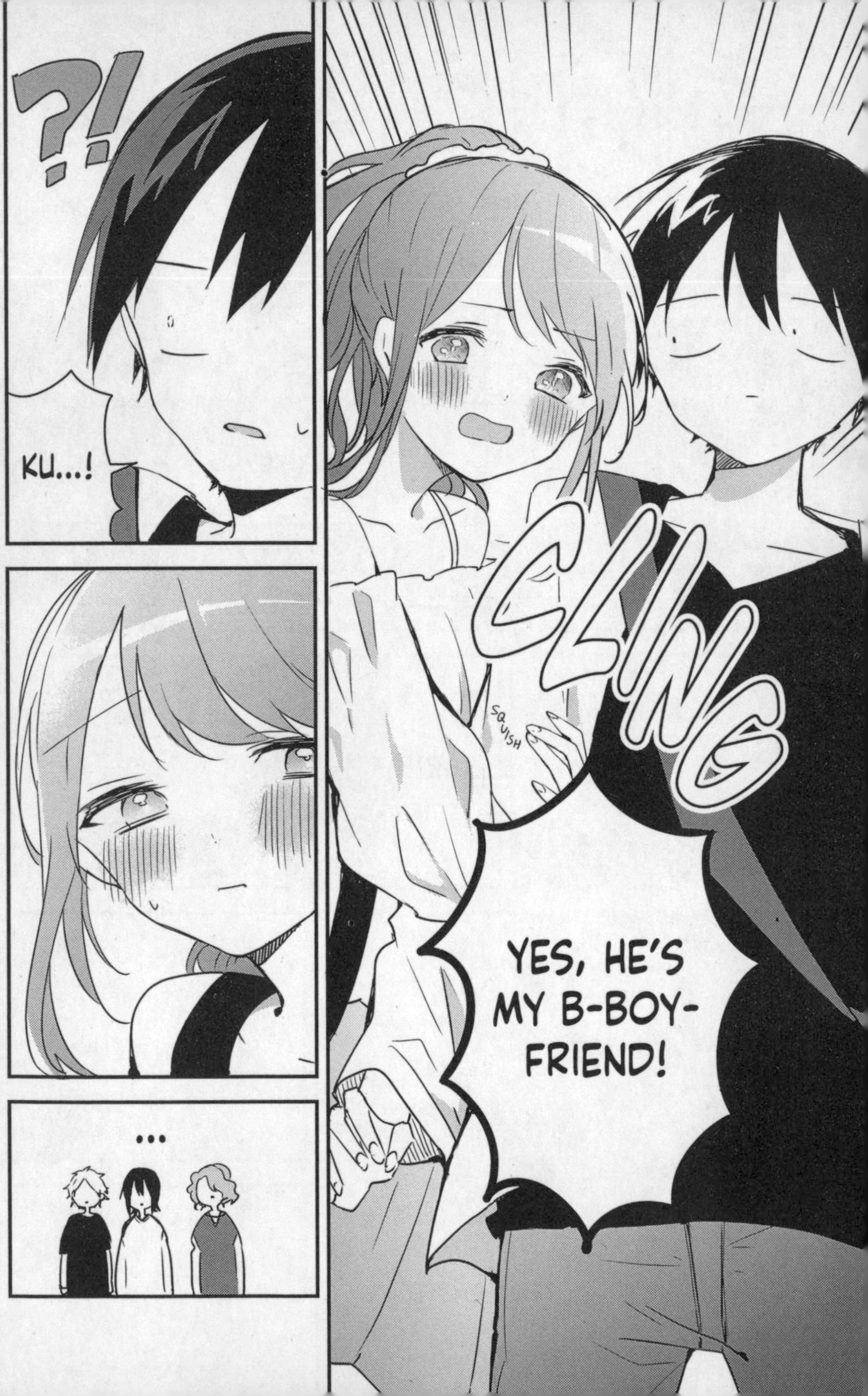
CLING
SQUISH
YES, HE'S MY B-BOY-FRIEND!
?!
KU...!
...

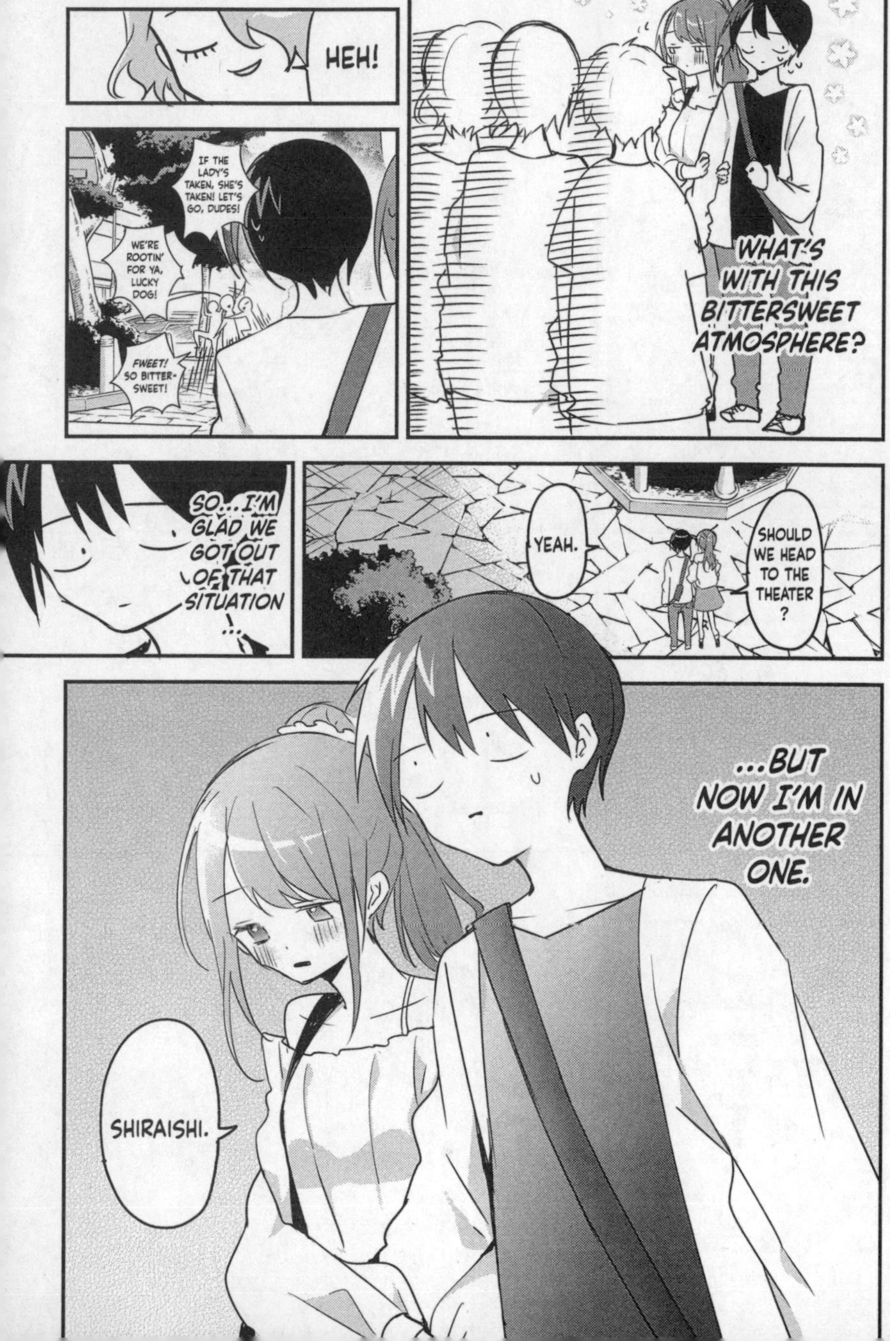
WHAT'S WITH THIS BITTERSWEET ATMOSPHERE?
HEH!
IF THE LADY'S TAKEN, SHE'S TAKEN! LET'S GO, DUDES!
WE'RE ROOTIN' FOR YA, LUCKY DOG!
FWEET! SO BITTER-SWEET!
SHOULD WE HEAD TO THE THEATER?
YEAH.
SO... I'M GLAD WE GOT OUT OF THAT SITUATION...
...BUT NOW I'M IN ANOTHER ONE.
SHIRAISHI.

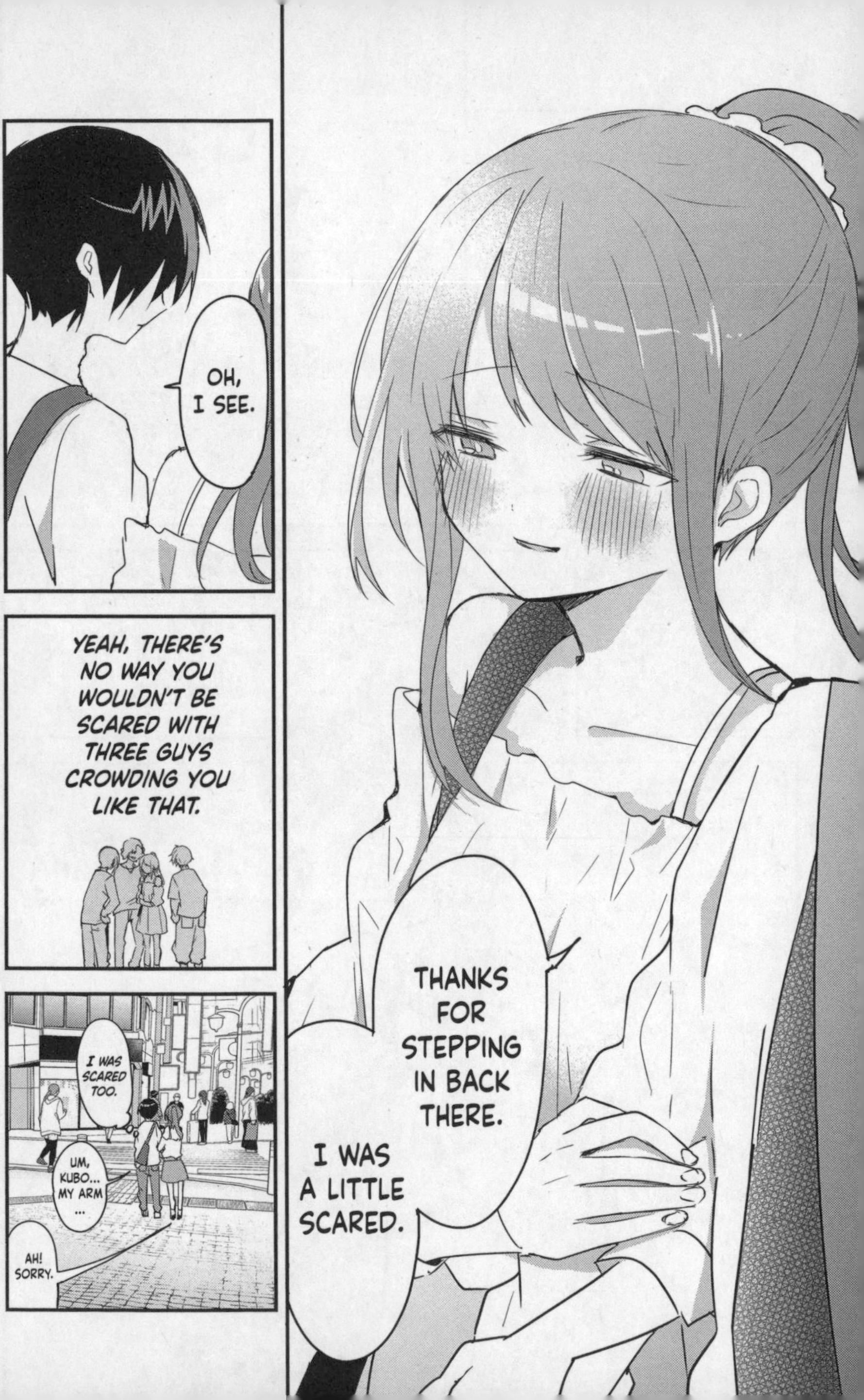
THANKS FOR STEPPING IN BACK THERE.
I WAS A LITTLE SCARED.
OH, I SEE.
YEAH, THERE'S NO WAY YOU WOULDN'T BE SCARED WITH THREE GUYS CROWDING YOU LIKE THAT.
I WAS SCARED TOO.
UM, KUBO... MY ARM ...
AH! SORRY.

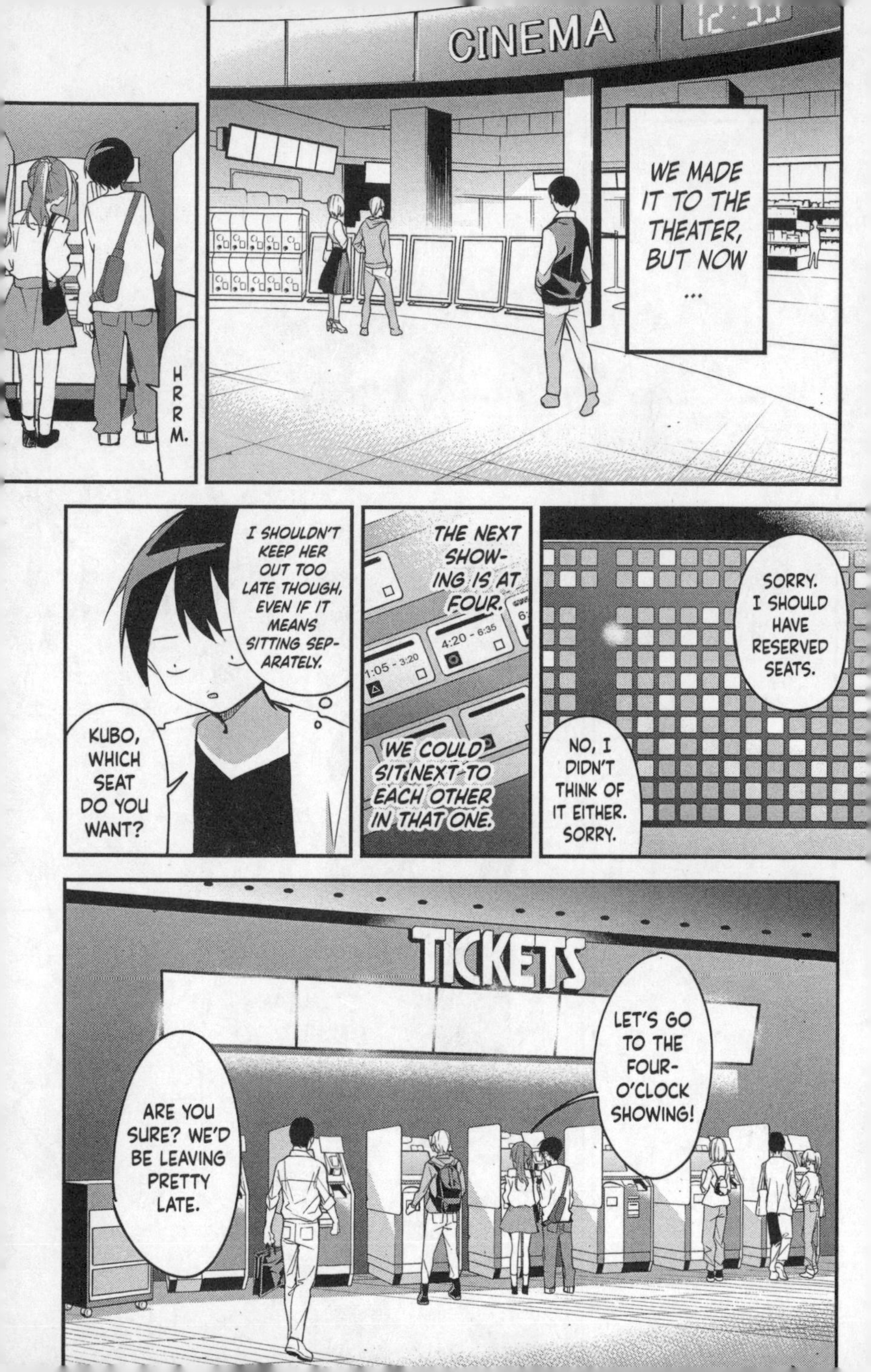
CINEMA
WE MADE IT TO THE THEATER, BUT NOW ...
HRRM.
SORRY. I SHOULD HAVE RESERVED SEATS.
NO, I DIDN'T THINK OF IT EITHER. SORRY.
THE NEXT SHOWING IS AT FOUR.
1:05 - 3:20
4:20 - 6:35
WE COULD SIT NEXT TO EACH OTHER IN THAT ONE.
I SHOULDN'T KEEP HER OUT TOO LATE THOUGH, EVEN IF IT MEANS SITTING SEPARATELY.
KUBO, WHICH SEAT DO YOU WANT?
TICKETS
LET'S GO TO THE FOUR-O'CLOCK SHOWING!
ARE YOU SURE? WE'D BE LEAVING PRETTY LATE.

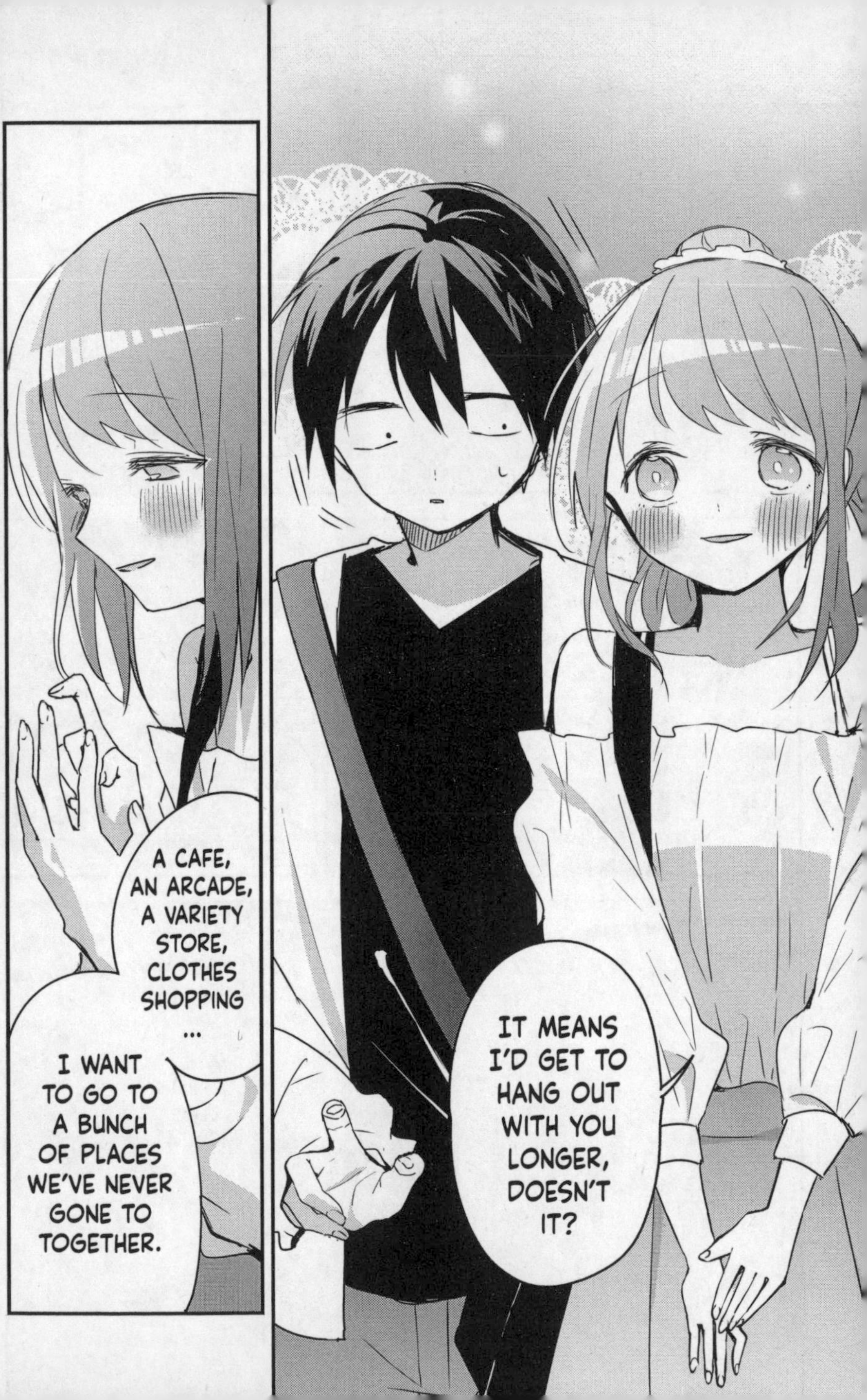
IT MEANS I'D GET TO HANG OUT WITH YOU LONGER, DOESN'T IT?
A CAFE, AN ARCADE, A VARIETY STORE, CLOTHES SHOPPING ...
I WANT TO GO TO A BUNCH OF PLACES WE'VE NEVER GONE TO TOGETHER.

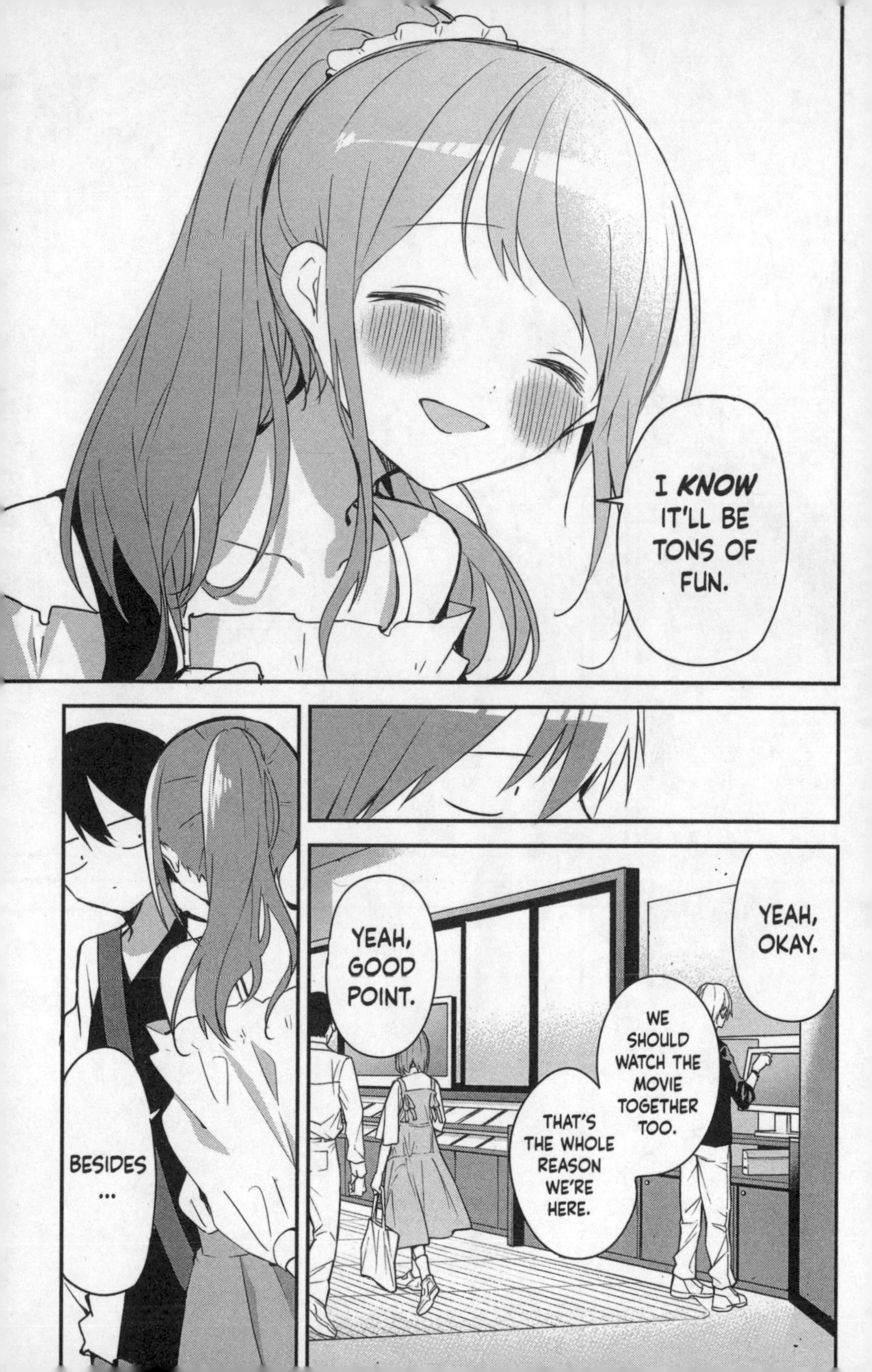
I *KNOW* IT'LL BE TONS OF FUN.
YEAH, OKAY.
WE SHOULD WATCH THE MOVIE TOGETHER TOO.
THAT'S THE WHOLE REASON WE'RE HERE.
YEAH, GOOD POINT.
BESIDES...

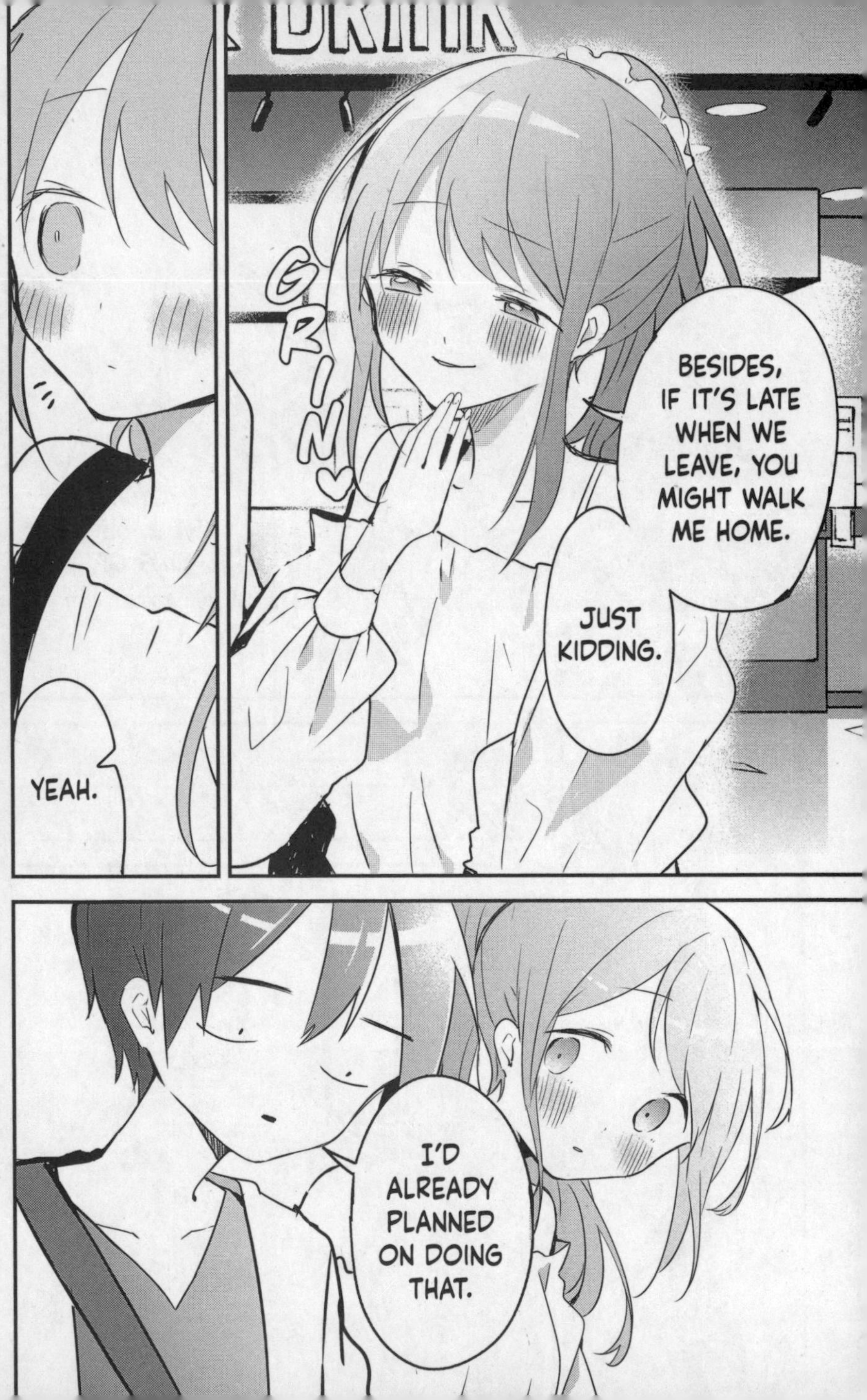
BESIDES, IF IT'S LATE WHEN WE LEAVE, YOU MIGHT WALK ME HOME.
GRIN♥
JUST KIDDING.
YEAH.
I'D ALREADY PLANNED ON DOING THAT.

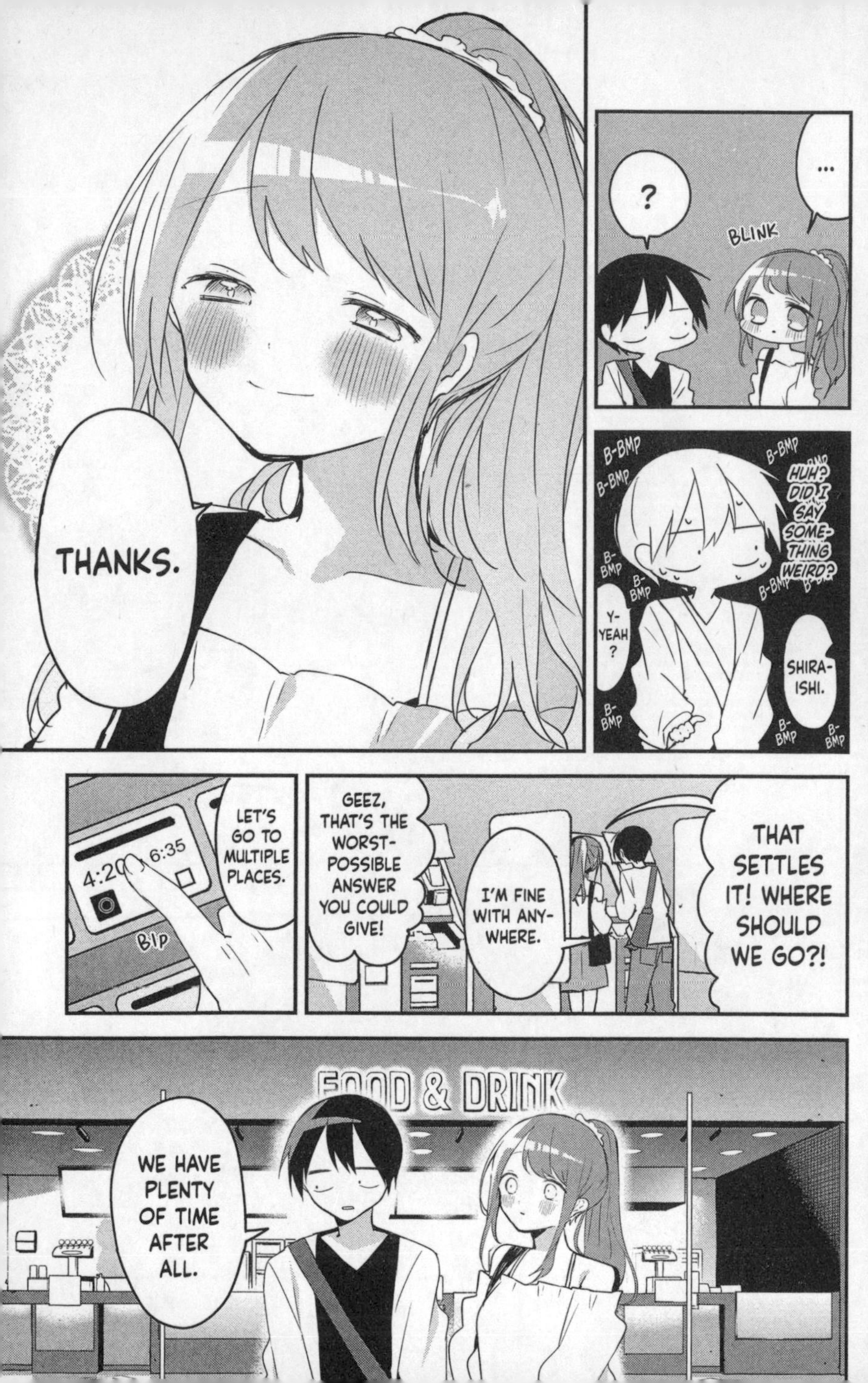
...
BLINK
?
B-BMP B-BMP
HUH? DID I SAY SOMETHING WEIRD?
SHIRA-ISHI.
Y-YEAH?
B-BMP
THANKS.
THAT SETTLES IT! WHERE SHOULD WE GO?!
I'M FINE WITH ANY-WHERE.
GEEZ, THAT'S THE WORST-POSSIBLE ANSWER YOU COULD GIVE!
LET'S GO TO MULTIPLE PLACES.
4:20
6:35
BIP
FOOD & DRINK
WE HAVE PLENTY OF TIME AFTER ALL.

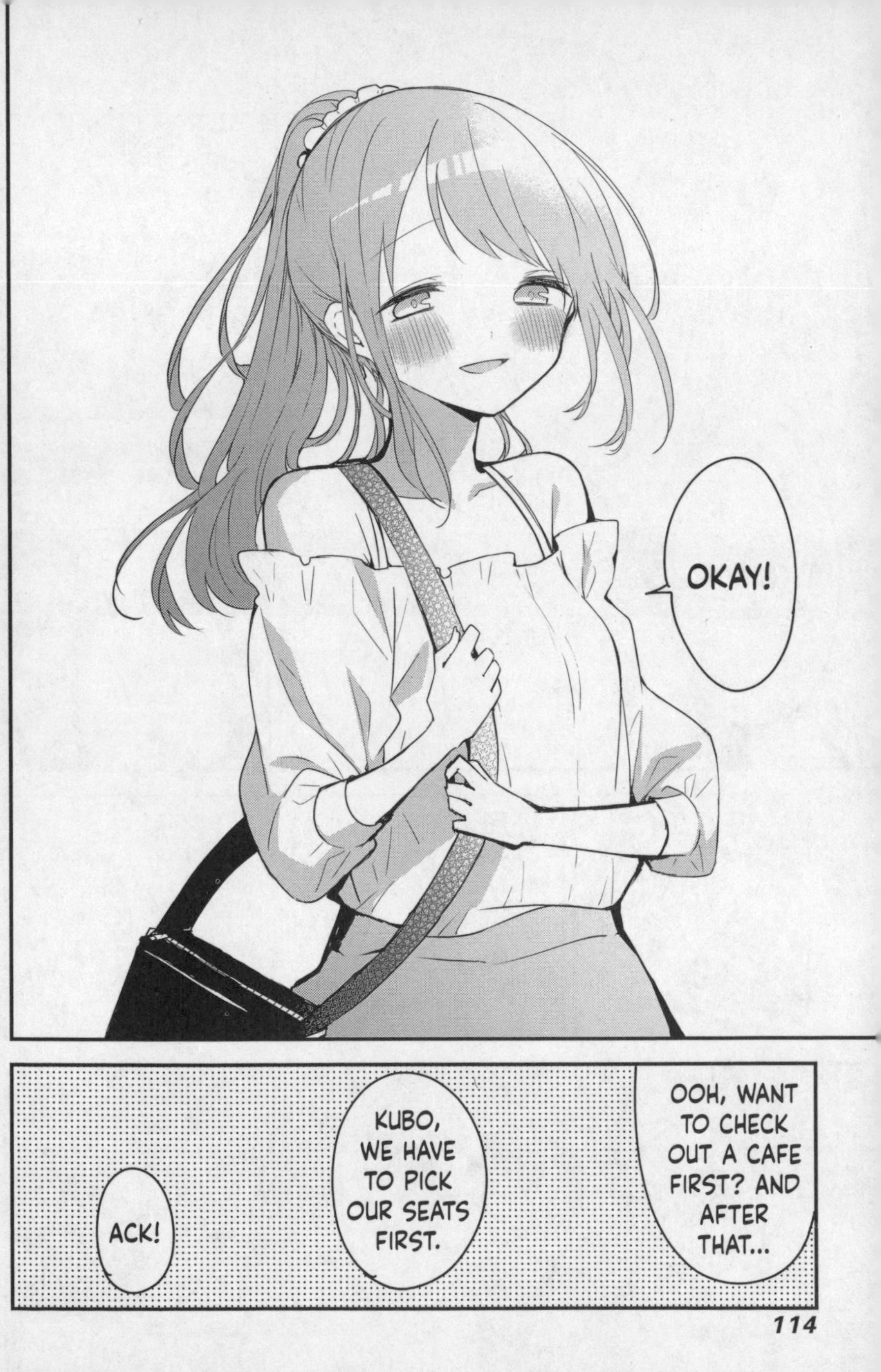
OKAY!
OOH, WANT TO CHECK OUT A CAFE FIRST? AND AFTER THAT...
KUBO, WE HAVE TO PICK OUR SEATS FIRST.
ACK!

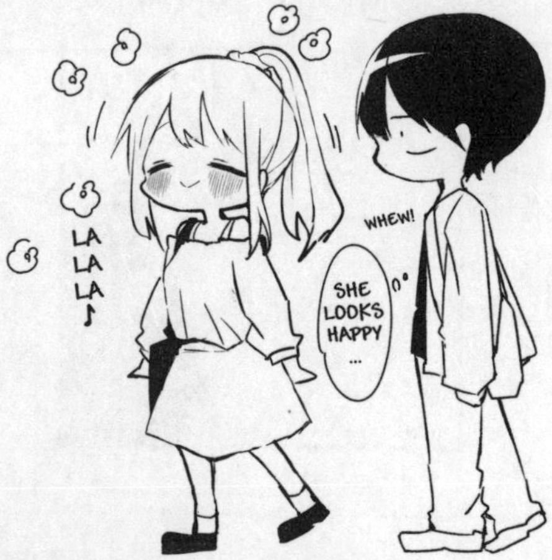
WHEW!
SHE LOOKS HAPPY...
LA LA LA♪

TOUCHING

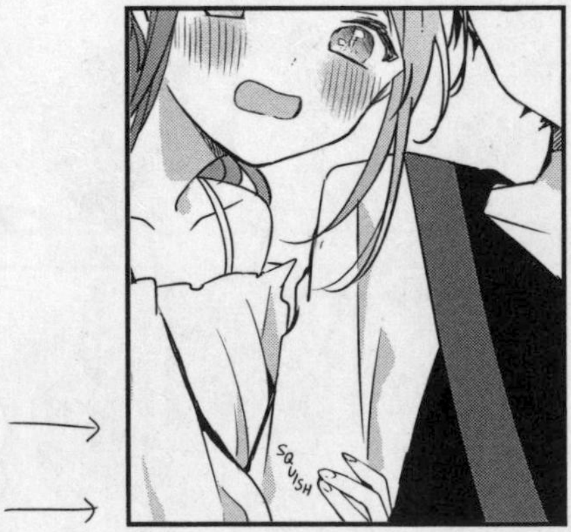
SQUISH

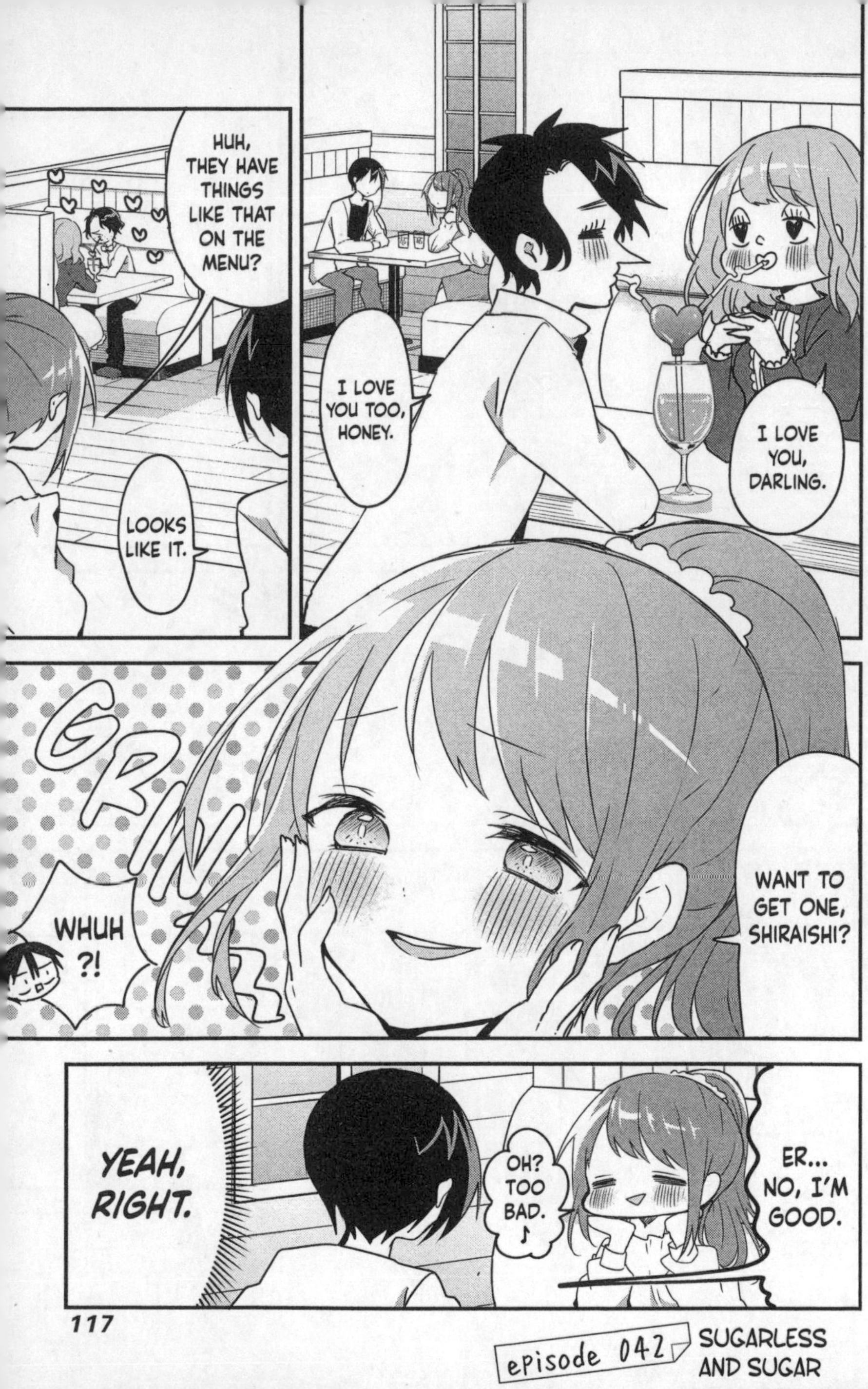
I LOVE YOU, DARLING.
I LOVE YOU TOO, HONEY.
HUH, THEY HAVE THINGS LIKE THAT ON THE MENU?
LOOKS LIKE IT.
WANT TO GET ONE, SHIRAISHI?
GRIN
WHUH ?!
ER... NO, I'M GOOD.
OH? TOO BAD. ♪
YEAH, RIGHT.

episode 042 SUGARLESS AND SUGAR

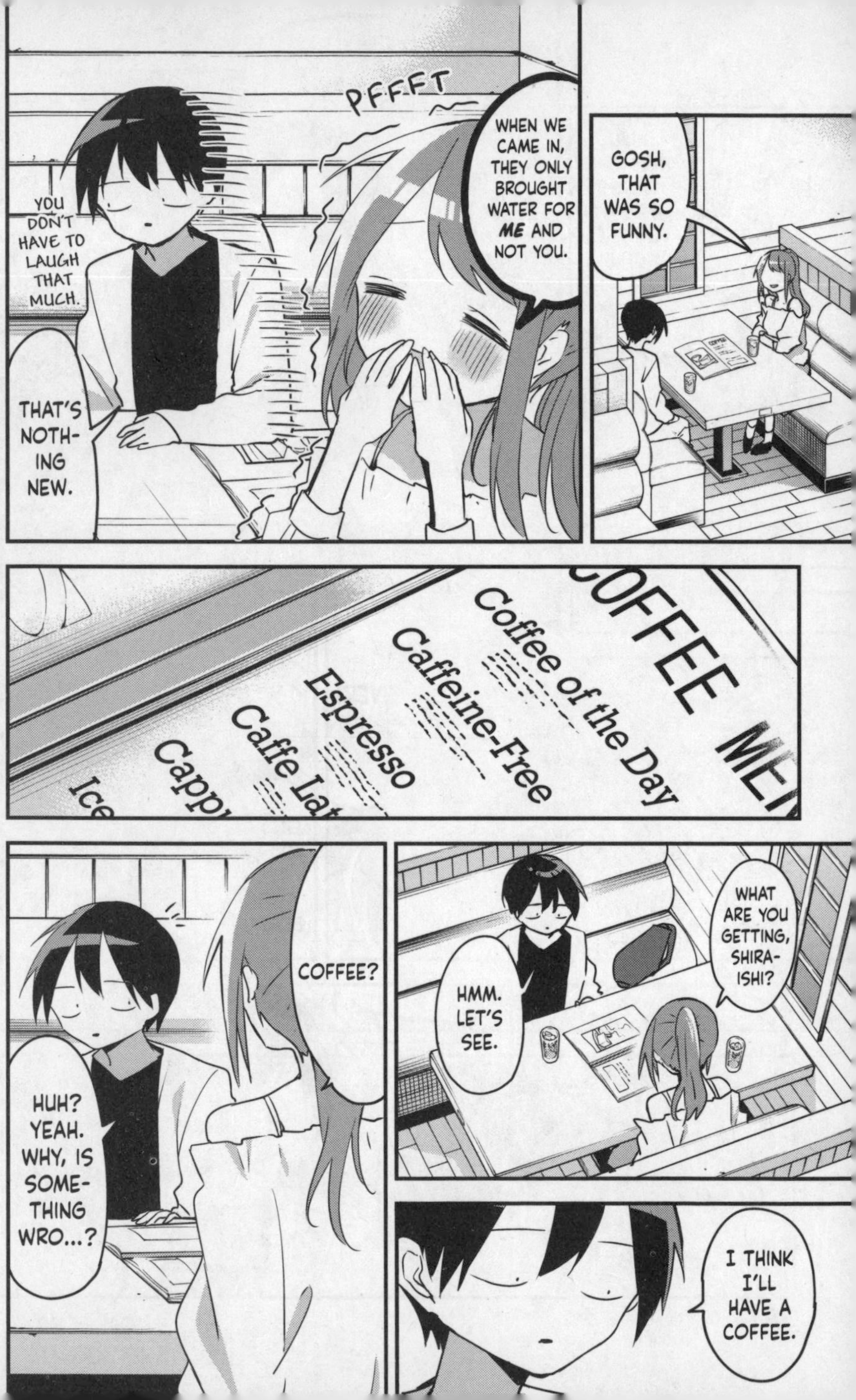
GOSH, THAT WAS SO FUNNY.
WHEN WE CAME IN, THEY ONLY BROUGHT WATER FOR *ME* AND NOT YOU.
PFFFT
YOU DON'T HAVE TO LAUGH THAT MUCH.
THAT'S NOTHING NEW.
COFFEE
Coffee of the Day
Caffeine-Free
Espresso
WHAT ARE YOU GETTING, SHIRAISHI?
HMM. LET'S SEE.
I THINK I'LL HAVE A COFFEE.
COFFEE?
HUH? YEAH. WHY, IS SOMETHING WRO...?

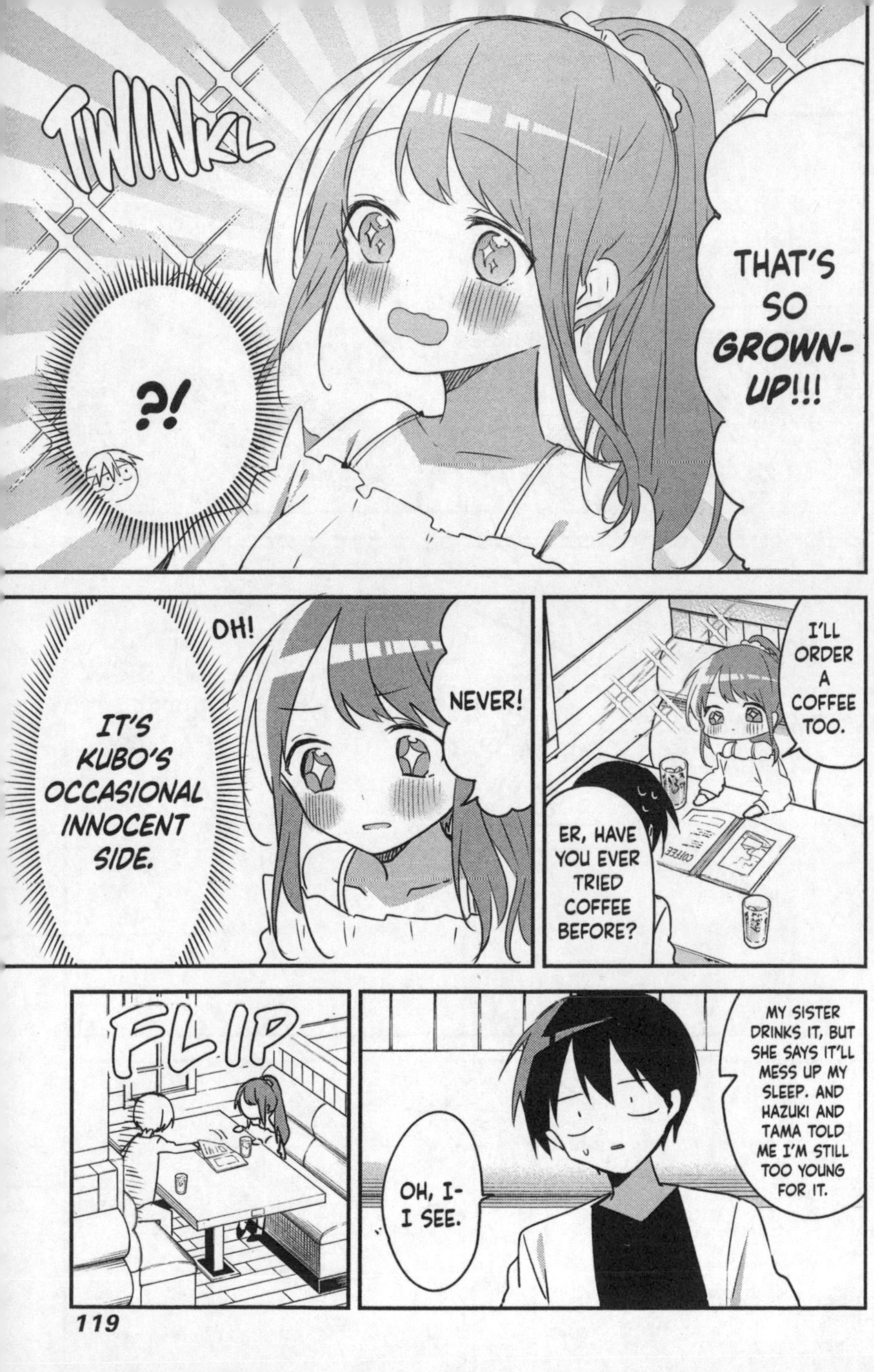
THAT'S SO GROWN-UP!!!
TWINKL
?!
I'LL ORDER A COFFEE TOO.
ER, HAVE YOU EVER TRIED COFFEE BEFORE?
OH!
NEVER!
IT'S KUBO'S OCCASIONAL INNOCENT SIDE.
MY SISTER DRINKS IT, BUT SHE SAYS IT'LL MESS UP MY SLEEP. AND HAZUKI AND TAMA TOLD ME I'M STILL TOO YOUNG FOR IT.
OH, I- I SEE.
FLIP

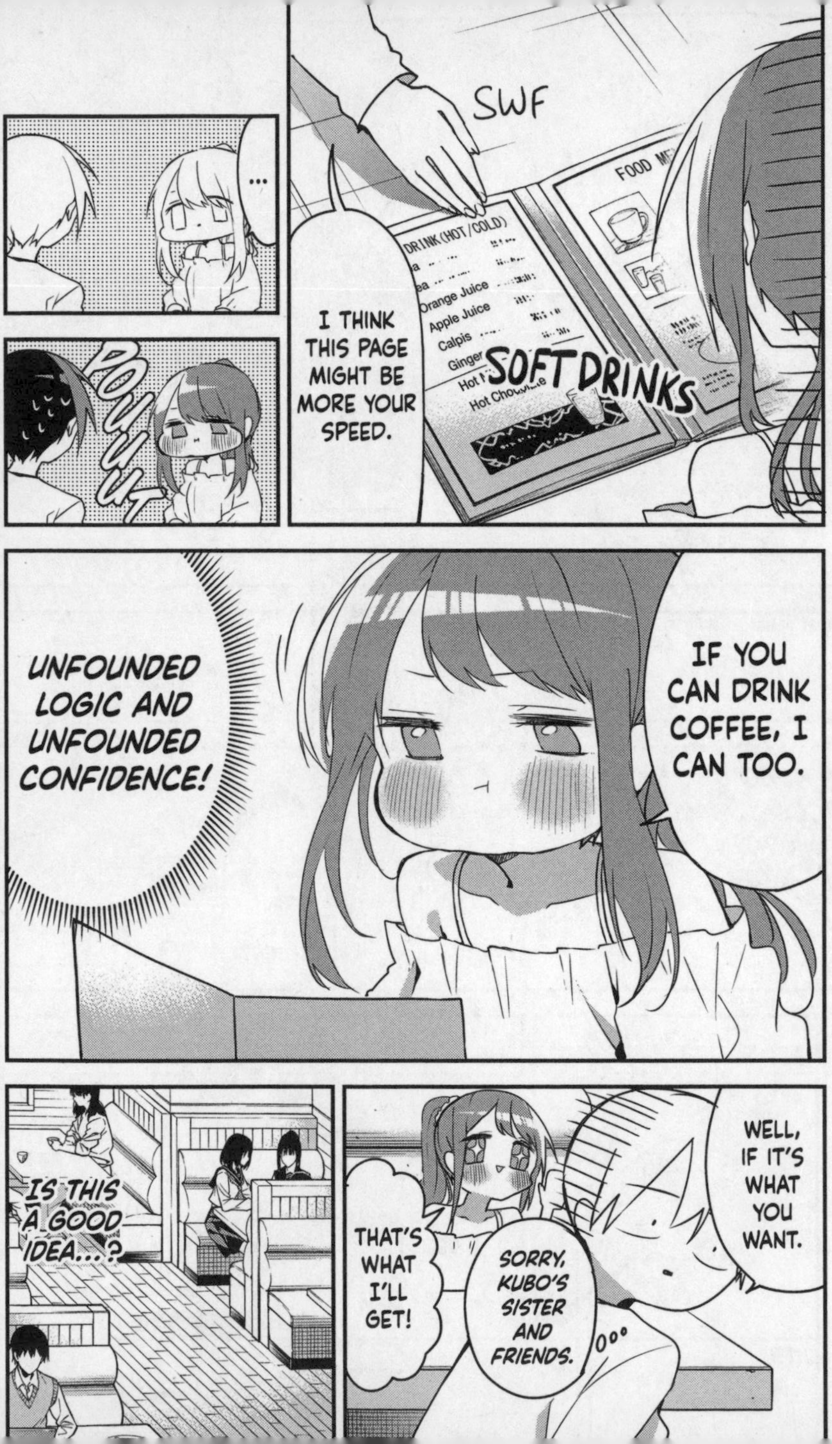
SWF
DRINK (HOT/COLD)
Orange Juice
Apple Juice
Calpis
I THINK THIS PAGE MIGHT BE MORE YOUR SPEED.
SOFT DRINKS
...
POUUUT
IF YOU CAN DRINK COFFEE, I CAN TOO.
UNFOUNDED LOGIC AND UNFOUNDED CONFIDENCE!
WELL, IF IT'S WHAT YOU WANT.
THAT'S WHAT I'LL GET!
SORRY, KUBO'S SISTER AND FRIENDS.
IS THIS A GOOD IDEA...?

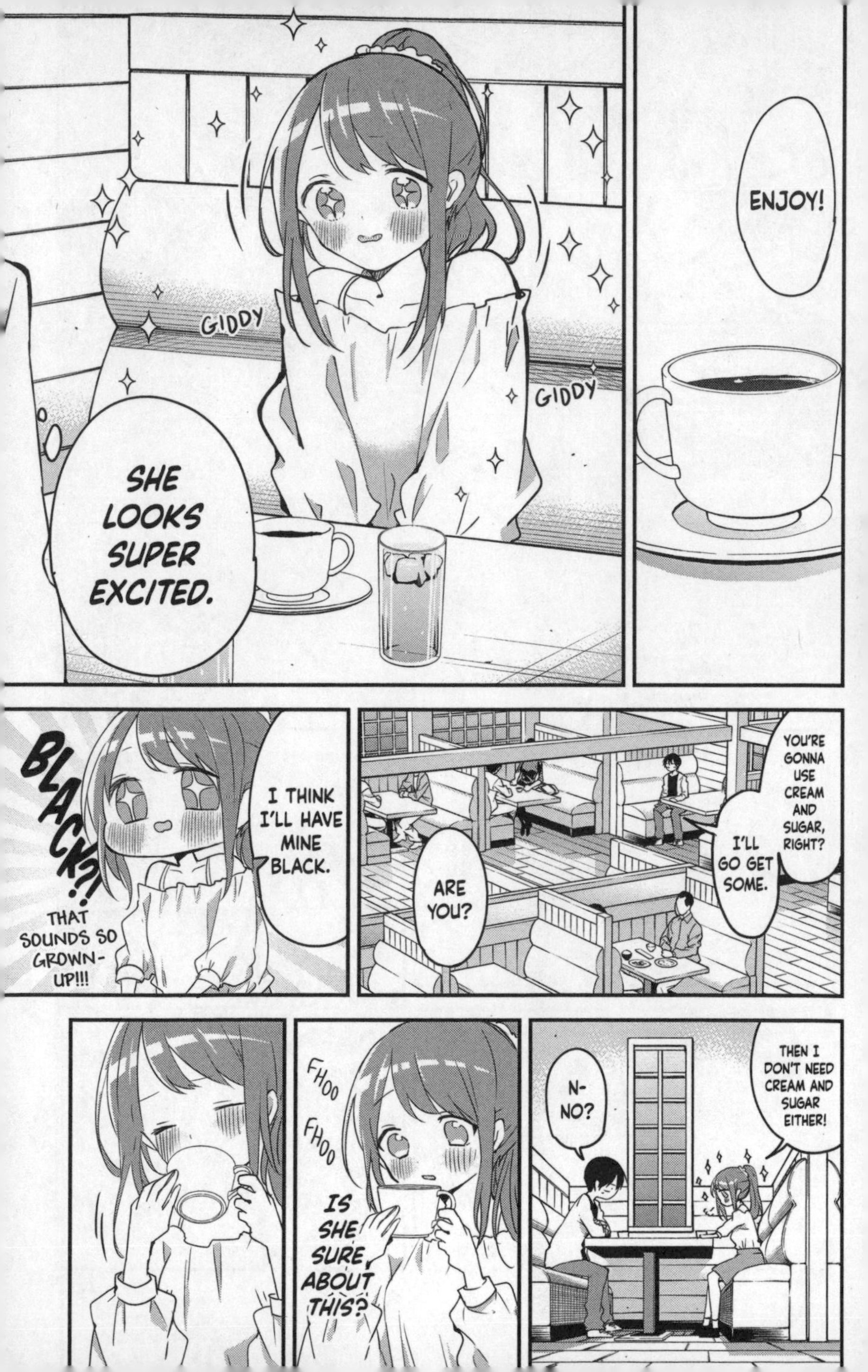
ENJOY!
GIDDY
GIDDY
SHE LOOKS SUPER EXCITED.
YOU'RE GONNA USE CREAM AND SUGAR, RIGHT?
I'LL GO GET SOME.
ARE YOU?
I THINK I'LL HAVE MINE BLACK.
BLACK?!
THAT SOUNDS SO GROWN-UP!!!
THEN I DON'T NEED CREAM AND SUGAR EITHER!
N-NO?
FHOO
FHOO
IS SHE SURE ABOUT THIS?

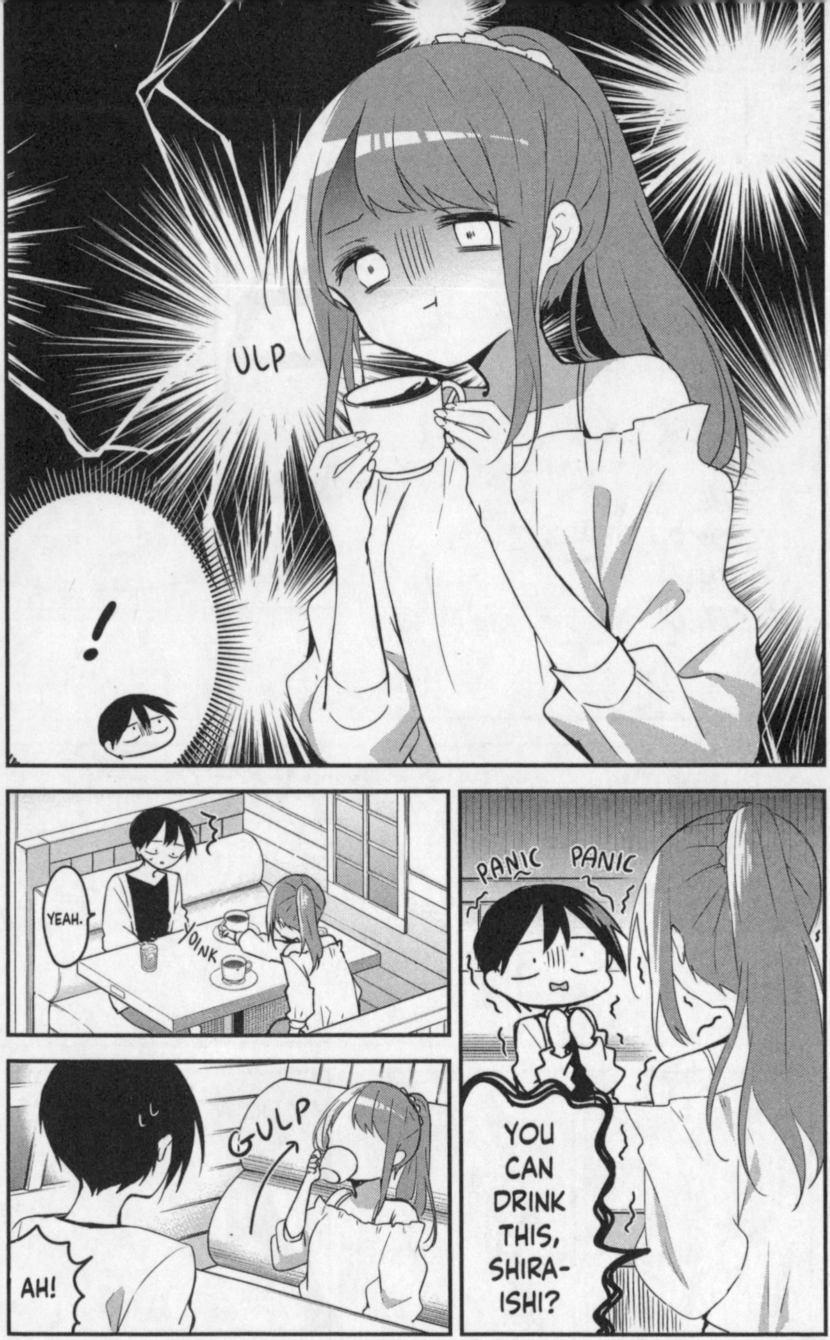
ULP
!
PANIC PANIC
YOU CAN DRINK THIS, SHIRA-ISHI?
YEAH.
YOINK
GULP
AH!

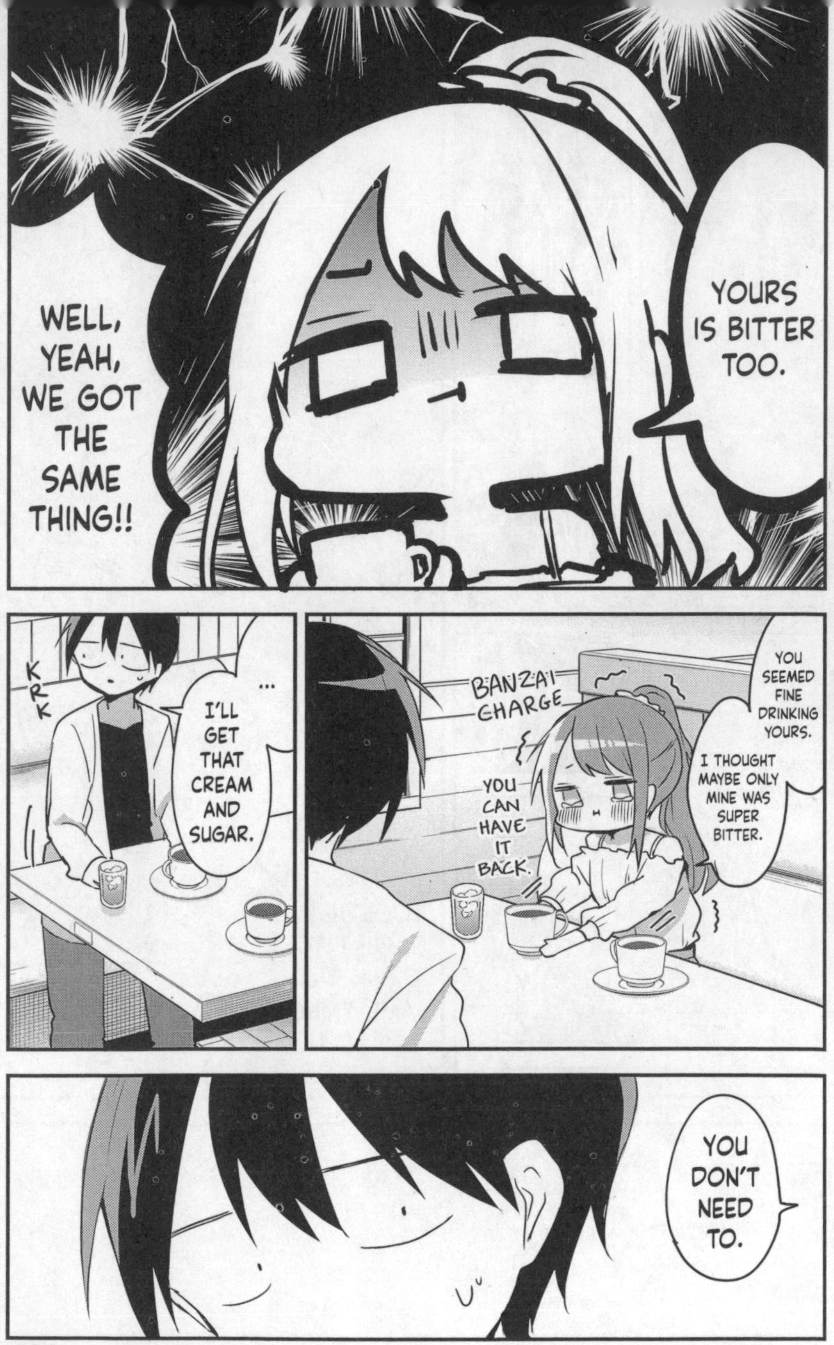
YOURS IS BITTER TOO.
WELL, YEAH, WE GOT THE SAME THING!!
YOU SEEMED FINE DRINKING YOURS.
I THOUGHT MAYBE ONLY MINE WAS SUPER BITTER.
BANZAI CHARGE
YOU CAN HAVE IT BACK.
...
I'LL GET THAT CREAM AND SUGAR.
KRK
YOU DON'T NEED TO.

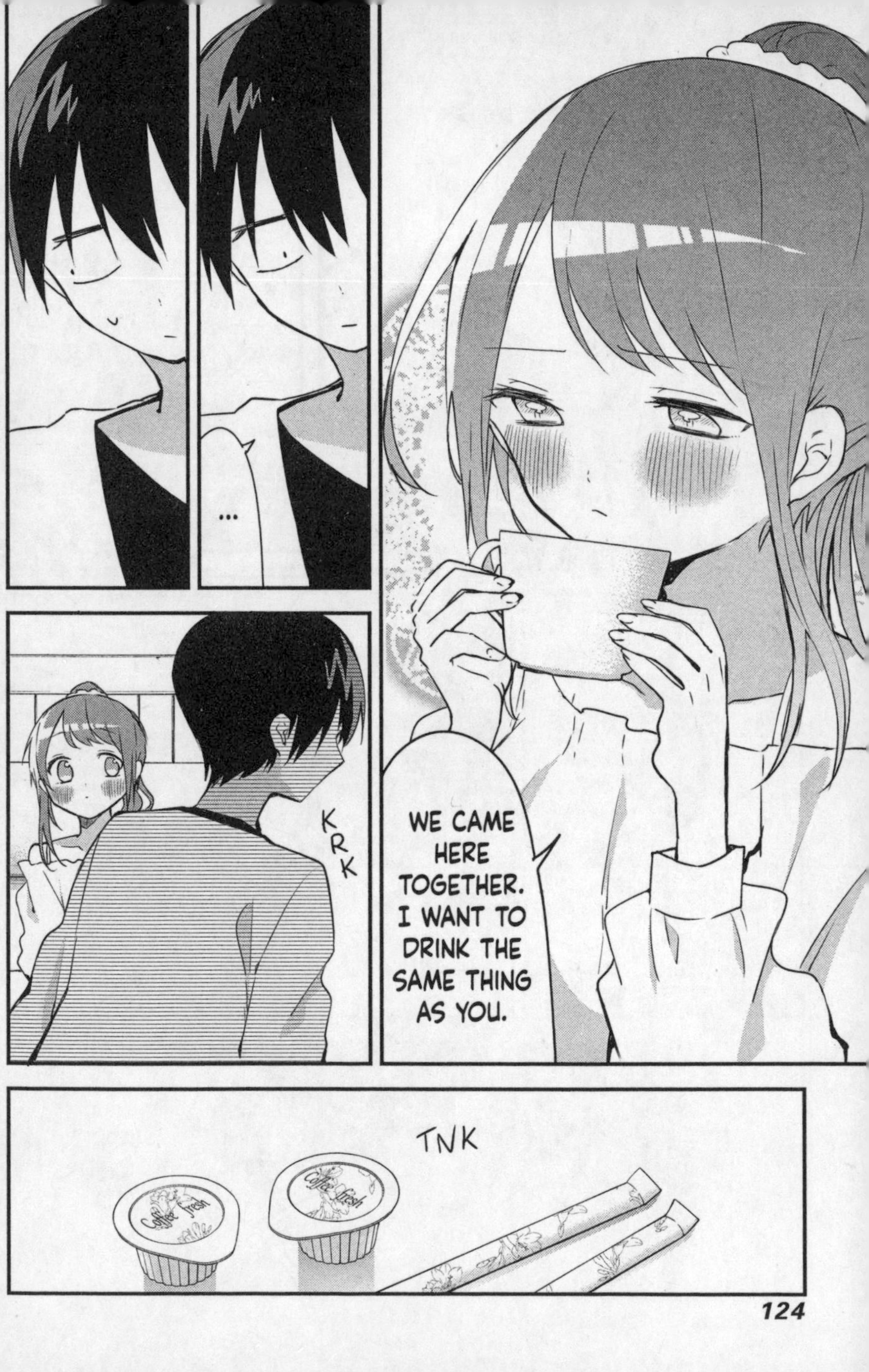
WE CAME HERE TOGETHER. I WANT TO DRINK THE SAME THING AS YOU.
...
KRK
TNK
Coffee fresh
Coffee fresh

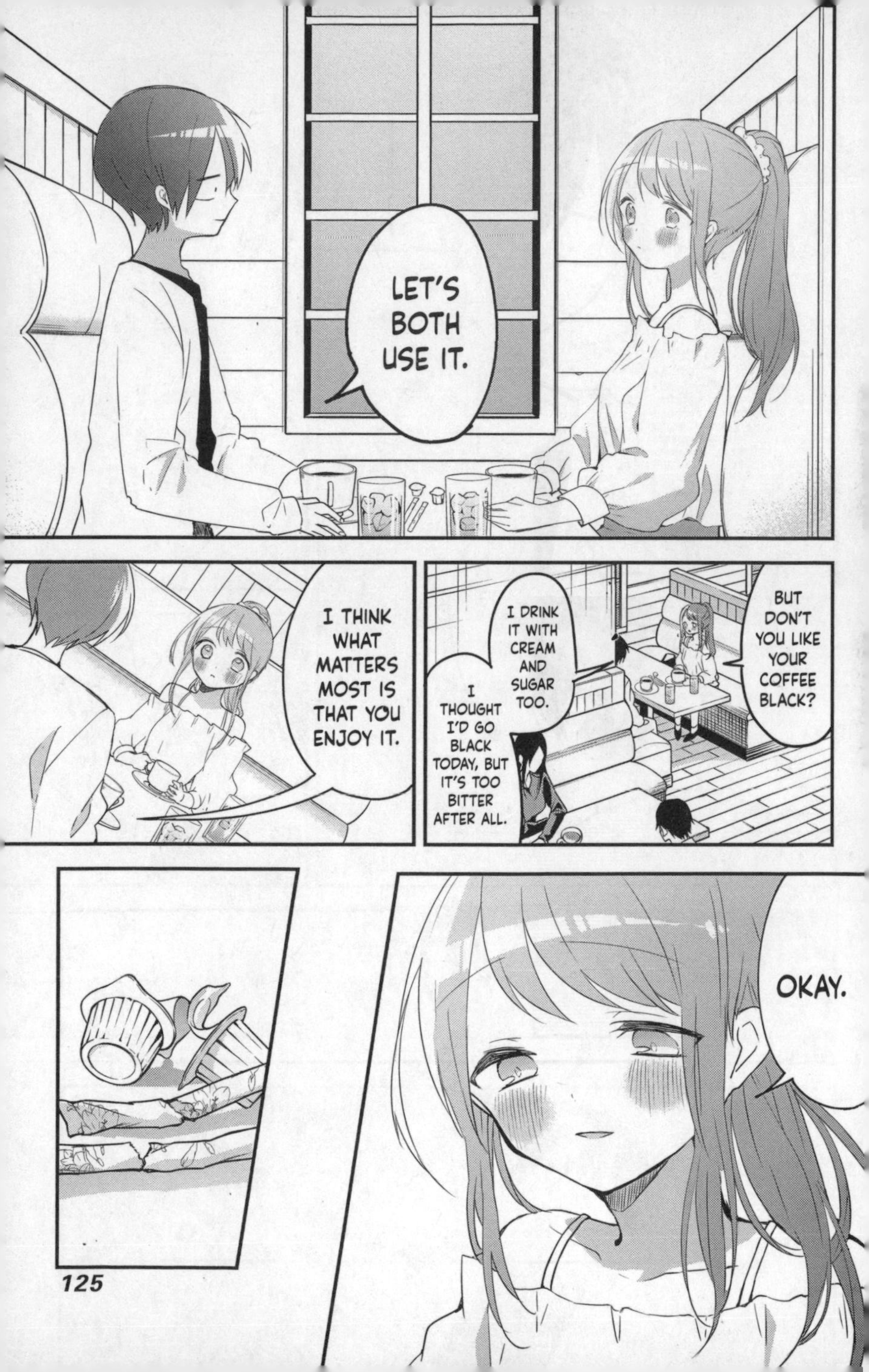
LET'S BOTH USE IT.
BUT DON'T YOU LIKE YOUR COFFEE BLACK?
I DRINK IT WITH CREAM AND SUGAR TOO.
I THOUGHT I'D GO BLACK TODAY, BUT IT'S TOO BITTER AFTER ALL.
I THINK WHAT MATTERS MOST IS THAT YOU ENJOY IT.
OKAY.

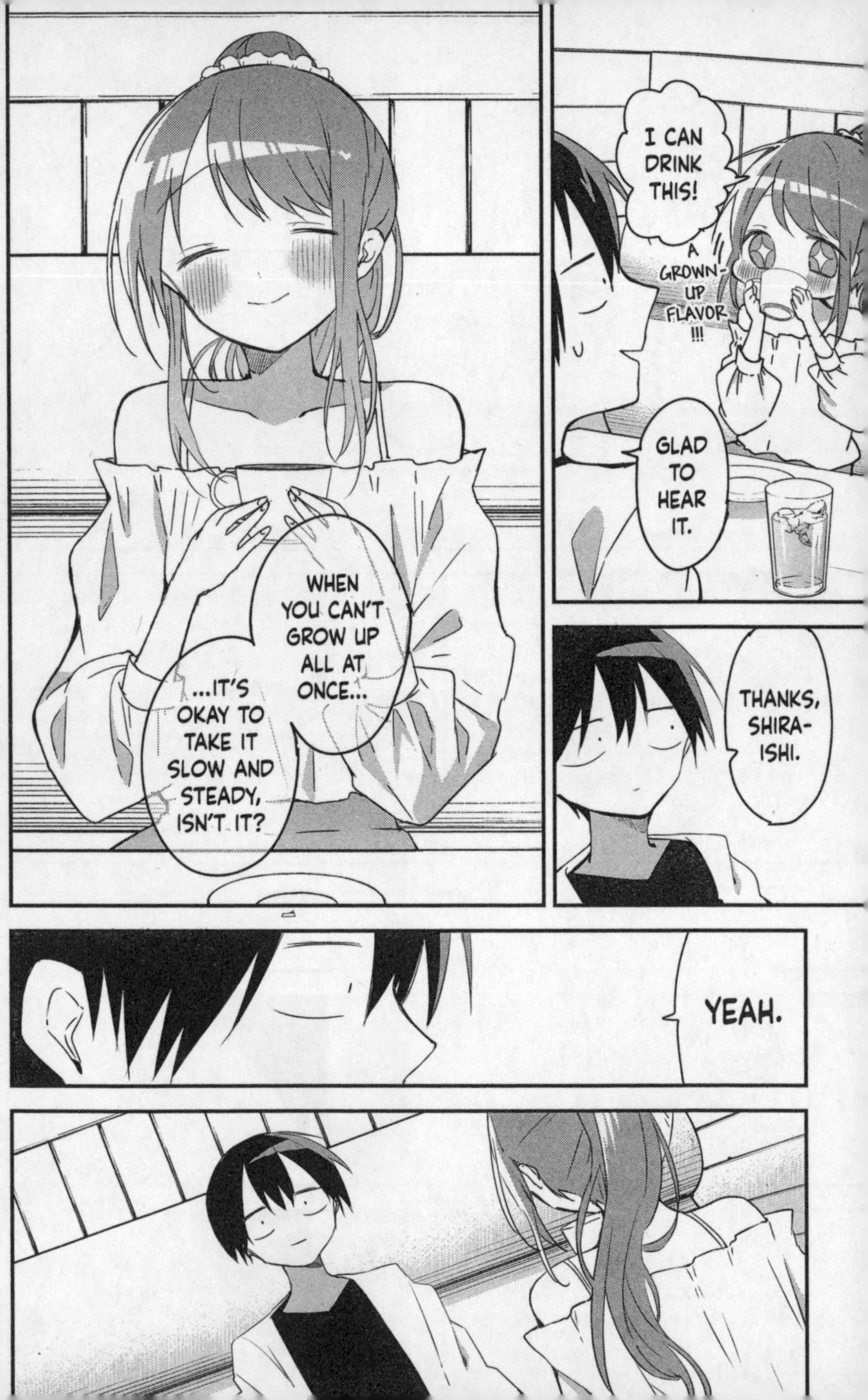
I CAN DRINK THIS!
A GROWN-UP FLAVOR!!!
GLAD TO HEAR IT.
THANKS, SHIRA-ISHI.
WHEN YOU CAN'T GROW UP ALL AT ONCE...
...IT'S OKAY TO TAKE IT SLOW AND STEADY, ISN'T IT?
YEAH.

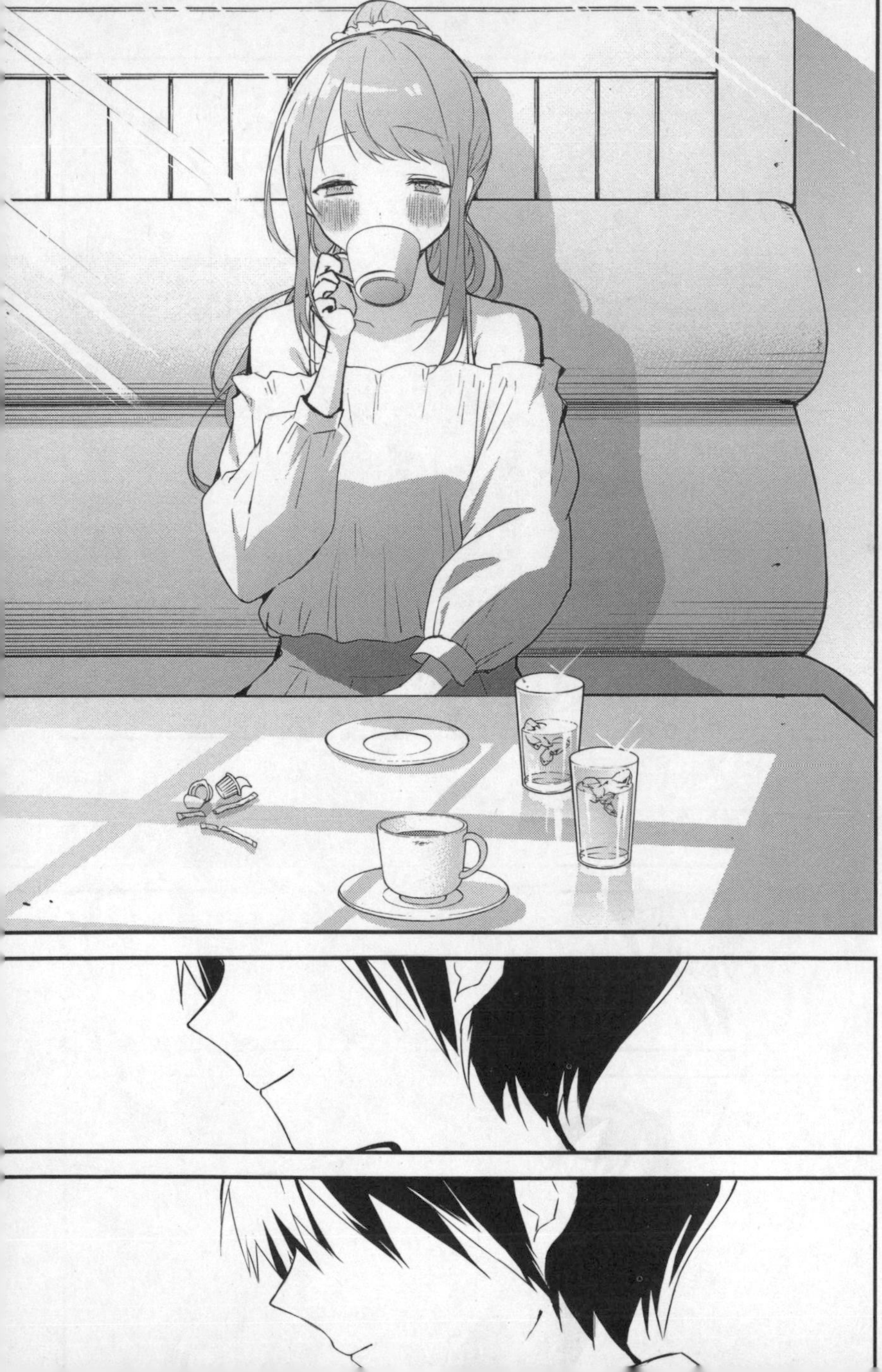

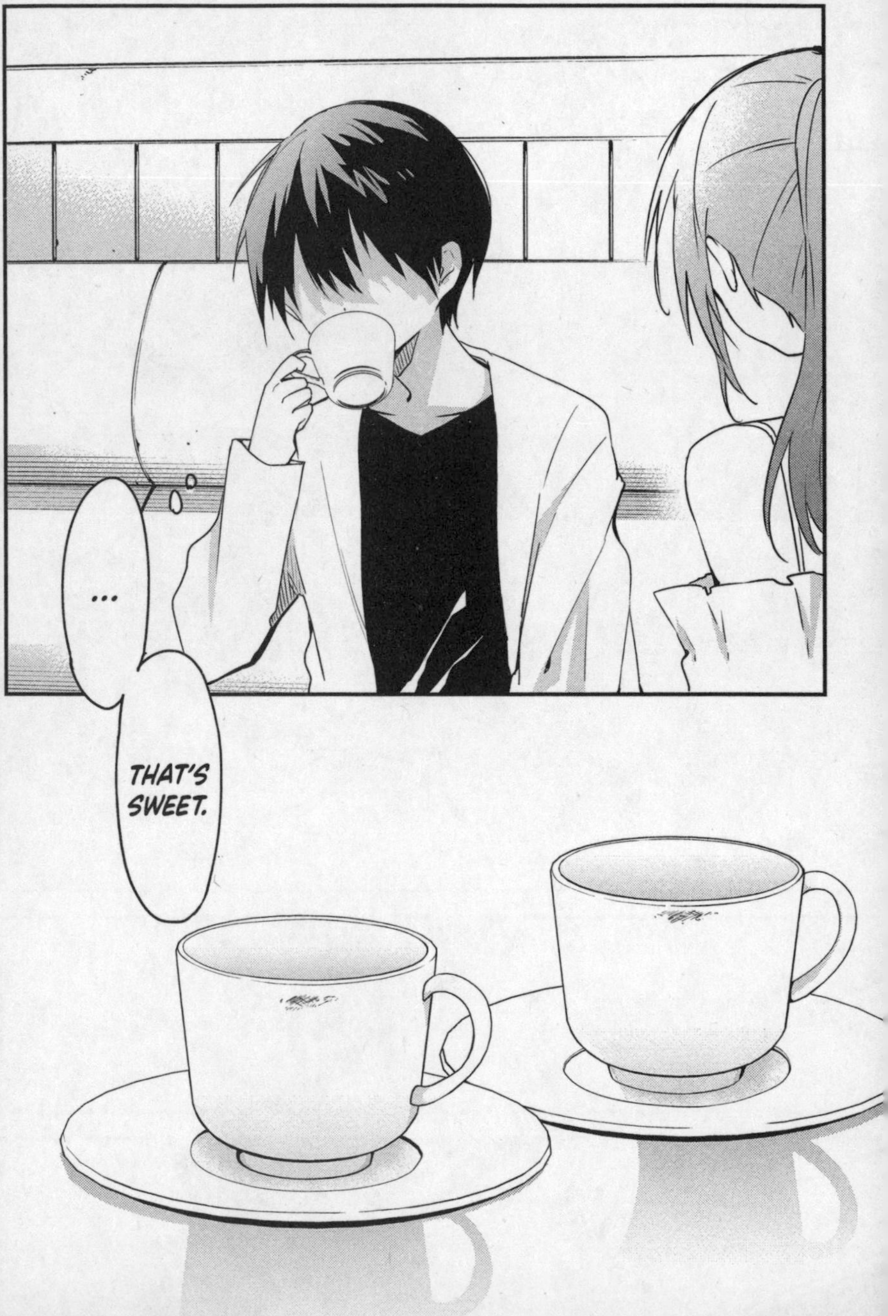
...
THAT'S SWEET.

episode 043 MOVIE THEATER AND FACIAL MUSCLES

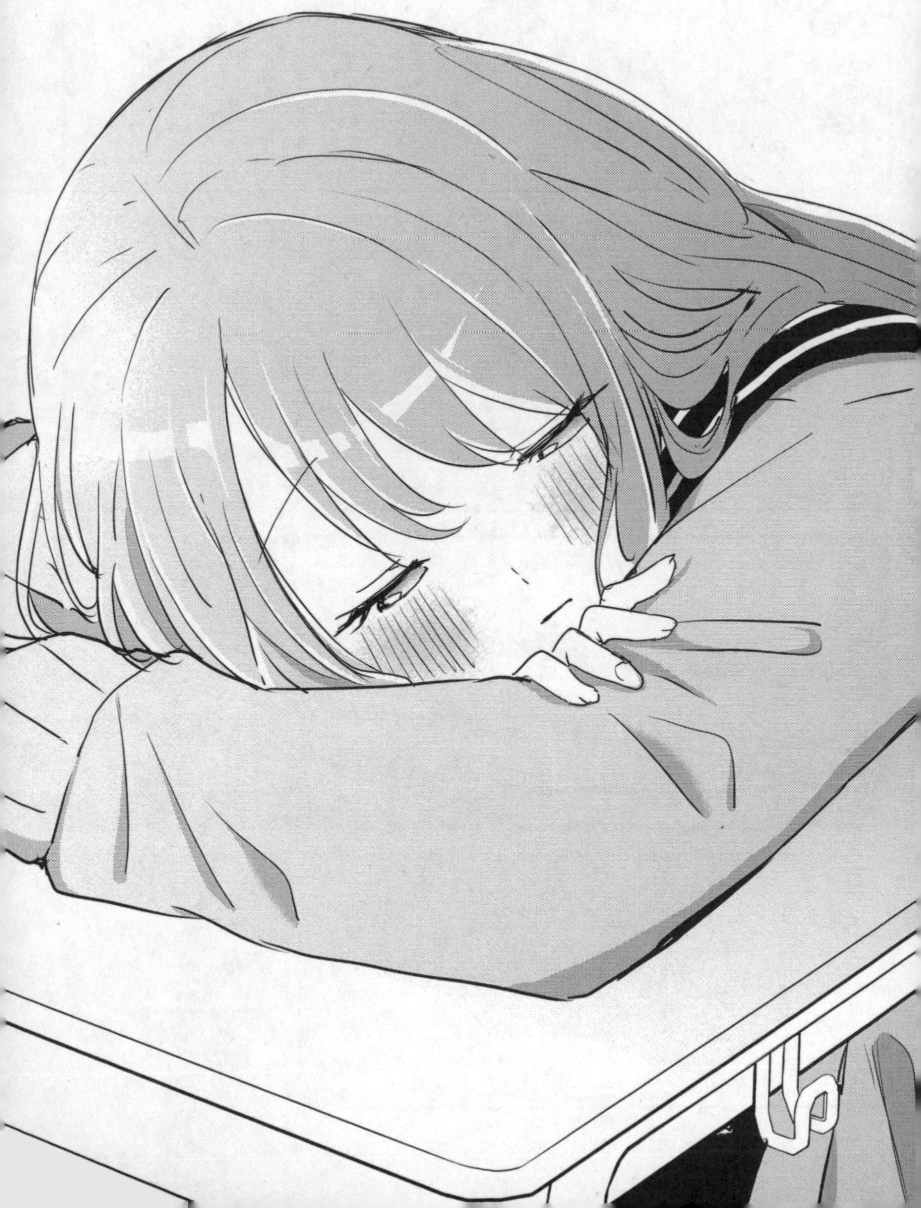

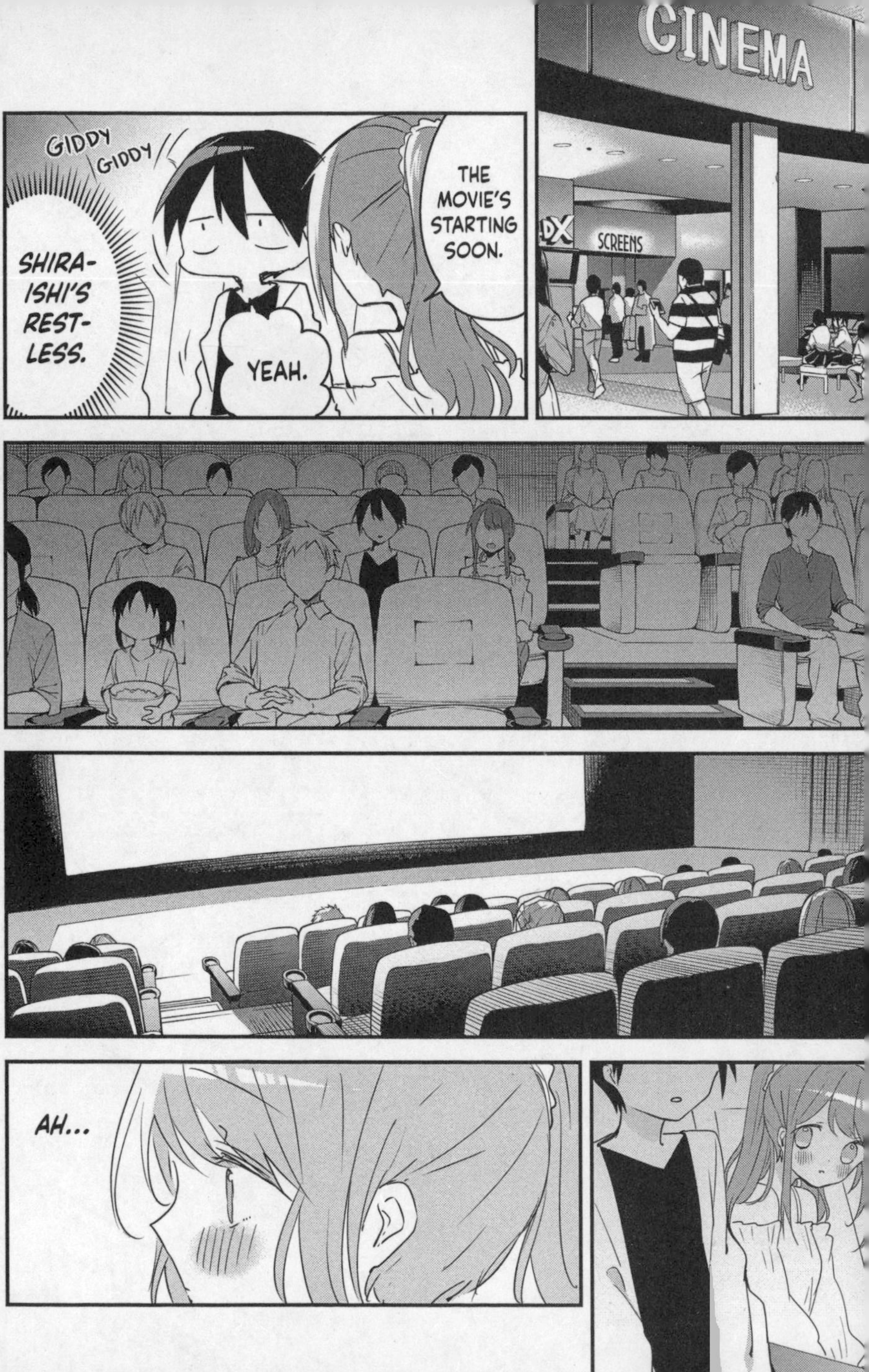
CINEMA
SCREENS
THE MOVIE'S STARTING SOON.
GIDDY GIDDY
YEAH.
SHIRA-ISHI'S REST-LESS.
AH...

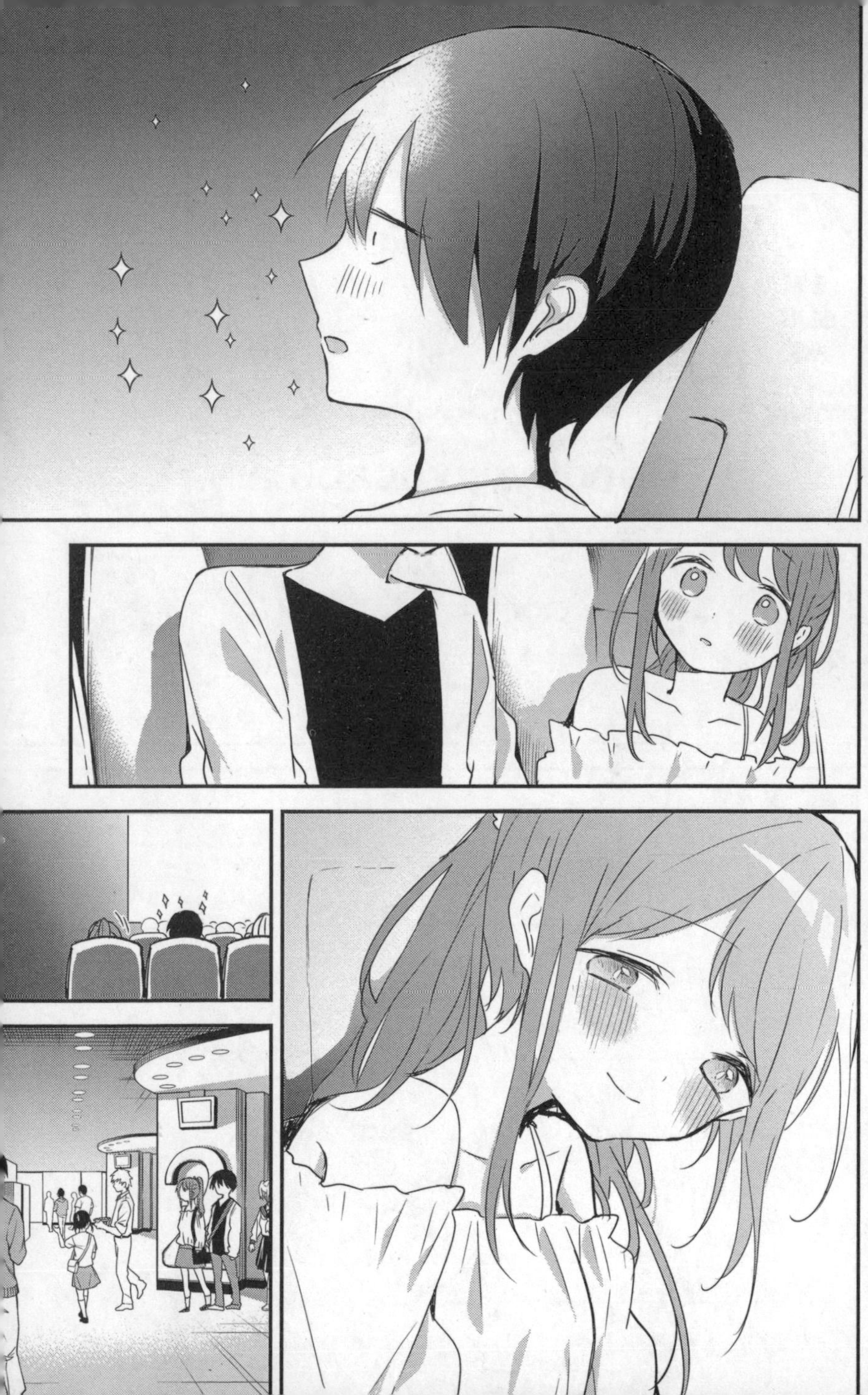

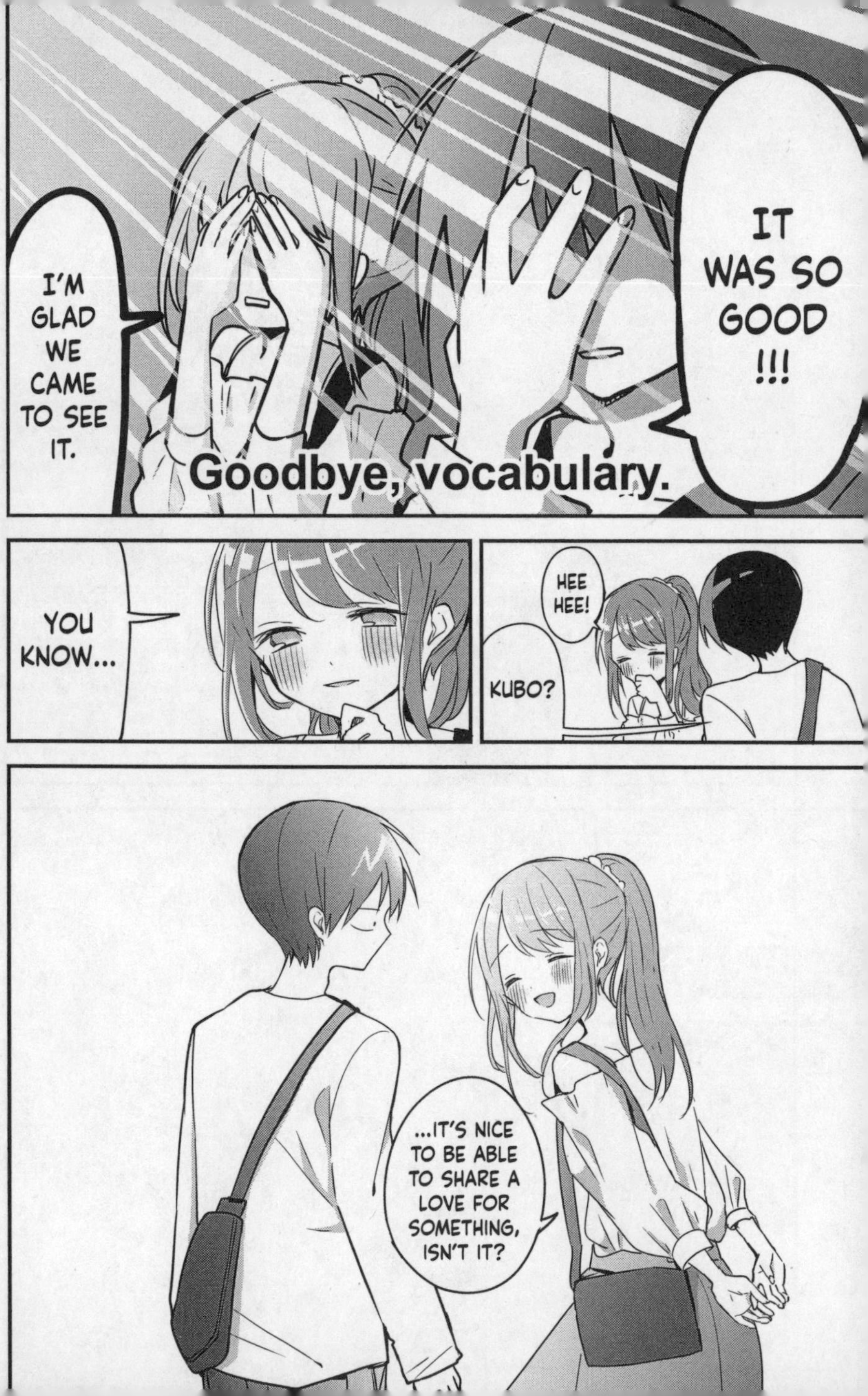
IT WAS SO GOOD !!!
I'M GLAD WE CAME TO SEE IT.
Goodbye, vocabulary.
HEE HEE!
KUBO?
YOU KNOW...
...IT'S NICE TO BE ABLE TO SHARE A LOVE FOR SOMETHING, ISN'T IT?

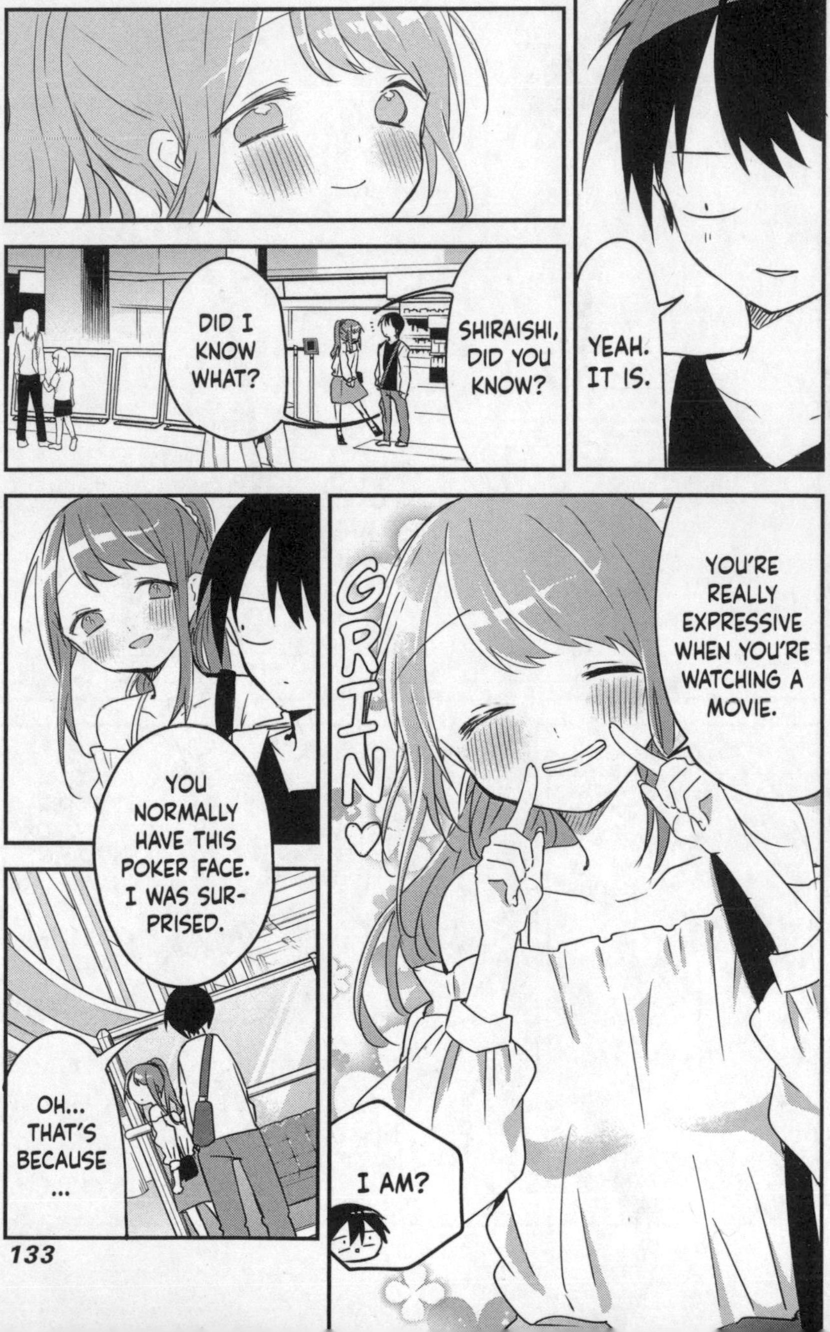
YEAH. IT IS.
SHIRAISHI, DID YOU KNOW?
DID I KNOW WHAT?
YOU'RE REALLY EXPRESSIVE WHEN YOU'RE WATCHING A MOVIE.
GRIN
I AM?
YOU NORMALLY HAVE THIS POKER FACE. I WAS SUR-PRISED.
OH... THAT'S BECAUSE ...

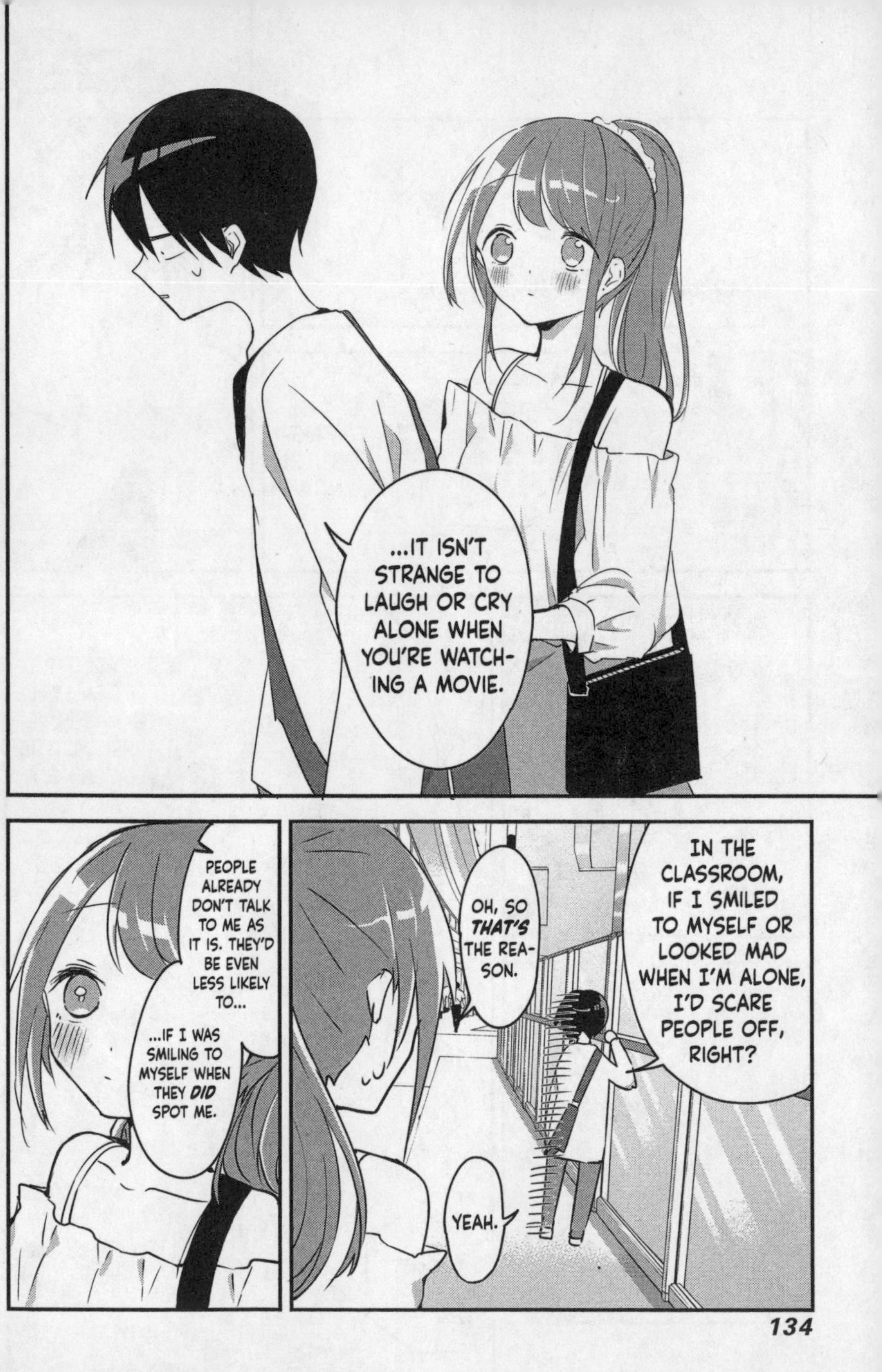
...IT ISN'T STRANGE TO LAUGH OR CRY ALONE WHEN YOU'RE WATCHING A MOVIE.
IN THE CLASSROOM, IF I SMILED TO MYSELF OR LOOKED MAD WHEN I'M ALONE, I'D SCARE PEOPLE OFF, RIGHT?
OH, SO *THAT'S* THE REASON.
YEAH.
PEOPLE ALREADY DON'T TALK TO ME AS IT IS. THEY'D BE EVEN LESS LIKELY TO...
...IF I WAS SMILING TO MYSELF WHEN THEY *DID* SPOT ME.

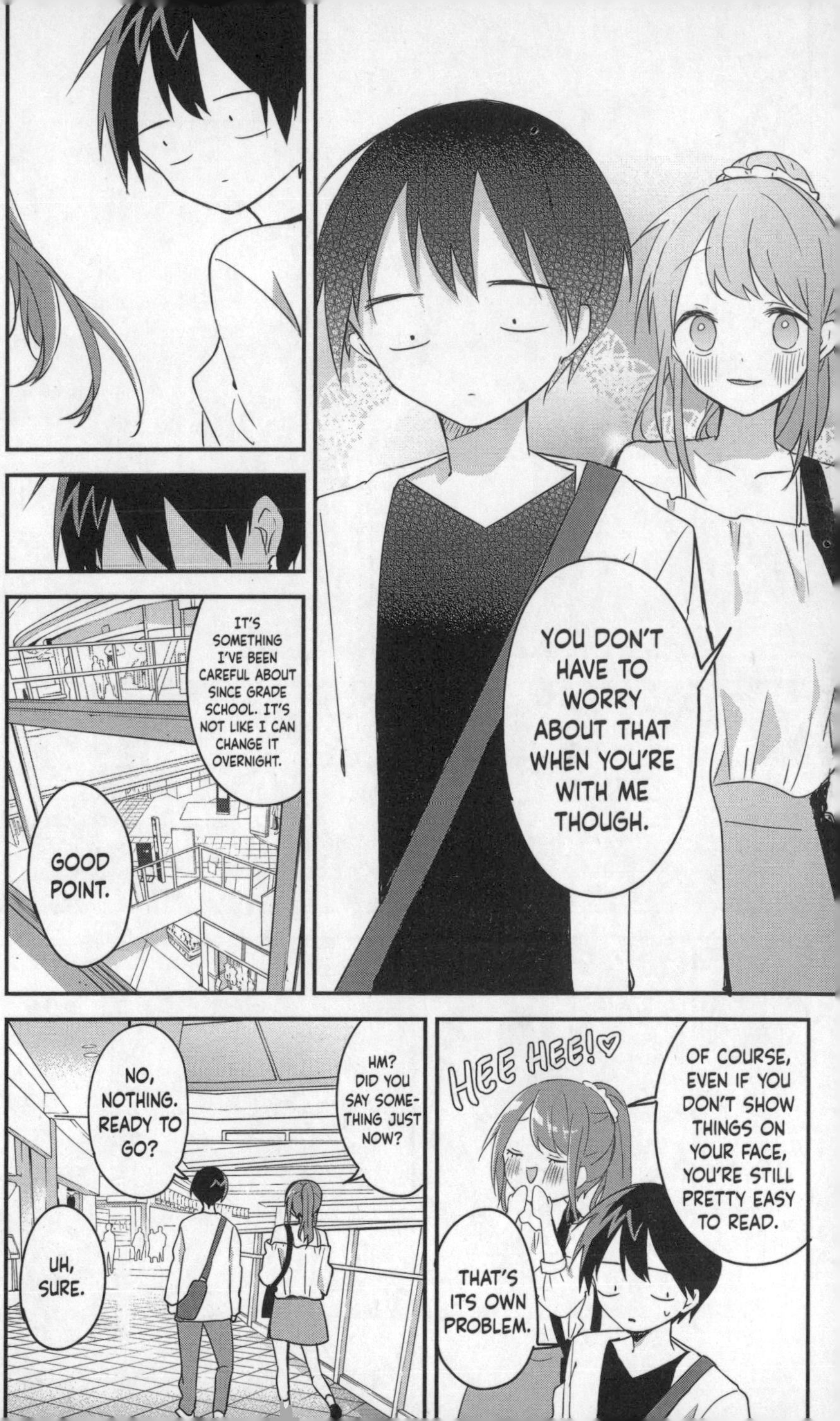
YOU DON'T HAVE TO WORRY ABOUT THAT WHEN YOU'RE WITH ME THOUGH.
IT'S SOMETHING I'VE BEEN CAREFUL ABOUT SINCE GRADE SCHOOL. IT'S NOT LIKE I CAN CHANGE IT OVERNIGHT.
GOOD POINT.
OF COURSE, EVEN IF YOU DON'T SHOW THINGS ON YOUR FACE, YOU'RE STILL PRETTY EASY TO READ.
HEE HEE!♡
THAT'S ITS OWN PROBLEM.
HM? DID YOU SAY SOME-THING JUST NOW?
NO, NOTHING. READY TO GO?
UH, SURE.

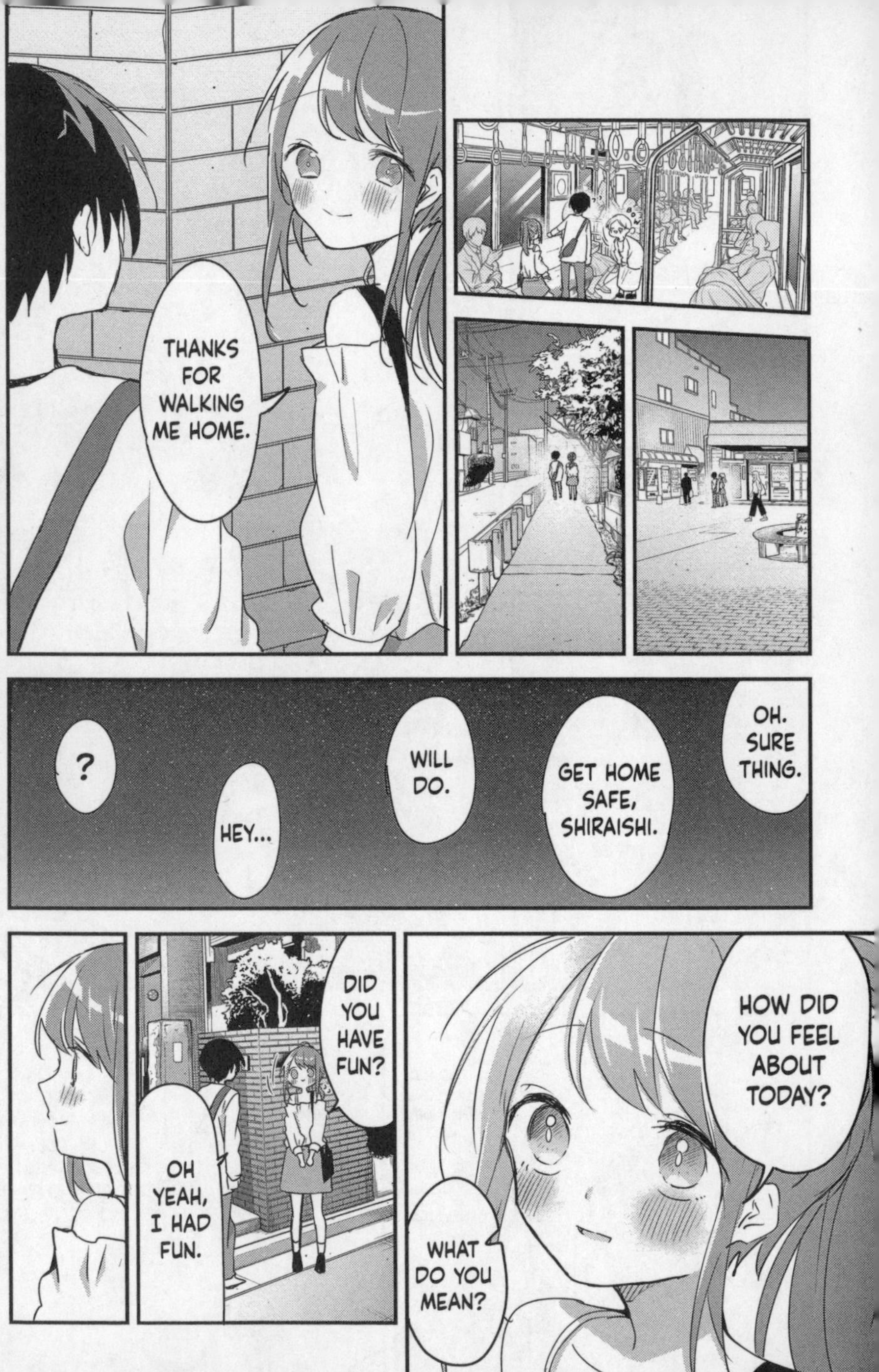
BOW
THANKS FOR WALKING ME HOME.
OH. SURE THING.
GET HOME SAFE, SHIRAISHI.
WILL DO.
HEY...
?
HOW DID YOU FEEL ABOUT TODAY?
WHAT DO YOU MEAN?
DID YOU HAVE FUN?
OH YEAH, I HAD FUN.

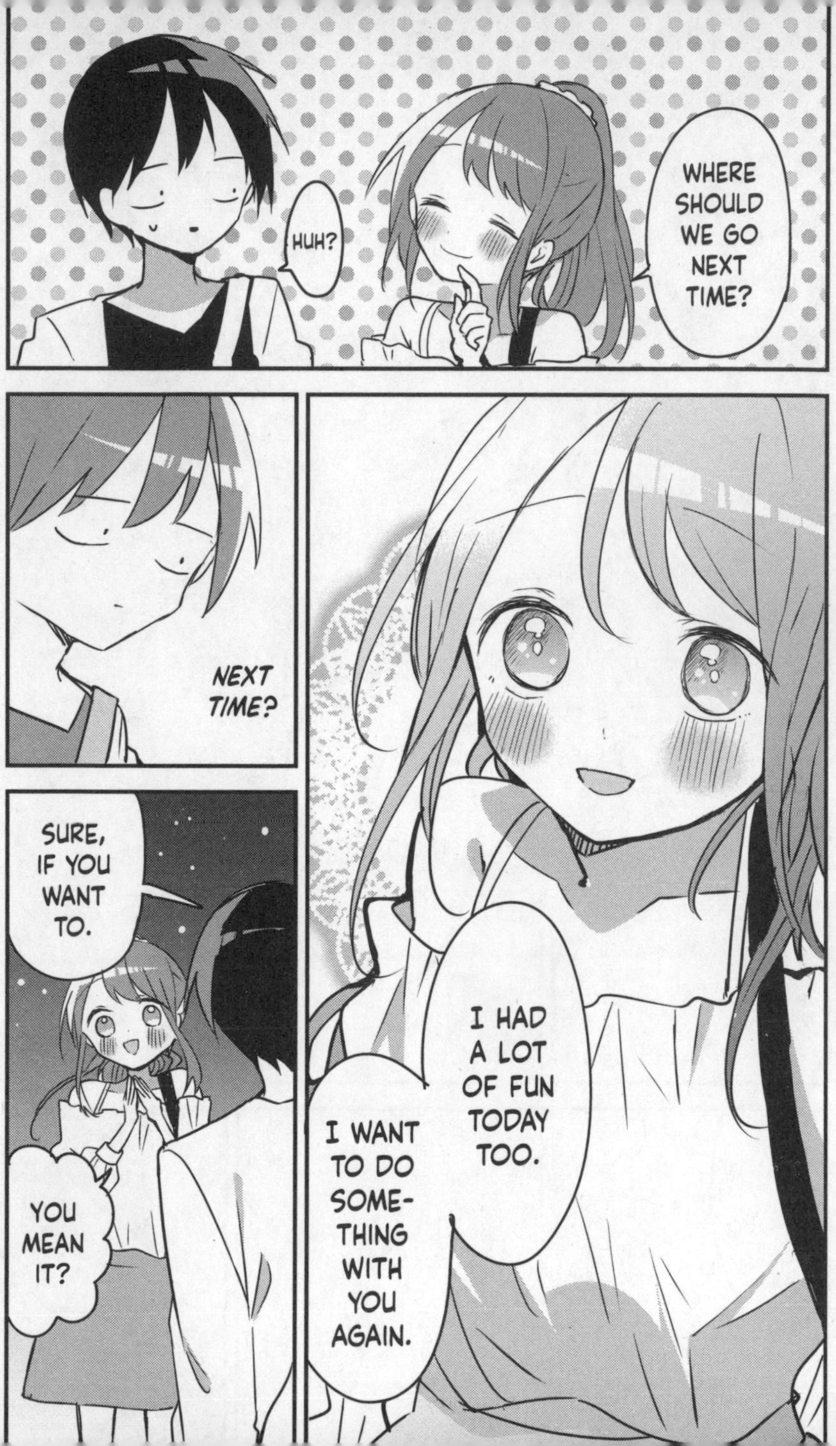
WHERE SHOULD WE GO NEXT TIME?
HUH?
I HAD A LOT OF FUN TODAY TOO.
I WANT TO DO SOME-THING WITH YOU AGAIN.
NEXT TIME?
SURE, IF YOU WANT TO.
YOU MEAN IT?

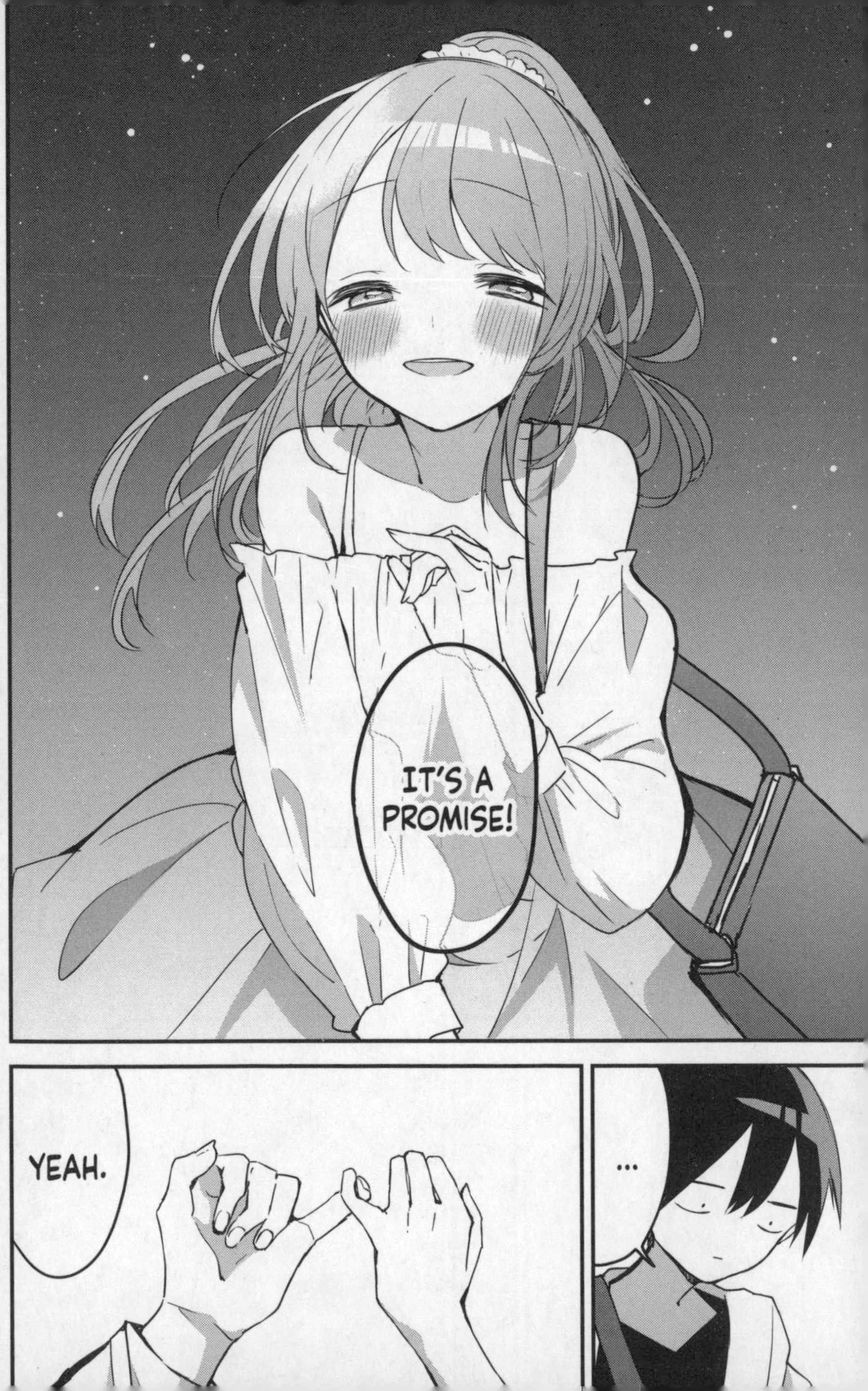
IT'S A PROMISE!
...
YEAH.

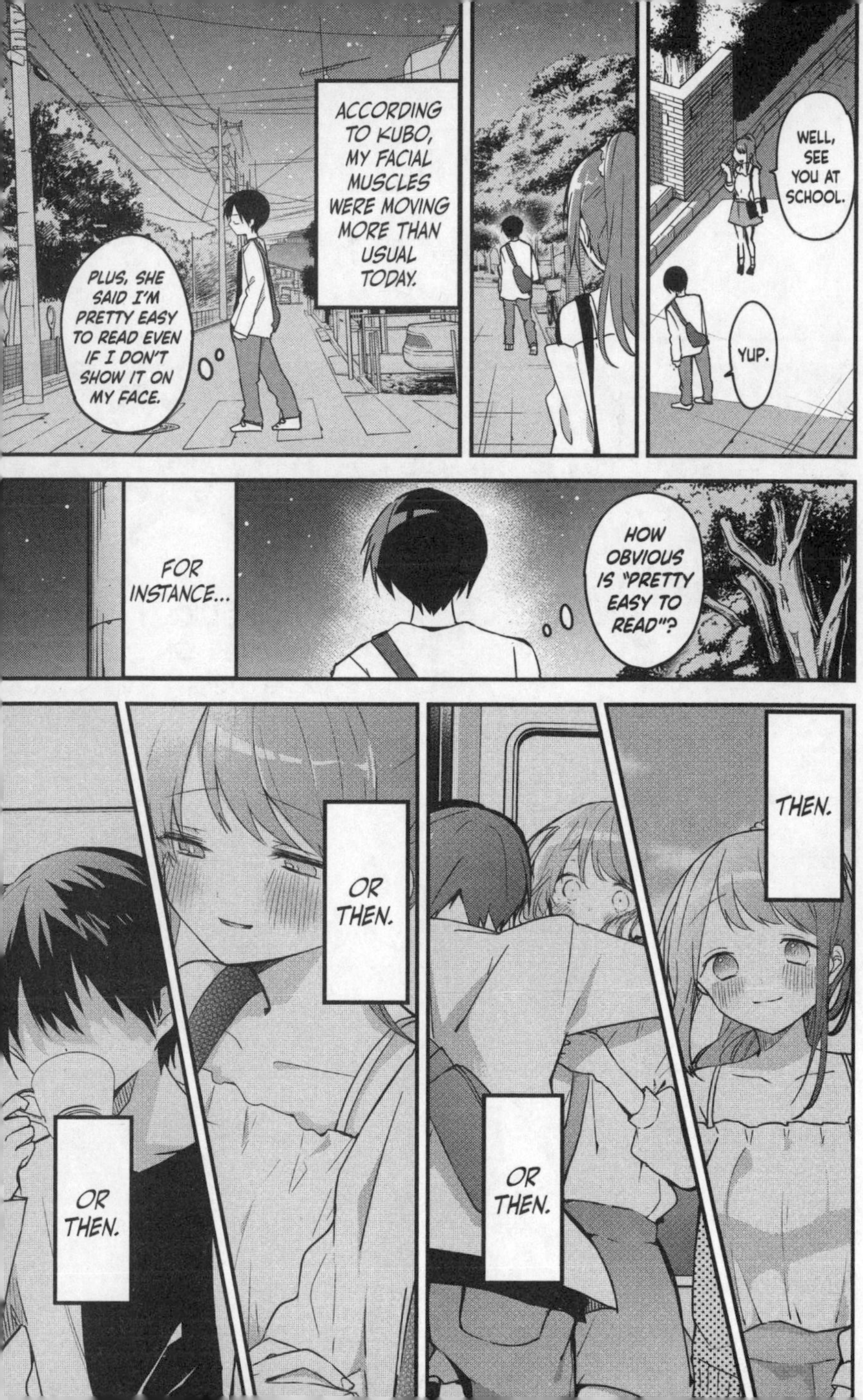
WELL, SEE YOU AT SCHOOL.
YUP.
ACCORDING TO KUBO, MY FACIAL MUSCLES WERE MOVING MORE THAN USUAL TODAY.
PLUS, SHE SAID I'M PRETTY EASY TO READ EVEN IF I DON'T SHOW IT ON MY FACE.
HOW OBVIOUS IS "PRETTY EASY TO READ"?
FOR INSTANCE...
THEN.
OR THEN.
OR THEN.
OR THEN.

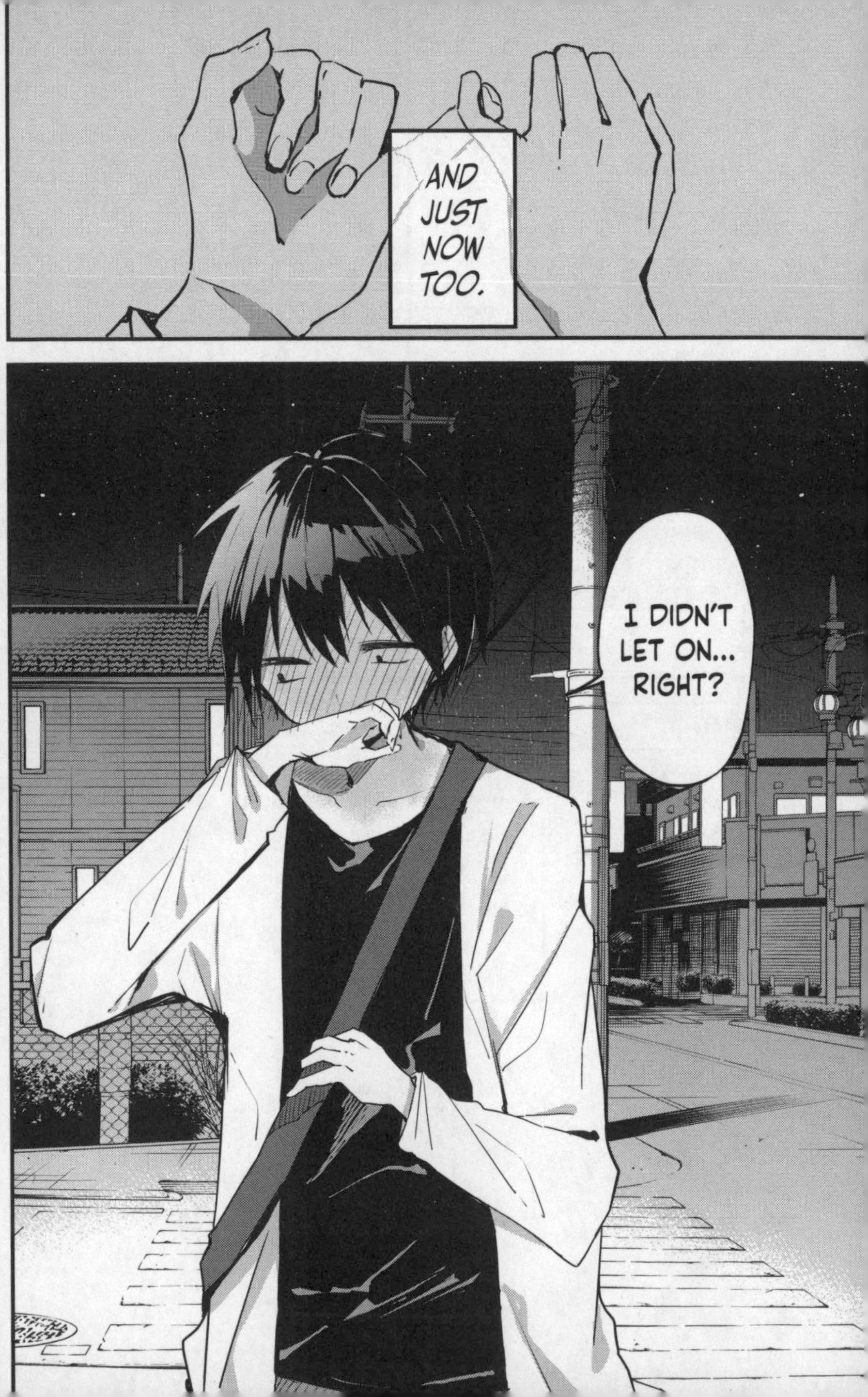
AND JUST NOW TOO.
I DIDN'T LET ON... RIGHT?

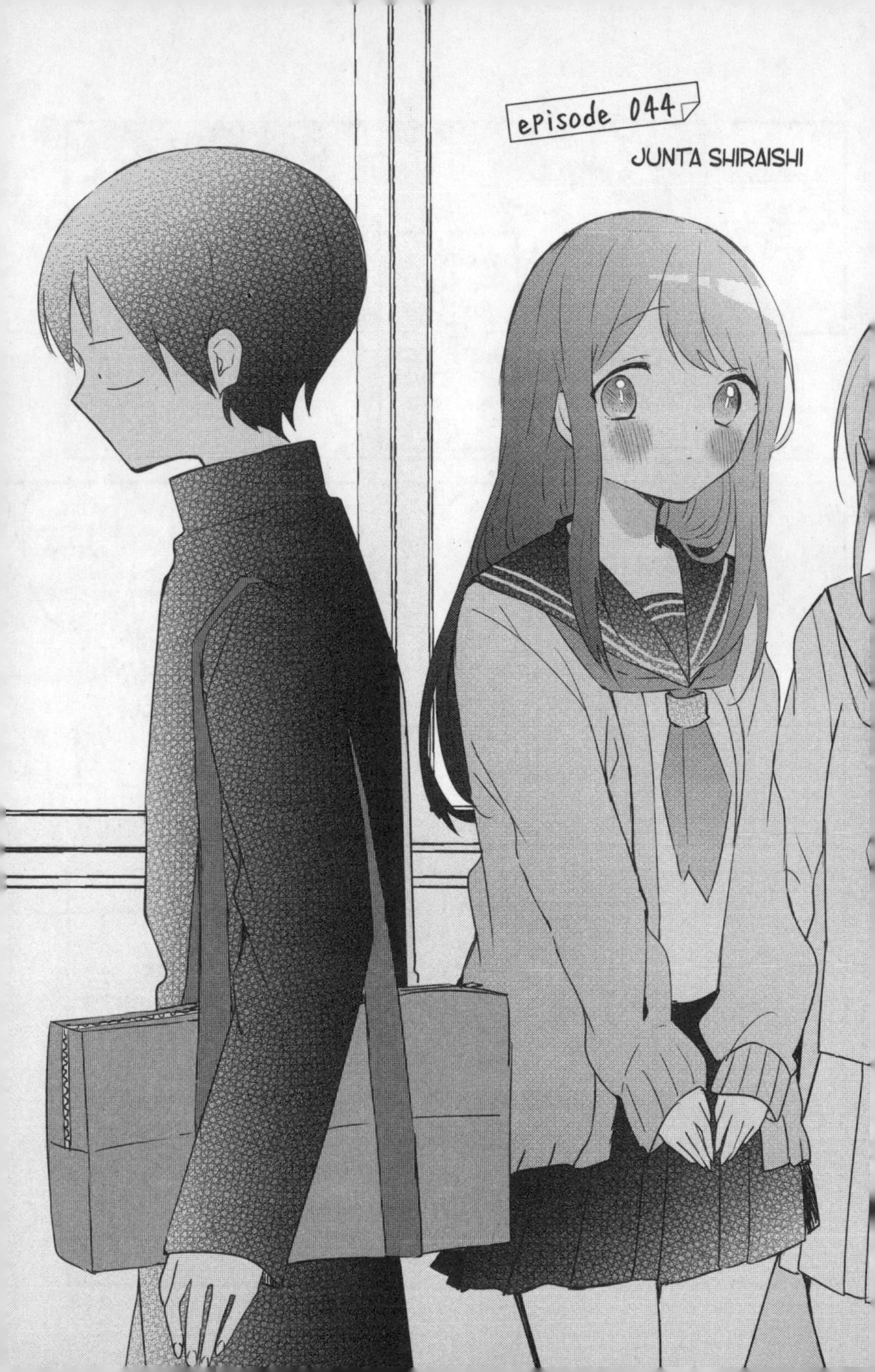
episode 044
JUNTA SHIRAISHI

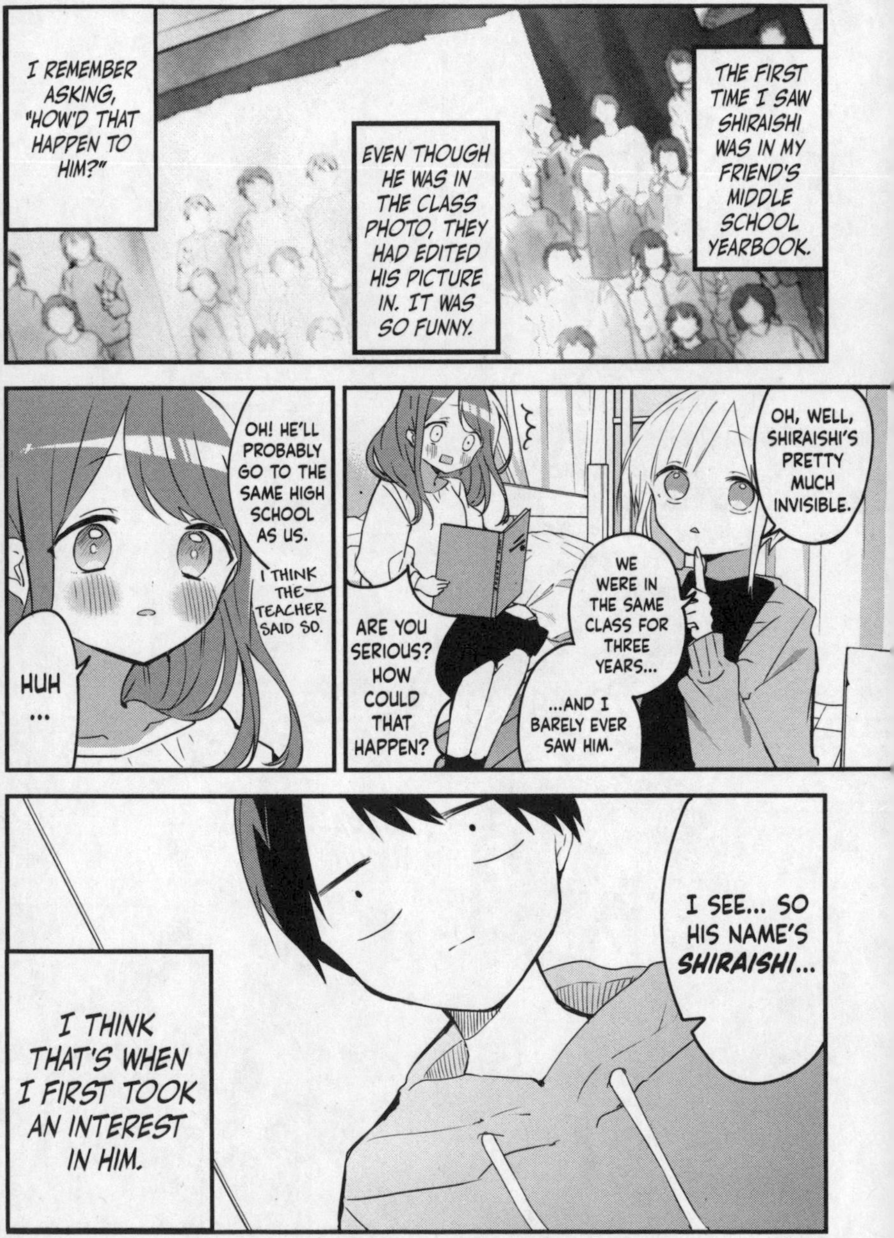
THE FIRST TIME I SAW SHIRAISHI WAS IN MY FRIEND'S MIDDLE SCHOOL YEARBOOK.
EVEN THOUGH HE WAS IN THE CLASS PHOTO, THEY HAD EDITED HIS PICTURE IN. IT WAS SO FUNNY.
I REMEMBER ASKING, "HOW'D THAT HAPPEN TO HIM?"
OH, WELL, SHIRAISHI'S PRETTY MUCH INVISIBLE.
WE WERE IN THE SAME CLASS FOR THREE YEARS...
...AND I BARELY EVER SAW HIM.
ARE YOU SERIOUS? HOW COULD THAT HAPPEN?
OH! HE'LL PROBABLY GO TO THE SAME HIGH SCHOOL AS US.
I THINK THE TEACHER SAID SO.
HUH ...
I SEE... SO HIS NAME'S **SHIRAISHI**...
I THINK THAT'S WHEN I FIRST TOOK AN INTEREST IN HIM.

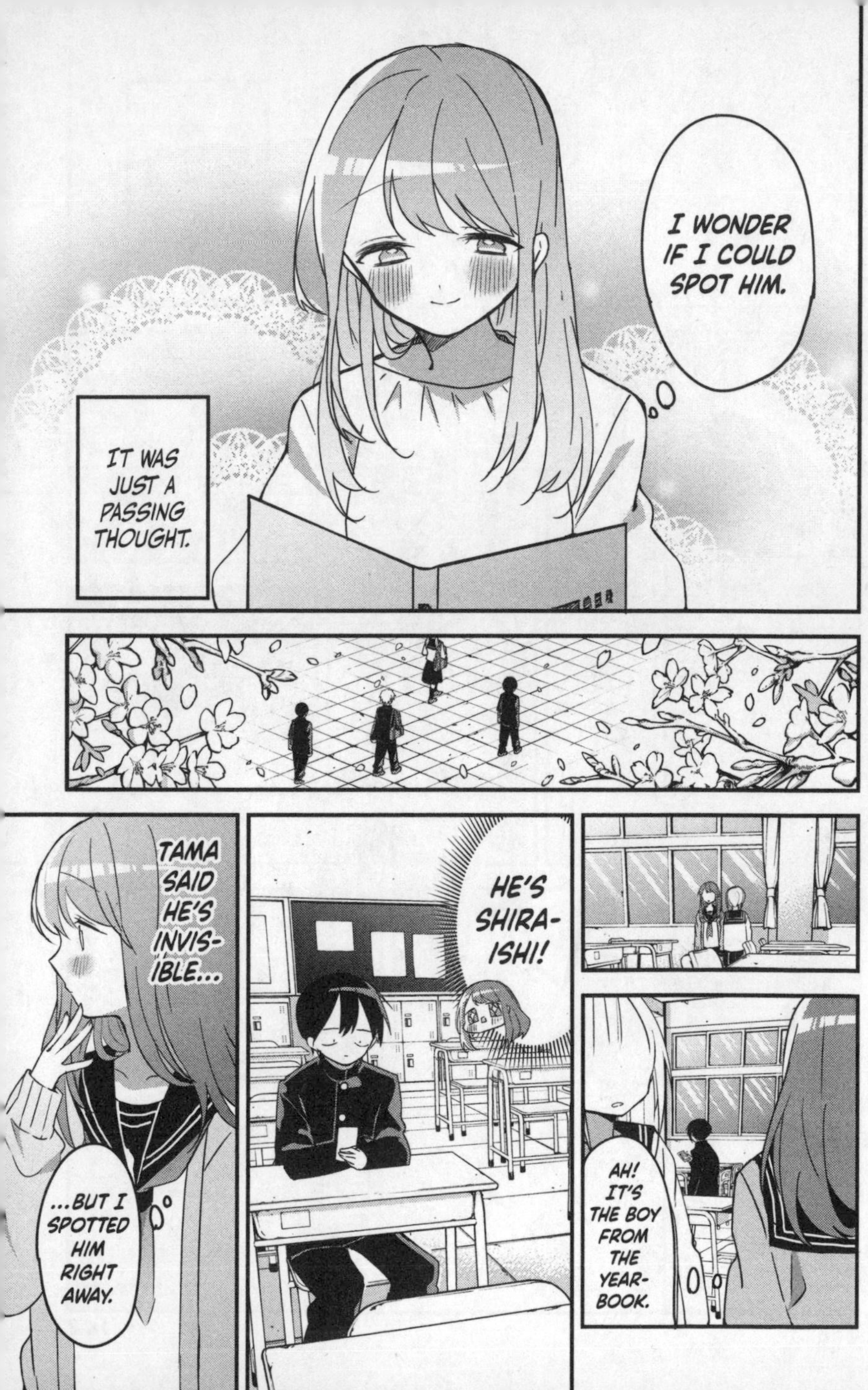
I WONDER IF I COULD SPOT HIM.
IT WAS JUST A PASSING THOUGHT.
AH! IT'S THE BOY FROM THE YEAR-BOOK.
HE'S SHIRA-ISHI!
TAMA SAID HE'S INVIS-IBLE...
...BUT I SPOTTED HIM RIGHT AWAY.

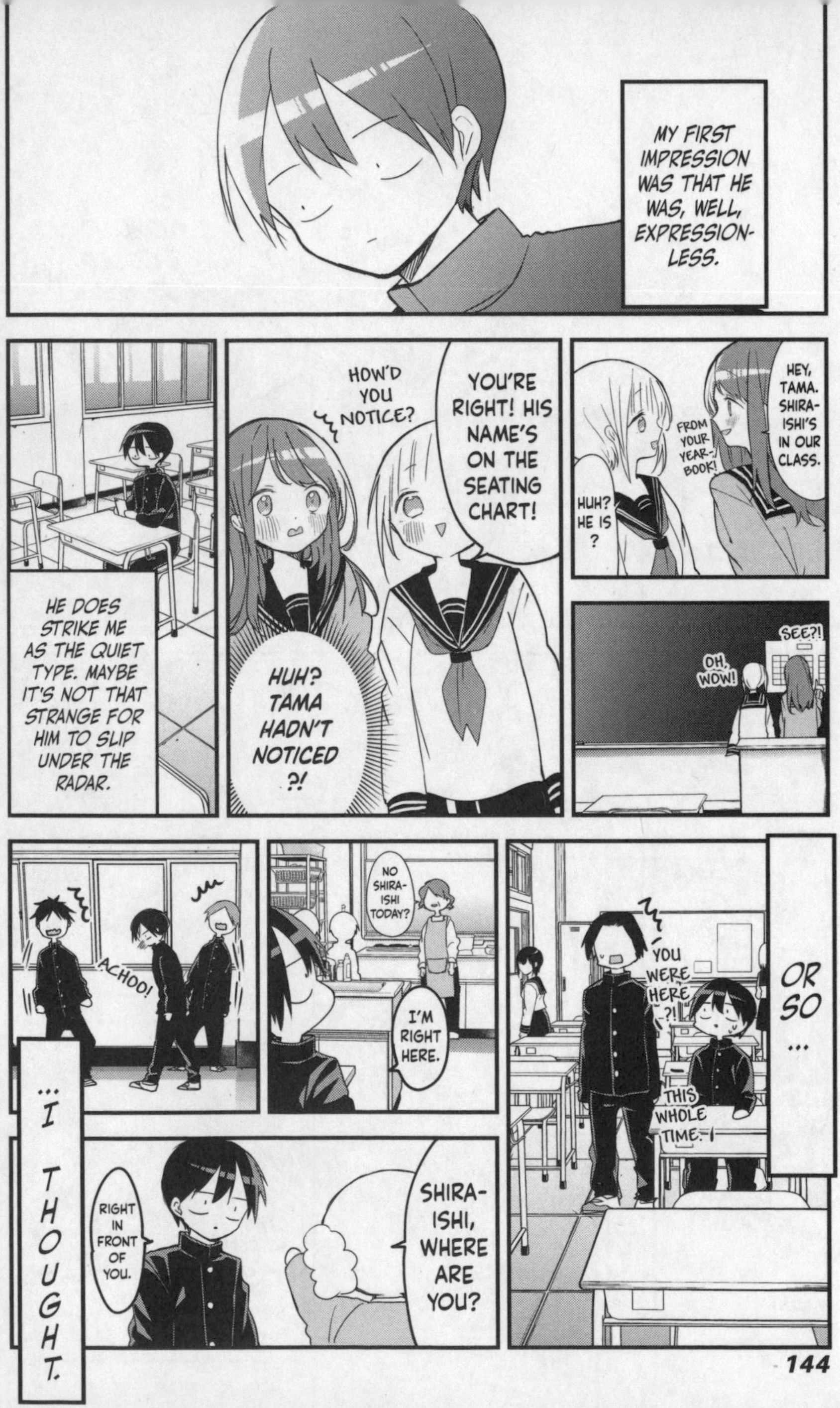
MY FIRST IMPRESSION WAS THAT HE WAS, WELL, EXPRESSION-LESS.
HEY, TAMA. SHIRA-ISHI'S IN OUR CLASS.
FROM YOUR YEAR-BOOK!
HUH? HE IS ?
SEE?!
OH, WOW!
YOU'RE RIGHT! HIS NAME'S ON THE SEATING CHART!
HOW'D YOU NOTICE?
HUH? TAMA HADN'T NOTICED ?!
HE DOES STRIKE ME AS THE QUIET TYPE. MAYBE IT'S NOT THAT STRANGE FOR HIM TO SLIP UNDER THE RADAR.
OR SO ...
YOU WERE HERE ?!
THIS WHOLE TIME.
NO SHIRA-ISHI TODAY?
I'M RIGHT HERE.
ACHOO!
SHIRA-ISHI, WHERE ARE YOU?
RIGHT IN FRONT OF YOU.
... I THOUGHT.

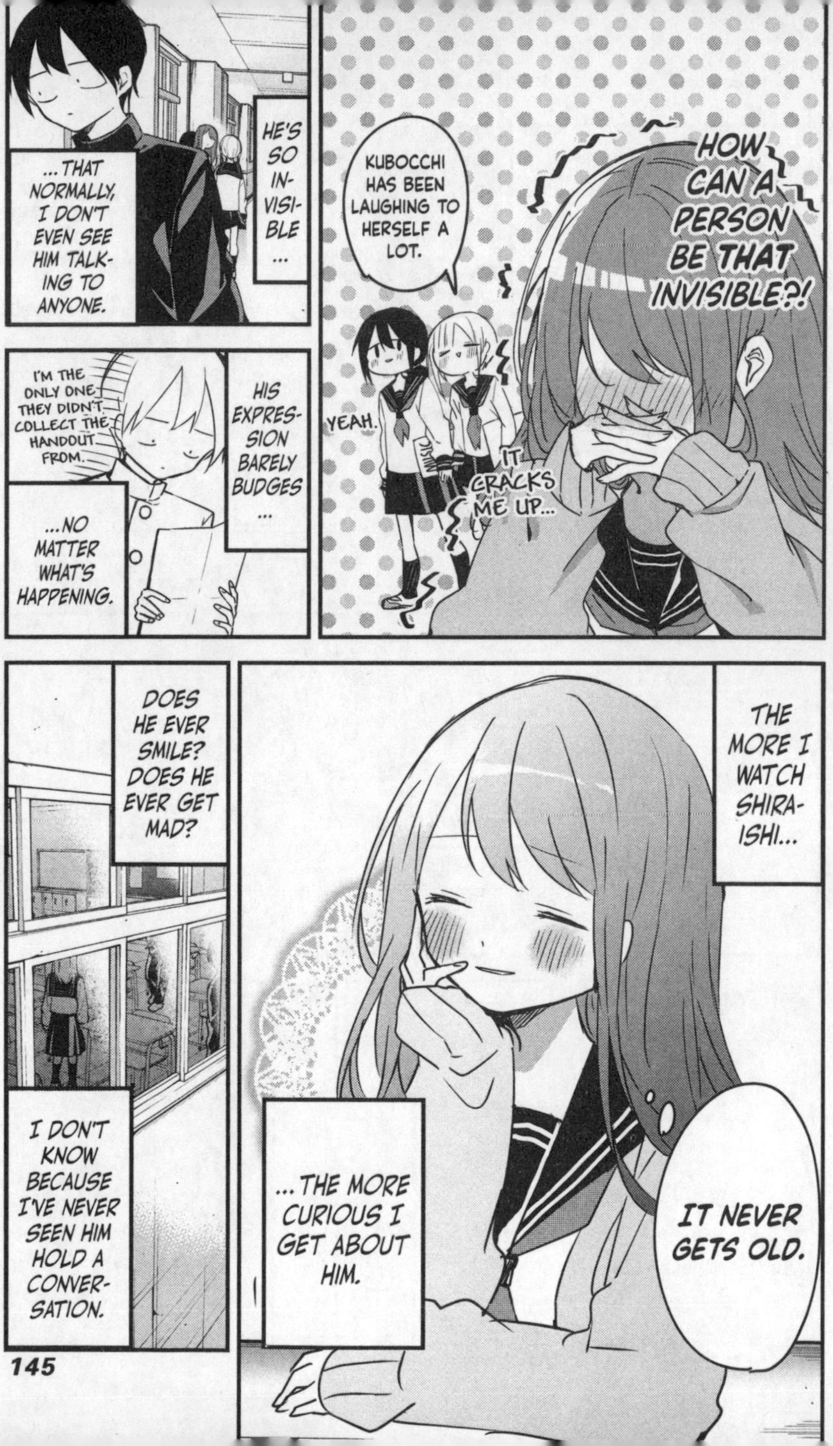
HOW CAN A PERSON BE THAT INVISIBLE?!
IT CRACKS ME UP...
KUBOCCHI HAS BEEN LAUGHING TO HERSELF A LOT.
YEAH.
HE'S SO INVISIBLE...
...THAT NORMALLY, I DON'T EVEN SEE HIM TALKING TO ANYONE.
HIS EXPRESSION BARELY BUDGES...
I'M THE ONLY ONE THEY DIDN'T COLLECT THE HANDOUT FROM.
...NO MATTER WHAT'S HAPPENING.
THE MORE I WATCH SHIRAISHI...
IT NEVER GETS OLD.
...THE MORE CURIOUS I GET ABOUT HIM.
DOES HE EVER SMILE? DOES HE EVER GET MAD?
I DON'T KNOW BECAUSE I'VE NEVER SEEN HIM HOLD A CONVERSATION.

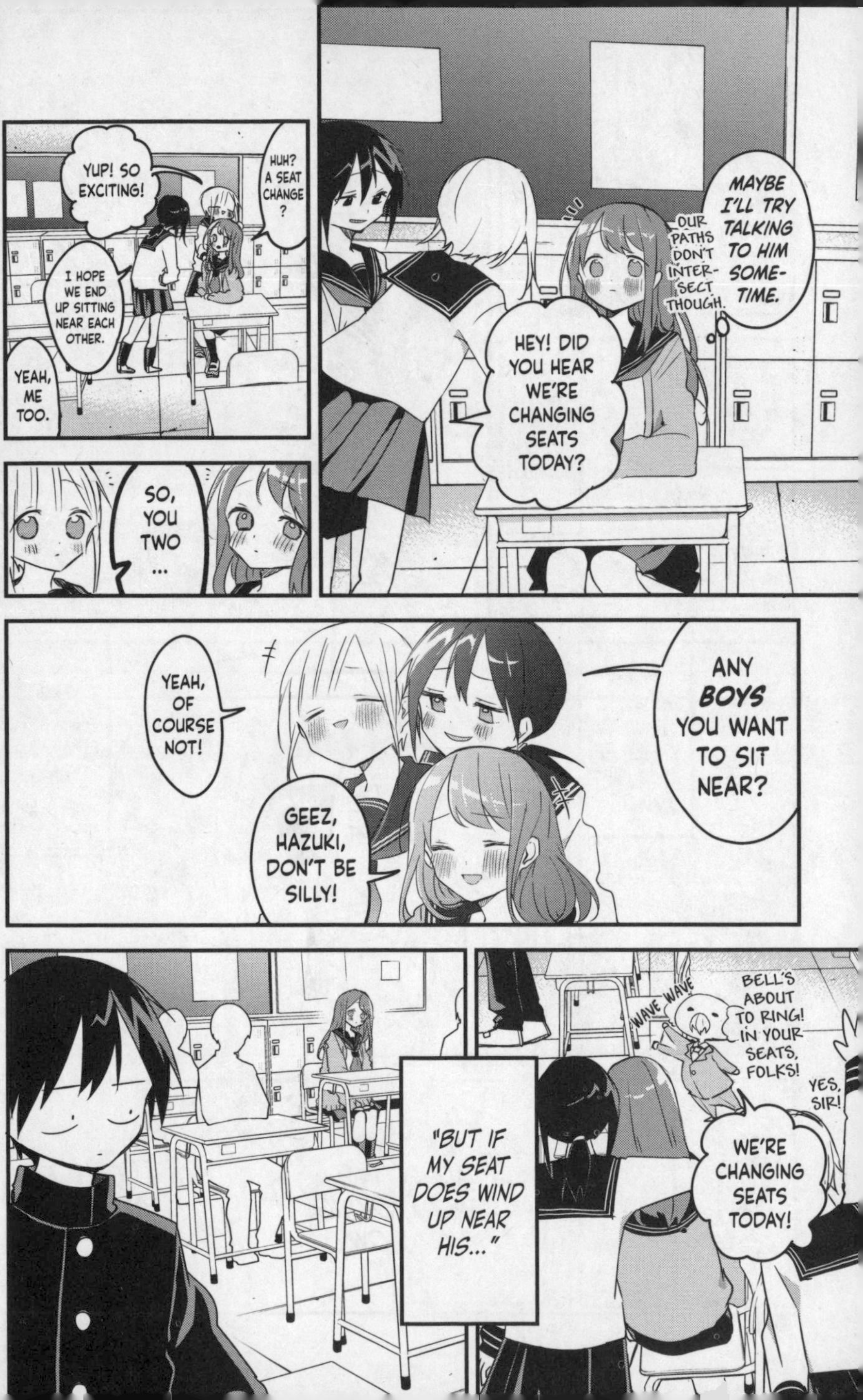
MAYBE I'LL TRY TALKING TO HIM SOMETIME.
OUR PATHS DON'T INTERSECT THOUGH.
HEY! DID YOU HEAR WE'RE CHANGING SEATS TODAY?
HUH? A SEAT CHANGE?
YUP! SO EXCITING!
I HOPE WE END UP SITTING NEAR EACH OTHER.
YEAH, ME TOO.
SO, YOU TWO...
ANY BOYS YOU WANT TO SIT NEAR?
YEAH, OF COURSE NOT!
GEEZ, HAZUKI, DON'T BE SILLY!
BELL'S ABOUT TO RING! IN YOUR SEATS, FOLKS!
WAVE WAVE
YES, SIR!
WE'RE CHANGING SEATS TODAY!
"BUT IF MY SEAT DOES WIND UP NEAR HIS..."

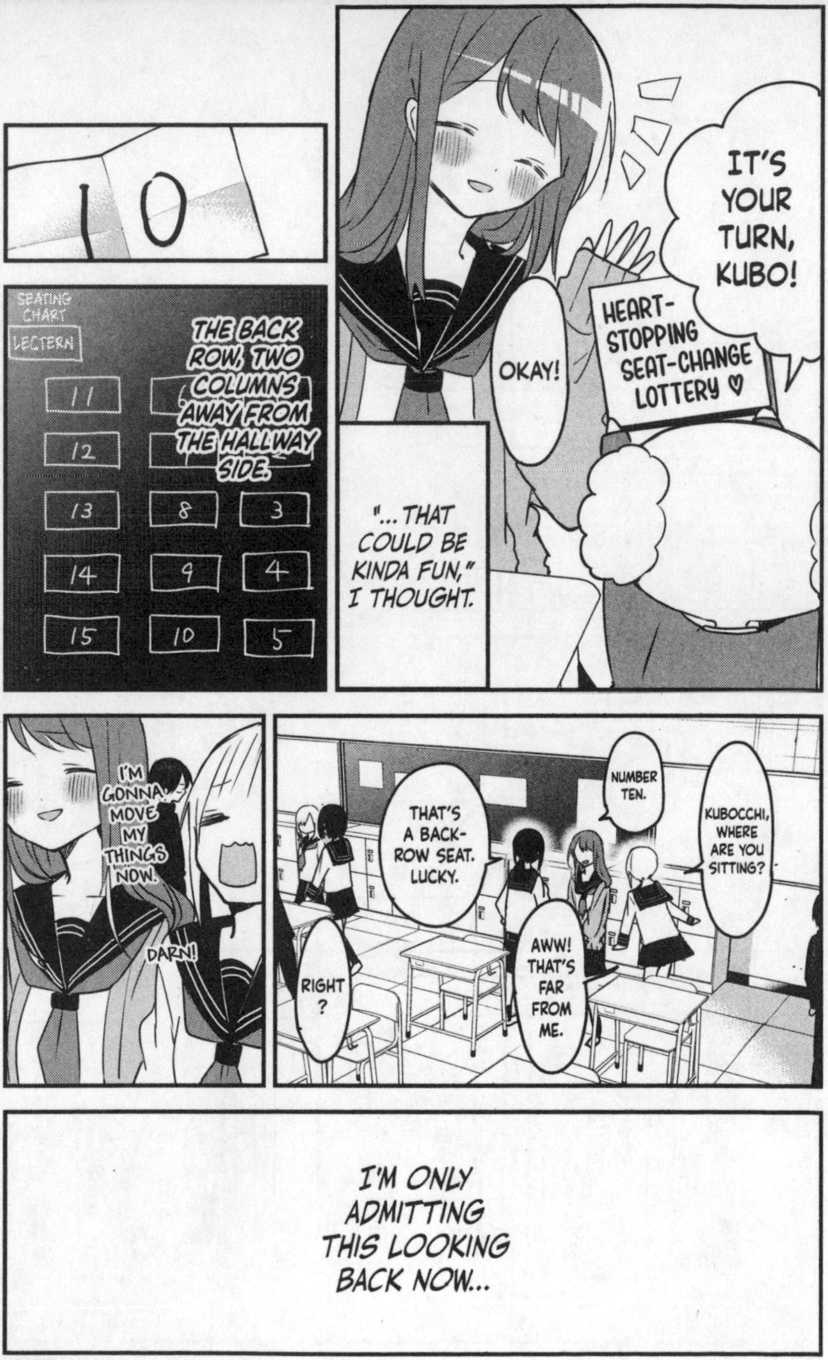
IT'S YOUR TURN, KUBO!
HEART-STOPPING SEAT-CHANGE LOTTERY ♡
OKAY!
"...THAT COULD BE KINDA FUN," I THOUGHT.
10
SEATING CHART
LECTERN
11
12
13 8 3
14 9 4
15 10 5
THE BACK ROW, TWO COLUMNS AWAY FROM THE HALLWAY SIDE.
KUBOCCHI, WHERE ARE YOU SITTING?
NUMBER TEN.
THAT'S A BACK-ROW SEAT. LUCKY.
AWW! THAT'S FAR FROM ME.
RIGHT?
I'M GONNA MOVE MY THINGS NOW.
DARN!
I'M ONLY ADMITTING THIS LOOKING BACK NOW...

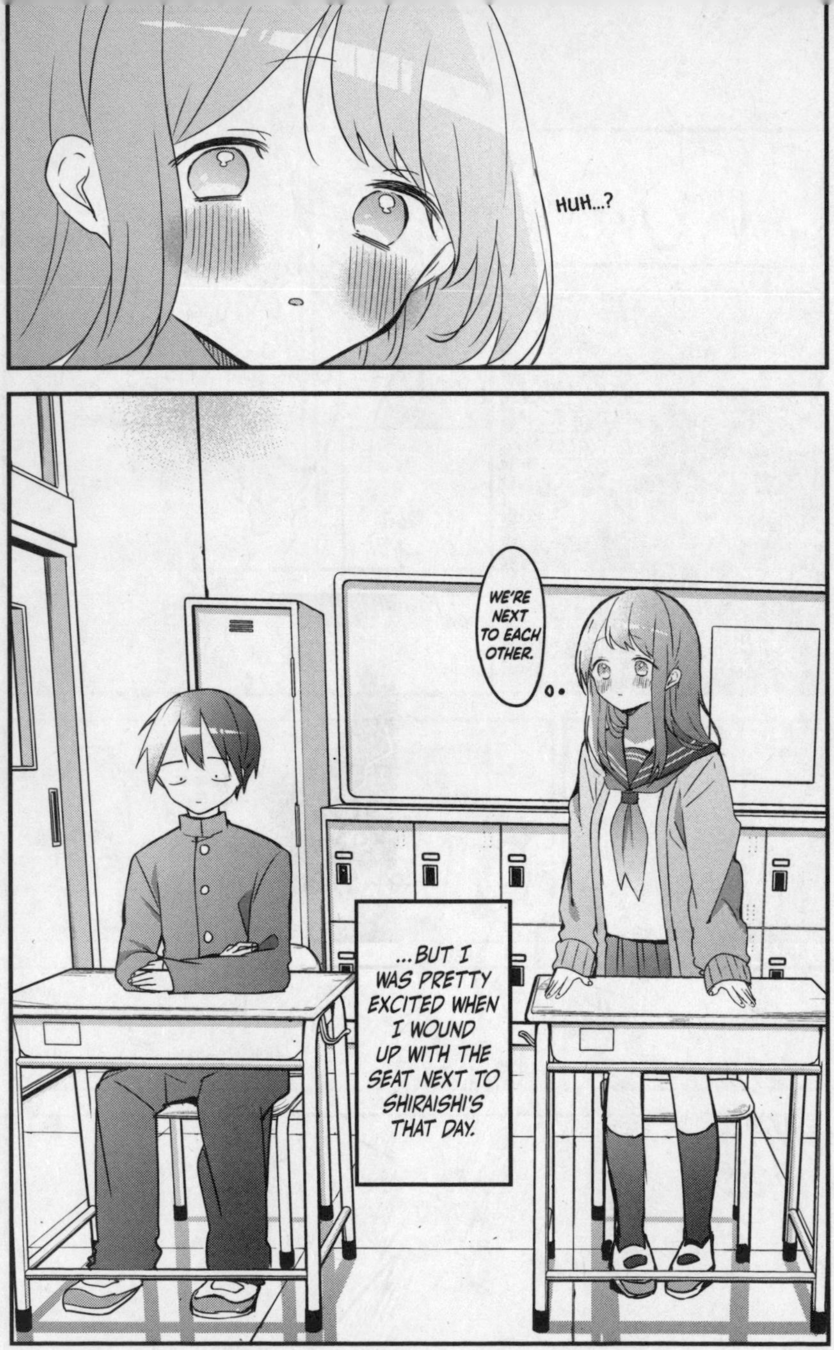
HUH...?
WE'RE NEXT TO EACH OTHER.
...BUT I WAS PRETTY EXCITED WHEN I WOUND UP WITH THE SEAT NEXT TO SHIRAISHI'S THAT DAY.

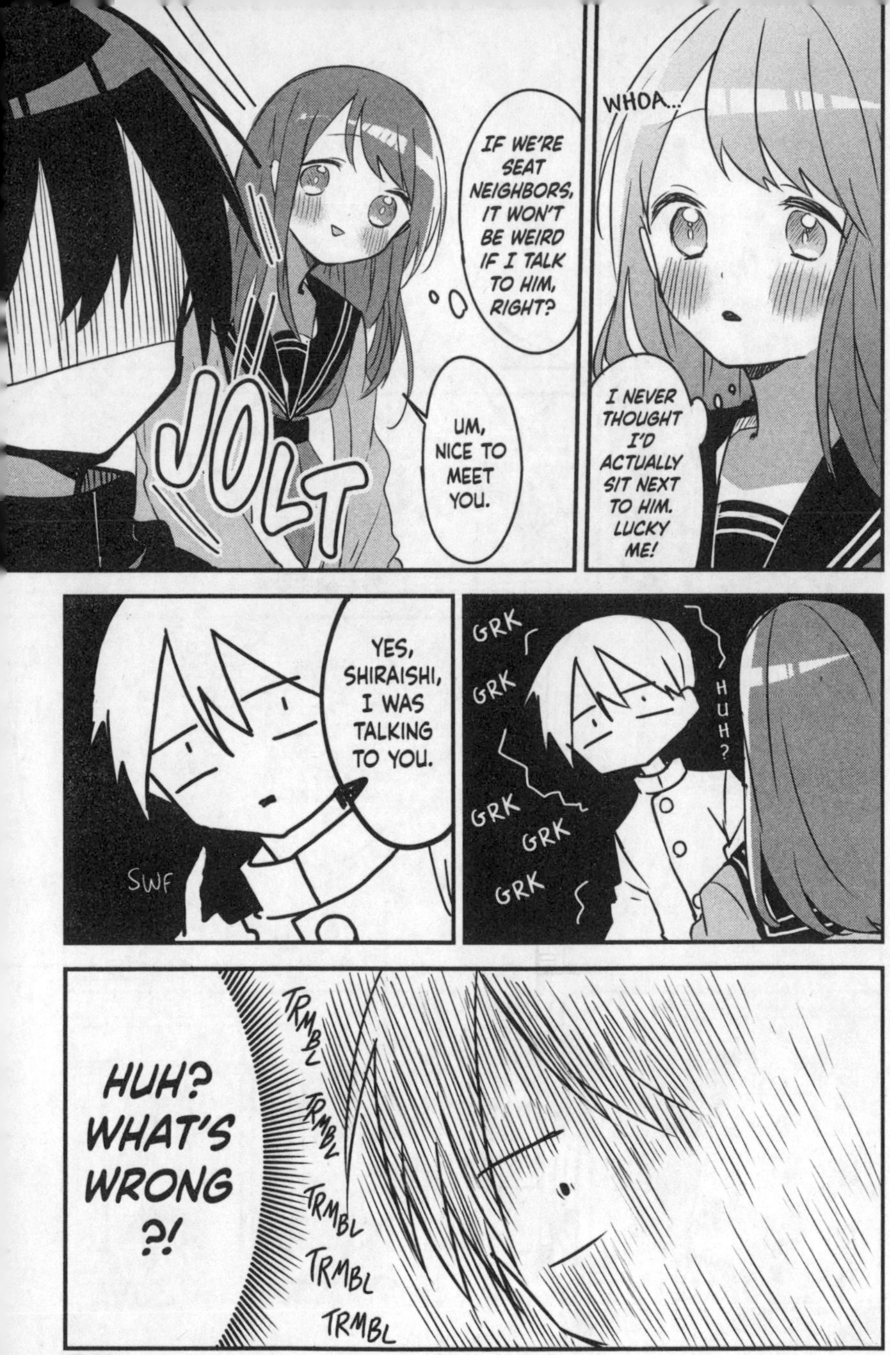
WHOA...
I NEVER THOUGHT I'D ACTUALLY SIT NEXT TO HIM. LUCKY ME!
IF WE'RE SEAT NEIGHBORS, IT WON'T BE WEIRD IF I TALK TO HIM, RIGHT?
UM, NICE TO MEET YOU.
JOLT
GRK
GRK
HUH?
GRK
GRK
GRK
YES, SHIRAISHI, I WAS TALKING TO YOU.
SWF
TRMBL
TRMBL
TRMBL
TRMBL
TRMBL
HUH? WHAT'S WRONG?!

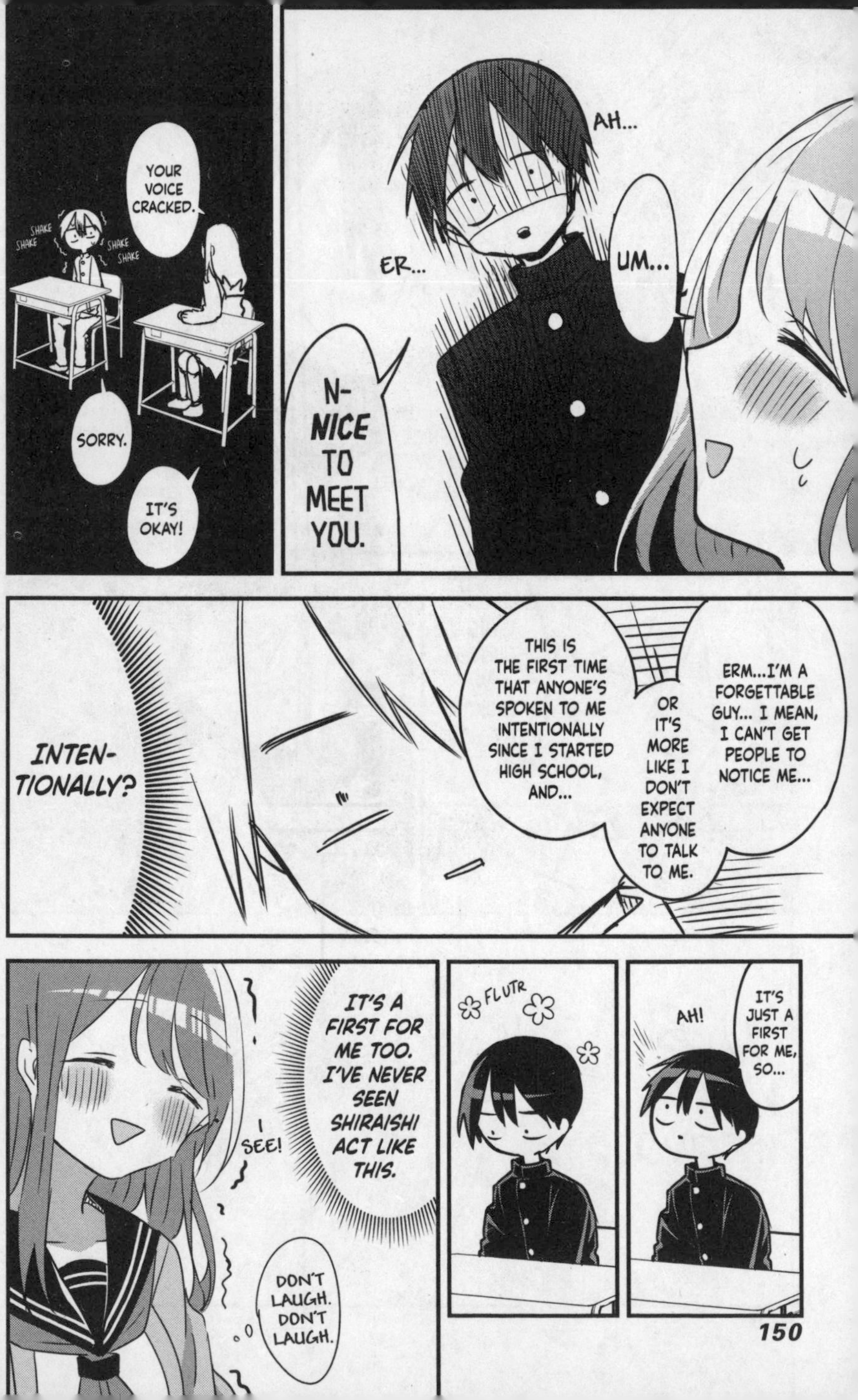
AH...
UM...
ER...
N-NICE TO MEET YOU.
YOUR VOICE CRACKED.
SHAKE SHAKE
SHAKE SHAKE
SORRY.
IT'S OKAY!
ERM...I'M A FORGETTABLE GUY... I MEAN, I CAN'T GET PEOPLE TO NOTICE ME...
OR IT'S MORE LIKE I DON'T EXPECT ANYONE TO TALK TO ME.
THIS IS THE FIRST TIME THAT ANYONE'S SPOKEN TO ME INTENTIONALLY SINCE I STARTED HIGH SCHOOL, AND...
INTEN-TIONALLY?
IT'S JUST A FIRST FOR ME, SO...
AH!
FLUTR
IT'S A FIRST FOR ME TOO. I'VE NEVER SEEN SHIRAISHI ACT LIKE THIS.
I SEE!
DON'T LAUGH. DON'T LAUGH.

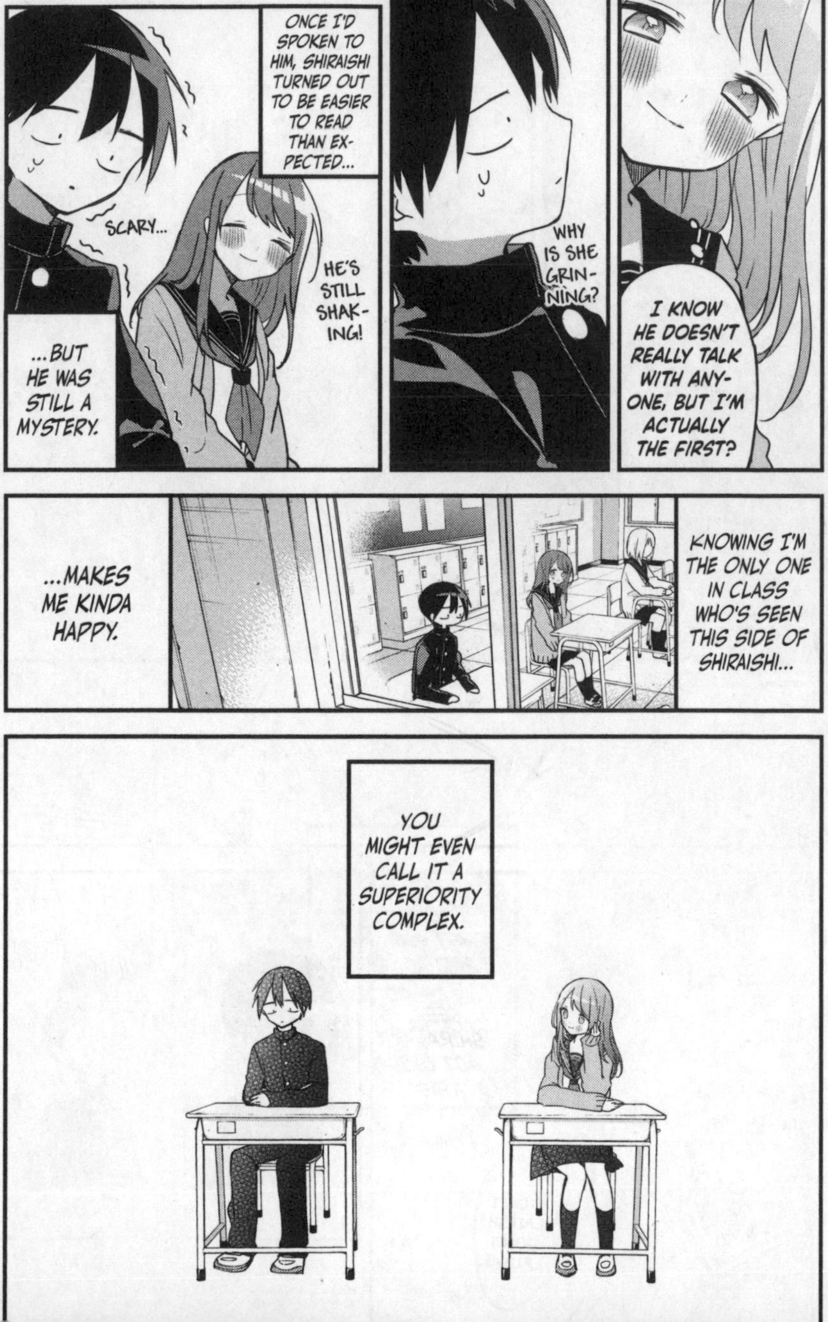
I KNOW HE DOESN'T REALLY TALK WITH ANYONE, BUT I'M ACTUALLY THE FIRST?
WHY IS SHE GRINNING?
ONCE I'D SPOKEN TO HIM, SHIRAISHI TURNED OUT TO BE EASIER TO READ THAN EXPECTED...
HE'S STILL SHAKING!
SCARY...
...BUT HE WAS STILL A MYSTERY.
KNOWING I'M THE ONLY ONE IN CLASS WHO'S SEEN THIS SIDE OF SHIRAISHI...
...MAKES ME KINDA HAPPY.
YOU MIGHT EVEN CALL IT A SUPERIORITY COMPLEX.

I'LL TRY SAYING "GOOD MORNING" TO HIM TOMORROW.

I WONDER HOW HE'LL REACT THEN.

I DON'T THINK I'LL BE ABLE TO TEAR MY EYES AWAY FROM SHIRAISHI FOR A WHILE.

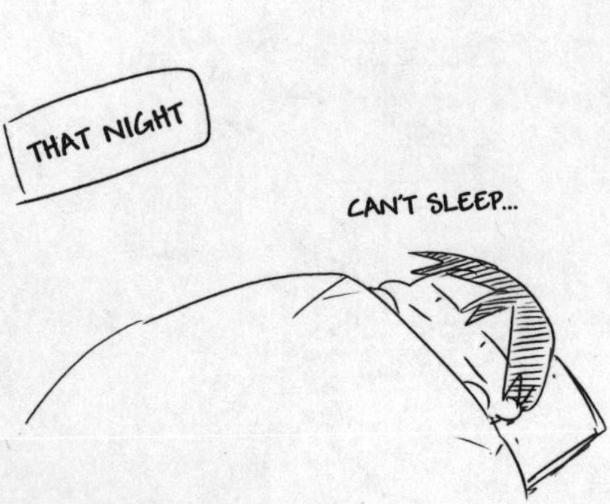
THAT NIGHT
CAN'T SLEEP...

THIS SHORT BONUS
MANGA IS...

THE STORY OF WHAT LED TO
SHIRAISHI GREETING KUBO BEFORE
SHE GREETED HIM FOR THE FIRST
TIME! IT TAKES PLACE BACK WHEN
THE PAIR WERE FIRST-YEARS! IT
BEGINS ON THE NEXT PAGE.

WE'RE HAVING A
STARING CONTEST!!

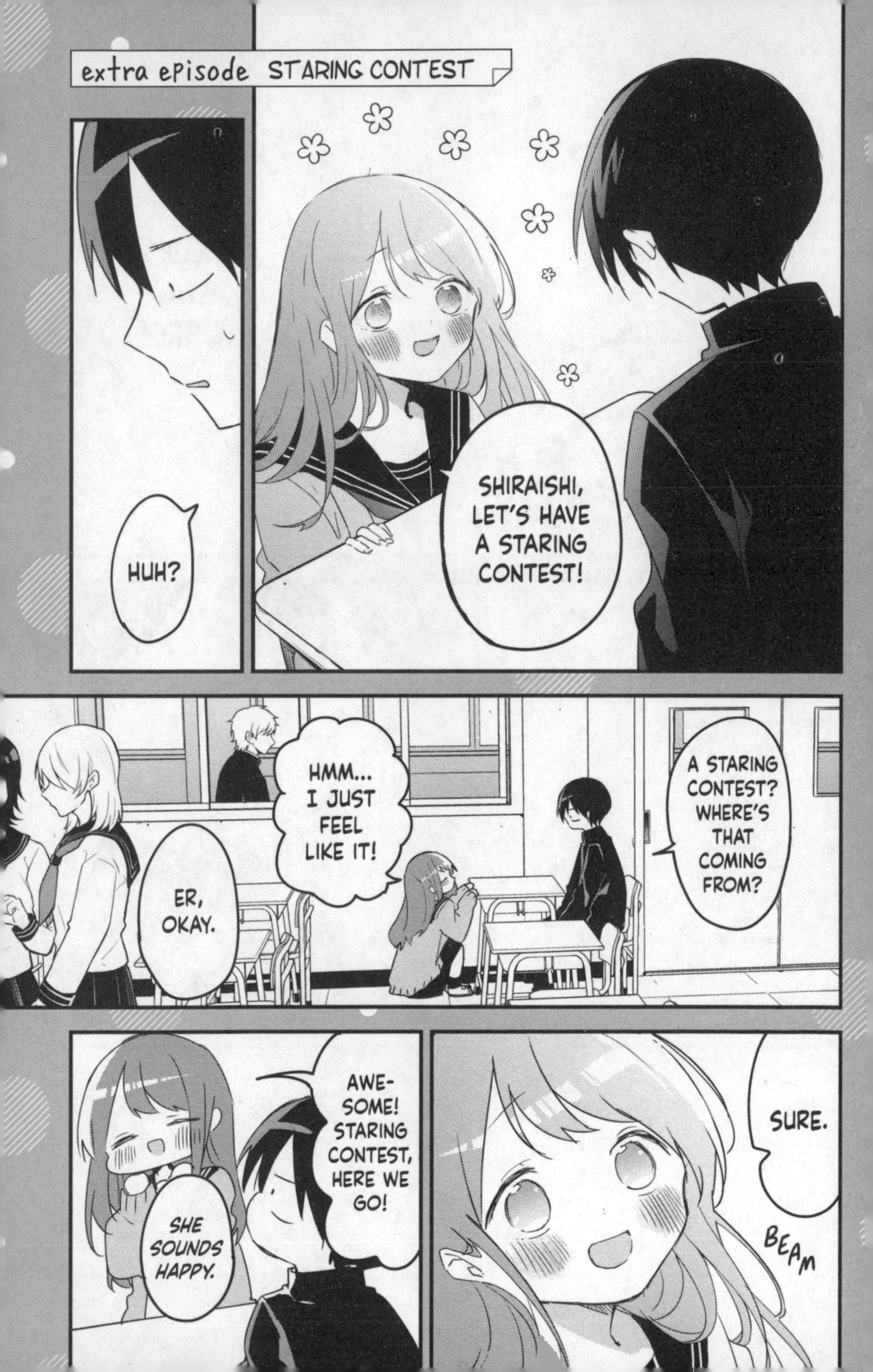
extra episode STARING CONTEST
SHIRAISHI, LET'S HAVE A STARING CONTEST!
HUH?
A STARING CONTEST? WHERE'S THAT COMING FROM?
HMM... I JUST FEEL LIKE IT!
ER, OKAY.
SURE.
BEAM
AWE-SOME! STARING CONTEST, HERE WE GO!
SHE SOUNDS HAPPY.

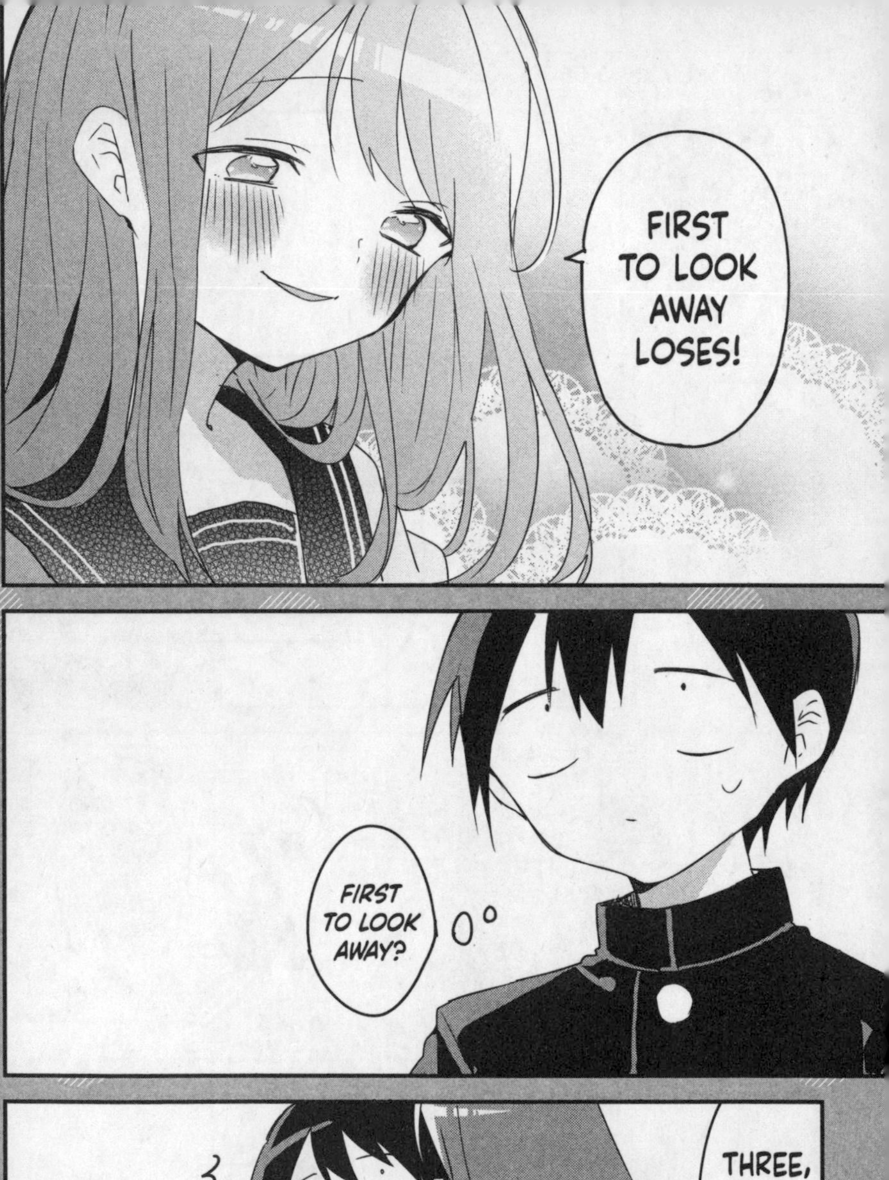
FIRST TO LOOK AWAY LOSES!
FIRST TO LOOK AWAY?
THREE, TWO, ONE, GO!

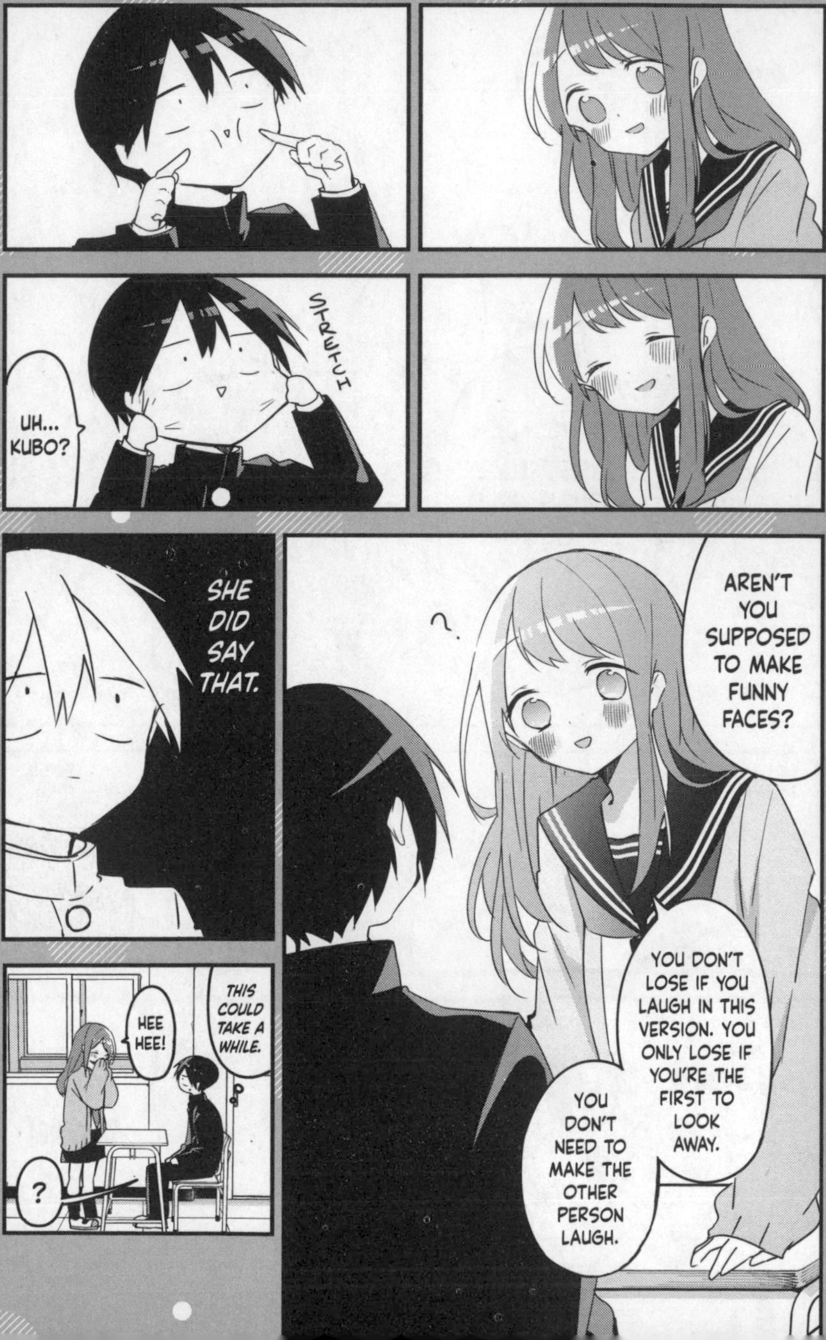
STRETCH
UH... KUBO?
AREN'T YOU SUPPOSED TO MAKE FUNNY FACES?
?
YOU DON'T LOSE IF YOU LAUGH IN THIS VERSION. YOU ONLY LOSE IF YOU'RE THE FIRST TO LOOK AWAY.
YOU DON'T NEED TO MAKE THE OTHER PERSON LAUGH.
SHE DID SAY THAT.
THIS COULD TAKE A WHILE.
HEE HEE!
?

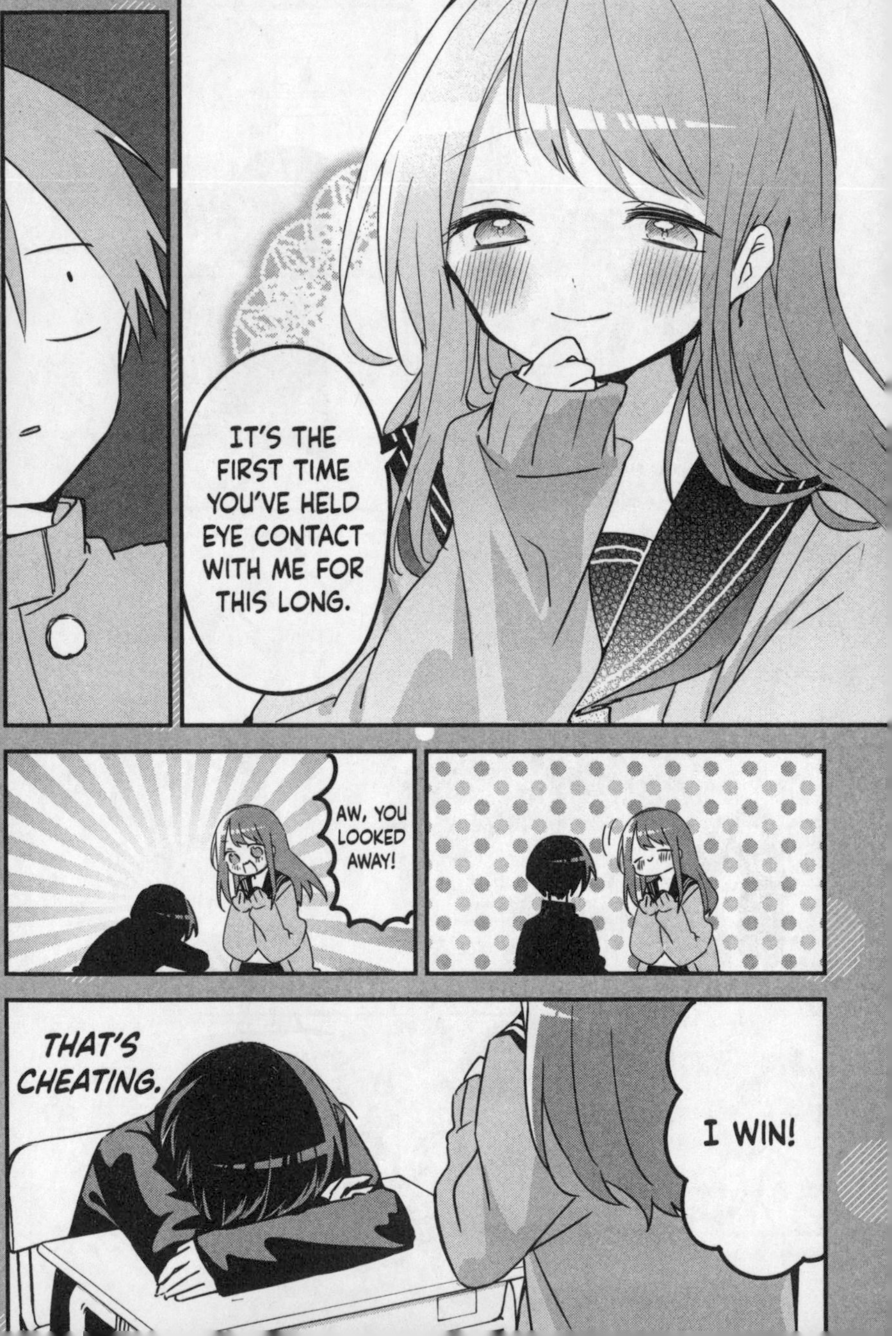
IT'S THE FIRST TIME YOU'VE HELD EYE CONTACT WITH ME FOR THIS LONG.
AW, YOU LOOKED AWAY!
I WIN!
THAT'S CHEATING.

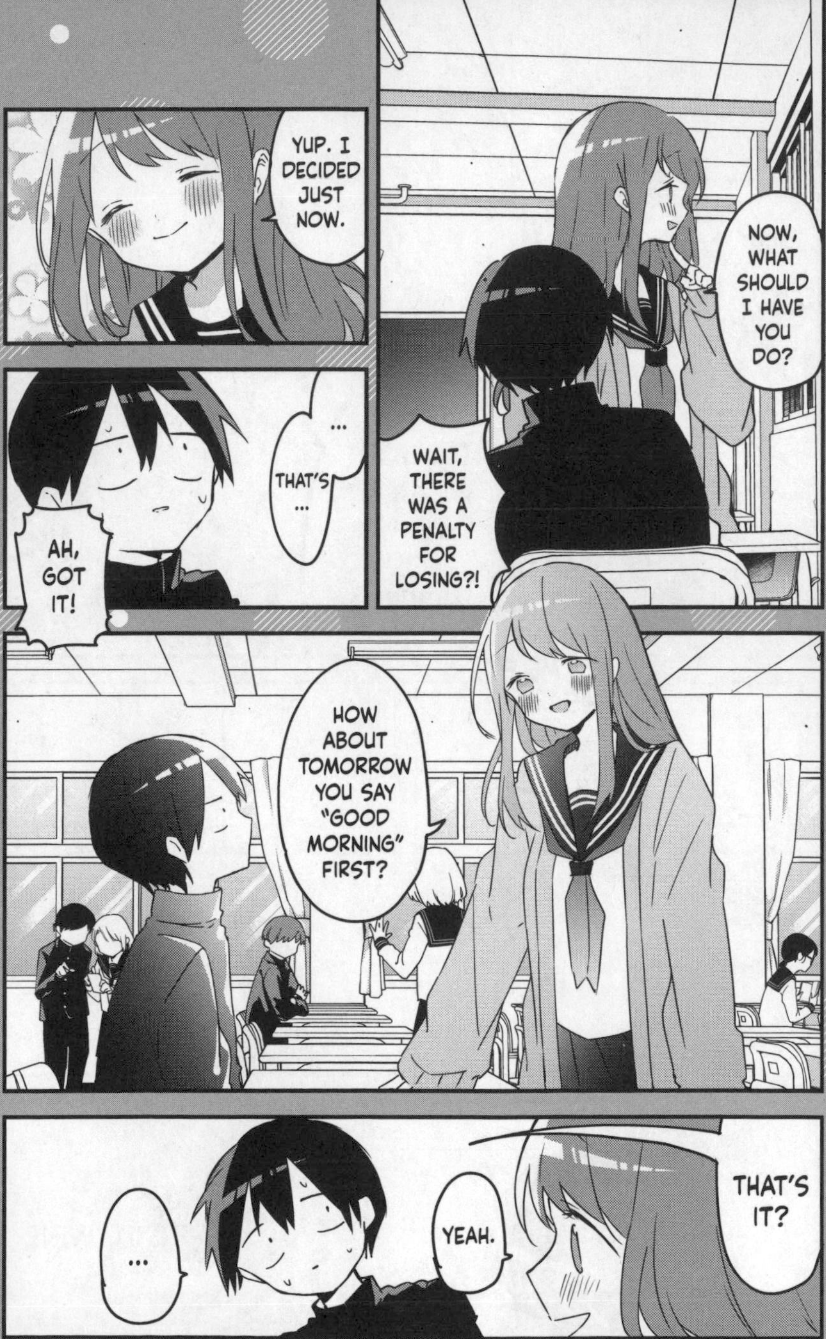
NOW, WHAT SHOULD I HAVE YOU DO?
WAIT, THERE WAS A PENALTY FOR LOSING?!
YUP. I DECIDED JUST NOW.
... THAT'S ...
AH, GOT IT!
HOW ABOUT TOMORROW YOU SAY "GOOD MORNING" FIRST?
THAT'S IT?
YEAH.
...

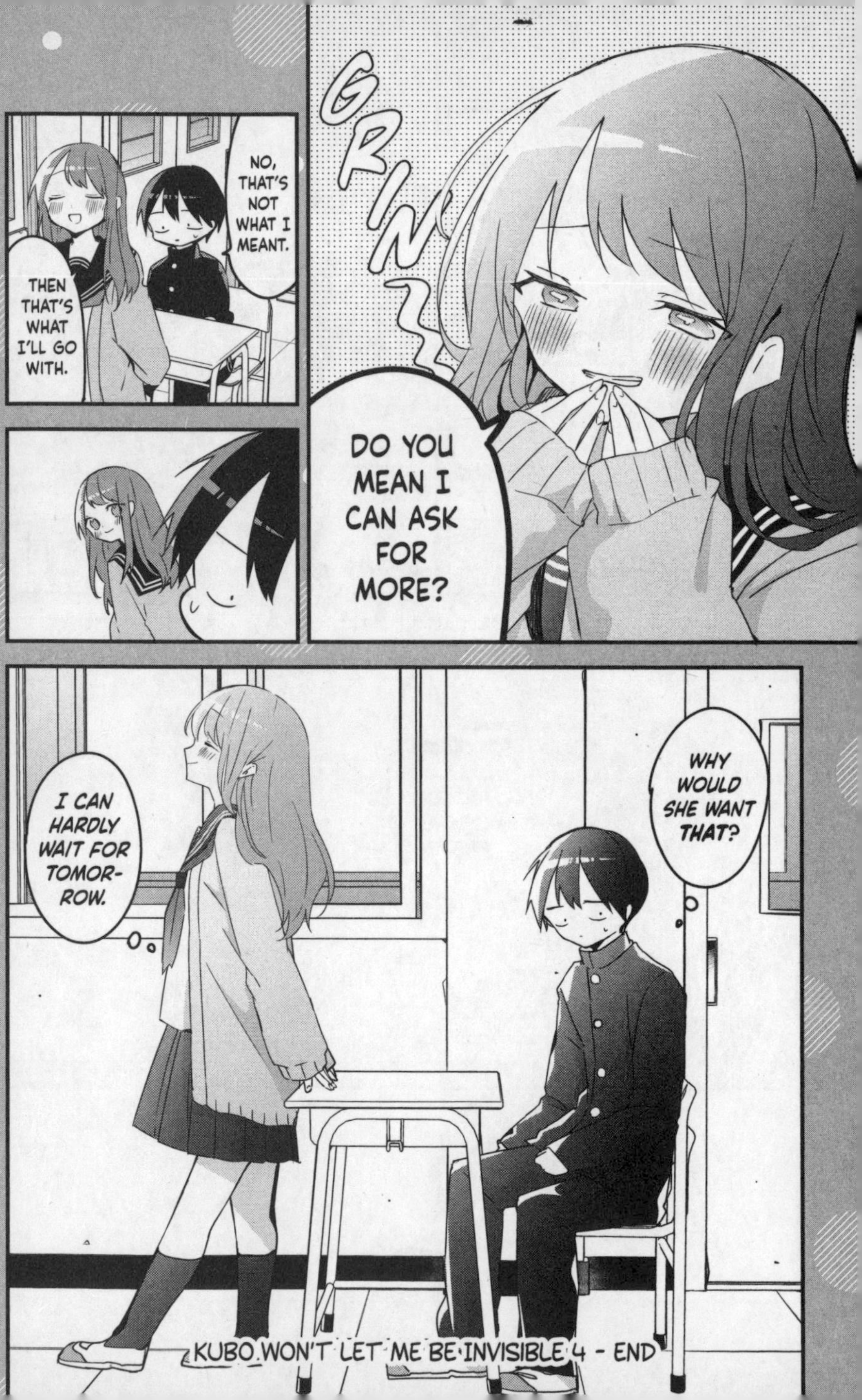
GRIN
DO YOU MEAN I CAN ASK FOR MORE?
NO, THAT'S NOT WHAT I MEANT.
THEN THAT'S WHAT I'LL GO WITH.
WHY WOULD SHE WANT THAT?
I CAN HARDLY WAIT FOR TOMOR-ROW.
KUBO WON'T LET ME BE INVISIBLE 4 - END

Kubo
Won't Let Me Be
Invisible

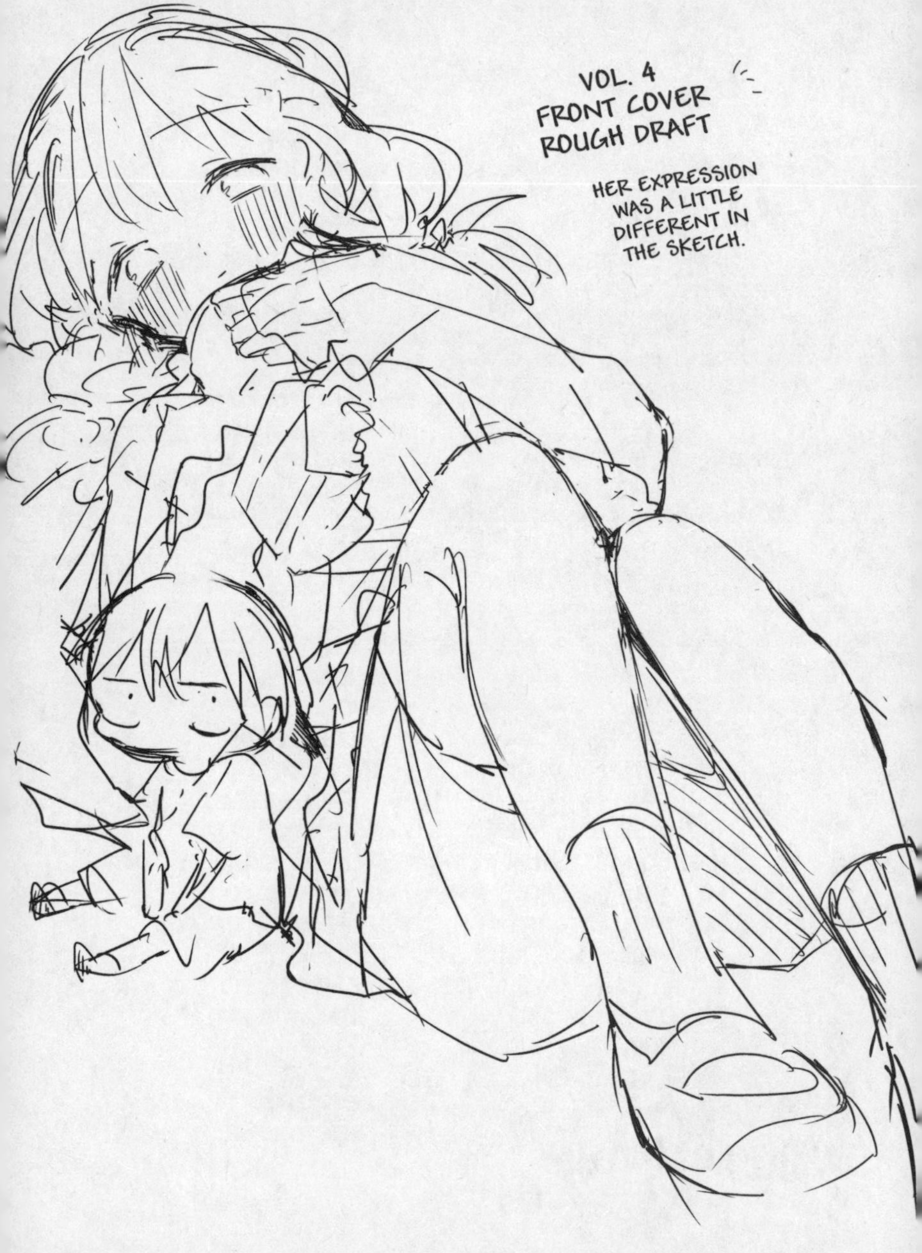
VOL. 4
FRONT COVER
ROUGH DRAFT
HER EXPRESSION
WAS A LITTLE
DIFFERENT IN
THE SKETCH.

AFTERWORD

IT'S VOLUME 4! THANK YOU FOR PICKING IT UP! WE REACHED VOLUME 4 IN NO TIME. TIME SURE FLIES. THANK YOU SO MUCH TO ALL MY SUPPORTERS. I'LL KEEP TRYING MY BEST WHILE NEVER FORGETTING THIS FEELING OF GRATITUDE.

I WAS LUCKY TO BE SO BUSY WITH WORK THAT ALL I REMEMBER OF 2020 IS MANGA. THAT MAKES ME A HAPPY CAMPER. ACTUALLY, IT SEEMS LIKE MY TWENTIES WILL BE ALL MANGA ALL THE TIME. IF I COULD GO BACK IN TIME TO MY STUDENT YEARS, I'D GRIN AT MY YOUNGER SELF AND SAY, "YOU'LL HAVE A WEEKLY SERIALIZATION!"

CHANGING THE SUBJECT, I BOUGHT A SWITCH ON MY ASSISTANTS' RECOMMENDATION. I GOT *SPLATOON 2*, *POKÉMON SWORD*, AND *THE LEGEND OF ZELDA: BREATH OF THE WILD*. I BEAT *POKÉMON* TOO FAST, BUT I PICKED IT UP AGAIN A WHILE LATER AND HAD A BLAST. I TRIED *SPLATOON 2* WITH MY ASSISTANTS AND HAD SO MUCH FUN I CRAMPED UP MY THUMBS. MY BRUSHSTROKES ARE WEAK, YET I HOLD MY CONTROLLER WITH AN IRON GRIP... *BREATH OF THE WILD*'S MAP IS ***HUGE***!!! MY GOSH!!! I LIKE ZELDA. IT ALWAYS MAKES MY HEART FLUTTER. VIDEO GAMES ARE SO GREAT. THANKS FOR READING THIS AFTERWORD!!!

MAY WE MEET AGAIN IN VOLUME 5! SEE YOU NEXT TIME!

NENE YUKIMORI

THANKS

NAKAO, EGUI, FUKATANI, EDITOR R, HACHIOJI HIGH SCHOOL, ALL MY SUPPORTERS

AND YOU!

I won't ask to go along
to all the places you're going.
But in exchange, when you grow weary,
I want you to always come back to me.

I can be any version of me you desire.
I want you to see me for all that I am,
no matter how clingy or selfish.

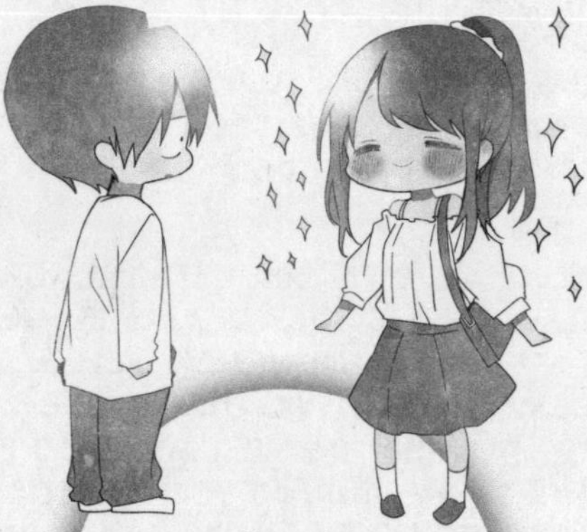

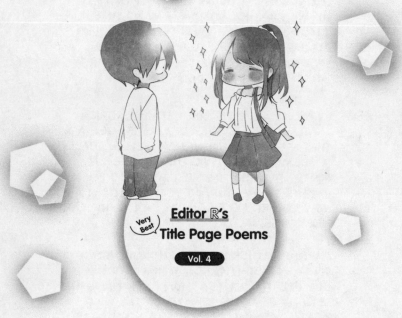

Editor R's Very Best Title Page Poems

Vol. 4

Everyone agrees "that" is a beautiful thing.
But no one will tell me
where to find its entrance.

You and I have different capacities in both mind and body.
Do you also feel
the love and loneliness that slips into that gap?

If I could use one magic spell,
more than enticing you,
more than stopping time,
more than changing the future,
I'd want to know about all the things you like.

Boldness and red cheeks:
I can blame them both on summer.

It's like how we project blue and crimson onto a colorless sky.
I project my feelings onto a colorless, transparent you and call it by that name.

A labyrinth of words, accidental deception.
Even if the correct answer turns inside out,
I can't escape Wonderland.

The chorus of chants stops.
The iridescent rays of summer's end.
In my memories, you fade to white.

I want to be the me I like.
I want to be the me you like.
That intersection of contradictions
is where I want my current self to be.

You can't notice the true start of love through something so silly as fate.

Love is like a jade green starch syrup.
An ephemeral color, a sweet fragrance,
and eventually, a gentle prison that locks you away.

●●●●●●●●●●●●●●●●●●●●●●●●●●●●●

This is Editor R's Very Best Poems Collection,
vol. 4. It's been one year since he started
writing these poems.

Happy poem birthday, Editor R.

He says he often comes up with them while
feeling the night breeze. What a romantic.
I think that's great.

I know I tease you here, but I'm grateful every
time. Thank you so much.

Nene
Yukimori

Nene Yukimori

Before the series began, I always thought, "If I can get a weekly serialization, I'll be Superman!" Once I got one, though, I realized I was merely at the starting line. I'm still a long way from Superman.

Nene Yukimori earned the right to serialize *Kubo Won't Let Me Be Invisible* in *Young Jump* after the manga's one-shot version won the magazine's Shinman GP 2019 Season 5 contest. The manga then began serialization in October 2019. The work is Yukimori's first to receive an English release.

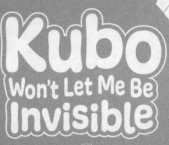

Kubo Won't Let Me Be Invisible

4

SHONEN JUMP EDITION

STORY AND ART BY
NENE YUKIMORI

TRANSLATION
AMANDA HALEY

TOUCH-UP ART & LETTERING
SNIR AHARON

DESIGN
ALICE LEWIS

EDITOR
JENNIFER SHERMAN

First published in Japan in 2019 by SHUEISHA Inc., Tokyo.
English translation rights arranged by SHUEISHA Inc.

Printed in the U.S.A.

Published by VIZ Media, LLC
P.O. Box 77010
San Francisco, CA 94107

10 9 8 7 6 5 4 3 2 1
First printing, November 2022

ratings.viz.com RATED T+ OLDER TEEN

PARENTAL ADVISORY
KUBO WON'T LET ME BE INVISIBLE is rated T+ for Older Teen and is recommended for ages 16 and up. This volume contains suggestive themes.

VIZ MEDIA
viz.com

SHONEN JUMP

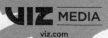

STOP!

YOU MAY BE READING THE WRONG WAY!

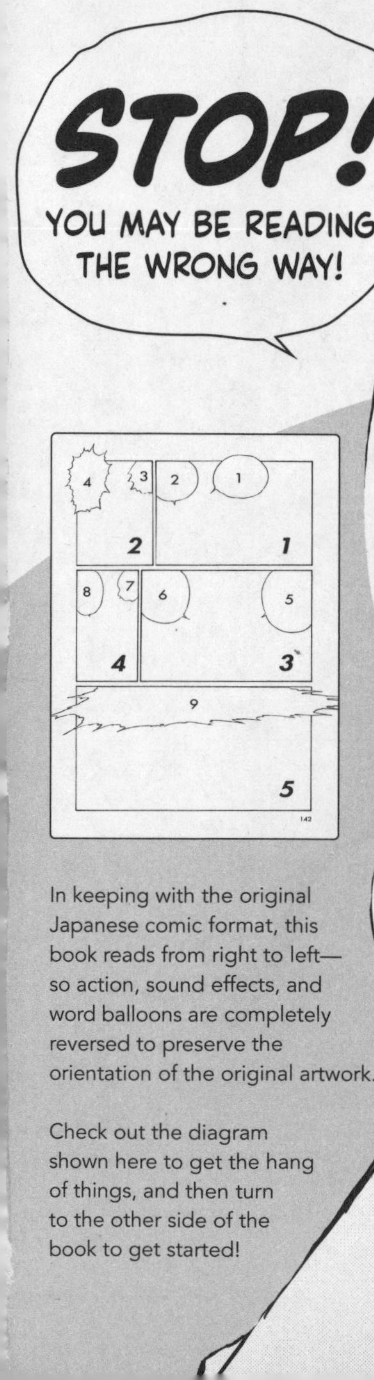

In keeping with the original Japanese comic format, this book reads from right to left—so action, sound effects, and word balloons are completely reversed to preserve the orientation of the original artwork.

Check out the diagram shown here to get the hang of things, and then turn to the other side of the book to get started!

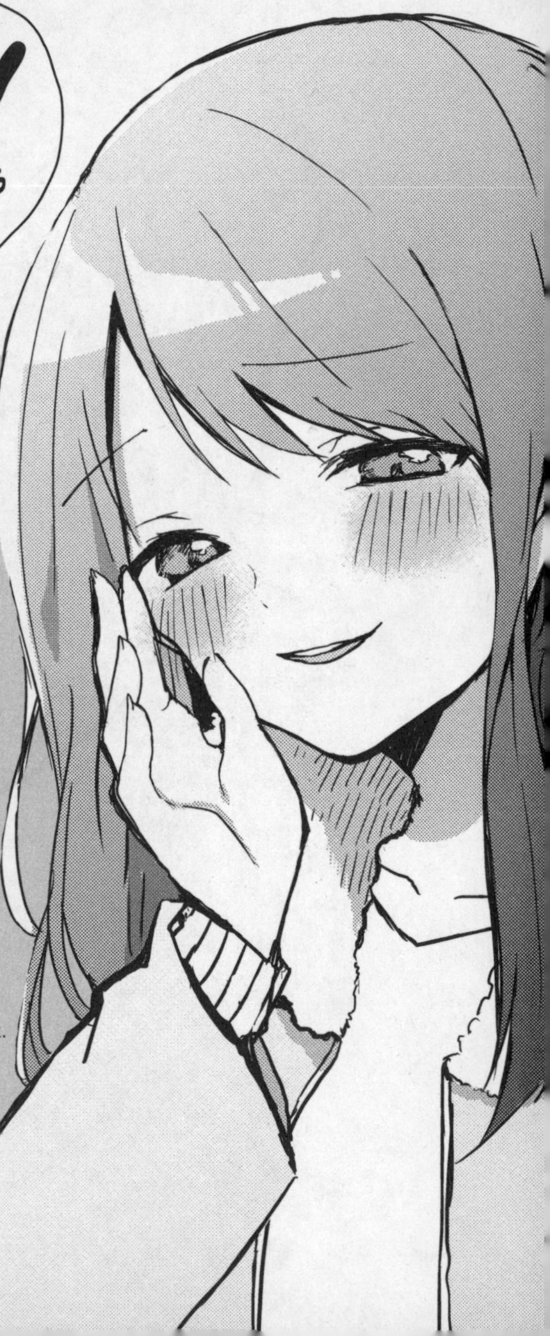